Kaplan Publishing are constantly finding new ways to make a difference to your stı exciting online resources really do oı different to students looking for exaı

This book comes with free MyKaplan online resources so that you can study anytime, anywhere. This free online resource is not sold separately and is included in the price of the book.

Having purchased this book, you have access to the following online study materials:

CONTENT	ACCA (including FFA,FAB,FMA)		FIA (excluding FFA,FAB,FMA)	
	Text	Kit	Text	Kit
iPaper version of the book	✓	✓	✓	✓
Interactive electronic version of the book	✓			
Check Your Understanding Test with instant answers				
Material updates		✓	✓	✓
Latest official ACCA exam questions*		✓		
Extra question assistance using the signpost icon**		✓		
Timed questions with an online tutor debrief using clock icon*		✓		
Interim assessment including questions and answers	✓		✓	
Technical answers	✓	✓	✓	✓

* Excludes F1, F2, F3, F4, FAB, FMA and FFA; for all other papers includes a selection of questions, as released by ACCA

** For ACCA P1-P7 only

How to access your online resources

Kaplan Financial students will already have a MyKaplan account and these extra resources will be available to you online. You do not need to register again, as this process was completed when you enrolled. If you are having problems accessing online materials, please ask your course administrator.

If you are already a registered MyKaplan user go to www.MyKaplan.co.uk and log in. Select the 'add a book' feature and enter the ISBN number of this book and the unique pass key at the bottom of this card. Then click 'finished' or 'add another book'. You may add as many books as you have purchased from this screen.

If you purchased through Kaplan Flexible Learning or via the Kaplan Publishing website you will automatically receive an e-mail invitation to MyKaplan. Please register your details using this email to gain access to your content. If you do not receive the e-mail or book content, please contact Kaplan Flexible Learning.

If you are a new MyKaplan user register at www.MyKaplan.co.uk and click on the link contained in the email we sent you to activate your account. Then select the 'add a book' feature, enter the ISBN number of this book and the unique pass key at the bottom of this card. Then click 'finished' or 'add another book'.

Your Code and Information

This code can only be used once for the registration of one book online. This registration and your online content will expire when the final sittings for the examinations covered by this book have taken place. Please allow one hour from the time you submit your book details for us to process your request.

Please scratch the film to access your MyKaplan code.

Please be aware that this code is case-sensitive and you will need to include the dashes within the passcode, but not when entering the ISBN. For further technical support, please visit www.MyKaplan.co

ACCA

Paper F8

Audit and Assurance

Complete Text

British library cataloguing-in-publication data

A catalogue record for this book is available from the British Library.

Published by:
Kaplan Publishing UK
Unit 2 The Business Centre
Molly Millars Lane
Wokingham
Berkshire
RG41 2QZ

ISBN 978-1-78415-680-0

Printed and bound in Great Britain.

Acknowledgements

We are grateful to the Association of Chartered Certified Accountants and the Chartered Institute of Management Accountants for permission to reproduce past examination questions. The answers have been prepared by Kaplan Publishing.

This Product includes content from the International Auditing and Assurance Standards Board (IAASB) and the International Ethics Standards Board for Accountants (IESBA), published by the International Federation of Accountants (IFAC) in 2015 and is used with permission of IFAC.

Contents

chapter
Intro

Paper Introduction

How to Use the Materials

These Kaplan Publishing learning materials have been carefully designed to make your learning experience as easy as possible and to give you the best chances of success in your examinations.

The product range contains a number of features to help you in the study process. They include:

(1) Detailed study guide and syllabus objectives

(2) Description of the examination

(3) Study skills and revision guidance

(4) Complete text or study notes

(5) Question practice

The sections on the study guide, the syllabus objectives, the examination and study skills should all be read before you commence your studies. They are designed to familiarise you with the nature and content of the examination and give you tips on how to best to approach your learning.

The **complete text or study notes** comprises the main learning materials and gives guidance as to the importance of topics and where other related resources can be found. Each chapter includes:

- The **learning objectives** contained in each chapter, which have been carefully mapped to the examining body's own syllabus learning objectives or outcomes. You should use these to check you have a clear understanding of all the topics on which you might be assessed in the examination.
- The **chapter diagram** provides a visual reference for the content in the chapter, giving an overview of the topics and how they link together.
- The **content** for each topic area commences with a brief explanation or definition to put the topic into context before covering the topic in detail. You should follow your studying of the content with a review of the illustration/s. These are worked examples which will help you to understand better how to apply the content for the topic.

- **Test your understanding** sections provide an opportunity to assess your understanding of the key topics by applying what you have learned to short questions. Answers can be found at the back of each chapter.
- **Summary diagrams** complete each chapter to show the important links between topics and the overall content of the paper. These diagrams should be used to check that you have covered and understood the core topics before moving on.
- **Question practice** is provided at the back of each text.

Quality and accuracy are of the utmost importance to us so if you spot an error in any of our products, please send an email to mykaplanreporting@kaplan.com with full details, or follow the link to the feedback form in MyKaplan.

Our Quality Co-ordinator will work with our technical team to verify the error and take action to ensure it is corrected in future editions.

Icon Explanations

Definition – Key definitions that you will need to learn from the core content.

Key Point – Identifies topics that are key to success and are often examined.

New – Identifies topics that are brand new in papers that build on, and therefore also contain, learning covered in earlier papers.

Expandable Text – Expandable text provides you with additional information about a topic area and may help you gain a better understanding of the core content. Essential text users can access this additional content on-line (read it where you need further guidance or skip over when you are happy with the topic)

Test Your Understanding – Exercises for you to complete to ensure that you have understood the topics just learned.

Illustration – Worked examples help you understand the core content better.

Tricky topic – When reviewing these areas care should be taken and all illustrations and test your understanding exercises should be completed to ensure that the topic is understood.

Tutorial note – Included to explain some of the technical points in more detail.

Footsteps – Helpful tutor tips.

On-line subscribers

Our on-line resources are designed to increase the flexibility of your learning materials and provide you with immediate feedback on how your studies are progressing.

If you are subscribed to our on-line resources you will find:

(1) On-line referenceware: reproduces your Complete Text on-line, giving you anytime, anywhere access.

(2) On-line testing: provides you with additional on-line objective testing so you can practice what you have learned further.

(3) On-line performance management: immediate access to your on-line testing results. Review your performance by key topics and chart your achievement through the course relative to your peer group.

Ask your local customer services staff if you are not already a subscriber and wish to join.

Syllabus for September 2016 to June 2017

Paper background

The aim of ACCA Paper F8, Audit and Assurance, is to develop knowledge and understanding of the process of carrying out the assurance engagement and its application in the context of the professional regulatory framework.

Objectives of the syllabus

- Explain the concept of audit and assurance and the functions of audit, corporate governance, including ethics and professional conduct, describing the scope and distinguishing between the functions of internal and external audit.
- Demonstrate how the auditor obtains and accepts audit engagements, obtains an understanding of the entity and its environment, assesses the risk of material misstatement (whether arising from fraud or other irregularities) and plans an audit of financial statements.
- Describe and evaluate internal controls, techniques and audit tests, including IT systems to identify and communicate control risks and their potential consequences, making appropriate recommendations.
- Identify and describe the work and evidence obtained by the auditor and others required to meet the objectives of audit engagements and the application of the International Standards on Auditing.
- Explain how consideration of subsequent events and the going concern principle can inform the conclusions from audit work and are reflected in different types of audit report, written representations and the final review and report.

Core areas of the syllabus

- Audit framework and regulation.
- Planning and risk assessment.
- Internal control.
- Audit evidence.
- Review and reporting.

Syllabus objectives and chapter references

We have reproduced the ACCA's syllabus below, showing where the objectives are explored within this book. Within the chapters, we have broken down the extensive information found in the syllabus into easily digestible and relevant sections, called Content Objectives. These correspond to the objectives at the beginning of each chapter.

Syllabus learning objective

A AUDIT FRAMEWORK AND REGULATION

1 The concept of audit and other assurance engagements

(a) Identify and describe the objective and general principles of external audit engagements. [2] **Ch. 1**

(b) Explain the nature and development of audit and other assurance engagements. [1] **Ch. 1**

(c) Discuss the concepts of accountability, stewardship and agency. [2] **Ch. 1**

(d) Define and provide the objectives of an assurance engagement. [1] **Ch. 1**

(e) Explain the five elements of an assurance engagement. [2] **Ch. 1**

(f) Describe the types of assurance engagement. [2] **Ch. 1**

(g) Explain the level of assurance provided by an external audit and other review engagements and the concept of true and fair presentation. [1] **Ch. 1**

2 External audits

(a) Describe the regulatory environment within which external audits take place. [1] **Ch. 2**

(b) Discuss the reasons and mechanisms for the regulation of auditors. [1] **Ch. 2**

(c) Explain the statutory regulations governing the appointment, rights, removal and resignation of auditors. [1] **Ch. 2**

(d) Explain the regulations governing the rights and duties of auditors. [1] **Ch. 2**

(e) Describe the limitations of external audits. [1] **Ch. 1**

(f) Explain the development and status of International Standards on Auditing (ISAs). [1] **Ch. 2**

(g) Explain the relationship between International Standards on Auditing and national standards. [1] **Ch. 2**

3 Corporate governance

(a) Discuss the objectives, relevance and importance of corporate governance. [2] **Ch. 11**

(b) Discuss the provisions of international codes of corporate governance (such as OECD) that are most relevant to auditors. [2] **Ch. 11**

(c) Describe good corporate governance requirements relating to directors' responsibilities (e.g. for risk management and internal control) and the reporting responsibilities of auditors. [2] **Ch. 11**

(d) Evaluate corporate governance deficiencies and provide recommendations to allow compliance with international codes of corporate governance. [2] **Ch. 11**

(e) Analyse the structure and roles of audit committees and discuss their benefits and limitations. [2] **Ch. 11**

(f) Explain the importance of internal control and risk management. [1] **Ch. 11**

(g) Discuss the need for auditors to communicate with those charged with governance. [2] **Ch. 10**

4 Professional ethics and ACCA's Code of Ethics and Conduct

(a) Define and apply the fundamental principles of professional ethics of integrity, objectivity, professional competence and due care, confidentiality and professional behaviour. [2] **Ch. 3**

(b) Define and apply the conceptual framework, including the threats to the fundamental principles of self-interest, self-review, advocacy, familiarity, and intimidation. [2] **Ch. 3**

(c) Discuss the safeguards to offset the threats to the fundamental principles. [2] **Ch. 3**

(d) Describe the auditor's responsibility with regard to auditor independence, conflicts of interest and confidentiality. [1] **Ch. 3**

5 Internal audit and governance, and the differences between external audit and internal audit

(a) Discuss the factors to be taken into account when assessing the need for internal audit. [2] **Ch. 12**

(b) Discuss the elements of best practice in the structure and operations of internal audit with reference to appropriate international codes of corporate governance. [2] **Ch. 12**

(c) Compare and contrast the role of external and internal audit. [2] **Ch. 12**

6 The scope of the internal audit function, outsourcing and internal audit assignments

(a) Discuss the scope of internal audit and the limitations of the internal audit function. [2] **Ch. 12**

(b) Explain outsourcing and the associated advantages and disadvantages of outsourcing the internal audit function. [1] **Ch. 12**

(c) Discuss the nature and purpose of internal audit assignments including value for money, IT, financial, regulatory compliance, fraud investigations and customer experience. [2] **Ch. 12**

(d) Discuss the nature and purpose of operational internal audit assignments. [2] **Ch. 12**

(e) Describe the format and content of audit review reports and make appropriate recommendations to management and those charged with governance. [2] **Ch. 12**

B PLANNING AND RISK ASSESSMENT

1 Obtaining, accepting and continuing audit engagements

(a) Discuss the requirements of professional ethics and ISAs in relation to the acceptance / continuance of audit engagements. [2] **Ch. 3**

(b) Explain the preconditions for an audit. [2] **Ch. 3**

(c) Explain the process by which an auditor obtains an audit engagement. [2] **Ch. 3**

(d) Discuss the importance of engagement letters and their contents. [1] **Ch. 3**

(e) Explain the quality control procedures that should be in place over engagement performance, monitoring quality and compliance with ethical requirements. [2] **Ch. 5**

2 Objective and general principles

(a) Identify the overall objectives of the auditor and the need to conduct an audit in accordance with ISAs. [2] **Ch. 2 and 5**

(b) Explain the need to plan and perform audits with an attitude of professional scepticism, and to exercise professional judgment. [2] **Ch. 4**

3 Assessing audit risks

(a) Explain the components of audit risk. [1] **Ch. 4**

(b) Explain the audit risks in the financial statements and explain the auditor's response to each risk. [2] **Ch. 4**

(c) Define and explain the concepts of materiality and performance materiality. [2] **Ch. 4**

(d) Explain and calculate materiality levels from financial information. [2] **Ch. 4**

4 Understanding the entity and its environment

(a) Explain how auditors obtain an initial understanding of the entity and its environment. [2] **Ch. 4**

(b) Describe and explain the nature and purpose of analytical procedures in planning. [2] **Ch. 4**

(c) Compute and interpret key ratios used in analytical procedures. [2] **Ch. 4**

5 Fraud, laws and regulations

(a) Discuss the effect of fraud and misstatements on the audit strategy and extent of audit work. [2] **Ch. 5**

(b) Discuss the responsibilities of internal and external auditors for the prevention and detection of fraud and error. [2] **Ch. 5**

(c) Explain the auditor's responsibility to consider laws and regulations. [2] **Ch. 5**

6 Audit planning and documentation

(a) Identify and explain the need for and importance of planning an audit. [2] **Ch. 5**

(b) Identify and describe the contents of the overall audit strategy and audit plan. [2] **Ch. 5**

(c) Explain and describe the relationship between the overall audit strategy and the audit plan. [2] **Ch. 5**

(d) Explain the difference between interim and final audit. [1] **Ch. 5**

(e) Describe the purpose of an interim audit, and the procedures likely to be adopted at this stage in the audit. [2] **Ch. 5**

(f) Describe the impact of the work performed during the interim audit on the final audit. [2] **Ch. 5**

(g) Explain the need for and the importance of audit documentation. [1] **Ch. 5**

(h) Describe the form and contents of working papers and supporting documentation. [2] **Ch. 5**

(i) Explain the procedures to ensure safe custody and retention of working papers. [1] **Ch. 5**

C INTERNAL CONTROL

1 Internal control systems

(a) Explain why an auditor needs to obtain an understanding of internal control relevant to the audit. [1] **Ch. 6**

(b) Describe and explain the five key components of internal control. [2] **Ch. 7**

- (i) the control environment
- (ii) the entity's risk assessment process
- (iii) the information system, including related business processes, relevant to financial reporting, and communication
- (iv) control activities relevant to the audit
- (v) monitoring of controls

2 The use and evaluation of internal control systems by auditors

(a) Explain how auditors record internal control systems including the use of, narrative notes, flowcharts, internal control questionnaires and internal control evaluation questionnaires. [2] **Ch. 7**

(b) Evaluate internal control components, including deficiencies and significant deficiencies in internal control. [2] **Ch. 7**

(c) Discuss the limitations of internal control components. [2] **Ch. 7**

3 Tests of controls

(a) Describe computer systems controls including general IT controls and application controls. [2] **Ch. 7**

(b) Describe control objectives, control procedures, activities and tests of control in relation to:

(i) The sales system

(ii) The purchases system

(iii) The payroll system

(iv) The inventory system

(v) The cash system

(vi) Non-current assets

4 Communication on internal control

(a) Discuss the requirements and methods of how reporting significant deficiencies in internal control are provided to management and those charged with governance. [2] **Ch. 7**

(b) Explain, in a format suitable for inclusion in a report to management significant deficiencies within an internal control system and provide recommendations for overcoming these deficiencies to management. [2] **Ch. 7**

D AUDIT EVIDENCE

1 Financial statement assertions and audit evidence

(a) Explain the assertions contained in the financial statements about: [2] **Ch. 6**

  (i) Classes of transactions and events and related disclosures;

  (ii) Account balances and related disclosures at the period end.

(b) Describe audit procedures to obtain audit evidence, including inspection, observation, external confirmation, recalculation, re-performance, analytical procedures and enquiry. [2] **Ch. 6**

(c) Discuss the quality and quantity of audit evidence. [2] **Ch. 6**

(d) Discuss the relevance and reliability of audit evidence. [2] **Ch. 6**

2 Audit procedures

(a) Discuss substantive procedures for obtaining audit evidence. [2] **Ch. 6**

(b) Discuss and provide examples of how analytical procedures are used as substantive procedures. [2] **Ch. 6**

(c) Discuss the problems associated with the audit and review of accounting estimates. [2] **Ch. 8**

(d) Describe why smaller entities may have different control environments and describe the types of evidence likely to be available in smaller entities. [1] **Ch. 8**

(e) Discuss the difference between tests of control and substantive procedures. [2] **Ch. 9**

3 Audit sampling and other means of testing

(a) Define audit sampling and explain the need for sampling. [1] **Ch. 6**

(b) Identify and discuss the differences between statistical and non-statistical sampling. [2] **Ch. 6**

(c) Discuss and provide relevant examples of, the application of the basic principles of statistical sampling and other selective testing procedures. [2] **Ch. 6**

(d) Discuss the results of statistical sampling, including consideration of whether additional testing is required. [2] **Ch. 6**

4 The audit of specific items

For each of the account balances stated in this sub-capability:

Explain the audit objectives and the audit procedures to obtain sufficient, appropriate evidence in relation to:

(a) Receivables:[2] **Ch. 8**

- (i) direct confirmation of accounts receivable
- (ii) other evidence in relation to receivables and prepayments, and
- (iii) completeness and occurrence of revenue.

(b) Inventory:[2] **Ch. 8**

- (i) inventory counting procedures in relation to year-end and continuous inventory systems
- (ii) cut-off testing
- (iii) auditor's attendance at inventory counting
- (iv) direct confirmation of inventory held by third parties
- (v) valuation
- (vi) other evidence in relation to inventory.

(c) Payables and accruals:[2] **Ch. 8**

- (i) supplier statement reconciliations and direct confirmation of accounts payable
- (ii) obtain evidence in relation to payables and accruals, and
- (iii) purchases and other expenses.

(d) Bank and cash:[2] **Ch. 8**

- (i) bank confirmation reports used in obtaining evidence in relation to bank and cash
- (ii) other evidence in relation to bank
- (iii) other evidence in relation to cash.

(e) Tangible and intangible non-current assets:[2] **Ch. 8**

   (i) evidence in relation to non-current assets

   (ii) depreciation

   (iii) profit/loss on disposal

(f) Non-current liabilities, provisions and contingencies:[2] **Ch. 8**

   (i) evidence in relation to non-current liabilities

   (ii) provisions and contingencies

(g) Share capital, reserves and directors' emoluments: [2] **Ch. 8**

   (i) evidence in relation to share capital, reserves and directors' emoluments

5 Computer-assisted audit techniques

(a) Explain the use of computer-assisted audit techniques in the context of an audit. [1] **Ch. 6**

(b) Discuss and provide relevant examples of the use of test data and audit software. [2] **Ch. 6**

6 The work of others

(a) Discuss why auditors rely on the work of others. [2] **Ch. 6**

(b) Discuss the extent to which external auditors are able to rely on the work of experts, including the work of internal audit. [2] **Ch. 6**

(c) Explain the audit considerations relating to entities using service organisations. [2] **Ch. 6**

(d) Explain the extent to which reference to the work of others can be made in audit reports. [1] **Ch. 6**

7 Not-for-profit organisations

(a) Apply audit techniques to not-for-profit organisations. [2] **Ch. 8**

E REVIEW AND REPORTING

1 Subsequent events

(a) Explain the purpose of a subsequent events review. [1] **Ch. 9**

(b) Explain the responsibilities of auditors regarding subsequent events. [1] **Ch. 9**

(c) Discuss the procedures to be undertaken in performing a subsequent events review. [2] **Ch. 9**

2 Going concern

(a) Define and discuss the significance of the concept of going concern. [2] **Ch. 9**

(b) Explain the importance of and the need for going concern reviews. [2] **Ch. 9**

(c) Explain the respective responsibilities of auditors and management regarding going concern. [1] **Ch. 9**

(d) Identify and explain potential indicators that an entity is not a going concern. [2] **Ch. 9**

(e) Discuss the procedures to be applied in performing going concern reviews. [2] **Ch. 9**

(f) Discuss the disclosure requirements in relation to going concern issues. [2] **Ch. 9**

(g) Discuss the reporting implications of the findings of going concern reviews. [2] **Ch. 9**

3 Written representations

(a) Explain the purpose of and procedure for obtaining written representations. [2] **Ch. 9**

(b) Discuss the quality and reliability of written representations as audit evidence. [2] **Ch. 9**

(c) Discuss the circumstances where written representations are necessary and the matters on which representations are commonly obtained. [2] **Ch. 9**

4 Audit finalisation and the final review

(a) Discuss the importance of the overall review in ensuring that sufficient, appropriate evidence has been obtained. [2] **Ch. 9**

(b) Describe procedures an auditor should perform in conducting their overall review of financial statements. [2] **Ch. 9**

(c) Explain the significance of uncorrected misstatements. [1] **Ch. 9**

(d) Evaluate the effect of dealing with uncorrected misstatements. [2] **Ch. 9**

5 Audit reports

(a) Identify and describe the basic elements contained in the independent auditor's report. [1] **Ch. 10**

(b) Explain unmodified audit opinions in the auditor's report. [2] **Ch. 10**

(c) Explain modified audit opinions in the audit report. [2] **Ch. 10**

(d) Describe the format and content of emphasis of matter and other matter paragraphs. [2] **Ch. 10**

The superscript numbers in square brackets indicate the intellectual depth at which the subject area could be assessed within the examination. Level 1 (knowledge and comprehension) broadly equates with the Knowledge module, Level 2 (application and analysis) with the Skills module and Level 3 (synthesis and evaluation) to the Professional level. However, lower level skills can continue to be assessed as you progress through each module and level.

For a list of examinable documents, see the ACCA web site: (www.accaglobal.com/en/student).

The Examination

Examination format

The syllabus is assessed by a three-hour 15 minute examination. All questions are compulsory.

Section A of the examination comprises three objective test cases (OT cases), each of which includes five OT questions of 2 marks each.

The Section A OT case questions can cover any areas of the syllabus.

Section B of the examination comprises two 20 mark and one 30 mark constructed response (long) questions.

Section B of the exam will predominantly examine one or more aspects of audit and assurance from planning and risk assessment, internal control or audit evidence, although topics from other syllabus areas may also be included.

Examination tips

Spend time reading the examination paper carefully. We recommend that 15 minutes should be spent reading the paper, paying particular attention to section B, where questions will be based on longer scenarios than the 2 mark OT cases in section A.

If 15 minutes are spent reading the examination paper, this leaves three hours to attempt the questions:

- Divide the time you spend on questions in proportion to the marks on offer.
- One suggestion for this examination is to allocate 1.8 minutes to each mark available (180 minutes/100 marks), so a 20 mark question should be completed in approximately 36 minutes. If you plan to spend more or less time than 15 minutes reading the paper, your time allocation per mark will be different.

Section A

You should begin by reading the OT questions that relate to the case, so that when you read through the information for the first time, you know what it is that you are required to do.

Each OT question is worth two marks. Therefore you have 18 minutes (1.8 minutes per mark) to answer the five OT questions relating to each case. It is likely that all of the cases will take the same length of time to answer, although some of the OT questions within a case may be quicker than other OT questions within that same case.

Once you have read through the information, you should first answer any of the OT questions that can be quickly answered. You should then attempt the other OT questions utilising the remaining time for that case.

Work steadily. Rushing leads to careless mistakes and the OT questions are designed to include answers which result from careless mistakes.

If you don't know the answer, eliminate those options you know are incorrect and see if the answer becomes more obvious.

Remember that there is no negative marking for an incorrect answer. After you have eliminated the options that you know to be wrong, if you are still unsure, guess.

Practice section A questions can be found at the end of each chapter.

Section B

The constructed response questions in section B will require a written response rather than being OT questions. Therefore, different techniques need to be used to score well.

Unless you know exactly how to answer the question, spend some time planning your answer. Stick to the question and tailor your answer to what you are asked. Pay particular attention to the verbs in the question e.g. 'Describe', 'State', 'Explain'.

If you get completely stuck with a question, leave space in your answer book and return to it later.

If you do not understand what a question is asking, state your assumptions. Even if you do not answer in precisely the way the examining team hoped, you may be given some credit, provided that your assumptions are reasonable.

You should do everything you can to make things easy for the marker. The marker will find it easier to identify the points you have made if your answers are legible.

When answering the constructed response questions, be concise. It is better to write a little about a lot of different points than a great deal about one or two points. Make sure that each point is clearly identifiable by leaving a line space between each of your points. DO NOT write an essay.

Some questions ask you to present your answer in the form of a report or letter. Use the correct format as there are easy marks to gain here for presentation.

Practice section B style questions can be found in most chapters and also in Chapter 15.

All sections

Don't skip parts of the syllabus. The F8 paper has 18 different questions so the examination can cover a very broad selection of the syllabus each sitting.

Spend time learning definitions.

Practice plenty of questions to improve your ability to apply the techniques.

Spend the last five minutes reading through your answers and making any additions or corrections.

Method of Examination

For examinations from September 2016, computer-based testing (CBT) will be available in respect of the ACCA Fundamental Skills Level papers (F5 – F9).

Students will have a choice of CBT or paper examinations.

The CBT and paper examinations will follow the same format, with the following exceptions:

OT questions in section A of the paper examination will be of multiple choice style only. This means there will be four possible answers to choose from for each OT, with only one answer being correct.

OT questions in section A of the CBT examination will be of varying styles. These styles include multiple choice, number entry, pull down list, multiple response, hot area, and drag and drop. A full explanation of these question types is included in the Kaplan Exam Kit.

Section B will be in the same format for both the CBT and paper examinations.

If you would like further information on sitting a CBT F8 examination please contact either Kaplan, or the ACCA.

Study skills and revision guidance

This section aims to give guidance on how to study for your ACCA exams and to give ideas on how to improve your existing study techniques.

Preparing to study

Set your objectives

Before starting to study decide what you want to achieve i.e. the type of pass you wish to obtain. This will decide the level of commitment and time you need to dedicate to your studies.

Devise a study plan

Determine which times of the week you will study.

Split these times into sessions of at least one hour for study of new material. Any shorter periods could be used for revision or practice.

Put the times you plan to study onto a study plan for the weeks from now until the exam and set yourself targets for each period of study. In your sessions make sure you cover the course, course assignments and revision.

If you are studying for more than one paper at a time, try to vary your subjects as this can help you to keep interested and see subjects as part of wider knowledge.

When working through your course, compare your progress with your plan and, if necessary, re-plan your work (perhaps including extra sessions) or, if you are ahead, do some extra revision/practice questions.

Effective studying

Active reading

You are not expected to learn the text by rote, rather, you must understand what you are reading and be able to use it to pass the exam and develop good practice. A good technique to use is SQ3Rs – Survey, Question, Read, Recall, Review:

(1) **Survey the chapter** – look at the headings and read the introduction, summary and objectives, to get an overview of what the chapter deals with.

(2) **Question** – whilst undertaking the survey, ask yourself the questions that you hope the chapter will answer for you.

(3) **Read** through the chapter thoroughly, answering the questions and making sure you can meet the objectives. Attempt the exercises and activities in the text, and work through all the examples.

(4) **Recall** – at the end of each section and at the end of the chapter, try to recall the main ideas of the section/chapter without referring to the text. This is best done after a short break of a couple of minutes after the reading stage.

(5) **Review** – check that your recall notes are correct.

You may also find it helpful to re-read the chapter to try to see the topic(s) it deals with as a whole.

Note-taking

Taking notes is a useful way of learning, but do not simply copy out the text. The notes must:

- be in your own words
- be concise
- cover the key points
- be well-organised
- be modified as you study further chapters in this text or in related ones.

Trying to summarise a chapter without referring to the text can be a useful way of determining which areas you know and which you don't.

Three ways of taking notes:

Summarise the key points of a chapter.

Make linear notes – a list of headings, divided up with subheadings listing the key points. If you use linear notes, you can use different colours to highlight key points and keep topic areas together. Use plenty of space to make your notes easy to use.

Try a diagrammatic form – the most common of which is a mind-map. To make a mind-map, put the main heading in the centre of the paper and put a circle around it. Then draw short lines radiating from this to the main sub-headings, which again have circles around them. Then continue the process from the sub-headings to sub-sub-headings, advantages, disadvantages, etc.

Highlighting and underlining

You may find it useful to underline or highlight key points in your study text – but do be selective. You may also wish to make notes in the margins.

Revision

The best approach to revision is to revise the course as you work through it. Also try to leave four to six weeks before the exam for final revision. Make sure you cover the whole syllabus and pay special attention to those areas where your knowledge is weak. Here are some recommendations:

Read through the text and your notes again and condense your notes into key phrases. It may help to put key revision points onto index cards to look at when you have a few minutes to spare.

Review any assessments you have completed and look at where you lost marks – put more work into those areas where you were weak.

Practise exam standard questions under timed conditions. If you are short of time, list the points that you would cover in your answer and then read the model answer, but do try to complete at least a few questions under exam conditions.

Also practise producing answer plans and comparing them to the model answer.

If you are stuck on a topic find somebody (a tutor) to explain it to you.

Read good newspapers and professional journals, especially ACCA's Student Accountant – this can give you an advantage in the exam.

Ensure you know the structure of the exam – how many questions and of what type you will be expected to answer. During your revision attempt all the different styles of questions you may be asked.

Further reading

You can find further reading and technical articles under the student section of ACCA's website.

chapter

1

Introduction to assurance

Chapter learning objectives

This chapter covers syllabus areas:

- A1 – The concept of audit and other assurance engagements
- A2e – Limitations of external audits

Detailed syllabus objectives are provided in the introduction section of the text book.

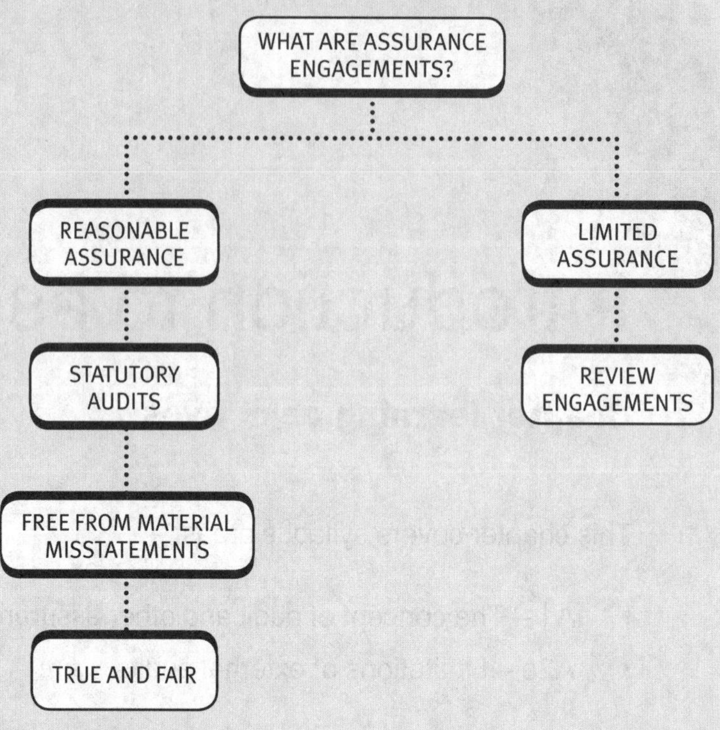

1 What is assurance?

An assurance engagement is: 'An engagement in which a practitioner expresses a conclusion designed to enhance the degree of confidence of the intended users other than the responsible party about the outcome of the evaluation or measurement of a subject matter against criteria.' (International Audit and Assurance Standards Board Handbook)

Giving assurance means: offering an opinion about specific information so the users of that information are able to make **confident decisions** knowing that the **risk** of the information being 'incorrect' is **reduced**.

There are five elements of an assurance engagement:

(i) the three parties involved:
   - the practitioner (i.e. the reviewer of the subject matter who provides the assurance)
   - the intended users (of the information)
   - the responsible party (i.e. those responsible for preparing the subject matter)

(ii) an appropriate subject matter

(iii) suitable criteria, against which the subject matter is evaluated/measured

(iv) sufficient appropriate evidence

(v) a written assurance report in an appropriate form.

Illustration 1: Buying a house

Consider someone who is buying a house.

Most members of the public lack the technical expertise to assess the structural condition of property. There is a risk that someone pays a large sum of money to purchase a structurally unsafe property which needs further expenditure to make it useable.

To reduce this risk, it is normal for house buyers (the users) to pay a property surveyor (the practitioner) to perform a structural assessment of the house (the subject matter). The surveyor would then report back (written report) to the house buyer identifying any structural deficiencies (measured against building regulations/best practice and other criteria). With this information the potential buyer can then make their decision to buy or not to buy the house with confidence that they know the structural condition of the house.

In this example, the responsible party is the current house owner, and the evidence would largely be obtained by visually inspecting the property.

The elements of an audit engagement

The five elements of an external audit engagement

(i) The three parties involved:
- the preparers – management/directors
- the users – shareholders
- the practitioner – the auditors

(ii) The subject matter: the financial statements (prepared by management).

(iii) Sufficient appropriate evidence: obtained by performing audit procedures and reviewing the financial statements.

(iv) This includes evaluating whether the FS are prepared in accordance with a relevant financial reporting framework (i.e. suitable criteria).

(v) The audit report: which is presented to the shareholders. This report summarises the auditor's opinion as to whether the financial statements are "presented fairly" (or "true and fair").

Assurance services

- Audit of financial statements
- Review of financial statements
- Risk assessment reviews
- Systems reliability reports
- Verification of social and environmental information (e.g. to validate an employer's claims about being an equal opportunities employer or a company's claims about sustainable sourcing of materials)
- Reviews of internal controls
- Value for money audit in public sector organisations.

2 Types of assurance engagement

The IAASB International Framework for Assurance Engagements permits two types of assurance engagement:

- reasonable
- limited.

Reasonable assurance engagements

In a reasonable assurance engagement, the practitioner:

- Gathers **sufficient appropriate evidence** to be able to draw reasonable conclusions.
- Concludes that the subject matter **conforms in all material respects** with identified suitable criteria.
- Gives a **positively** worded assurance **opinion**.
- Gives a **high** level of assurance (confidence).
- Performs very thorough procedures to obtain sufficient appropriate evidence – tests of controls and substantive procedures.

Illustration 2: Positively worded assurance opinion

In our opinion, the financial statements give a true and fair view of (or *present fairly, in all material respects*) the financial position of Murray Company as at December 31 20X4, and of its financial performance and its cash flows for the year then ended in accordance with International Financial Reporting Standards.

Limited assurance engagement

In a limited assurance assignment, the practitioner:

- Gathers **sufficient appropriate evidence** to be able to draw limited conclusions.
- Concludes that the subject matter, with respect to identified suitable criteria, **is plausible in the circumstances**.
- Gives a **negatively** worded assurance **conclusion**.
- Gives a **moderate** or lower level of assurance than that of an audit.
- Performs significantly fewer procedures – mainly enquiries and analytical procedures.

Illustration 3: Negatively worded assurance opinion

Nothing has come to our attention that causes us to believe that the financial statements of Murray Company as of 31 December 20X4 are not prepared, in all material respects, in accordance with an applicable financial reporting framework.

The confidence inspired by a reasonable assurance report is designed to be greater than that inspired by a limited assurance report.

Therefore:

- there are more regulations/standards governing a reasonable assurance assignment
- the procedures carried out in a reasonable assignment will be more thorough
- the evidence gathered will need to be of a higher quality.

3 External audit engagements

Objective of an external audit engagement

The objective of an **external audit engagement** is to enable the auditor to express an opinion on whether the financial statements:

- Give a true and fair view (or present fairly in all material respects).
- Are prepared, in all material respects, in accordance with an applicable financial reporting framework.

The financial reporting framework to be applied will vary from country to country. In F8, it is assumed that International Financial Reporting Standards are the basis of preparing the financial statements.

ISA 200 *Overall objectives of the independent auditor and the conduct of an audit in accordance with International Standards on Auditing* states: the objectives of an **auditor** are to:

- Obtain reasonable assurance about whether the financial statements as a whole are free from material misstatement, whether due to fraud or error.
- Express an opinion on whether the financial statements are prepared, in all material respects, in accordance with an applicable financial reporting framework.
- Report on the financial statements, and communicate as required by ISAs, in accordance with the auditor's findings.

An **external audit** is an example of a **reasonable assurance** engagement.

The purpose of an audit is to enhance the degree of confidence of the intended users in the financial statements.

Need for external audit

- Shareholders provide the finance for a company and may or may not be involved in the day to day running of the company.
- Directors manage the company on behalf of the shareholders in order to achieve the objectives of that company (normally the maximisation of shareholder wealth).
- The directors must prepare financial statements to provide information on performance and financial position to the shareholders.
- The directors have various incentives to manipulate the financial statements and show a different level of performance.
- Hence the need for an independent review of the financial statements to ensure they give a true and fair view – the external audit.

In most developed countries, publicly quoted companies and large companies are required by law to produce annual financial statements and have them audited by an external auditor.

Companies that are not required to have a statutory audit may choose to have an external audit because the company's shareholders or other influential stakeholders want one and because of the benefits of an audit.

Benefits of an audit

- Improves the quality and reliability of information, giving investors faith in and improving the reputation of the market.
- Independent scrutiny and verification may be valuable to management.
- May reduce the risk of management bias, fraud and error by acting as a deterrent.
- May detect bias, fraud and error.
- Enhances the credibility of the financial statements, e.g. for tax authorities or lenders.
- Deficiencies in the internal control system may be highlighted by the auditor.

Expectations gap

Some users incorrectly believe that an audit provides absolute assurance; that the audit opinion is a guarantee the financial statements are 'correct'. This and other misconceptions about the role of an auditor are referred to as the '**expectations gap**'.

Examples of the expectations gap

- A belief that auditors test **all** transactions and balances; they test on a sample basis.
- A belief that auditors are required to detect **all** fraud; auditors are required to provide reasonable assurance that the financial statements are free from **material** misstatement, which may be caused by fraud.
- A belief that auditors are responsible for **preparing** the financial statements; this is the responsibility of management.

Auditors provide reasonable assurance which is not absolute assurance. The **limitations of an audit** mean that it is not possible to provide a 100% guarantee.

Limitations of an audit:

- **F**inancial statements include subjective estimates and other judgmental matters.
- **I**nternal controls may be relied on which have their own inherent limitations.
- **R**epresentations from management may have to be relied upon as the only source of evidence in some areas.
- **E**vidence is often persuasive not conclusive.
- **D**o not test all transactions and balances. Auditors test on a sample basis.

4 Review engagements

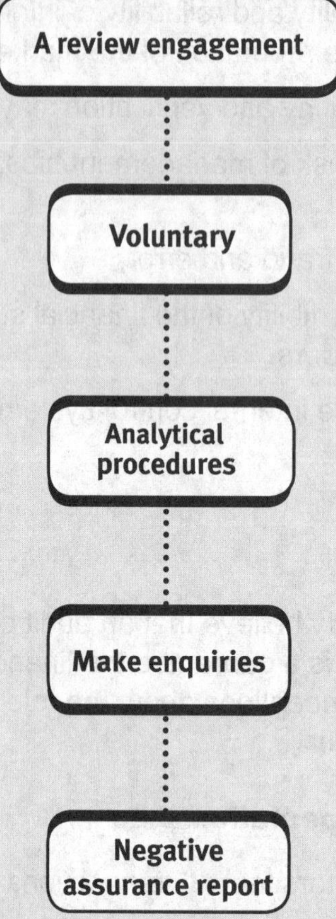

The **objective of a review of financial statements** is to enable an auditor to state whether, on the basis of procedures which do not provide all the evidence required in an audit, anything has come to the auditor's attention that causes the auditor to believe that the financial statements are not prepared in accordance with the applicable financial reporting framework (i.e. negative/limited assurance).

A **review engagement** is an example of a **limited assurance** engagement.

A company which is not legally required to have an audit may choose to have a review of their financial statements instead. The review will still provide some assurance to users but is likely to cost less and be less disruptive than an audit.

The procedures will mainly focus on analytical procedures and enquiries of management. In particular, no tests of controls will be performed. As only limited assurance is being expressed, the work does not need to be as in depth as for an audit.

Accountability, agency and stewardship

Key definitions:

Accountability means that people in a position of power can be held to account for their actions, i.e. they can be compelled to explain their decisions and can be criticised or punished if they have abused their position.

Accountability is central to the concept of good corporate governance – the process of ensuring that companies are well run – which we will look at in more detail in a later chapter.

Agency occurs when one party, the principal, employs another party, the agent, to perform a task on their behalf.

Stewardship is the responsibility to take good care of resources. A steward is a person entrusted with management of another person's property, for example, when one person is paid to look after another person's house while the owner goes abroad on holiday. The steward is **accountable** for the way he carries out his role.

This relationship, where one person has a duty of care towards someone else is known as a '**fiduciary relationship**'.

A **fiduciary relationship** is a relationship of 'good faith' such as that between the directors of a company and the shareholders of the company. There is a 'separation of ownership and control' in the sense that the shareholders own the company, while the directors make the decisions. The directors must make their decisions in the interests of the shareholders rather than in their own selfish personal interests.

Therefore:

- The directors are the stewards of the company.
- The shareholder is the principal, employing the directors (the agents) to run the company on their behalf.
- The directors are accountable to the shareholders for the way in which they run the company.

The development of assurance engagements

Incorporation and the separation of ownership and control

Businesses can operate through a number of different vehicles. It is common for investors in those businesses to seek the protection of limited company status. This means that whilst they could lose the funds they invest in a business they cannot be held personally responsible for satisfying the remaining corporate debts. The creation of a limited company is referred to as **incorporation**.

Incorporation has the following implications:

- the creation of a legal distinction between the owners of the business and the business itself;
- the opportunity for the owners/investors to detach themselves from the operation of the business; and
- the need for managers to operate the business on a daily basis.

Whilst this has provided financial protection for shareholders it does lead to one significant conflict:

- Shareholders seek to maximise their wealth through the increasing value of their shareholding. This is driven by the profitability (both current and potential) of the company.
- Directors/management seek to maximise their wealth through salary, bonuses and other employment benefits. This reduces company profitability.

This conflict led to the legal requirement for **financial statements** to be produced by directors to account for their **stewardship** of the company. These are sent to shareholders to allow them to assess the performance of management.

True and fair

- **True**: factual, conforms with accounting standards and relevant legislation and agrees with underlying records.
- **Fair**: clear, impartial and unbiased and reflects the commercial substance of the transactions of the entity.

Examples of stakeholder groups

Examples of stakeholder groups and their use of corporate information are:

- Shareholders can decide whether to alter their shareholdings.
- Employees may be able to judge whether they think their levels of pay are adequate compared to the directors and results of the company, and to enable them to make career decisions.
- Those charged with governance can see whether they think management have struck the right balance between their own need for reward (remuneration, share options, etc) and the needs of other stakeholders.
- Customers can make judgments about whether the company has sufficient financial strength (i.e. liquidity) to justify future trading.
- Suppliers and lenders can assess financial stability before giving credit.
- The government can decide whether the right amounts of tax have been paid and whether the company appears to be compliant with the relevant laws and regulations.

Test your understanding 1

Auditors are frequently required to provide assurance for a range of non-audit engagements.

Required:

List and explain the elements of an assurance engagement.

(5 marks)

Test your understanding 2

Explain the term 'limited assurance' in the context of a review of a company's cash flow forecast and explain how this differs from the assurance provided by a statutory audit.

(5 marks)

Test your understanding 3 – OT Case

Your firm has been approached to perform the external audit of Perth Co. As this is the first year the company has required an audit, the directors are unsure about the purpose of the audit, the level of assurance provided and the benefits of having an audit.

(1) Auditors aim to give absolute assurance over the accuracy of the financial statements. True or False?

A True

B False

(2) Which of the following is not one of the five elements of an assurance engagement?

A Subject matter

B Suitable criteria

C Assurance file

D Written report

(3) Which of the following is NOT a benefit of an audit?

A Increased credibility of the financial statements

B Deficiencies in controls may be identified during testing

C Fraud may be detected during the audit

D Sampling is used

(4) Which of the following statements is false?

A The auditor will express an opinion as to whether the financial statements show a true and fair view

B The audit opinion will provide reasonable assurance

C If the financial statements are found to contain material misstatements a negative audit opinion will be given

D An audit may not detect all fraud and error in the financial statements

(5) Which of the following are examples of the expectations gap?

(i) The audit report confirms the financial statements are accurate

(ii) An unmodified opinion means the company is a going concern

(iii) The auditor tests all transactions

(iv) The auditor can be sued for negligence if they issue an inappropriate opinion

A (i), (ii) and (iii)

B (i), (ii) and (iv)

C (i) and (ii) only

D (ii) and (iii) only

5 Chapter summary

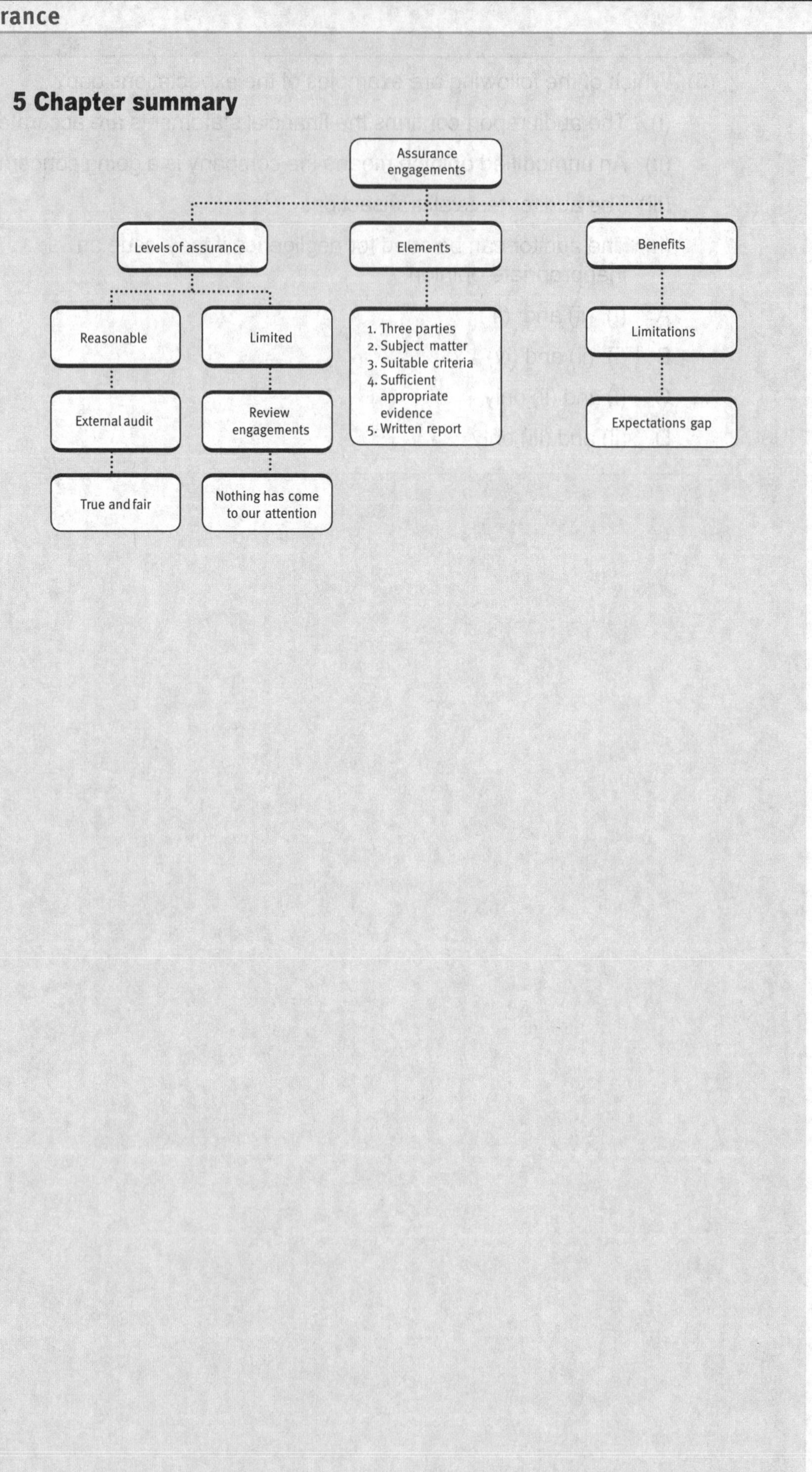

Test your understanding answers

Test your understanding 1

(1) An assurance engagement will involve three separate parties:

- (i) the intended user who is the person who requires the assurance report
- (ii) the responsible party, which is the organisation responsible for preparing the subject matter to be reviewed and
- (iii) the practitioner (i.e. an accountant) who is the professional, who will review the subject matter and provide the assurance.

(2) A second element is a suitable subject matter. The subject matter is the data that the responsible party has prepared and which requires verification.

(3) Suitable criteria are required in an assurance engagement. The subject matter is compared to the criteria in order for it to be assessed and an opinion provided.

(4) Appropriate evidence has to be obtained by the practitioner in order to give the required level of assurance.

(5) An assurance report is the opinion that is given by the practitioner to the intended user and the responsible party.

Test your understanding 2

Limited Assurance	**Assurance provided by statutory audit**
Limited assurance is a moderate level of assurance.	A statutory audit provides reasonable assurance, which is a high level.
The objective of a limited assurance engagement is to obtain sufficient appropriate evidence that the cash flow forecast is plausible in the circumstances.	The objective of a statutory audit is to obtain sufficient appropriate evidence that the financial statements conform in all material respects with the relevant financial reporting framework.
A limited assurance report provides a negative opinion. The practitioner will state that nothing has come to their attention which indicates that the cash flow forecast contains any material errors. The assurance is therefore given on the absence of any indication to the contrary.	The statutory audit report provides a positive opinion; that is the financial statements do show a true and fair view.
With limited assurance, limited procedures are performed; often only enquiry and analytical procedures.	More evidence will need to be obtained to provide reasonable assurance, and a wider range of procedures performed, including tests of controls.
A cash flow relates to the future, which is inherently uncertain, and therefore it would not be possible to obtain assurance that it is free from material misstatement.	Financial statements relate to the past, and so the auditor should be able to obtain sufficient appropriate evidence.
Less reliance can therefore be placed on the forecast than the financial statements, where the positive assurance was given.	

Test your understanding 3 – OT Case

(1)	B	False. Only reasonable assurance can be given as all transactions are not tested.
(2)	C	Assurance file.
(3)	D	Sampling provides a limitation of the audit process, not a benefit.
(4)	C	A negative opinion is used for limited assurance engagements.
(5)	A	The auditor cannot confirm the accuracy of the financial statements as they contain estimates and judgments of management. The company may not be a going concern and the financial statements may correctly reflect this resulting in an unmodified audit opinion. The auditor does not test all transactions.

chapter

2

Rules and regulation

Chapter learning objectives

This chapter covers syllabus areas:

- A2 – External audits

Detailed syllabus objectives are provided in the introduction section of the text book.

1 The need for regulation

The role of the auditor has come under increased scrutiny over the last thirty years due to an increase in high profile audit failures. The most high profile case, and the catalyst for regulatory change, was the collapse of Enron and its auditor Arthur Andersen.

In order to try and regain trust in the auditing profession national and international standard setters and regulators have tried to introduce three initiatives:

- **Harmonisation** of auditing procedures, so that users of audit services are confident in the nature of audits being conducted around the world.
- Focus **on audit quality**, so that the expectations of users are met.
- Adherence to a strict **ethical code** of conduct, to try and improve the perception of auditors as independent, unbiased service providers.

In order to achieve this practitioners have to follow regulatory guidance:

- **National corporate law (e.g. The Companies Act 2006 in the UK and The Sarbanes Oxley Act in the US).**
- **Auditing Standards** (the basis of this text is International Standards on Auditing).
- **Code of Ethics**. Covered in the chapter 'Ethics and acceptance'.

2 Legal requirements for audits and auditors

In this section, the law referred to in most cases is UK law and the Companies Act 2006. Different countries may have different requirements but generally the same principles will apply across the world.

National law includes:

- which companies are required to have an audit
- who can and cannot carry out an audit
- auditor appointment, resignation and removal
- the rights and duties of an auditor.

Who needs an audit and why?

In most countries, companies are required by law to have an audit.

Small or owner-managed companies are often exempt. This is because there is less value in an audit for these companies.

Note that these exemptions often do not apply to companies in certain regulated sectors, e.g. financial services companies or companies listed on a stock exchange.

Reasons for exempting small companies from audit

The main reasons for exempting small companies are:

- The owners and managers of the company are often the same people.
- The advice and value which accountants can add to a small company is more likely to concern other services, such as accounting and tax.
- The impact of misstatements in the accounts of small companies is unlikely to be material to the wider economy.
- The audit fee and disruption of an audit are seen as too great a cost for any benefits the audit might bring.

Who may act as auditor?

To be **eligible to act as auditor**, a person must be:

- a member of a Recognised Supervisory Body (RSB), e.g. ACCA, and allowed by the rules of that body to be an auditor **or**
- someone directly authorised by the state.

Conducting audit work

Individuals who are authorised to conduct audit work may be:

- sole practitioners
- partners in a partnership
- members of a limited liability partnership
- directors of an audit company.

To be eligible to offer audit services, a firm must be:

- controlled by members of a suitably authorised supervisory body or
- a firm directly authorised by the state.

Note: In some countries only individuals can be authorised to act as auditor and need to be directly authorised by the state.

Who may not act as auditor?

Excluded by law: The law in most countries excludes those involved with managing the company and those who have business or personal connections with them from auditing that company.

Excluded by the Code of Ethics: Auditors must also comply with a Code of Ethics. The Code of Ethics requires the auditor to consider any factors that would prevent them acting as auditor, such as independence, competence or issues regarding confidentiality. This is considered in more detail in the next chapter.

Excluded by law: UK example

For example, in the UK the following are excluded by company law:

- an officer (director or secretary) of the company
- an employee of the company
- a business partner or employee of the above.

Who appoints the auditor?

Members (shareholders) – in most jurisdictions of the company appoint the auditor by voting them in.

Directors – can appoint the first auditor or to fill a 'casual vacancy' this requires the members' approval at a members meeting. In some countries the auditors may be appointed by the directors as a matter of course.

Secretary of State – if no auditors are appointed by the members or directors.

Auditors of public companies are appointed from one AGM to the next one.

Auditors of private companies are appointed until they are removed.

Removing the auditor

Arrangements for removing the auditor have to be structured in such a way that:

- the auditor has sufficiently secure tenure of office, to maintain independence of management.
- auditors can be removed if there are doubts about their continuing abilities to carry out their duties effectively.

Removal of auditors can usually be achieved by a simple majority at a general meeting of the company. There are some safeguards, such as a specified notice period, to prevent the resolution to remove the auditors being 'sprung' on the meeting.

Auditors can circulate representations stating why they should not be removed if applicable.

A statement of circumstances must be sent to the company and the regulatory authority to set out issues surrounding the cessation of office.

Resigning as auditor

In practice, if the auditors and management find it difficult to work together, the auditors will usually resign.

The auditor issues written notice of the resignation and a statement of circumstances to the members and regulatory authority.

Notifying ACCA

If an auditor resigns or is removed from office before the end of their term of office, they must notify the ACCA.

The auditor's responsibilities on removal/resignation

The following is taken from UK law, but provides an example of the typical responsibilities of the auditor.

- Deposit at the company's registered office:
  - a statement of the circumstances connected with the removal/resignation or
  - a statement that there are no such circumstances.
- Deal promptly with requests for clearance from new auditors.

The auditor's rights

During appointment as auditor

- Access to the company's books and records at any reasonable time.
- To receive information and explanations necessary for the audit.
- To receive notice of and attend any general meeting of members of the company.
- To be heard at such meetings on matters of concern to the auditor.
- To receive copies of any written resolutions of the company.

On resignation

- To request a General Meeting of the company to explain the circumstances of the resignation.
- To require the company to circulate the notice of circumstances relating to the resignation.

The auditor's duties

The auditor's primary statutory duty is to audit the financial statements and provide an opinion on whether the financial statements, as presented to the shareholders at the general meeting of the company give a true and fair view (or are fairly presented in all material respects).

They may have additional reporting responsibilities required by local national law, such as confirming that the financial statements are properly prepared in accordance with those laws.

3 Auditing standards

IFAC

The International Federation of Accountants (IFAC) is the global organisation for the accountancy profession.

IFAC promotes international regulation of the accountancy profession. By ensuring minimum requirements for accountancy qualifications, post qualification experience and guidance on accounting and assurance for accountants around the world, there will be greater public confidence in the profession as a whole.

International Audit and Assurance Standards Board

One of the subsidiary boards of IFAC is the International Audit and Assurance Standards Board (IAASB). It is their responsibility to develop and promote International Standards on Auditing (ISAs). There are currently 36 ISAs and one International Standard of Quality Control, although not all are examinable for this syllabus. A list of examinable documents is available on the ACCA website.

You do not need to learn the names or numbers of the ISAs but you will need to know and be able to apply the key principles and requirements of the standards.

- ISAs are written in the context of an audit of the financial statements but can be applied to the audit of other historical financial information.
- ISAs must be applied in all but exceptional cases. Where the auditor deems it necessary to depart from an ISA to achieve the overall aim of the audit, this departure must be justified.
- The ISAs contain basic principles and requirements followed by application and other explanatory material.

Development of ISAs

For an ISA to be issued, a lengthy process of discussion and debate occurs to ensure the members affected by the guidance have had an input.

An exposure draft (ED) is issued for public comment and these comments may result in revisions to the ED.

Approval of two thirds of IAASB members is required for the ISA to come into force.

The relationship between international and national standards and regulation

Because IFAC is simply a grouping of accountancy bodies, it has no legal standing in individual countries. Countries therefore need to have arrangements in place for:

- Regulating the audit profession
- Implementing auditing standards.

National standard setters

- May set their own auditing standards and ethical standards (such as the FRC Ethical Standards in the UK)
- May adopt and implement ISAs, possibly after modifying them to suit national needs.

In the event of a conflict between the two sets of guidance, local regulations will apply. However, in such a situation, IFAC members are encouraged to amend their local regulations to bring them in line with ISAs to avoid such conflicts.

In the UK, the national standard setter (the Financial Reporting Council, Codes and Standards division) decided to adopt and modify ISAs.

More about IFAC

IFAC is a non governmental, non political organisation. IFAC's overall mission is to serve the public interest, strengthen the worldwide accountancy profession, and contribute to the development of strong international economies by establishing and promoting adherence to high quality professional standards.

IFAC was formed in 1977 and is based in New York. As of January 2015, IFAC has over 175 member bodies of accountants (including the ACCA), representing 2.5 million accountants from over 130 separate countries.

IFAC supports the following standard setting boards:

- International Auditing and Assurance Standards Board (issues audit and assurance guidance for all types of assurance services e.g. ISAs).
- International Ethics Standards Board for Accountants (sets ethical standards for accountants and auditors).
- International Public Sector Accounting Standards Board (issues financial reporting standards and guidance for Public Sector entities).
- International Accounting Education Standards Board (provides guidance to accountancy bodies for entry requirements, exam content and experience requirements for their students, and continuing professional development for members. This is to ensure minimum requirements for accountancy qualifications are in place and the competence of accountants around the world is more consistent).

National regulatory bodies

National regulatory bodies:

- enforce the implementation of auditing standards
- have disciplinary powers to enforce quality of audit work
- have rights to inspect audit files to monitor audit quality.

There are two possible schemes for regulation at the national level:

- self regulation by the audit/accountancy profession
- regulation by government or by some independent body set up by government for the purpose.

The UK is primarily self regulated by the FRC. In European countries, there is considerably more government involvement.

Whilst self regulation is working effectively it is likely to continue. However, if a major audit failure occurs which damages the reputation of the profession as a whole, then it is likely that the government will get involved.

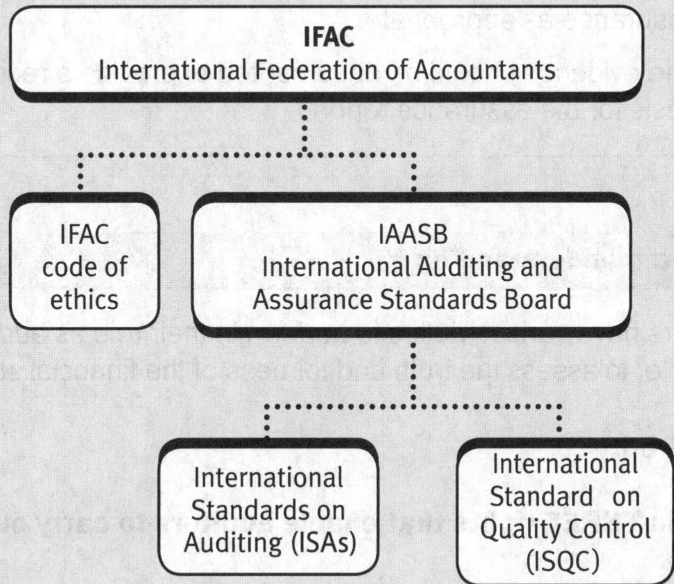

Assurance engagements other than audits

ISAE 3000 *Assurance engagements other than audits or reviews of historical financial information* is the International Standard on Assurance Engagements (ISAE) that 'establishes the basic principles and essential procedures for, and provides guidance to, professional accountants... for the performance of assurance engagements other than audits or reviews of historical financial information.'

This requires the practitioner to:

- Comply with ethical requirements.
- Apply professional scepticism and judgment.
- Perform acceptance and continuance procedures to ensure only work of acceptable risk is accepted.
- Agree the terms of engagement.
- Comply with quality control requirements (ISQC 1).
- Plan and perform the engagement so it will be conducted in an effective manner.
- Obtain sufficient appropriate evidence to be able to form a conclusion.
- Consider the effect of subsequent events on the subject matter.
- Form a conclusion expressing either reasonable or limited assurance as appropriate.
- The evidence should be documented to provide a record of the basis for the assurance report.

Test your understanding 1

Auditors have various duties to perform in their role as auditors, for example, to assess the truth and fairness of the financial statements.

Required:

Explain THREE rights that enable auditors to carry out their duties.

(3 marks)

Test your understanding 2

The purpose of an external audit and its role are not well understood. You have been asked to write some material for inclusion in your firm's training materials dealing with these issues in the audit of large companies.

Required:

Draft an explanation dealing with the purpose of an external audit and its role in the audit of large companies, for inclusion in your firm's training materials.

(10 marks)

Test your understanding 3 – OT Case

You have been approached by some new trainees recruited by your firm to answer some queries regarding the appointment and removal of auditors and the regulatory environment surrounding the auditing profession.

(1) There is a legal requirement for an auditor to follow auditing standards when performing the audit. Is this statement false or true?

A False

B True

(2) Which of the following are reasons for the audit profession issuing auditing standards?

(i) To ensure consistency of audits across different firms

(ii) To provide bureaucracy for auditors

(iii) To ensure quality in the standard of audits performed

A All of them

B (i) and (ii) only

C (i) and (iii) only

D (ii) and (iii) only

(3) A person may not act as auditor if they are an officer or employee of the company. Is this statement true or false?

A True

B False

(4) In most jurisdictions, the auditors of a company will be appointed by which party?

A Directors

B Audit committee

C Government

D Shareholders

(5) Which of the following statements is true?

A The shareholders of most companies will also be the directors

B The directors are the stewards of the company responsible for looking after the company on behalf of the owners

C Directors will always have a vested interest in the company doing well because they own shares in the company they work for

D Auditors are allowed to be business partners of the company directors

4 Chapter summary

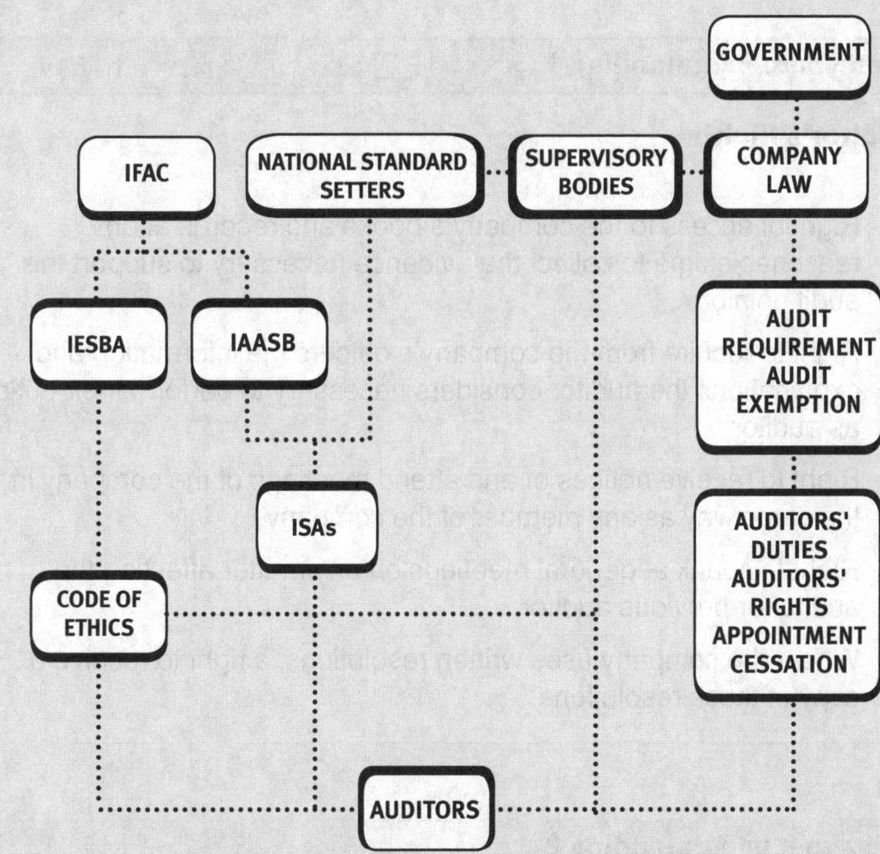

Test your understanding answers

Test your understanding 1

Auditor's Rights

- Right of access to the company's books and records at any reasonable time to collect the evidence necessary to support the audit opinion.
- Right to require from the company's officers the information and explanations the auditor considers necessary to perform their duties as auditors.
- Right to receive notices of and attend meetings of the company in the same way as any member of the company.
- Right to speak at general meetings on any matter affecting the auditor or previous auditor.
- Where the company uses written resolutions, a right to receive a copy of those resolutions.

Test your understanding 2

Training material: purpose of external audit and its role

(i) The external audit has a long history that derives largely from the separation of the ownership and management of assets. Those who own assets wish to ensure that those to whom they have entrusted control are using those assets wisely. This is known as the 'stewardship' function.

(ii) The requirement for an independent audit helps ensure that financial statements are free of bias and manipulation for the benefit of users of financial information.

(iii) Companies are owned by shareholders but they are managed by directors (in very small companies, owners and managers are the same, but many such companies are not subject to statutory audit requirements).

(iv) The requirement for a statutory audit is a public interest issue: the public is invited to invest in enterprises, it is in the interests of the capital markets (and society as a whole) that those investing do so in the knowledge that they will be provided with 'true and fair' information about the enterprise. This should result in the efficient allocation of capital as investors are able to make rational decisions on the basis of transparent financial information.

(v) The requirement for an audit can help prevent investors from being defrauded, although there is no guarantee of this because the external audit has inherent limitations. Reducing the possibility of false information being provided by managers to owners is achieved by the requirement for external auditors to be independent of the managers upon whose financial statements they are reporting.

(vi) The purpose of the external audit under International Standards on Auditing is for the auditor to obtain sufficient appropriate audit evidence on which to base the audit opinion. This opinion is on whether the financial statements give a 'true and fair view' (or 'present fairly in all material respects') of the position, performance (and cash flows) of the entity. This opinion is prepared for the benefit of shareholders.

Test your understanding 3 – OT Case

(1)	A	Auditing standards are professional guidance, not law.
(2)	C	By issuing standards, audits should be performed more consistently which should improve quality.
(3)	A	True.
(4)	D	Shareholders.
(5)	B	Whilst directors may be shareholders of the company they work for, large public companies will have a significant number of shareholders who are not involved in the operations of the company. Auditors are not allowed to be business partners of the directors of a company they audit.

chapter

3

Ethics and acceptance

Chapter learning objectives

This chapter covers syllabus areas:

- A4 – Professional ethics and ACCA's Code of Ethics and Conduct
- B1 – Obtaining, accepting and continuing audit engagements

Detailed syllabus objectives are provided in the introduction section of the text book.

1 The need for professional ethics

Professional accountants have a responsibility to act in the public interest. The purpose of assurance engagements is to increase the confidence of the intended users, therefore the users need to trust the professional who is providing the assurance.

In order to be trusted the assurance provider needs to be **independent** of their client.

Independence can be defined as having 'freedom from situations and relationships where objectivity would be perceived to be impaired by a reasonable and informed third party.'

Practitioners need to **behave and be seen to behave** in an ethical, professional manner. This means taking active steps to comply with the Code of Ethics in every professional situation.

2 The IFAC and ACCA codes and the conceptual framework

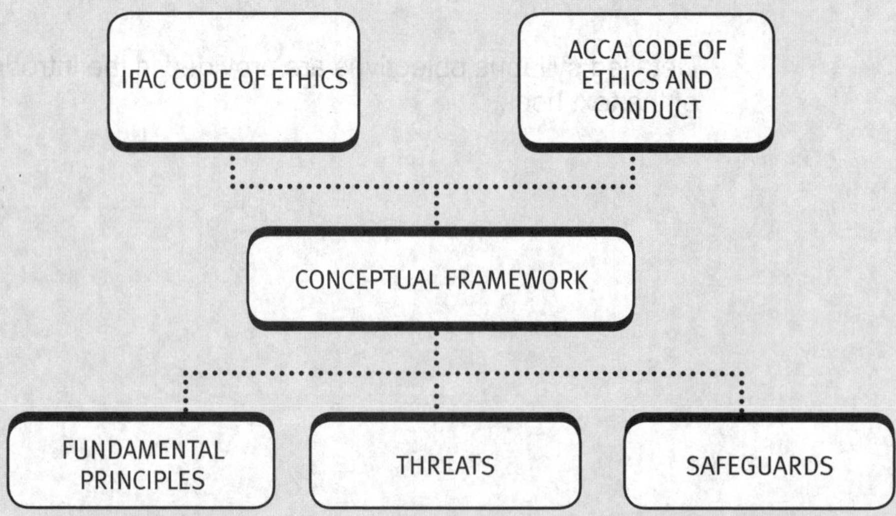

IFAC, through the IESBA, has issued a code of ethics, as has the ACCA. The ACCA Code of Ethics is covered in this chapter. However, both the IESBA and ACCA codes have the same roots and are, to all intents and purposes identical.

Both follow a conceptual framework which identifies:

- fundamental principles of ethical behaviour
- potential threats to compliance with these fundamental principles
- possible safeguards which can be implemented to eliminate the threats identified, or reduce them to an acceptable level.

A conceptual framework relies on a principles rather than a rules based approach. This provides guidance so that the principles may be applied to wide ranging and potentially unique circumstances.

This requires the assurance provider to apply **professional judgment** in applying the code of ethics.

Consequences

Practitioners should apply the spirit of the code to every day practice. However, the framework and principles would be of little use if they could not be enforced.

Professional bodies like the ACCA therefore reserve the right to discipline members who fail to comply with the code of ethics through a process of:

- Disciplinary hearings which can result in:
  - fines
  - suspension of membership
  - withdrawal of membership.

3 The fundamental principles

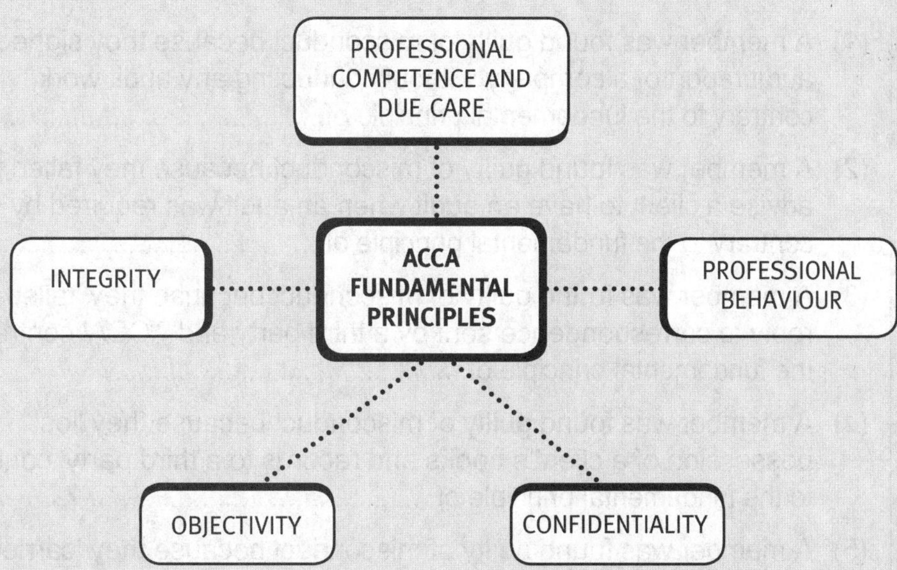

The formal definitions of the fundamental principles are as follows:

- **Objectivity**: Members should not allow bias, conflicts of interest or undue influence of others to override professional or business judgments.
- **Professional behaviour**: Members should comply with relevant laws and regulations and should avoid any action that discredits the profession.

- **Professional competence and due care**: Members should maintain professional knowledge and skill at a level required to ensure that a client or employer receives competent professional services based on current developments in practice, legislation and techniques.

  Members should act diligently and in accordance with applicable technical and professional standards.

- **Integrity**: Members should be straightforward and honest in all professional and business relationships.
- **Confidentiality**: Members should respect the confidentiality of information acquired as a result of professional and business relationships and should not disclose any such information to third parties without proper and specific authority or unless there is a legal or professional right or duty to disclose. Confidential information acquired as a result of professional and business relationships should not be used for the personal advantage of members or third parties.

Illustration 1: Fundamental principles

The following are real précis hearings held and decisions made and published by the ACCA Disciplinary Committee:

(1) A member was found guilty of misconduct because they signed the audit report of a company without conducting any audit work, contrary to the fundamental principle of..?

(2) A member was found guilty of misconduct because they failed to advise a client to have an audit when an audit was required by law, contrary to the fundamental principle of..?

(3) A member was found guilty of misconduct because they 'failed to reply to correspondence sent by a third party and ACCA' contrary to the fundamental principle of..?

(4) A member was found guilty of misconduct because they 'lost possession of a client's books and records to a third party' contrary to the fundamental principle of..?

(5) A member was found guilty of misconduct because they 'carried out an audit of a company' in which they owned shares 'without implementing appropriate safeguards' contrary to the fundamental principle of..?

Exercise:

Discuss the scenarios described above and identify which of the fundamental principles has been breached in each circumstance.

Illustration 1 Solution: Fundamental principles

The following are real précis hearings held and decisions made by the ACCA Disciplinary Committee:

(1) A member was found guilty of misconduct because they signed the audit report of a company without conducting any audit work, contrary to the fundamental principle of **integrity**.

(2) A member was found guilty of misconduct because they failed to advise a client to have an audit when an audit was required by law, contrary to the fundamental principle of **professional competence and due care**.

(3) A member was found guilty of misconduct because they 'failed to reply to correspondence sent by a third party and ACCA' contrary to the fundamental principle of **professional behaviour**.

(4) A member was found guilty of misconduct because they 'lost possession of a client's books and records to a third party' contrary to the fundamental principle of **confidentiality**.

(5) A member was found guilty of misconduct because they 'carried out an audit of a company' in which they owned shares 'without implementing appropriate safeguards' contrary to the fundamental principle of **objectivity**.

As a result, a combination of the following sanctions were ordered by ACCA Disciplinary Committee in each case:

- suspension of membership
- exclusion from ACCA
- a fine
- a costs order
- publication of the results of the decision and the member's name on the ACCA website
- publication of the results of the decision and the member's name in the local press.

4 Threats and safeguards

Self Interest

- Own shares
- Fee dependency
- Gifts & hospitality
- Loans
- Business and personal relationships
- Employment with client
- Overdue fees
- Contingency fees
- Litigation with a client

Self Review

- Accounts preparation
- Internal audit
- Tax computations
- Valuation services
- Client staff joins the audit firm

Familiarity

- Long association
- Personal relationships
- Movement of staff between the firm and client
- Gifts & hospitality

Threats to objectivity

Intimidation

- Fee dependency
- Personal relationships
- Audit partner leaves to join client
- Litigation with a client

Advocacy

- Representing the client
- Promoting the client
- Negotiating on behalf of the client

Definitions and examples of threats

Self interest threats

Where the auditor has a financial or other interest in the client. A financial or other interest that will inappropriately influence the judgment or behaviour of the assurance provider.

Threat	Safeguards
Owning shares/financial interests Holding a beneficial interest in the shares, or some other form of investment in a client. The auditor will want to maximise return from the investment and overlook audit adjustments which would affect the value of their investment.	• Dispose of the shares immediately if a member of the audit team; or • Remove the individual from the engagement team. • Any employee who is not a member of the audit team must dispose of the share as soon as possible. • Note, if a partner of the firm (whether on the engagement team or not) has such a financial interest, the shares must be disposed of, or the engagement declined.
Fee dependency Over-dependence on an audit client could lead the auditor to ignore adjustments required in the financial statements for fear of losing the client.	A firm's independence is threatened, and should be reviewed if total fees from a listed audit client exceed 15% of the firm's total fees for two consecutive years. • Disclosure to those charged with governance at the client. • An independent engagement quality control review should be performed by a person not a member of the audit firm expressing the opinion or by the professional regulatory body.

Gifts and hospitality Acceptance of goods, services or hospitality from an audit client can create self-interest and familiarity threats as the auditor may feel indebted to the client.	Only gifts which are trivial and inconsequential should ever be accepted and even these should be approved by a partner. The offer of gifts and hospitality must be documented on the audit file even if refused. **Note:** The purchase of goods and services from an assurance client would not normally give rise to a threat to independence, provided the transaction is in the normal course of business and on commercial terms.
Loans and guarantees	A loan or guarantee from (or deposit with) an assurance client will not create a threat to independence provided that: • it is on commercial terms; and • made in the normal course of business. If the loan is made to the firm (rather than a member), it must be immaterial to both the firm and the client. If it is material, a self-interest threat may arise and appropriate safeguards should be put into place, e.g. an external review of the work performed. Loans and guarantees to/from audit clients that are **not in the normal course of business** or **not on commercial terms** are **not permitted** (i.e. the self-interest threat is so significant, no safeguards could reduce the threat to an acceptable level).
Overdue fees The overdue fees may be regarded as a loan (loans are not permitted to an audit client).	Do not perform any further work for the client until the outstanding fees are paid or arrangements have been agreed with the client for repayment.

Business and personal relationships If audit firms (or members) enter into business relationships (e.g. joint ventures, marketing arrangements) with clients this leads to self-interest because the auditor would have an interest in the successful operation of the client. In the case of audit firms, or partners of those firms.	Unless immaterial, no safeguard can reduce this threat to an acceptable level. For personal relationships, the individual with the connection to the audit client should be removed from the audit team.
Potential employment with an audit client If a member of the engagement team has reason to believe they may become an employee of the client they will not wish to do anything to affect their potential future employment.	• The policies and procedures of the firm should require such individuals to notify the firm of the possibility of employment with the client. • Removal of the individual from the assurance engagement. • Performing an independent review of any significant judgments made by that individual.
Contingent fees The auditor would have incentive to ensure a particular outcome is achieved in order to maximise the audit fee. E.g. overlook audit adjustments that would reduce profit if the fee is a percentage of the profit.	Fees based on particular outcome, e.g. level of profits of the company are not permitted for assurance services.

Actual or threatened litigation	The firm must resign from or decline the audit.
Litigation could represent a breakdown in the relationship of trust between auditor and client. This may affect the impartiality of the auditor, and lead to a reluctance of management to disclose relevant information to the auditor.	It may be possible to continue other assurance engagements, depending on the significance of the threat by: • Discussing the matter with the client's audit committee. • If the litigation involves an individual, removing that individual from the engagement team. • Obtaining an external review of the work done.

Self review threats

Where non-audit work is provided to an audit client and is then subject to audit, the auditor will be unlikely to admit to errors in their own work, or may not identify the errors in their own work.

Threat	Safeguards
Accounting and bookkeeping services	• A firm can provide an audit client that is not listed with accounting and bookkeeping services, including payroll services, of a 'routine or mechanical nature', as long as adequate safeguards are implemented. • A firm cannot provide an audit client that is listed with accounting and bookkeeping services. • Where services are provided, separate teams must be used. • Managerial decisions must not be made by the firm, and the source data, underlying assumptions, and subsequent adjustments must be originated or approved by the client.

Internal audit services	A firm cannot provide internal audit services for an audit client that is listed, where the service relates to internal controls over financial reporting, financial accounting systems, or in relation to amounts or disclosures that are material to the financial statements. Where services are provided, separate teams must be used.
Taxation services Tax calculations for inclusion in the financial statements and tax planning advice creates a self review threat. Completion of tax returns is not deemed to create a self review threat.	• A firm **cannot prepare tax calculations** for an **audit client** that is **listed**. • Where services are provided, separate teams must be used.
Valuation services	• Valuation of matters that are material to the financial statements and involve a significant degree of subjectivity should not be provided. • For listed audit clients, valuation services that are material to the financial statements (regardless of subjectivity) should not be provided.

Client staff joins audit firm A self interest, self-review, or familiarity threat may arise where a director or employee of an assurance client (in a position to exert significant influence over the financial statements or subject matter of another assurance engagement) becomes an employee of the firm.	• Such individuals should not be assigned to an engagement team until at least two years have elapsed (after the end of their employment with the client). • An employee or partner of a firm **cannot** also be an employee or director of an assurance client, as the self-interest and self-review threats created would be so significant that no safeguard could reduce the threats to an acceptable level.

Familiarity threats

The auditor becomes too sympathetic to or too trusting of a client and loses professional scepticism.

Threat	Safeguards
Long-association of senior personnel Using the same senior personnel in an engagement team over a long period may cause the auditor to become too trusting/less sceptical of the client.	• Rotation of senior personnel. • Independent partner/quality control reviews. • Note that it is a requirement to rotate key audit partners on listed clients after no more than seven years (with a minimum break of two years), unless in exceptional circumstances where necessary to maintain audit quality, in which case a maximum one year extension is permitted. • Note: In April 2014, the EU voted in favour of compulsory tendering of large listed companies every ten years.

Family and other personal relationships A familiarity threat (and self-interest threat or intimidation threat) may occur when a member of the engagement team has a family or personal relationship with someone at the client who is able to exert significant influence over the financial statements (or subject matter of another assurance engagement). Consideration should be given to the possibility that such a threat may also arise when a partner (or employee) of the firm has a family or personal relationship with someone at the client who is able to exert significant influence over the subject matter, even when the individual is not a member of the engagement team.	• Remove the individual from the engagement team. • Structure the engagement team so that the individual does not deal with matters that are the responsibility of the close family member.

Audit staff leave the firm to join the client A self interest, familiarity or intimidation threat may arise where an employee of the firm becomes a director or employee of an assurance client (in a position to exert significant influence over the financial statements or subject matter of another assurance engagement). The threat is significant if significant connection remains between the employee and the firm such as entitlement to benefits or payments from the firm, or participates in the firms business and professional activities. For public interest entities, independence would be deemed to be compromised unless, subsequent to the partner ceasing to be a key audit partner, the public interest entity had issued audited financial statements covering a period of not less than twelve months and the partner was not a member of the audit team with respect to the audit of those financial statements.	• Reviewing (and revising) the composition of the engagement team. • Performing an independent partner/quality control review of the engagement.

Advocacy threats

Promoting the position of a client or representing them in some way would mean the audit firm is seen to be 'taking sides' with the client.

Examples include:

- Promoting a share issue for an audit client.
- Representing the client in court or in any dispute where the matter is material to the financial statements.
- Negotiating on the client's behalf for finance.

The audit firm must not act for the audit client in this way. Any request for such services must be politely declined.

Intimidation threats

Actual or perceived pressures from the client, or attempts to exercise undue influence over the assurance provider, e.g. actual or threatened litigation between the auditor and audit client (in which case it may be necessary to resign from the engagement).

Intimidation can arise from some of the same situations mentioned above. The safeguards to address these threats are the same as to address the other threats.

- Fee dependency
- Personal relationships
- Audit partner joining the client
- Litigation with between the audit firm and client.

Identifying the threats

Firms must establish procedures to:

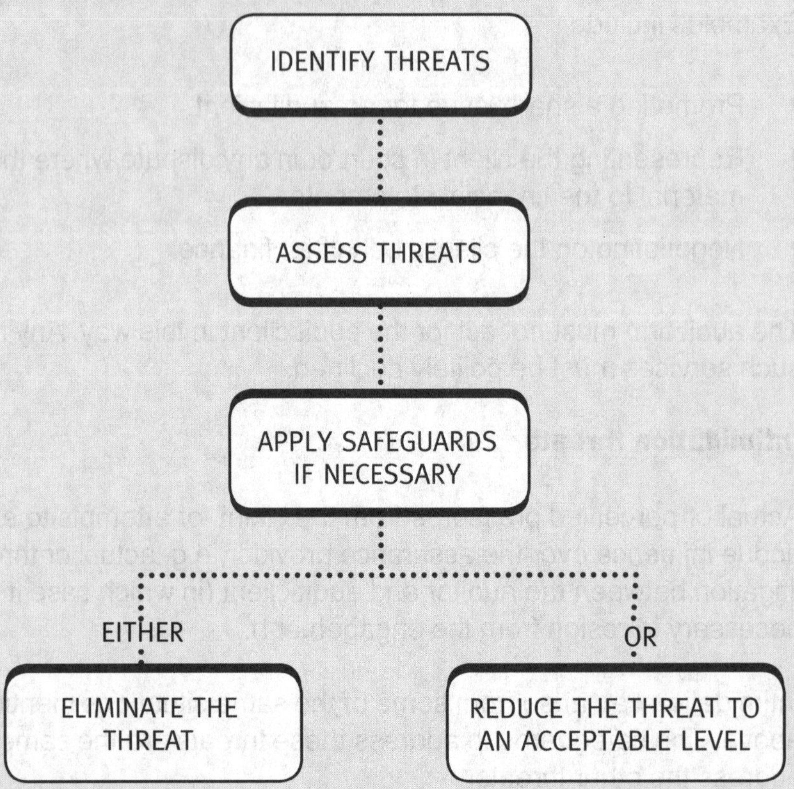

A **safeguard** is an action or measure that eliminates a threat, or reduces it to an acceptable level.

If the threat cannot be eliminated or reduced to an acceptable level, the assurance provider must decline or resign from the engagement.

The ACCA Code of Ethics divides safeguards into two broad categories:

- **Safeguards created by the profession, legislation or regulation**, these include: requirements for entry into the profession, continuing professional development, corporate governance, professional standards, and monitoring and disciplinary procedures, etc.
- **Safeguards created by the work environment**, these include: rotation/removal of relevant staff from the engagement team, independent quality control reviews, using separate teams, etc.

5 Confidentiality

External auditors are in a unique position of having a legal right of access to all information about their clients. The client must be able to trust the auditor not to disclose anything about their business to anyone as it could be detrimental to their operations.

Members of an assurance team should not disclose any information to anyone outside of the engagement team, whether or not they work for the same firm.

Information should only be disclosed with proper and specific authority or when there is a legal or professional right or duty to disclose.

The following are circumstances where professional accountants are or may be required to disclose confidential information or when such disclosure may be appropriate:

(a) Disclosure is permitted by law and is authorised by the client or the employer.

(b) Disclosure is required by law, for example:

- Production of documents or other provision of evidence in the course of legal proceedings.
- Disclosure to the appropriate public authorities of infringements of the law that come to light.

(c) There is a professional duty or right to disclose, when not prohibited by law:

- To comply with the quality review of ACCA or another professional body.
- To respond to an inquiry or investigation by ACCA or a regulatory body.
- To protect the professional interests of a professional accountant in legal proceedings.
- To comply with technical standards and ethics requirements.

Public interest

The auditor may feel disclosure is required in the public interest. Maintaining confidentiality in such circumstances may be considered unethical. Examples could include significant fraud, environmental pollution, or simply companies acting against the public good.

Legal advice should be sought beforehand to avoid the risk of being sued for breach of confidentiality. Matters should only be reported to an appropriate authority.

Before disclosing information in the public interest, the auditor should consider, for example, whether that matter is likely to be repeated and how serious the effects of the client's actions are.

Conflicts of interest

Professional accountants should always act in the best interests of the client. However, where conflicts of interest exist, such as when a firm acts for competing clients (which is common) the firm's work should be arranged to **avoid the interests of one being adversely affected** by those of another and to prevent a breach of **confidentiality**.

In order to ensure this, the firm must notify all affected clients of the conflict and **obtain their consent to act**.

The following additional safeguards should be considered:

- separate engagement teams (with different engagement partners and team members).
- procedures to prevent access to information, e.g. physical separation of the team members by using teams from different offices of the firm, and confidential/secure data filing.
- signed confidentiality agreements by audit staff.
- regular review of the application of safeguards by an independent person of appropriate seniority.
- advise the clients to seek independent advice.

If adequate safeguards cannot be implemented, the firm must decline, or resign from one or more conflicting engagements.

Test your understanding 1

Murray case study: Ethical issues

You are an audit manager in Wimble & Co, a large audit firm which specialises in providing audit and accountancy services to manufacturing companies. Murray Co has asked your firm to accept appointment as external auditor. Murray Co manufactures sports equipment. Your firm also audits Barker Co, another manufacturer of sports equipment, and therefore your firm is confident it has the experience to carry out the audit.

You have been asked to take on the role of audit manager for Murray Co, should your firm accept the engagement. You own a small number of shares in Murray Co, as you used to be an employee of the company. Don Henman, who has been the engagement partner for Barker Co for twelve years, will take the role of engagement partner for Murray Co. The audit senior will be Tim Andrews, as his sister is the Financial Controller at Murray Co and therefore he knows the business well.

Your firm recently purchased some bibs, footballs and other equipment from Murray Co for the firm's annual football tournament. Murray Co has offered to provide this equipment free of charge to the firm if they accept the role as auditor.

Murray Co would also like your firm to provide taxation and accounting services. Specifically, the company would like you to prepare the financial statements and represent the company in a dispute with the taxation authorities.

The fees for last year's audit of Barker Co have not yet been paid, and you have been asked by Don Henman to look into the matter.

Required:

Using the information provided, explain the ethical threats which may affect the independence of Wimble & Co in respect of the audit of Murray Co or Barker Co, and for each threat identify ways in which the threat might be reduced.

6 Accepting/continuing an audit engagement

Accepting new work

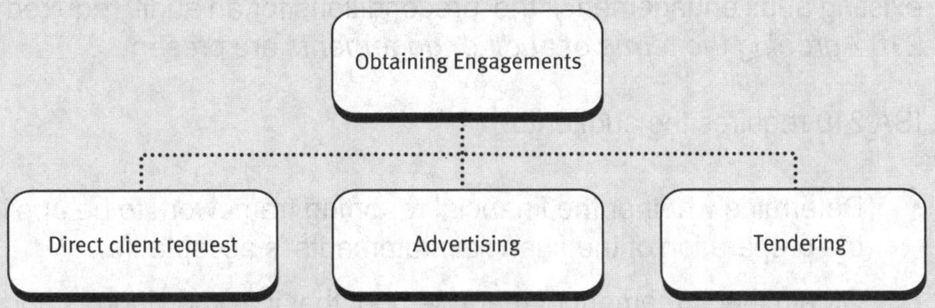

Audit clients may be obtained through 3 main methods:

- Direct client request – where the prospective client approaches the audit firm, may be as a result of a recommendation.
- Advertising – where the audit firm has recently advertised its services and the prospective client responds to the advert.
- Tendering – where the prospective client asks several audit firms to bid for their audit. The firms will put together a tender proposal in which the firm tries to sell itself to the prospective client to win the work. The proposed audit fee will be included in the tender proposal along with any specific aspects the firm believes will encourage the prospective client to give the work to them.

An audit firm should only take on clients and work of appropriate level of risk. For this reason, the firm will perform 'client screening'. The firm will consider the following matters before accepting a new engagement or client:

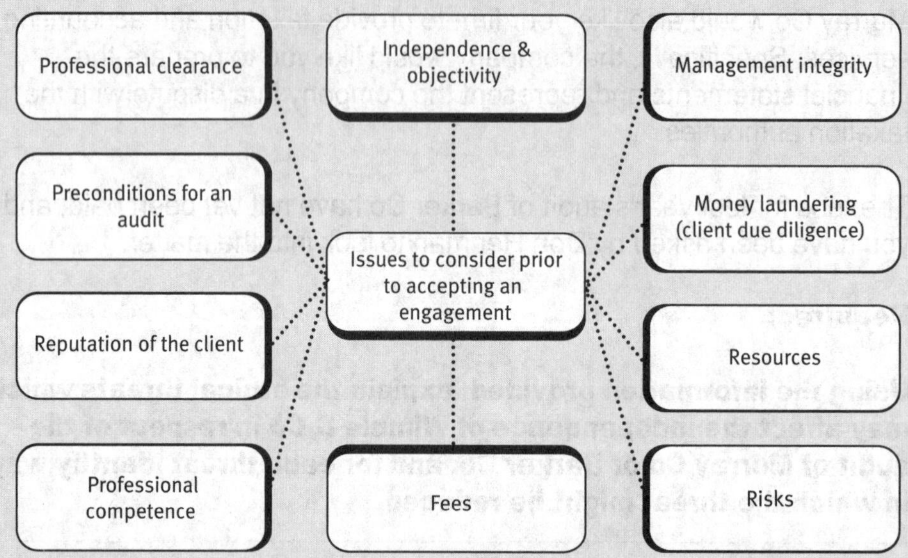

Preconditions for an audit

Auditors should only accept a new audit engagement, or continue an existing audit engagement if the 'preconditions for an audit' required by ISA 210 *Agreeing the terms of audit engagements* are present.

ISA 210 requires the auditor to:

- Determine whether the financial reporting framework to be applied in the preparation of the financial statements is acceptable.
- Obtain the agreement of management that it acknowledges and understands its responsibilities for the following:
  - Preparing the financial statements in accordance with the applicable financial reporting framework.
  - Internal control necessary for the preparation of the financial statements to be free from material misstatement.
  - Providing the auditor with access to information relevant for the audit and access to staff within the entity to obtain audit evidence.

If the preconditions for an audit are not present, the auditor should discuss the matter with management, and should not accept the engagement unless required to do so by law or regulation.

Continuance

Once the audit is complete, the audit firm must revisit the acceptance considerations again to ensure it is appropriate to continue with the engagement for the following year. If any significant issues have arisen during the year such as disagreements with management or doubts over management integrity, the auditor may consider resigning.

Acceptance considerations

Professional clearance

If offered an audit role, the prospective audit firm must:

- Ask the **client** for **permission** to **contact the existing auditor** (and refuse engagement if client refuses).
- Contact the outgoing auditor, asking for **all information relevant** to the decision **whether or not to accept** appointment (e.g. overdue fees, disagreements with management, breaches of laws & regulations).
- If a reply is not received, the prospective auditor should try and contact the outgoing auditor by other means e.g. by telephone.
- If a reply is still not received the prospective auditor may still choose to accept but must proceed with care.
- Consider the outgoing auditor's response and assess if there are any ethical or professional reasons why they should not accept appointment.

The existing auditor must:

- Ask the **client** for **permission** to **respond to the prospective auditor**.
- If the client refuses permission, the existing auditor should notify the prospective auditor of this fact.

Independence and objectivity

If the auditor is aware, prior to accepting an engagement, that the threats to objectivity cannot be managed to an acceptable level, the audit should not be accepted.

Management integrity

If the audit firm has reason to believe the client lacks integrity there is a greater risk of fraud and intimidation.

Money laundering (client due diligence)

The audit firm must comply with Money Laundering Regulations which requires client due diligence to be carried out. If there is any suspicion of money laundering, or actual money laundering committed by the prospective client, the audit firm cannot accept the engagement.

Resources

The firm should consider whether there are adequate resources available at the time the audit is likely to take place to perform the work properly. If there is insufficient time to conduct the work with the resources available the quality of the audit could be impacted.

Risks

Any risks identified with the prospective client (e.g. poor performance, poor controls, unusual transactions) should be considered. These risks can increase the level of audit risk, i.e. the risk the auditor issues an inappropriate opinion. The auditor should only take on clients of acceptable risk.

Fees

The audit firm should consider the acceptability of the fee. The fee should be commensurate with the level of risk.

In addition, the creditworthiness of the prospective client should be considered as non payment of fees can create a self interest threat.

Professional competence

An engagement should only be accepted if the audit firm has the necessary skill and experience to perform the work competently.

Reputation of the client

The audit firm should consider the reputation of the client and whether its own reputation could be damaged by association.

7 Engagement letters

The engagement letter specifies the nature of the **contract** between the audit firm and client.

Its purpose is to

- minimise the risk of any misunderstanding between the auditor and client
- confirm acceptance of the engagement
- set out the terms and conditions of the engagement.

The letter will be **sent before the audit commences**.

It should be **reviewed every year** to ensure that it is up to date but does not need to be reissued every year unless there are changes to the terms of the engagement. The auditor must issue a **new engagement letter if the scope or context** of the assignment **changes** after initial appointment.

ISA 210 requires the auditor to consider whether there is a need to remind the entity of the existing terms of the audit engagement for recurring audits and many firms choose to send a new letter every year, to emphasise its importance to clients.

Reasons for changes

Reasons for changes include:

- Changes to statutory duties due to new legislation.
- Changes to professional duties, perhaps due to new ISAs.
- Changes to 'other services' as requested by clients.

The contents of the engagement letter

The contents of a letter of engagement for audit services are listed in ISA 210 *Agreeing the Terms of Audit Engagements*.

The main contents should include:

- the objective and scope of the audit.
- the responsibilities of the auditor.

- the responsibilities of management.
- the identification of an applicable financial reporting framework.
- reference to the expected form and content of any reports to be issued.

In addition the following items will be included:

- Reference to professional standards, regulations and legislation applicable to the audit.
- Limitations of an audit.
- Expectation that management will provide written representations.
- Basis on which the fees are calculated.
- Agreement of management to notify the auditor of subsequent events after the audit report is signed.
- Agreement of management to provide draft financial statements in time to allow the audit to be completed by the deadline.
- Form (and timing) of any other communication during the audit.

Other matters that the engagement letter may cover include:

- Arrangements concerning the involvement of internal auditors and other staff of the entity.
- Limitations to the auditor's liability.

Illustration 2: Murray Co engagement letter

Wimble & Co
14 The Grove
Kingston
KI4 6AP

25 November 20X4

To the Board of Directors of Murray Company.

This letter and the attached terms of business dated 25 November 20X4 set out the basis on which we are to provide services as auditors and your and our respective responsibilities.

The objective and scope of the audit: You have requested that we audit the financial statements of Murray Company, which comprise the statement of financial position as at December 31, and the statement of profit or loss, statement of changes in equity and statement of cash flows for the year then ended, and a summary of significant accounting policies and other explanatory information.

We are pleased to confirm our acceptance and our understanding of this audit engagement by means of this letter. Our audit will be conducted with the objective of our expressing an opinion on the financial statements.

The responsibilities of the auditor: We will conduct our audit in accordance with International Standards on Auditing (ISAs). Those standards require that we comply with ethical requirements and plan and perform the audit to obtain reasonable assurance about whether the financial statements are free from material misstatement. An audit involves performing procedures to obtain audit evidence about the amounts and disclosures in the financial statements. The procedures selected depend on the auditor's judgment, including the assessment of the risks of material misstatement of the financial statements, whether due to fraud or error. An audit also includes evaluating the appropriateness of accounting policies used and the reasonableness of accounting estimates made by management, as well as evaluating the overall presentation of the financial statements.

Because of the inherent limitations of an audit, together with the inherent limitations of internal control, there is an unavoidable risk that some material misstatements may not be detected, even though the audit is properly planned and performed in accordance with ISAs.

In making our risk assessments, we consider internal control relevant to Murray Company's preparation of the financial statements in order to design audit procedures that are appropriate in the circumstances, but not for the purpose of expressing an opinion on the effectiveness of Murray Company's internal control. However, we will communicate to you in writing concerning any significant deficiencies in internal control relevant to the audit of the financial statements that we have identified during the audit.

The responsibilities of management: Our audit will be conducted on the basis that management acknowledge and understand that they have responsibility:

(a) For the preparation and fair presentation of the financial statements in accordance with International Financial Reporting Standards.

(b) For such internal control as management determines is necessary to enable the preparation of financial statements that are free from material misstatement, whether due to fraud or error.

(c) To provide us with:

(i) Access to all information of which management is aware that is relevant to the preparation of the financial statements such as records, documentation and other matters.

(ii) Additional information that we may request from management for the purpose of the audit.

(iii) Unrestricted access to persons within the entity from whom we determine it necessary to obtain audit evidence.

As part of our audit process, we will request from management written confirmation concerning representations made to us in connection with the audit.

We look forward to full cooperation from your staff during our audit.

Report: We will report to the members of Murray Company as a body, whether in our opinion the financial statements present fairly in all material respects, the financial position of Murray Company as at December 31, and its financial performance and its cash flows for the year then ended in accordance with International Financial Reporting Standards. The form and content of our report may need to be amended in the light of our audit findings.

Fees: Our fees, which will be billed as work progresses, are based on the time required by the individuals assigned to the engagement plus out-of-pocket expenses. Individual hourly rates vary according to the degree of responsibility involved and the experience and skill required.

Limitation of liability: To the fullest extent permitted by law, we will not be responsible for any losses, where you or others supply incorrect or incomplete information, or fail to supply any appropriate information or where you fail to act on our advice or respond promptly to communications from us.

Our work is not, unless there is a legal or regulatory requirement, to be made available to third parties without our written permission and we will accept no responsibility to third parties for any aspect of our professional services or work that is made available to them.

Confirmation of your agreement: Please sign and return the attached copy of this letter to indicate your acknowledgement of, and agreement with, the arrangements for our audit of the financial statements including our respective responsibilities.

If this letter and the attached terms of business are not in accordance with your understanding of our terms of appointment, please let us know.

Wimble & Co

Wimble & Co

Acknowledged and agreed on behalf of Murray Company by (signed)

....

Name and Title

Date

Murray Co engagement letter – further explanation

To the Board of Directors of Murray Company...

- Although the audit report is issued to the shareholders, the engagement letter is addressed to and signed by the directors of a company.

The responsibilities of the auditor... The responsibilities of management...

- It is important to set out the directors and auditors responsibilities for clarity and to reduce any expectation gap.
- The responsibilities of the auditor include the scope of the audit, i.e. the process by which the auditor will form their opinion. The same description of the scope of an audit is included in the audit report.

We will report to the members of Murray Company as a body...

- It is important to define who the intended users of the report are, i.e. who can place reliance on it.

Confirmation of your agreement...

- Both the client and the auditor must sign and retain a copy of the engagement letter for reference and to support the contract agreed.

Test your understanding 2

Explain each of the FIVE fundamental principles of ACCA's Code of Ethics and Conduct.

(5 marks)

Test your understanding 3

(a) There are legal and professional arrangements for the appointment and removal of auditors.

(i) **State the circumstances in which a person is not eligible to act as an auditor**

(2 marks)

(ii) **Describe the steps required to remove an auditor from an engagement.**

(3 marks)

You are a manager in the audit department of Whilling and Abel. A potential new client, Truckers Co, a haulage company, has approached your firm to do the statutory audit in addition to some other non-audit services for the financial year ended 30 September. Your audit firm was recommended to Truckers Co by an existing client, O&P, a shipping company who is also a major customer of Truckers Co.

You have been chosen to lead the assignment as you have experience of auditing haulage companies and you also manage the audit of O&P. Whilst arranging the initial meeting with the directors of Truckers Co you discover that you studied accountancy with the finance director at university.

During the meeting, you establish that Truckers Co has not made a profit for the last 2 years. The directors explain that this is largely due to escalating costs in the industry including fuel price rises. They are confident they have now controlled their costs for the current year. They have also been approached to tender for a large profitable contract which would improve their financial performance going forward. They would like you to assist them with the preparation of this tender and present with them on the day.

The current year's financial statements and audit are being finalised with another audit firm. The finance director tells you that the current auditors have identified material misstatements but the board of directors are refusing to make these adjustments. If adjusted, it would turn the break even position into a loss. The finance director told you this information informally whilst catching up on old times at the local pub.

The current auditors have replied to your professional clearance letter and have informed you that they are still owed fees relating to the prior year. This is under dispute with the client.

Once back from the meeting you calculate that the potential fees from Truckers Co would amount to about 14% of your firm's total fee income.

Required:

(b) **Identify and explain the threats to independence if Whilling and Abel accept Truckers Co as a new audit client. For each threat, recommend how the threat can be managed.**

(15 marks)

(Total: 20 marks)

Test your understanding 4

You are a manager in the audit firm of JT & Co and this is your first time you have worked on one of the firm's established clients, Pink Co. The main activity of Pink Co is providing investment advice to individuals regarding saving for retirement, purchase of shares and securities and investing in tax efficient savings schemes. Pink Co is a listed company regulated by the relevant financial services authority.

You have been asked to start the audit planning for Pink Co, by Mrs Goodall, a partner in JT & Co. Mrs Goodall has been the engagement partner for Pink Co, for the previous seven years and so has a sound knowledge of the client. Mrs Goodall has informed you that she would like her son Simon to be part of the audit team this year; Simon is currently studying for his first set of fundamentals papers for his ACCA qualification. Mrs Goodall also informs you that Mr Supper, the audit senior, received investment advice from Pink Co during the year and intends to do the same next year.

In an initial meeting with the finance director of Pink Co, you learn that the audit team will not be entertained on Pink Co's yacht this year as this could appear to be an attempt to influence the opinion of the audit. Instead, he has arranged a day at the horse races costing less than two fifth's of the expense of using the yacht and hopes this will be acceptable.

JT & Co have done some consultive work previously and the invoice is still outstanding.

Required:

Identify and explain the threats to independence in relation to the audit of Pink Co by JT & Co. For each threat, recommend how the threat can be managed.

(10 marks)

Test your understanding 5

Client confidentiality underpins the relationship between Chartered Certified Accountants in practice and their clients.

It is a core element of ACCA's Rules of Professional Conduct.

Required:

(a) **Explain the circumstances in which ACCA's Rules of Professional Conduct permit or require external auditors to disclose information relating to their clients to third parties without the knowledge or consent of the client.**

(8 marks)

(b) A waste disposal company has breached tax regulations, environmental regulations and health and safety regulations. The auditor has been approached by the tax authorities, the government body supervising the award of licences to such companies and a trade union representative. All of them have asked the auditor to provide them with information about the company. The auditor has also been approached by the police. They are investigating a suspected fraud perpetrated by the managing director of the company and they wish to ask the auditor certain questions about him.

Describe how the auditor should respond to these types of request.

(12 marks)

(Total: 20 marks)

Test your understanding 6 – OT Case 1

You are holding a training course for your firm's new recruits covering the topic of ethics. The training will focus on the fundamental principles of ethical behaviour with which accountants must comply. You have compiled the following quiz for the end of the session to test their understanding of the course content.

(1) Which of these is not a fundamental ethical principle?

A Integrity

B Independence

C Objectivity

D Professional competence and due care

(2) Which of these statements is the best explanation of integrity?

A Members should act diligently and in accordance with applicable technical and professional standards

B Members should not bring the profession into disrepute

C Members should not use client information for personal advantage

D Members should be straightforward and honest in all professional and business relationships

(3) A member was found guilty of ethical misconduct by failing to respond to the professional clearance requests from another audit firm. The members actions are primarily a breach of which fundamental principle?

A Integrity

B Independence

C Professional behaviour

D Professional competence and due care

(4) A principles based approach to ethics means that auditors must abide by specific rules and that no judgment is required. Is this statement true or false?

A True

B False

(5) What is the main reason auditors need to be independent?

A To ensure users of the audit report can place reliance on it and have faith it is not biased

B To ensure the financial statements give a true and fair view

C To provide more regulation for auditors so it looks like the audit is of higher quality

D The law requires it

Test your understanding 7 – OT Case 2

You are the audit manager responsible for the audit of Broome Co, a listed company. You have been informed by one of the audit juniors that the finance director has offered to take the audit team to a World Cup Final at the expense of the client as a thank you for an efficient audit with minimal disruption.

The finance director has requested that you attend a social event where the company will outline a new rights issue of ordinary shares to shareholders. The finance director believes that the presence of the external auditor will add credibility to the rights issue and increase the chance of raising the required finance.

(1) Which of the following is not a threat to objectivity?

A Independence

B Self-Review

C Advocacy

D Intimidation

(2) Which ethical threat would be created if the audit manager attends the social event where the client will outline a new rights issue to shareholders?

A Familiarity

B Advocacy

C Self-review

D Self-interest

(3) The offer of tickets to the World Cup Final creates which type of threat?

A Intimidation

B Advocacy

C Self-review

D Self-interest

(4) What is the restriction, if any, on the level of fee income that can be received from recurring work from Broome Co before a situation of dependency is presumed to exist?

A 5%

B 10%

C 15%

D No restriction

(5) For clients where the level of fees must be monitored, what safeguard can the firm apply to reduce the threat to an acceptable level?

(i) Rotation of audit team members on an annual basis

(ii) Discussion of the matter with the audit committee of Broome Co

(iii) Assign an engagement quality review partner

A (i) and (ii) only

B (i) and (iii) only

C (ii) and (iii) only

D (i), (ii) and (iii)

8 Chapter summary

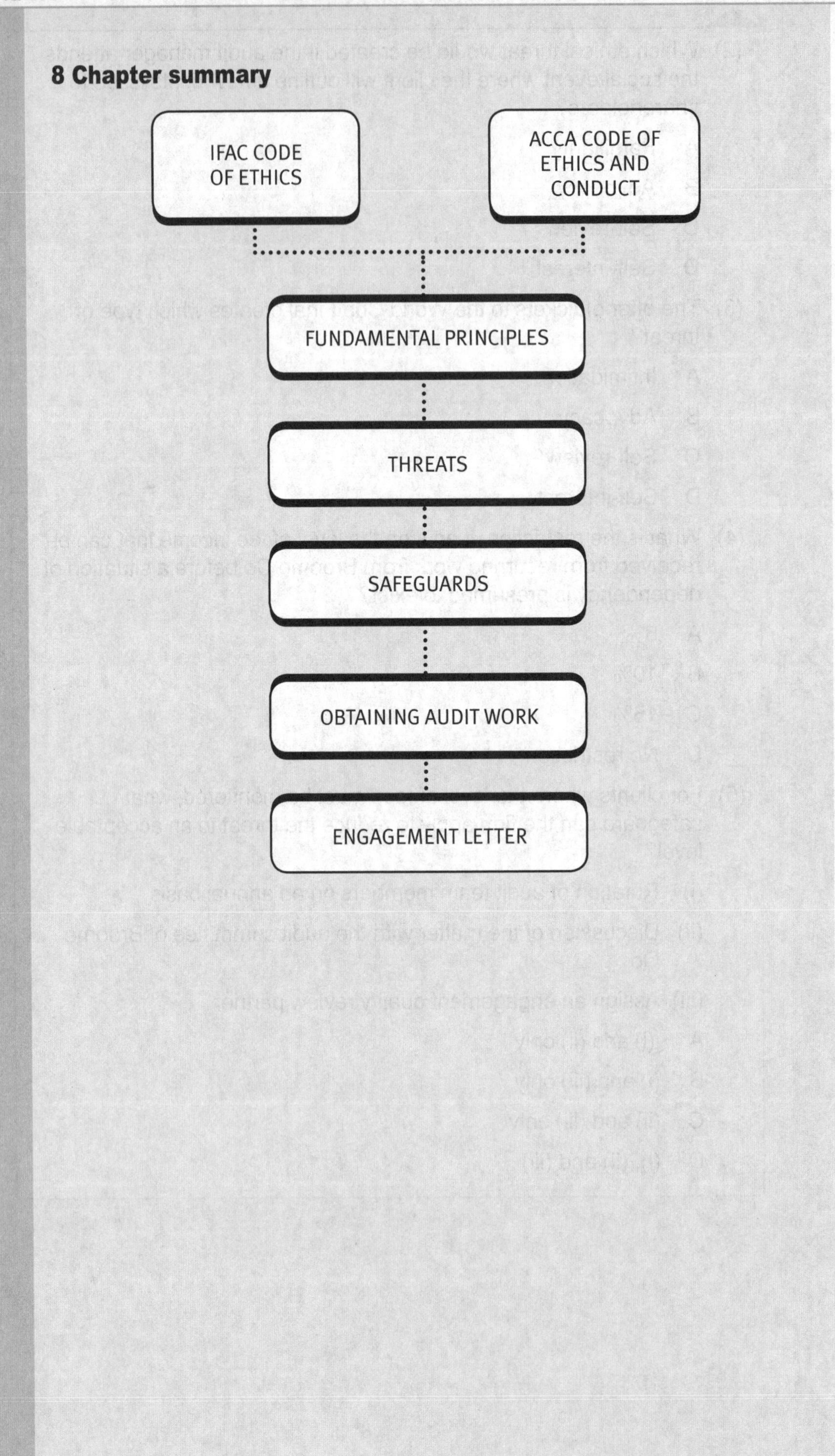

Test your understanding answers

Test your understanding 1

Threat	Managing the threat
Conflict of Interest Wimble & Co also audits Barker Co, another manufacturer of sports equipment. The engagement partner for Barker Co will be the engagement partner for Murray Co. Acting for directly competing clients is a threat to objectivity (and confidentiality). It is normal for firms to have clients that are in competition with each other; firms need relevant professional experience in the client's industry in order to comply with the fundamental principle of professional competence and accept appointment as auditor.	Wimble & Co should obtain consent from both clients to continue and ensure that separate teams are used for each engagement.
Financial interest The audit manager owns shares in Murray Co. This creates a **self-interest threat**: the audit manager may be reluctant to identify misstatements or modify the audit opinion for fear of damaging the value of their shareholding.	The audit manager must be required to dispose of the shares immediately, or another audit manager should be appointed to the engagement team instead.

Previous employment with the client The audit manager used to work for Murray Co. If the employment with the client was recent, the audit manager may be auditing work that they were responsible for when working for Murray Co. They may not identify errors in their own work or if they are identified may not be brought to the client's attention. This creates a **self review threat**. In addition, a familiarity threat may arise as the audit manager is likely to have friendships with previous colleagues which could result in the audit manager not applying sufficient professional scepticism and trusting the client too much.	The audit manager should not be assigned to the audit of Murray Co until a period of two years has elapsed.
Gifts and hospitality Murray Co has offered free equipment to the auditor. Accepting gifts or hospitality from an audit client may create **self-interest** and familiarity threats. The auditor may feel indebted to the client or the offer may be seen to be a bribe from the client for a clean audit opinion.	The partners of the firm should evaluate the gift offered and unless trivial and inconsequential, the audit team must not accept the equipment.

Long association The engagement partner for Barker Co has been in place for twelve years. **Familiarity** and **self-interest** threats are created by using the same senior personnel on an assurance engagement for a long period of time. The audit partner may be too trusting of the client and may be too complacent after so many years.	• Rotate the senior personnel off the assurance team. • Independent review of the senior personnel's work. • Independent quality control reviews of the engagement.
Personal relationship The audit senior's sister is the Financial Controller at Murray Co and is therefore in a position to exert significant influence over the financial statements. Family and personal relationships between a member of an assurance team and a director of the client, or an employee of the client in a position to exert significant influence over the subject matter, may create **familiarity, self-interest** or **intimidation threats**. The audit senior may be too trusting of his sister and not apply sufficient professional scepticism.	Tim Andrews should not be on the audit team for Murray Co.
Murray Co would like the audit firm to and represent the company in a dispute with the taxation authorities. This would create **advocacy** and **self-review** threats as the audit firm would be seen to be taking sides with their client.	Firms must not represent audit clients in such disputes.

Overdue fees The fee for last year's audit of Barker Co have not yet been paid. Overdue fees create a **self-interest threat** where they remain unpaid for some time. The auditor may be reluctant to raise issues with the client in case they refuse to pay. In addition, overdue fees could be perceived to be a loan. An audit firm must not enter into any loan arrangement with a client.	Do not perform any more work for the client until the outstanding fees have been paid.
Provision of other services Murray Co would like the audit firm to prepare the financial statements. Preparing the financial statements and then auditing them creates a significant **self-review** threat. If the auditor reviews work they were responsible for, they may not identify errors they have made.	• Use staff who are not part of the audit team to prepare the financial statements. • If performed by a member of the audit team, arrange an independent partner or senior staff member to review the work performed. • If an audit client is a **listed or other public-interest entity**, the firm **must not provide any accounting or bookkeeping services**, including payroll services or preparation of the financial statements.

Tutorial note:

The provision of other services may create additional threats to objectivity and independence. The threats, and significance of those threats is dependent on the services being provided.

- When the total fees from an audit client represent a large proportion of a firm's total income (or a specific partner or office's income), i.e. **fee dependence**, a **self-interest** or **intimidation** threat to objectivity may be created; the auditor may be reluctant to identify misstatements in the financial statements or to modify the audit opinion, for fear of losing the client. Possible safeguards include:
  - reducing dependence on the client
  - independent quality control reviews of the engagement.

- When the audit client is a **listed client or other public interest entity**, and the total fees represent **more than 15%** of the firm's total income for **two consecutive years**, the firm must:
  - disclose this to those charged with governance
  - arrange for an external quality control review of the engagement (either before or after issuing the audit report).
- Assuming management responsibilities for an assurance client may create threats to independence. The provision of other services may require the assurance firm to assume management responsibilities but an assurance firm **must not assume management responsibilities** as part of an assurance engagement or **for an audit client**.

Test your understanding 2

Fundamental principles

Integrity. A professional accountant should be honest and straightforward in performing professional services.

Objectivity. A professional accountant should be fair and not allow personal bias, conflict of interest or influence of others to override objectivity.

Professional competence and due care. When performing professional services, a professional accountant should show competence and duty of care by keeping up-to-date with developments in practice, legislation and techniques.

Confidentiality. A professional accountant should respect the confidentiality of information acquired during the course of providing professional services and should not use or disclose such information without obtaining client permission.

Professional behaviour. A professional accountant should act in a manner consistent with the good reputation of the profession and refrain from any conduct which might bring discredit to the profession.

Test your understanding 3

(a)

(i) A person is not eligible to act as an auditor in the following circumstances:

- They are not a member of an RSB (recognised supervisory body) or not allowed to practice under the rules of an RSB.
- They are an officer or employee of the company.
- They are a business partner or employee of the company.

(ii) Steps required to remove an auditor from an engagement

- A decision must be made by the shareholders at a general meeting usually with a majority vote being required.
- Advance notice must be given to the company and the auditors prior to any general meeting
- Auditors have the right to attend and speak at the general meeting or have representations read out on their behalf.

(b) **Threats to independence**

Threat	**Managing the threat**
Audit manager knows one of the directors socially. This creates a familiarity threat. The auditor may be too trusting of the client or too sympathetic to the client's needs.	A different audit manager should be assigned to the audit of Truckers Co.
You are the audit manager of one of Trucker Co's major customers. This creates a conflict of interest and a risk that confidential information may be passed between the clients.	A different audit manager should be assigned to the audit of Truckers Co. Different teams should be used for the audit of Truckers Co and O&P.
The audit manager has been asked to present at the tender for clients contract. This would give rise to an advocacy threat as the audit firm would be promoting the client.	The auditors should politely decline the invitation to present at the tender explaining their reasons.
There are outstanding fees still owed to the previous auditors. This situation could arise again for the new auditor leading to a self-interest threat where the auditor may not wish to identify misstatements or modify the audit opinion for fear of not receiving outstanding fees.	Discuss reasons for non payment with client and consider whether you should accept the assignment. If accepted new work should not be commenced when significant fees remain outstanding.

The audit firm will provide non audit services in addition to the statutory audit. This represents a self-review threat. The audit firm may ignore or overlook their own errors when auditing the financial statements.	The audit firm should ensure separate teams work on each engagement. An independent partner review of the files for each engagement should be arranged.
Total fees received from Trucker Co will represent 14% of the audit firm's total income. Fee dependence creates a self-interest threat.	Whilling & Abel should consider declining additional non-audit services from Trucker Co to reduce fee dependence. An independent partner review of the audit work should be arranged. NB: If the client is a listed company, fee dependency is presumed when fees exceed 15% for two consecutive years.

Test your understanding 4

Threat	Managing the threat
Mrs Goodall has been the engagement partner for the last seven years. This creates a familiarity threat. Mrs Goodall may be too trusting of or too close to the client to be able to make objective decisions due to this long association.	Mrs Goodall should be rotated from the engagement team. It may be possible to allow Mrs Goodall to continue as engagement partner for one further year in order to safeguard audit quality. Audit committee approval must be obtained in order to allow this and an independent partner review of the audit files for Pink Co should be arranged.

There is no ethical rule which stops Mrs Goodall recommending Simon for the audit, or letting Simon take part in the audit. However, there may be the impression of lack of independence as Simon is related to the engagement partner. Simon could be tempted not to identify errors in case this prejudiced his Mum's relationship with the client. In addition, if Mrs Goodall was reviewing Simon's work, she may not review it as thoroughly as the other audit staff due to their relationship.	To demonstrate complete independence, Simon should not be part of any audit or assurance team for which Mrs Goodall is partner.
As long as Mr Supper paid a full fee to Pink Co for the investment advice (i.e. it is on an arm's length basis) there is no ethical threat as investment advice is in the normal course of business for Pink Co. However, if Mr Supper were to receive a discount on the services of Pink Co as a benefit of being part of the audit team, this would create a self-interest threat. In either case, continued use of client services could be perceived as a lack of independence as Mr Supper could be given the investment advice for a reduced fee (or free) as a benefit of being part of the audit team.	Mr Supper should be asked not to use the services of Pink Co again unless this is first agreed with the engagement partner.
The audit team has been offered a day at the horse races at the end of the audit. Acceptance of gifts or hospitality from a client creates a self-interest threat, and unless of an insignificant amount, is not allowed. The fact that the horse race day costs less than the yacht expense is irrelevant, independence could still be impaired.	The day out should not be accepted. In addition, the rationale for accepting hospitality in previous years should be investigated.

There are outstanding fees. This creates a self-interest threat to objectivity. JT & Co may be reluctant to identify misstatements for fear of not getting paid. In addition, outstanding fees may be considered to be a loan. Loans to clients are not permitted.	Payment for work should be arranged before the audit is commenced, or a payment plan agreed.

Test your understanding 5

(a) **Disclosure of information relating to clients to third parties**

(i) Auditors are permitted or required to disclose information about their clients to third parties without their knowledge or consent in very limited circumstances.

(ii) Generally, auditors can be required to, or are permitted to, disclose information to certain regulatory bodies, including certain specialist units within police forces under legislation. Such legislation in many countries includes financial services legislation, legislation concerning banks and insurance companies, legislation concerning money laundering and legislation concerning the investigation of serious fraud or tax evasion.

(iii) Auditors are also permitted or required to disclose information where they are personally involved in litigation, including litigation that involves the recovery of fees from clients, or where they are subject to disciplinary proceedings brought by ACCA or other, similar professional bodies.

(iv) Auditors are also permitted to disclose information where they consider it to be in the 'public interest' or in the interests of national security. Factors to take into account include the seriousness of the matter, the likelihood of repetition and the extent to which the public is involved. This right is rarely used in practice.

(b) **Response to requests**

(i) It is not unusual in practice for various bodies to request information from auditors 'informally' because it relieves them of the obligation to obtain the necessary statutory authorities which may be time consuming or difficult.

(ii) Auditors must not disclose information without the consent of the client or unless the necessary statutory documentation is provided by the person(s) requesting the information.

(iii) Unless the auditor has reason to believe that there is a statutory duty not to inform the client that an approach has been made, the client should first be approached to see if consent can be obtained, and to see if the client is aware of the investigations, as should normally be the case. The auditor should ensure that the client is aware of the fact the voluntary disclosure may work in the client's favour, in the long run, but if the client refuses, the auditor should inform the client if the auditor has a statutory duty of disclosure.

(iv) Auditors should take legal advice in all of the cases described.

(v) Where the auditor is made aware of potential actions against the client that may have an effect on the financial statements, the auditor must consider the effect on the audit report. If the client is aware of the investigation, the auditor will be able to seek audit evidence to support any necessary provisions or disclosures in the financial statements.

(vi) The auditors should consider whether the suspected fraud relating to the managing director relates to the company and affects the financial statements.

(vii) Auditors will be in a very difficult situation if they become aware of an action that may materially affect the financial statements, but where the client is not, and where auditors are under a statutory duty not to inform the client. This situation will not be improved by the resignation of auditors as they may be obliged to make a statement on resignation. This puts auditors in a very difficult position and legal advice is essential in such circumstances.

(viii) Tax authorities normally have powers to ask clients to disclose information voluntarily. Such voluntary disclosure is often looked on favourably by the tax authorities and the courts. Tax authorities normally also have statutory powers to demand information from both clients and auditors. The same is generally true of environmental and health and safety inspectors.

(ix) The power of the police to demand information is sometimes less clear and auditors and clients should take care to ensure that the appropriate authorities are in place. Those sections of the police investigating serious frauds usually have more powers than the general police. It is unlikely that trade union representatives have any statutory powers to demand information.

Test your understanding 6 – OT Case 1

(1)	B	Whilst independence is an important characteristic for an auditor it is not one of the fundamental principles.
(2)	D	Integrity means straightforward and honest.
(3)	C	Professional behaviour incorporates professional courtesy e.g. responding promptly to requests from other auditors.
(4)	B	False. This describes a rules based approach.
(5)	A	Independence means freedom from bias and influence.

Test your understanding 7 – OT Case 2

(1)	A	Independence.
(2)	B	The audit manager may be seen to be promoting the company and encouraging the shareholders to subscribe to the rights issue.
(3)	D	Self-interest. The auditor may feel they owe the client something in return if they accept such an expensive gift.
(4)	C	15%
(5)	C	Independence matters should be discussed with the audit committee and an engagement quality review partner should be assigned. Rotation of the audit team would not provide a safeguard for a self-interest threat.

chapter

4

Risk

Chapter learning objectives

This chapter covers syllabus areas:

- B2b – Explain the need to plan and perform audits with an attitude of professional scepticism and to exercise professional judgment
- B3 – Assessing audit risks
- B4 – Understanding the entity and its environment

Detailed syllabus objectives are provided in the introduction section of the text book.

1 The importance of risk assessment

Objectives of an auditor

The overriding principle of auditing is introduced in ISA 200 *Overall Objectives of the Independent Auditor and the Conduct of an Audit in Accordance with ISAs*:

'To obtain reasonable assurance, **the auditor shall obtain sufficient appropriate evidence to reduce audit risk to an acceptably low level**...'

Audit risk is the risk that the auditor expresses an **inappropriate audit opinion**.

This is further developed by ISA 315 (Revised) *Identifying and Assessing the Risks of Material Misstatement Through Understanding the Entity and its Environment* which states:

'The **objective** of the auditor is **to identify and assess the risk of material misstatement,** whether due to fraud or error, at the financial statement and assertion levels, through understanding the entity and its environment, including the entity's internal control, thereby providing a basis for **designing and implementing responses to the assessed risks of material misstatement.**'

The auditor must identify the risks of material misstatement; and use this to guide the design of their audit procedures.

What is a misstatement?

'A **difference between** the amount, classification, presentation, or disclosure of a reported **financial statement** item and the amount, classification, presentation, or disclosure that is required for the item to be in accordance with the applicable **financial reporting framework**. Misstatements can arise from error or fraud.' (ISA 450 *Evaluation of Misstatements Identified during the Audit)*

In conducting a thorough assessment of risk, auditors will be able to:

- Identify areas of the financial statements where misstatements are likely to occur early in the audit.
- Plan procedures that address the significant risk areas identified.
- Carry out an efficient, focussed and effective audit.
- Minimise the risk of issuing an inappropriate audit opinion to an acceptable level.
- Reduce the risk of reputational and punitive damage.

Types of misstatements

There are three categories of misstatements:

(i) Factual misstatements: a misstatement about which there is no doubt.

(ii) Judgmental misstatements: a difference in an accounting estimate that the auditor considers unreasonable, or the selection or application of accounting policies that the auditor considers inappropriate.

(iii) Projected misstatements: a projected misstatement is the auditor's best estimate of the total misstatement in a population through the projection of misstatements identified in a sample.

2 Materiality

What is materiality?

'Misstatements, including omissions, are considered to be material if they, individually or in the aggregate, could reasonably be expected to influence the economic decisions of users taken on the basis of the financial statements'

(ISA 320 *Materiality in Planning and Performing an Audit*)

What is the significance of materiality?

If financial statements contain material misstatement they cannot be deemed to show a true and fair view.

As a result, the focus of an audit is identifying the significant risks of material misstatement in the financial statements and then designing procedures aimed at identifying and quantifying material misstatement.

How is materiality determined?

The guidance in ISA 320 states that the determination of materiality is a **matter of professional judgment** and that the auditor must consider:

- whether the misstatement would affect the economic decision of the users
- both the size and nature of misstatements
- the information needs of the users as a group.

Materiality is a subjective matter and as such should be considered in light of the client's circumstances.

Material by size

ISA 320 recognises the need to establish a financial threshold to guide audit planning and procedures. For this reason the following benchmarks may be used as a starting point:

- ½ – 1% of revenue
- 5% – 10% of profit before tax
- 1 – 2% of total assets.

The above are common benchmarks but different audit firms may use different benchmarks or different thresholds for each client.

Material by nature

Materiality is not just a purely financial concern. Some items may be material by nature i.e. the impact they have on the financial statements.

Examples of items which are material by nature or material by impact include:

- Misstatements that, when adjusted, would turn a reported profit into a loss for the year.
- Misstatements that, when adjusted, would turn a reported net-asset position into a net-liability position (or net-current asset to net-current liability).
- Transactions with directors, e.g. salary and benefits, personal use of assets, etc.
- Disclosures in the financial statements relating to possible future legal claims or going concern issues, for example, could influence users' decisions and may be purely narrative. In this case a numerical calculation is not relevant.

Illustration 1: Murray Co materiality

Financial Statement Extracts	**20X4**	**20X3**
	$000	$000
Revenue	21,960	19,580
Total assets	9,697	7,288
Profit before tax	1,048	248
Materiality		
Revenue	½%	1%
	110	220
Profit before taxation	5%	10%
	52	105
Total assets	1%	2%
	97	194

A suitable range for **preliminary materiality** is **$97,000 – $105,000**.

Murray Co materiality – further discussion

Materiality is not normally based on revenue, except in circumstances when it would not be meaningful to base materiality on profit, e.g. because the entity being audited is a not-for-profit entity or where there is a small profit (or a loss) as this will result in over-auditing of the financial statements (such as was the case for Murray Co in the prior year).

More than $105,000 profit is material to the statement of profit and loss, therefore preliminary materiality is likely to be set lower than this amount. Less than $52,000 is not material to profit (or to the statement of financial position) so preliminary materiality should not be less than this amount.

A suitable preliminary materiality level is most likely to be one that lies within the overlap of the ranges calculated for profit and total assets. $97,000 (1% of total assets) represents 9% profit. As this is at the lower end of the assets range, this would be a relatively prudent measure of materiality (resulting in a higher level of audit work).

$105,000 (10% of profit) represents 1.1% of total assets. Preliminary materiality might be set at this end of the range had this been a recurring audit. However, as this is a first audit, preliminary materiality is likely to be lower.

The financial statements are draft and therefore greater errors should be expected than if they were actual. Consequently, sample sizes for audit testing should be increased (i.e. preliminary materiality should be set at a relatively lower level).

Preliminary materiality is therefore likely to be set at $97,000.

Performance materiality

It is unlikely, in practice, that auditors will be able to design tests that identify individually material misstatements. It is much more common that misstatements are material in aggregate (i.e. in combination). This is also referred to as 'creeping materiality'.

For this reason, ISA 320 introduces a further concept: **performance materiality**.

Performance materiality is defined as:

'The amount set by the auditor at less than materiality for the financial statements as a whole to reduce to an appropriately low level the probability that the aggregate of uncorrected and undetected misstatements exceeds materiality for the financial statements as a whole.'

- The auditor sets **performance materiality** at a **value lower than overall materiality**, and uses this lower threshold when designing and performing audit procedures.
- This **reduces** the **risk** that the auditor will fail to identify misstatements that are material when added together.

Murray Co performance materiality

The audit engagement team is planning the audit of the financial statements for the year ended 31 December. The team has determined a materiality level for the financial statements as a whole, of $97,000. Performance materiality needs to be applied to work-in-progress inventories, as this is an area of audit risk.

Performance materiality could be determined as a percentage of financial statement materiality, say 75%, i.e. a performance materiality of ($97,000 × 75%) $72,750 (the audit team could use a higher or lower percentage, or use a different calculation, depending on their professional judgment).

The aim of performance materiality is to reduce the risk that the aggregate of immaterial misstatements exceed materiality for the financial statements as a whole.

For example, if a misstatement was identified of, say $80,000, without performance materiality the auditor would conclude that work-in-progress is not materially misstated. However, the audit may not have detected further misstatements which when added to the $80,000 identified would result in a material misstatement. By using performance materiality, the auditor would conclude that a misstatement of $80,000 is material, and consequently would require the directors to amend the financial statements to correct this misstatement, reducing the risk of giving an inappropriate opinion.

3 Audit Risk

Audit risk is the risk that the auditor expresses an **inappropriate audit opinion**, i.e. that they give an unmodified audit opinion when the financial statements contain a material misstatement.

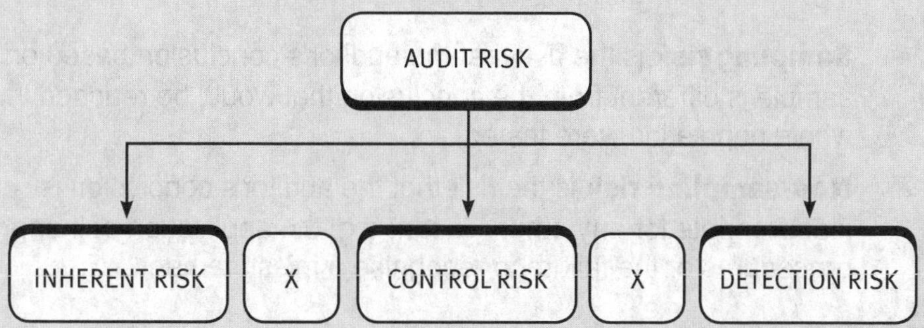

Audit risk is made up of three components: **inherent risk, control risk** and **detection risk**.

Inherent risk is the susceptibility of an assertion about a class of transaction, account balance or disclosure to misstatement that could be material, before consideration of any related controls.

- Inherent risk is the risk of a material misstatement in the financial statements because of the nature of the industry, entity or the nature of the item itself.
- Complex accounting treatment is an example of an inherent risk. For example, where an accounting standard provides guidance on a specific accounting treatment this might not be understood by the client and material misstatement could result.
- Inventory is inherently risky if it quickly becomes obsolete as it may not be valued appropriately at the lower of cost and NRV.

Control risk is the risk that a misstatement that could occur and that could be material will not be prevented, or detected and corrected on a timely basis by the entity's internal controls.

- Control risk may be high either because the design of the internal control system is insufficient in the circumstances of the business or because the controls have not been applied effectively during the period. This is covered in more detail in the chapter 'Systems and controls'.

Together, inherent risk and control risk make up the **risk of material misstatement.** This is the risk that the financial statements are materially misstated prior to the audit commencing. This will be due to fraud or errors occurring during the year when transactions have been processed or when the financial statements have been prepared.

Detection risk is the risk that the procedures performed by the auditor to reduce audit risk to an acceptably low level will not detect a misstatement that exists and that could be material.

Detection risk comprises **sampling risk** and **non-sampling risk**:

- **Sampling risk** is the risk that the auditor's conclusion based on a sample is different from the conclusion that would be reached if the whole population were tested.
- **Non-sampling risk** is the risk that the auditor's conclusion is inappropriate for any other reason, e.g. the application of inappropriate procedures or the failure to recognise a misstatement.

Auditor's response

The auditor must amend the audit approach in response to risk assessment. They can achieve this by:

- assigning more experienced staff to risk areas
- increasing supervision levels
- increasing the element of unpredictability in sample selection
- changing the nature, timing and extent of procedures
- increasing the emphasis on substantive tests of detail
- emphasising the need for **professional scepticism**.

Professional scepticism is: 'An attitude that includes a **questioning mind**, being alert to conditions which may indicate possible misstatement due to fraud or error, and a **critical assessment of audit evidence**.' (ISA 200 *Overall Objectives of the Independent Auditor and the Conduct of an Audit in Accordance with International Standards on Auditing*).

Clearly this requires the audit team to have a good knowledge of how the client's activities are likely to affect its financial statements, and the audit team should discuss these matters in a **planning meeting** before deciding on the detailed approach and audit work to be used.

How to apply professional scepticism

Professional scepticism requires the auditor to **be alert to**:

- Audit **evidence that contradicts other** audit **evidence**.
- Information that brings into question **the reliability of documents and responses to enquiries** to be used as audit evidence.
- Conditions that may indicate **possible fraud**.
- Circumstances that suggest **the need for audit procedures in addition to those required by ISAs**.

4 Risk assessment procedures

ISA 315 (Revised) requires auditors to perform the following risk assessment procedures:

- **Enquiries** with management, of appropriate individuals within the internal audit function (if there is one), and others (with relevant information) within the client entity (e.g. about external and internal changes the company has experienced)
- **Analytical procedures**
- **Observation** (e.g. of control procedures) and **inspection** (e.g. of key strategic documents and procedural manuals).

Understanding the entity and its environment

In order to identify the risks of material misstatement in the financial statements the auditor is required to obtain an understanding of: their clients; their clients' environments; and their clients' internal controls. This generally includes:

- relevant industry, regulatory and other external factors (including the financial reporting framework)
- the nature of the entity, including:
  - its operations
  - its ownership and governance structures
  - the types of investment it makes
  - the way it is structured and financed
- the entity's selection and application of accounting policies
- the entity's objectives, strategies and related business risks
- the measurement and review of the entity's financial performance
- the internal controls relevant to the audit.

(ISA 315 (Revised) *Identifying and Assessing the Risks of Material Misstatement through understanding the entity and its environment*)

If the entity has an internal audit function, obtaining an understanding of that function also contributes to the auditor's understanding in particular the role that the function plays in the entity's monitoring of internal control over financial reporting.

The information used to obtain this understanding can come from a wide range of sources, including:

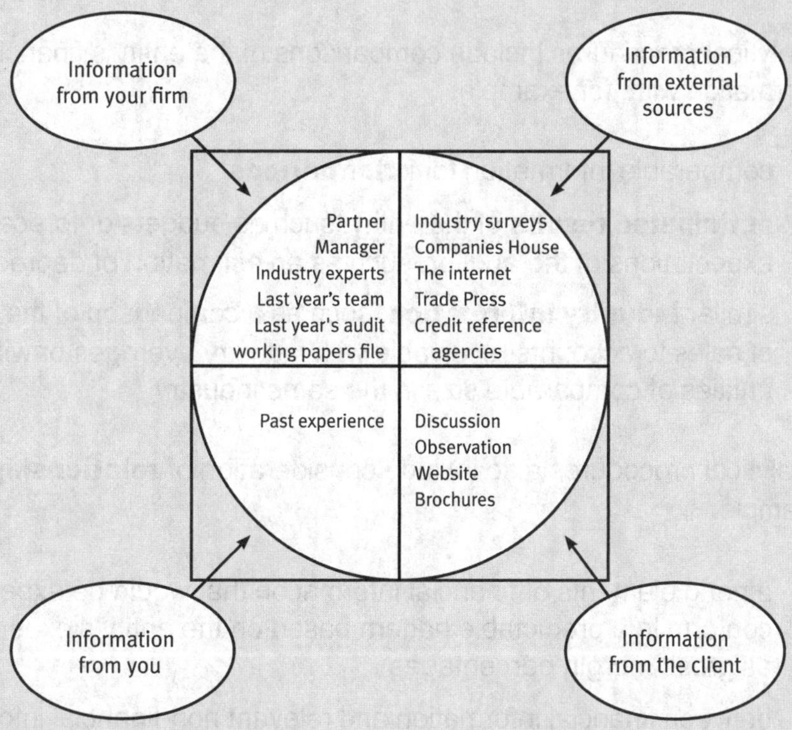

Analytical procedures

Analytical procedures are defined in ISA 520 *Analytical Procedures* as:

'Evaluations of financial information through **analysis of plausible relationships** among both financial and non-financial data' and investigation of identified fluctuations, inconsistent relationships or amounts that differ from expected values.

Analytical procedures are fundamental to the auditing process.

The auditor is **required to perform analytical procedures as risk assessment procedures in accordance with ISA 315** in order to:

- assist in **assessing the risks of material misstatement** in order to provide a basis for designing and implementing responses to the assessed risks
- help **identify** the existence of **unusual transactions or events, and amounts, ratios, and trends** that might indicate matters that have audit implications
- assist the auditor in identifying risks of material misstatement due to **fraud**.

Analytical procedures include comparisons of the entity's financial information with, for example:

- comparable information for **prior periods**.
- **anticipated results** of the entity, such as budgets or forecasts, or expectations of the auditor, such as an estimation of depreciation
- similar **industry information**, such as a comparison of the entity's ratio of sales to accounts receivable with industry averages or with other entities of comparable size in the same industry.

Analytical procedures also include consideration of **relationships**, for example:

- among elements of financial information that would be expected to conform to a predictable pattern based on the entity's experience, such as gross margin percentages
- between financial information and relevant non-financial information, such as payroll costs to number of employees.

Computer assisted auditing techniques are now often used to perform data analysis.

Analytical procedures during the audit

Analytical procedures can be used at all stages of an audit.

However, ISA 315 *Identifying and Assessing the Risks of Material Misstatement through Understanding the Entity and Its Environment* requires the auditor to perform analytical procedures as risk assessment procedures in order to help the auditor to obtain an understanding of the entity and assess the risk of material misstatement.

The auditor can choose to use analytical procedures as substantive procedures during the final audit to obtain relevant and reliable audit evidence.

The auditor must also use analytical procedures at the final review stage, near the end of the audit, when forming an overall conclusion as to whether the financial statements are consistent with the auditor's understanding of the entity.

Ratios

Key ratios

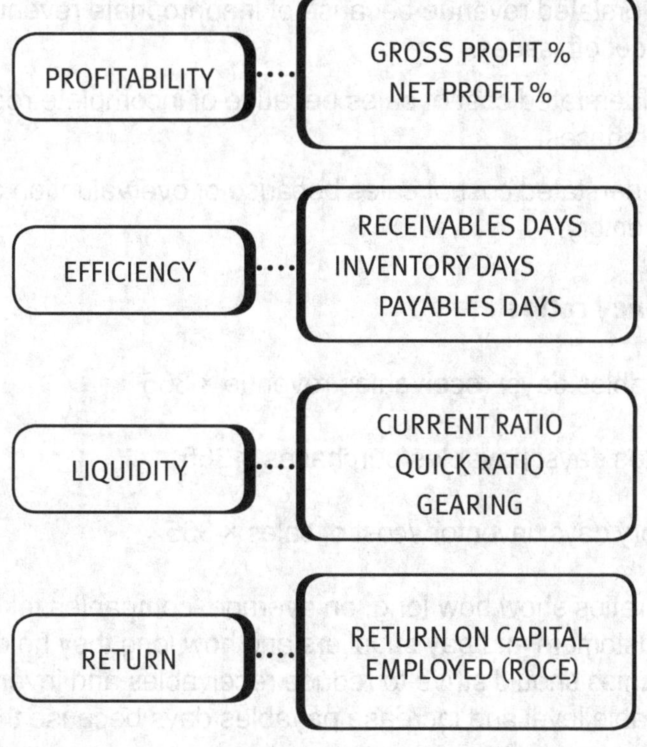

Profitability ratios

Gross margin: gross profit/sales revenue × 100%

Net margin: profit before tax/sales revenue × 100%

Auditors would expect the relationships between costs and revenues to stay relatively stable. Things that can affect these ratios include: changes in sales prices, bulk purchase discounts, economies of scale, new marketing initiatives, changing energy costs, wage inflation.

Therefore, any unusual fluctuation in the profitability ratio could mean that the figures are materially misstated. For example, if gross profit margin improves, this could be caused by any or all of the following:

- Overstated revenue because of inappropriate revenue recognition or cut off issues.
- Understated cost of sales because of incomplete recording of purchases.
- Understated cost of sales because of overvaluation of closing inventory.

Efficiency ratios

Receivables days: receivables/revenue × 365

Payables days: payables/purchases × 365

Inventory days: inventory/cost of sales × 365

These ratios show how long, on average, companies take to collect cash from customers and pay suppliers and how long they hold inventory for. Companies should strive to reduce receivables and inventory days to an acceptable level and increase payables days because this strategy maximises cash flow.

Any changes can indicate significant issues to the auditor, such as:

- worsening credit control and increased need for receivables allowance
- ageing and possible obsolete inventory that could be overvalued
- poor cash flow leading to going concern problems which would require disclosure.

Liquidity ratios

Current ratio: current assets/current liabilities

Quick ratio: (current assets-inventory)/current liabilities

These ratios indicate how able a company is to meet its short term debts. As a result these are key indicators when assessing going concern.

Investor ratios

Gearing: borrowings/share capital + reserves

Return on capital employed (ROCE): profit before interest and tax/(share capital + reserves + borrowings)

Gearing is a measure of external debt finance to internal equity finance. ROCE indicates the returns those investments generate.

Any change in gearing or ROCE could indicate a change in the financing structure of the business or it could indicate changes in overall performance of the business. These ratios are important for identifying potentially material changes to the statement of financial position (new/repaid loans or share issues) and for obtaining an overall picture of the annual performance of the business.

5 Exam focus – Audit risk questions

Audit risk identification and explanation

Audit risk is regularly examined and it is important to answer the question from an auditor's perspective rather than the perspective of the client.

The auditor is trying to detect material misstatements in the financial statements to avoid issuing the wrong opinion. The auditor is not looking to identify risks which affect the profitability of the client, they are not business consultants.

A common mistake that students make in exams is to explain business risks rather than audit risks. Business risks are not examinable in this syllabus. Therefore take care to ensure your answer is relevant to the requirement.

For example

Factor	Audit risk	NOT Audit risk (business risk)
Customers are struggling to pay debts.	Receivables may be overstated if bad debts are not written off.	Bad debts may arise reducing the profits of the company.
The client operates in a fast paced industry.	Inventory may be overstated if the inventory is obsolete and NRV is lower than cost.	Inventory may have to be written off reducing the profits of the company.
Revenue is falling due to recession.	If other factors are present, this could mean the company is unable to continue to trade for the foreseeable future and going concern disclosures may be required. There is a risk that adequate disclosure is not made.	Falling revenue will result in reduced profits and possible going concern issues.

In the exam make sure your risks link with a risk of material misstatement or a detection risk.

A risk of material misstatement will affect either a balance in the financial statements, a disclosure in the notes to the financial statements or the basis of preparation.

Auditor responses to risks

Once the risks are identified, you must suggest a **relevant** audit response to the risk identified.

The response must specifically deal with the risk. You should not suggest audit responses that address the balance generally.

For example

Audit risk	Relevant response	Irrelevant response	Explanation
Overstatement of receivables due to bad [illegible]	Inspect after date cash receipts from customers to see if [illegible] year end [illegible] e debt is [illegible] tely valued.	Obtain the receivables listing and cast it. Obtain external confirmation from customers to confirm existence	The risk identified is overvaluation. Obtaining the listing does not provide evidence that the debts are appropriately stated. External confirmation is providing evidence for the existence but not the valuation.
[illegible]	[illegible] aged [illegible] listing and [illegible] old items. [illegible] with [illegible] ent the [illegible] hese to be [illegible] wn in the [illegible] tatements.	Attend the inventory count to confirm existence of the inventory.	As written, the response of attending the inventory count is confirming existence, not valuation. This should be re-worded to say attend the inventory count and look out for old or obsolete items that should be written down in the financial statements.

Going concern disclosures may not be adequate if the company has trading difficulties.	Assess the client's ability to continue as a going concern by examining the forecasts prepared by management and assess the reasonableness of the assumptions used in the forecast.	Perform an analysis of past performance and assess the profitability of the company. Calculate liquidity ratios.	Analysing past performance does not help indicate how the company will perform in the future. Profitability is not the best indicator of going concern. Profits can be distorted by accounting policies. A company can be profitable but not have sufficient cash available to pay its suppliers and employees. Calculation of ratios can help identify indicators of going concern problems but further procedures would need to be performed to obtain evidence of the company's ability to continue to trade.

Test your understanding 1

Murray case study: Audit risks

Your firm Wimble & Co has recently accepted appointment as auditor of Murray Co (a manufacturer of sports equipment).

Having sold your shares in Murray Co, you have been assigned as audit manager and you have started planning the audit (although you were an employee of Murray Co, this was many years ago and you did not have any involvement in preparation of the financial statements). You have held a meeting with the client and have ascertained the following:

Murray Co manufactures sports equipment. Most items of equipment, such as tennis rackets, hockey sticks and goals, take less than one day to manufacture. Murray Co's largest revenue generating product, ergometers (rowing machines), takes up to one week to manufacture. Murray Co refurbished the assembly line for the ergometers during the year. Murray Co uses a third party warehouse provider to store the manufactured ergometers and approximately one quarter of the other equipment.

Historically, Murray Co has only sold to retailers. For the first time this year, Murray Co has made sales directly to consumers, via a new website. The website is directly linked to the finance system, recording sales automatically. Website customers pay on ordering. The website development costs have been capitalised. This initiative was implemented to respond to market demands, as retailer sales have fallen dramatically in the last two years. Some of Murray Co's retail customers are struggling to pay their outstanding balances. Several of the sales team were made redundant last month as a result of the falling retailer sales.

Murray Co is planning to list on the stock exchange next year.

Required:

Using the information provided, describe SIX audit risks and explain the auditor's response to each risk in planning the audit of Murray Co.

Test your understanding 2

Murray Case Study: Analytical procedures

Draft Statement of Financial Position as at 31 December 20X4

	20X4	20X3
	$000	$000
Non-current assets		
Property plant and equipment	5,350	4,900
Website development	150	0
	5,500	4,900
Current assets		
Inventory	2,109	1,300
Trade receivables	2,040	1,050
Cash and cash equivalents	48	38
	4,197	2,388
	9,697	7,288
Equity		
Share capital (50c shares)	2,100	2,100
Retained earnings	2,959	2,156
	5,059	4,256
Non current liabilities		
Long term loan	2,800	1,500
Current liabilities		
Provisions	240	195
Trade and other payables	1,400	1,205
Accruals	18	12
Bank overdraft	180	120
	1,838	1,532
	9,697	7,288

Draft Statement of Profit or Loss for the year ended 31 December 20X4

	20X4	20X3
	$000	$000
Revenue	21,960	19,580
Cost of sales	(18,560)	(17,080)
Gross profit	3,400	2,500
Operating expenses	(2,012)	(2,012)
Finance cost	(340)	(240)
Profit before tax	1,048	248
Taxation	(245)	(24)
Profit for the period	803	224

Required:

Using the financial information provided, and the information from TYU 1, perform analytical procedures on the draft financial statements of Murray Co and explain the audit risks that arise.

Test your understanding 3

You are an audit senior at JPR Edwards & Co and you are currently planning the statutory audit of Hook Co for the year ending 30 June. Your firm was appointed as auditor in January after a successful tender to provide audit and tax services. JPR Edward & Co were asked to tender after the lead partner, Neisha Selvaratalm, met Hook Co's CEO, Pete Tucker, at a charity cricket match. Neisha explained that they were unhappy with the previous auditors as Pete Tucker felt their audit didn't add much value to Hook Co.

Hook Co manufacturers electrical goods such as MP3 players, smart phones and personal computers for the entertainment market. They do not retail their goods under their own name but manufacture for larger companies with established brands. Their key client, who represents 70% of their revenue, was the market leader in smart phones and MP3 players last year with 60% market share.

Hook Co uses a number of suppliers to source components for their products. Most suppliers are based in the UK however Hook Co imports microchips, a key component in all their goods, from a number of suppliers based in San Jose, Costa Rica. They assemble their goods in their one factory in Staines, UK, and package their products for their customers before distribution across the UK.

During the year Hook Co started developing applications which can be downloaded onto their smart phones. They have spent $1 million on an application called "snore-o-meter" which allows the users to record the sounds they make while they are asleep. There was a technical difficulty in production which meant the launch of "snore-o-meter" was delayed from the 31 March to its anticipated release on the 31 July.

To fund their expansion into Smartphone applications Hook is seeking a listing on the London Stock Exchange in the fourth quarter of the year.

Required:

Using the information provided, describe FIVE audit risks and explain the auditor's response to each risk in planning the audit of Hook Co.

(10 marks)

Test your understanding 4

(a) **With reference to ISA 520 *Analytical Procedures* explain**

(i) **what is meant by the term 'analytical procedures'**

(1 marks)

(ii) **the different types of analytical procedures available to the auditor**

(3 marks)

(iii) **the situations in the audit when analytical procedures are used.**

(3 marks)

Tribe Co sells bathrooms from 15 retail outlets. Sales are made to individuals, with income being in the form of cash and debit cards. All items purchased are delivered to the customer using Tribe's own delivery vans; most bathrooms are too big for individual's to transport in their own motor vehicles. The directors of Tribe indicate that the company has had a difficult year, but are pleased to present some acceptable results to the members.

The statement of profit or loss for the last two financial years are shown below:

Statement of profit or loss

	31 March 20X4	*31 March 20X3*
	$000	$000
Revenue	11,223	9,546
Cost of sales	(5,280)	(6,380)
	5,943	3,166
Operating expenses		
Administration	(1,853)	(1,980)
Selling and distribution	(1,472)	(1,034)
Interest payable	(152)	(158)
Investment income	218	–
	2,684	(6)

Statement of financial position extract

Cash and bank	380	(1,425)

Required:

(b) **As part of your risk assessment procedures for Tribe Co, identify and provide a possible explanation for unusual changes in the statement of profit or loss.**

(9 marks)

Test your understanding 5 – OT Case 1

Audit risk is the risk the auditor issues an inappropriate opinion on the financial statements. The auditor aims to reduce audit risk to an acceptably low level by assessing the risks of material misstatement and designing audit procedures to respond to those risks. The auditor has different types of procedures available to them to achieve this including analytical procedures.

You have received the latest management accounts from your client, Esperence Co, to help with your risk assessment for the forthcoming audit. The management accounts show actual results for the year to date, January to October inclusive. In October Esperence Co received a claim from a customer as a result of a defective product.

(1) Which of the following is an example of an audit risk for Esperence Co?

A The client is being sued by a customer for a defective product and if they lose the compensation awarded is likely to be significant

B The client is being sued by a customer for a defective product with the publicity of the case damaging their reputation

C The client will have to spend a significant amount of money on improving their quality control procedures to avoid the same defects occurring again

D Provisions may be understated if the probable payment resulting from the court case is not recognised as a liability in the financial statements

(2) Which of the following is the correct formula for calculating the payables days ratio using the management accounts of Esperence Co?

A Payables/Cost of sales × 304

B Payables/Cost of sales × 365

C Payables/Revenue × 304

D Payables/Revenue × 365

(3) Which of the following is not an analytical procedure?

A Calculation of gross profit margin and comparison with prior year

B Recalculation of a depreciation charge

C Comparison of revenue month by month

D Comparison of expenditure for current year with prior year

(4) Which of the following is not a ratio?

A Gross profit margin

B Acid test

C Inventory turnover

D Revenue growth

(5) You have used the management accounts to calculate the gross profit margin and found it to be higher than the prior year figure. Which of the following would provide a possible explanation?

A Sales prices have been reduced to increase sales volumes

B Prices charged by suppliers have increased but the company has absorbed these rather than increase sales prices to customers

C Closing inventory has been overvalued

D Administration expenses have reduced increasing profitability of the company

Test your understanding 6 – OT Case 2

You are the audit manager responsible for planning the audit of Fremantle Co. The draft financial statements show profit before tax of $3m and total assets of $50m. You have held a planning meeting with the client and have performed preliminary analytical procedures on the draft financial statements. You are currently assessing preliminary materiality for the audit and performing further risk assessment procedures.

(1) Which of the following statements is false in relation to materiality?

A Materiality can be assessed by size or nature

B A balance which is omitted from the financial statements cannot be material

C Materiality is a matter of professional judgment for the auditor

D There is an inverse relationship between risk and materiality. If audit risk is high, the materiality level set by the audit will be lower

(2) Which of the following procedures will not be performed in accordance with ISA 315 to identify risks of material misstatements?

A Inspection

B Observation

C External confirmation

D Enquiry

(3) Based on the above draft figures, what would be an appropriate level at which to set preliminary materiality?

A $150,000 for the statement of profit and loss and $500,000 for the statement of financial position

B $500,000 for the statement of profit and loss and $150,000 for the statement of financial position

C $1,500 for the statement of profit and loss and $50,000 for the statement of financial position

D $50,000 for the statement of profit and loss and $1,500 for the statement of financial position

(4) Performance materiality should be used by the auditor when performing substantive testing during the audit. Which of the following best describes performance materiality?

A The maximum amount of misstatement the auditor is willing to accept

B The amount at which the auditor deems the misstatement to be trivial

C An amount which could influence the economic decisions of the users taken on the basis of the financial statements

D An amount set below materiality for the financial statements as a whole to reduce, to an acceptably low level, the risk that misstatements could be material in aggregate

(5) Professional scepticism must be applied by auditors during the audit. Which of the following is not an application of professional scepticism?

A A critical evaluation of the evidence

B An open and questioning mind

C The auditor should not believe anything the client tells them

D The auditor must be alert to fraud and error

6 Chapter summary

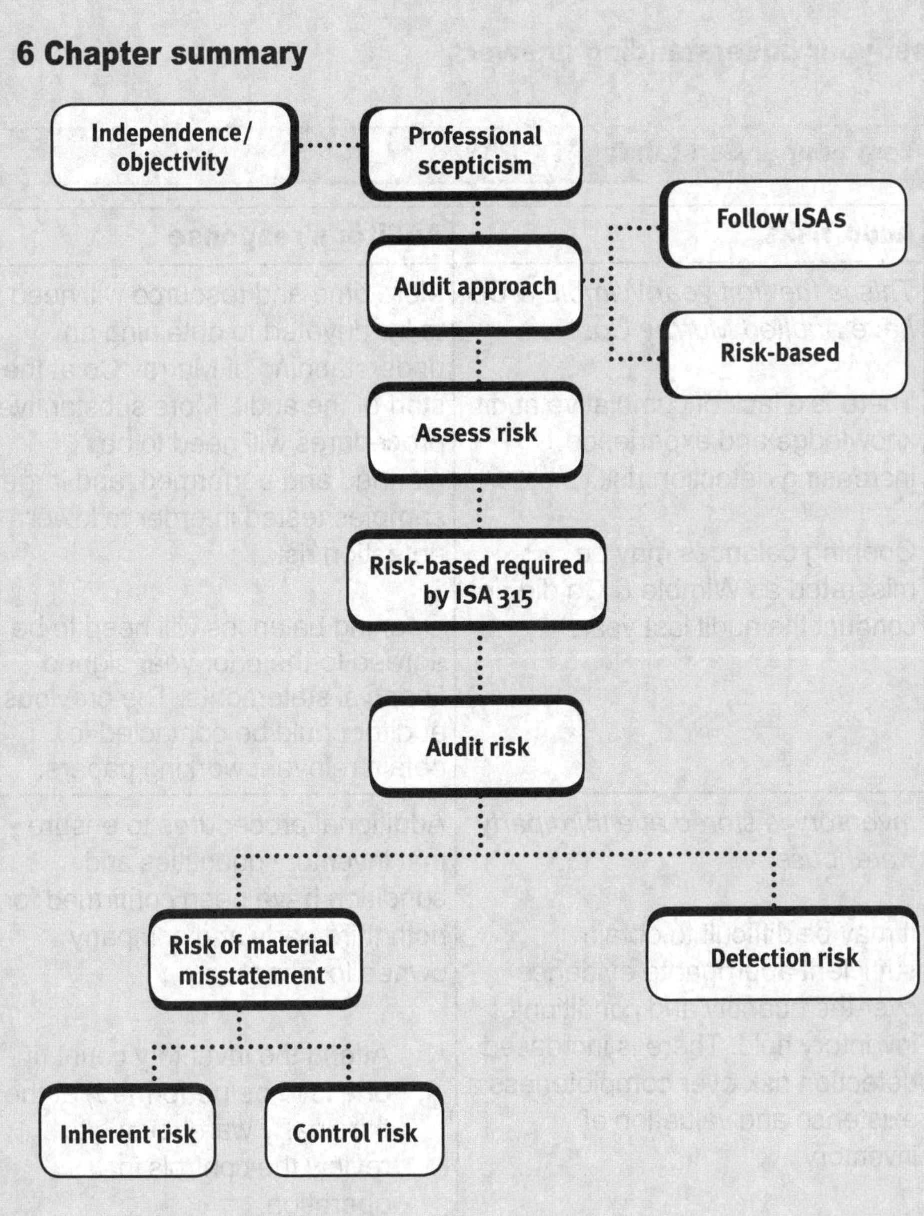

Test your understanding answers

Test your understanding 1

Audit risks	Auditor's response
This is the first year Wimble & Co have audited Murray Co. There is a lack of cumulative audit knowledge and experience, increasing detection risk. Opening balances may be misstated as Wimble & Co did not conduct the audit last year.	More time and resource will need to be devoted to obtaining an understanding of Murray Co at the start of the audit. More substantive procedures will need to be planned and performed, and larger samples tested in order to lower detection risk. Opening balances will need to be agreed to the prior year signed financial statements. The previous auditor could be contacted to obtain relevant working papers.
Inventory is stored at a third party warehouse. It may be difficult to obtain sufficient appropriate evidence over the quantity and condition of inventory held. There is increased detection risk over completeness, existence and valuation of inventory.	Additional procedures to ensure that inventory quantities and condition have been confirmed for both third party and company owned locations, e.g.: • Attend the inventory count (if one is to be performed) at the third party warehouses to review the controls in operation. • Inspect any reports produced by the auditors of third party warehouses in relation to the adequacy of controls over inventory. • Obtain external confirmation from the third party regarding the quantity and condition of the inventory.

Ergometers take up to one week to manufacture. There is likely to be a material work in progress (WIP) inventory balance at the year end. Determining the value and quantity of WIP is complex. There is a risk of misstatement of WIP inventory.	The percentage of completion basis should be discussed with the client and assessed for reasonableness. The WIP calculation should be agreed to supporting documentation such as purchase invoices for materials and timesheets and payroll records for labour. The overhead calculation should be recalculated and reviewed for any non-production overheads.
Murray Co refurbished the assembly line for the ergometers during the year. There is a risk that the expenditure incurred has been incorrectly treated as capital in nature and included within assets or expensed as repairs.	Review a breakdown of the costs and agree to invoices to assess the nature of the expenditure and if capital agree to inclusion within the asset register, and if repairs agree to expense in the statement of profit or loss.
There is a new website directly linked to the finance system which records sales automatically. There is increased risk over completeness of income if the system fails to record all sales made on the website. Revenue may be understated.	Extended controls testing to be performed over the sales cycle, including the use of test data where possible. Detailed testing to be performed over the completeness of income.
The website development costs have been capitalised. In order to be capitalised, it must meet all of the criteria under IAS 38 *Intangible Assets.* Research costs should be expensed rather than capitalised. There is a risk that intangible assets and profits are overstated.	A breakdown of the development expenditure should be reviewed and tested in detail to ensure that only projects which meet the capitalisation criteria are included as an intangible asset, with the balance being expensed.

Retailer sales have fallen dramatically in the last two years. If retailer sales continue to fall and direct consumer sales do not compensate for the loss of retailer revenue, Murray Co may not be able to continue to operate for the foreseeable future. There is a risk that disclosures of material uncertainties relating to going concern may be inadequate.	Perform a detailed going concern review, including: obtain and review the company's cash flow forecast and evaluate the reasonableness of the assumptions used to understand if management will have sufficient cash. Review post year end order books from retailers and post year end direct consumer sales to assess if the revenue figures in the cash flow are reasonable.
Several of the sales team were made redundant last month as a result of the falling retailer sales. Under IAS 37 *Provisions, Contingent Liabilities and Contingent Assets,* a redundancy provision will be required for any staff not yet paid at the year end. There is a risk of understated liabilities.	Discuss with management the progress of the redundancy programme and review and recalculate the redundancy provision.
Some retail customers are struggling to pay their outstanding balances to Murray Co. There is a risk of overstatement of receivables and understatement of irrecoverable debt allowance.	Extended post-year end cash receipts testing to assess valuation. Review of the aged receivables ledger to identify long outstanding debts. Allowance for receivables should be discussed with management if it is considered inadequate.
Murray Co is planning to list on the stock exchange next year. There is an increased risk of manipulation of the financial statements. There is a risk of overstatement of assets and profits, and understatement of expenses and liabilities.	Plan and perform procedures to ensure accounting estimates and judgmental areas are reasonable. Maintain professional scepticism and be alert to the risks identified in order to achieve a successful listing.

Test your understanding 2

Audit risks identified using analytical procedures:

Revenue has increased by 12%.	Retailer sales at Murray Co have fallen dramatically in the last two years. The increase in revenue is not consistent with this. Although Murray Co has begun selling directly to consumers for the first time this year, it is unlikely that these sales will have compensated for the loss in retailer sales at this early stage. In addition, revenue may be deliberately overstated by Murray Co in order to increase the chances of a successful listing. There is a risk that revenue is overstated.
Gross profit margin has increased from 13% to 15%.	The margins for direct consumer sales are likely to be higher than retailer sales, which may explain this increase. However, the increase could also be caused by overstatement of revenue, as explained above, or understatement of cost of sales due to incomplete recording of costs or overvaluation of closing inventory.
Operating expenses has no movement.	This is unusual given the increase in revenue and cost of sales. There is a risk that the prior year figure has been incorrectly presented in the current year column.
Net margin has increased from 1% to 4%.	Net margin has increased at a greater rate than gross profit margin. Given that this is the first year of direct consumer sales, the net margin would not be expected to increase significantly as the level of operating expenses would normally be higher at this early stage. This indicates potential overstatement of revenue and understatement of operating expenses.
Inventory days has increased from 28 (1,300/17,080×365) to 41 (2,109/18,560×365) days.	As sales have increased, this could be because of an increase in demand and therefore the need to hold more inventory. However, as retailer sales at Murray Co have fallen dramatically, there is a risk that some of the inventory is bespoke, and may therefore be obsolete. There is a risk that inventory is overstated.

Trade receivables days has increased from 20 (1,050/19,580×365) to 34 (2,040/21,960×365) days.	Given that website customers pay on ordering, trade receivables days would be expected to fall. However, some of Murray Co's retail customers are struggling to pay their outstanding balances. Trade receivables may be overstated, and the allowance for doubtful debts understated.
Trade payables days has increased from 26 (1,205/17,080×365) to 28 (1,400/18,560×365) days.	An increase in trade payables days could be caused by understatement of cost of sales. The increase in gross profit margin also highlighted this as a potential risk.
Current ratio has improved from 1.6:1 to 2.3:1.	Murray Co appears to be managing its working capital effectively. However, given the plans to list on the stock exchange next year, this may be indicative of manipulation of the financial statements in order to increase the chances of a successful listing. In addition, Murray Co has increased its long and short-term finance during the year.

Test your understanding 3

(a) **Audit risks and effect on audit approach**

Risk and explanation	**Effect on audit approach**
This is the first year JPR Edwards & Co have audited Hook Co. There may not be as deep an understanding of Hook Co's business as if they had audited in previous years and therefore detection risk is increased. Opening balances may be misstated as JPR Edwards & Co were not the auditors last year and cannot rely on their own previous work.	More time should be devoted to understanding the business at the start of the audit. More substantive procedures may be planned to lower detection risk. JPR Edwards & Co will have to design specific audit procedures to obtain sufficient evidence regarding opening balances. This includes agreeing the opening balances to the prior year signed financial statements and obtaining relevant working papers from the prior year auditors.

Hook Co is a manufacturing business. Hook will have a combination of raw materials, work in progress and finished goods in inventory. The calculation and valuation of work in progress and finished goods is subjective and therefore at risk of possible overstatement.	Appropriate time should be allocated to attending the inventory count and understanding the inventory valuation process for work in progress and finished goods. The basis for assessing the percentage of completion of WIP should be discussed with management to ensure it is reasonable. Purchase invoices should be inspected to verify cost, payroll records and job cards should be inspected to verify the labour element of WIP and finished goods. Overheads included in WIP and finished goods should be recalculated and reviewed to ensure only production overheads are included.
Hook Co manufactures electrical goods for the entertainment market. This is a rapidly changing market and goods can become obsolete quickly and therefore be valued incorrectly in the financial statements.	Hook Co's process for identifying obsolete items should be reviewed thoroughly as changes in technology are likely to render items obsolete quicker than in a more stable market. The aged inventory listing should be reviewed for old or obsolete items and compared with the allowance made to write the inventory down to NRV. If the allowance does not appear adequate, it should be discussed with management.

Their key client represents 70% of their revenue. Hook Co may be over reliant on this client which could threaten its going concern status if this key client was lost. There is a risk that disclosures of material uncertainties relating to going concern are inadequate.	Procedures should be designed at the planning stage to allow the auditor to assess the going concern risk faced by Hook Co. Contracts and other correspondence from the key customer should be reviewed to identify any specific risks that the client may be lost. Analytical procedures should be designed to assess the impact on Hook Co's financial position if the contract was not renewed.
Hook Co spent $1m on developing a new product. There is a risk that Hook Co have capitalised development expenditure which should have been expensed through the statement of profit or loss as research costs. If the application does not meet the criteria required to classify as development costs they should be expensed to the statement of profit or loss in the year they were incurred. There is a risk overstatement of intangible assets.	Enquiries should be made as to how Hook Co identifies whether the criteria for capitalisation has been met in accordance with accounting standards (IAS 38). Where amounts have been capitalised further procedures should be designed, for example, to assess how Hook Co measures whether the project would be profitable.
Hook Co is aiming to list on the London Stock Exchange this year. The directors may have greater incentive to 'window dress' the accounts to show a more favourable position in order to increase the proceeds generated from flotation. Assets and profits may be overstated and liabilities understated to make the company appear a more attractive investment.	Increased professional scepticism is required when performing the audit. Procedures should be planned to ensure areas of judgment and estimates exercised by the directors are reasonable and can be justified. *Special consideration should be given to sales cut-off testing.*

Test your understanding 4

(a) (i) Explanation of analytical procedures

Analytical procedures are used in obtaining an understanding of an entity and its environment and in the overall review at the end of the audit. They can also be used as a substantive procedure.

'Analytical procedures' means the evaluation of financial and other information and the review of plausible relationships in that information. The review also includes identifying fluctuations and relationships that do not appear consistent with other relevant information or results.

(ii) Types of analytical procedures

Analytical procedures can be used as:

- Comparison of comparable information to prior periods to identify unusual changes or fluctuations in amounts.
- Comparison of actual or anticipated results of the entity with budgets and/or forecasts, or the expectations of the auditor in order to determine the potential accuracy of those results.
- Comparison to industry information either for the industry as a whole or by comparison to entities of similar size to the client to determine whether receivable days, for example, are reasonable.

(iii) Use of analytical procedures

Risk assessment procedures

Analytical procedures are used at the beginning of the audit to help the auditor obtain an understanding of the entity and assess the risk of material misstatement. Audit procedures can then be directed to these 'risky' areas.

Analytical procedures as substantive procedures

Analytical procedures can be used as substantive procedures in determining the risk of material misstatement at the assertion level during work on the statement of profit or loss and statement of financial position.

Analytical procedures in the overall review at the end of the audit

Analytical procedures help the auditor at the end of the audit in forming an overall conclusion as to whether the financial statements as a whole are consistent with the auditor's understanding of the entity.

(b) Net profit

Overall, Tribe's result has changed from a net loss to a net profit. Given that revenue has only increased by 17% and that expenses, at least administration expenses, appear low, then there is the possibility that expenditure may be understated.

Revenue – increase 17%

According to the directors, Tribe has had a 'difficult year'. Reasons for the increase in revenue must be ascertained as the change does not conform to the directors' comments. It is possible that the industry as a whole, has been growing allowing Tribe to produce this good result. Alternatively, incorrect revenue recognition may have been applied.

Cost of sales – fall 17%

A fall in cost of sales is unusual given that revenue has increased significantly. This may have been caused by an incorrect inventory valuation and the use of different (cheaper) suppliers which may cause problems with faulty goods in the next year.

Gross profit (GP) – increase 88%

This is a significant increase with the GP% changing from 33% last year to 53% this year. Identifying reasons for this change will need to focus initially on the change in revenue and cost of sales.

Administration – fall 6%

A fall is unusual given that revenue is increasing and so an increase in administration to support those sales would be expected. Expenditure may be understated, or there has been a decrease in the number of administration staff.

Selling and distribution – increase 42%

This increase does not appear to be in line with the increase in revenue as selling and distribution would be expected to increase in line with revenue. There may be mis-allocation of expenses from administration or the age of Tribe's delivery vans is increasing resulting in additional service costs.

Interest payable – small fall

Given that Tribe has a considerable cash surplus this year, continuing to pay interest is surprising. The amount may be overstated. Reasons for lack of fall in interest payment e.g. loans that cannot be repaid early, must be determined. If the interest is associated with the overdraft that was in the SFP last year, this may have only been paid off just before the year end.

Investment income – new this year

This is expected given cash surplus on the year, although the amount is still very high indicating possible errors in the amount or other income generating assets not disclosed on the statement of financial position extract.

Test your understanding 5 – OT Case 1

(1)	D	A, B and C are business risks. An audit risk must be described in terms of a risk of material misstatement (i.e. the impact on the financial statements) or a detection risk (why the auditor may not detect the misstatement).
(2)	A	Payables/Cost of sales × 304. There are 304 days in the period January to October.
(3)	B	Recalculation is not an analytical procedure. An analytical procedure evaluates relationships between data.
(4)	D	Revenue growth is a trend rather than a ratio.
(5)	C	If closing inventory is overvalued, a larger figure will be deducted from cost of sales and, therefore, cost of sales will be lower and gross profit will be higher. A and B would both cause gross profit margin to fall. D would have no impact as administrative expenses do not affect gross profit.

Test your understanding 6 – OT Case 2

(1)	B	The financial statements can be materially misstated by the omission of a balance or disclosure.
(2)	C	External confirmation is not listed in ISA 315 as a risk assessment procedure. It is usually used as a substantive procedure.
(3)	A	Using 5% of PBT and 1% of total assets an appropriate level of materiality would be $150,000 for the statement of profit or loss and $500,000 for the statement of financial position.
(4)	D	A and B both refer to tolerable misstatement. C is a description of materiality for the financial statements as a whole.
(5)	C	Professional scepticism involves being alert to possible frauds and errors but does not require complete mistrust of the client.

chapter

5

Planning

Chapter learning objectives

This chapter covers syllabus areas:

- B1e – Quality control procedures
- B2 – Planning and risk assessment: objective and general principles
- B5 – Fraud, laws and regulations
- B6 – Audit planning and documentation

Detailed syllabus objectives are provided in the introduction section of the text book.

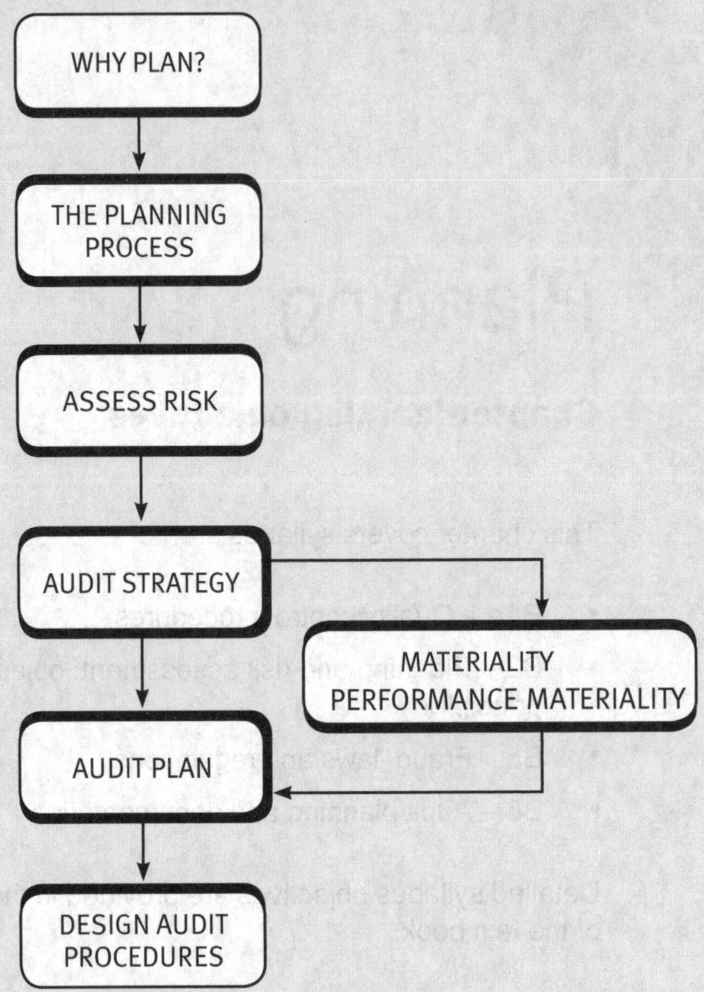

1 Purpose of planning

'The objective of the auditor is to plan the audit so that it will be performed in an effective manner.' (ISA 300 *Planning an Audit of Financial Statements).*

Audits are potentially complex, risky and expensive processes. Although firms have internal manuals and standardised procedures it is vital that engagements are planned to ensure that the auditor:

- devotes appropriate attention to important areas of the audit
- identifies and resolves potential problems on a timely basis
- organises and manages the audit so that it is performed in an effective and efficient manner
- selects team members with appropriate capabilities and competencies
- directs and supervises the team and reviews their work
- effectively coordinates the work of others, such as experts and internal audit.

Planning ensures that the risk of performing a poor quality audit (and ultimately giving an inappropriate audit opinion) is reduced to an acceptable level.

In order to achieve the overall objectives of the auditor, the audit must be conducted in accordance with ISAs.

Conducting the audit in accordance with ISAs:

- ensures that the auditor is fulfilling all of their responsibilities.
- allows a user to have as much confidence in one auditor's opinion as another's and therefore to rely on one audited set of financial statements to the same extent that they rely on another.
- ensures that the quality of audits internationally, is maintained to a high standard (thereby upholding the reputation of the profession).
- provides a measure to assess the standard of an auditor's work (necessary when determining their suitability as an authorised practitioner).

Auditors are also required to perform audits with an attitude of **professional scepticism**. Having an enquiring mind in itself is not sufficient to comply with a risk based method of auditing. In order to fulfil this responsibility auditors must also use **professional judgment**. This means the application of relevant training, knowledge and experience in making informed decisions about the courses of action that are appropriate to the unique circumstances of the audit engagement.

Therefore the use of a risk based approach requires skill, knowledge, experience and an inquisitive, open mind.

Although risk assessment is a fundamental element of the planning process, risks can be uncovered at any stage of the audit and procedures must be adapted in light of revelations that indicate further risks of material misstatement. It is, ultimately, the responsibility of the most senior reviewer (usually the engagement partner) to confirm that the risk of material misstatement has been reduced to an acceptable level.

The planning process

Planning consists of a number of elements. They can be summarised as:

- Preliminary engagement activities:
  - evaluating compliance with ethical requirements
  - establishing the terms of the engagement.
- Planning activities:
  - developing the audit strategy
  - developing an audit plan.

2 The audit strategy

Considerations in establishing the overall strategy

In determining the audit strategy the auditor should:

(i) Identify the characteristics of the engagement.

(ii) Ascertain the reporting objectives to plan the timing of the audit and the nature of communications.

(iii) Consider the significant factors and results of preliminary engagement activities that will direct the team's efforts.

(iv) Ascertain the nature, timing and extent of resources necessary to perform the engagement.

The audit strategy sets the scope, timing and direction of the audit. It allows the auditor to determine the following:

- the resources to deploy for specific audit areas (e.g. experience level, external experts)
- the amount of resources to allocate (i.e. number of team members)
- when the resources are to be deployed
- how the resources are managed, directed and supervised, including the timings of meetings, debriefs and reviews.

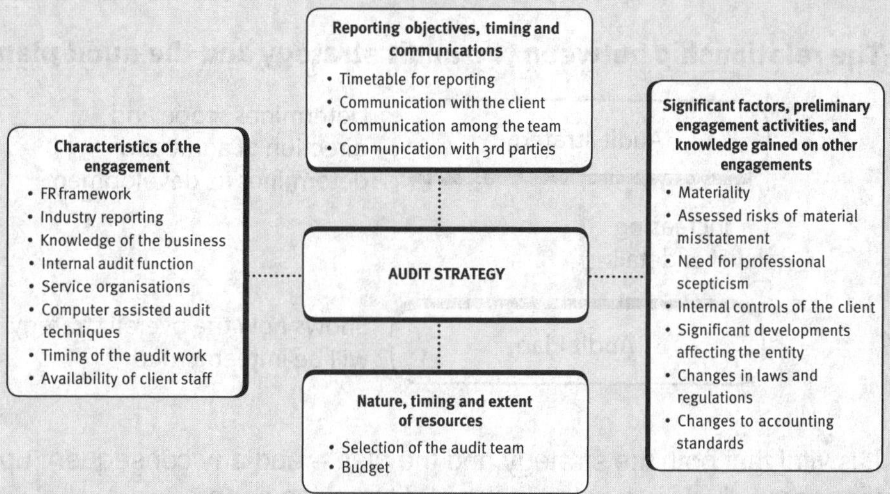

3 The audit plan

Once the audit strategy has been established, the next stage is to develop a specific, detailed plan to address how the various matters identified in the overall strategy will be applied.

The strategy sets the overall approach to the audit, the plan fills in the operational details of how the strategy is to be achieved.

The plan itself

The audit plan should include specific descriptions of:

- the nature, timing and extent of risk assessment procedures.
- the nature, timing and extent of further audit procedures, including:
  - **what** audit procedures are to be carried out
  - **who** should do them
  - **how much** work should be done (sample sizes, etc.)
  - **when** the work should be done (interim vs. final)
- any other procedures necessary to conform to ISAs.

The relationship between the audit strategy and the audit plan

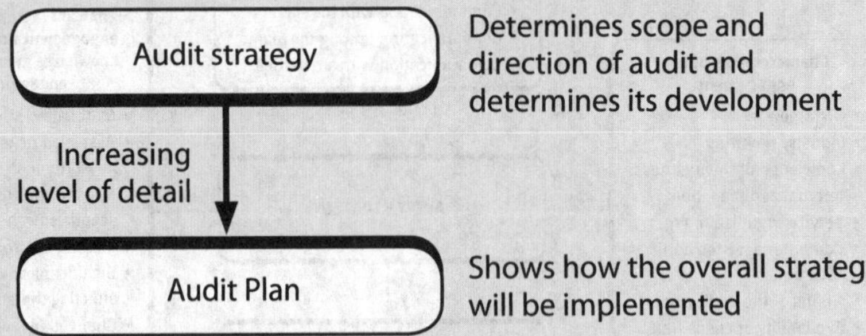

It is vital that both the strategy and the plan – and any consequent updates to them are fully documented in the audit working papers.

4 Interim and final audit

The auditor must consider the timing of audit procedures: whether to carry out an interim audit and a final audit, or just a final audit.

Interim audits

- Completed part way through a client's accounting year (i.e. before the year end).
- Allows the auditor to spread out their procedures and enables more effective planning for the final stage of the audit.
- Useful when there is a tight reporting deadline which increases detection risk.

Interim audits normally focus on:

- documenting systems and
- evaluating controls.

The interim audit can also be used to:

- test specific and complete material transactions, e.g. purchasing new non-current assets
- test transactions such as sales, purchases and payroll for the year to date
- assess risks that will impact work conducted at the final audit
- attend perpetual inventory counts.

For an interim audit to be justified the client normally needs to be of a sufficient size because this may increase costs. In argument to this, an interim audit should improve risk assessment and make final procedures more efficient. If there is to be an interim as well as a final audit the timing has to be:

- Early enough:
  - not to interfere with year-end procedures at the client and
  - to give adequate warning of specific problems that need to be addressed in planning the final audit.
- Late enough:
  - to enable sufficient work to be done to ease the pressure on the final audit.

The **final audit** takes place after the year-end and focuses on the remaining tests and areas that pose significant risk of material misstatement. This usually involves concentration on:

- statement of financial position balances which will only be known at the year end
- transaction testing for transactions that have occurred since the interim audit took place
- year end journals which may include adjustments to the transactions tested at the interim audit
- obtaining evidence that the controls tested at the interim audit have continued to operate during the period since the interim audit took place.

Impact of interim audit work on the final audit

If an interim audit is carried out this will have the following impacts:

- if the controls tested at the interim stage provided evidence that control risk is low, fewer substantive procedures can be performed
- if substantive procedures were performed at the interim stage, fewer procedures will be required at the final audit in general
- as fewer procedures are being performed, the final audit will require less time to perform
- the audit report can be signed closer to the year end resulting in more timely reporting to shareholders
- if the interim audit identified areas of increased risk, for example, controls were found not to be working effectively, increased substantive procedures will be required at the final audit.

5 Fraud and error

Fraud is an **intentional** act by one or more individuals among management, those charged with governance, employees or third parties, involving the use of **deception** to obtain an unjust or illegal advantage.

Fraud can be split into two types:

- Fraudulent financial reporting – deliberately misstating the accounts to make the company look better/worse than it actually is.
- Misappropriation – the theft of the company's assets such as cash or inventory.

The directors' responsibilities

The primary responsibility for the prevention and detection of fraud rests with those charged with governance and the management of an entity. This is achieved by:

- implementing an **effective system of internal control**, reducing opportunities for fraud to take place and increasing the likelihood of detection (and punishment)
- creating a **culture** of honesty, ethical behaviour, and active oversight by those charged with governance.

The directors should be aware of the potential for fraud and this should feature as an element of their risk assessment and corporate governance procedures.

The audit committee should review these procedures to ensure that they are in place and working effectively. This will normally be done in conjunction with the internal auditors.

Responsibilities of internal auditors in respect of fraud

Typical functions the internal auditor can perform in relation to fraud and error:

- Test the effectiveness of the internal controls at preventing and detecting fraud and error and provide recommendations for improvements to the controls.

- Perform fraud investigations to identify:
  - how the fraud was committed
  - the extent of the fraud
  - provide recommendations on how to prevent the fraud from happening again.
- Perform surprise asset counts to identify misappropriation.

The presence of an internal audit department may act as a deterrent to fraud in itself as there is a greater chance of being discovered.

The external auditor's responsibilities

ISA 240 the *Auditor's Responsibilities Relating to Fraud in an Audit of Financial Statements* recognises that misstatement in the financial statements can arise from either fraud or error.

The distinguishing factor is whether the underlying action that resulted in the misstatement was intentional or unintentional.

The external auditor is responsible for obtaining reasonable assurance that the financial statements, taken as a whole, are free from material misstatement, whether caused by fraud or error. Therefore, the external auditor has some responsibility for considering the risk of material misstatement due to fraud.

In order to achieve this the auditor must:

- Maintain an attitude of professional scepticism. This means that the auditor must recognise the possibility that a material misstatement due to fraud could occur, regardless of the auditor's prior experience of the client's integrity and honesty.
- Consider any incentives to commit fraud, e.g. profit related bonuses or applications for finance.
- Discuss among the engagement team, the client's susceptibility to fraud.
- Identify and assess the risks of material misstatement due to fraud.
- Identify, through enquiry, how management assesses and responds to the risk of fraud.
- Enquire of management, internal auditors and those charged with governance if they are aware of any actual or suspected fraudulent activity.

Responses to assessed fraud risks:

- Obtain written representation from management that they have informed the auditor of all known or suspected frauds.
- Test year end journals and adjustments as these may be used to manipulate the figures in the financial statements.
- Test accounting estimates and areas of management judgment for reasonableness.
- Make audit procedures unpredictable so the client cannot hide fraud in areas the auditor is not expected to test.
- Use suitably experienced staff to audit areas of particular risk.

There is an unavoidable risk that some material misstatements may not be detected even if properly planned in accordance with ISAs as fraud is likely to be concealed.

The ability to detect fraud depends on the skill of the perpetrator, collusion, relative size of amounts manipulated, and the seniority of the people involved.

Reporting of fraud

If the auditor identifies a fraud they must communicate the matter on a timely basis to the appropriate level of management (i.e. those with the primary responsibility for prevention and detection of fraud).

If the suspected fraud involves management the auditor must communicate the matter to those charged with governance. If the auditor has doubts about the integrity of those charged with governance they should seek legal advice regarding an appropriate course of action.

In addition to these responsibilities the auditor must also consider whether they have a responsibility to report the occurrence of a suspicion to a party outside the entity. Whilst the auditor does have an ethical duty to maintain confidentiality, it is likely that any legal responsibility will take precedence. In these circumstances it is advisable to seek legal advice.

If the fraud has a material impact on the financial statements the audit report will be modified. When the audit report is modified, the auditor will explain why the audit report has been modified and this will make the shareholders aware of the fraud.

6 Laws and regulations

Responsibilities of management

Management are responsible for ensuring the entity complies with relevant laws and regulations.

This requires management to **monitor legal requirements**, develop **systems of internal control** to ensure compliance with those legal requirements and **monitor** the **effectiveness** of those **control systems**.

Responsibilities of the auditor

- The auditor must **obtain sufficient, appropriate evidence** of **compliance** with those **laws and regulations** generally recognised to have a **direct effect** on the determination of material amounts and disclosures in the financial statements.
- The auditor must also **perform specified audit procedures** to help **identify** instances of **non-compliance** with **other laws and regulations** that may have a **material impact** on the financial statements. If non-compliance is identified (or suspected) the auditor must then respond appropriately.

Specified procedures

ISA 250 *Consideration of Laws and Regulations in an Audit of Financial Statements* requires an auditor to:

- Obtain a general understanding of the client's legal and regulatory environment.
- Inspect correspondence with relevant licensing and regulatory authorities.
- Enquire of management and those charged with governance as to whether the entity is compliant with laws and regulation.
- Remain alert to possible instances of non-compliance e.g. reading board minutes, making inquiries of lawyers and through performing substantive procedures.
- Obtain written representations that the directors have disclosed all instances of known and possible non-compliance to the auditor.

Effect of laws and regulations

ISA 250 distinguishes between two types of laws and regulations: those which are generally recognised to have a **direct effect** on the determination of material amounts and disclosures in the financial statements; and **other laws and regulations**.

Examples of laws and regulations with a **direct effect** include:

- Financial reporting regulations
- Company law (e.g. the Companies Act in the UK)
- Taxation legislation.

Examples of **other laws and regulations** include:

- Environmental legislation
- Health and safety law
- Employment law.

Non-compliance with other laws and regulations can impact the financial statements because companies in breach of the law may need to make provisions for future legal costs and fines. In the worst case scenario this could affect the ability of the company to continue as a going concern.

In addition, the auditor may need to report identified non-compliance with laws and regulations either to management or to a regulatory body, if the issue requires such action.

7 Quality control

ISA 220 *Quality control for an audit of financial statements*

The firm has an obligation to establish a system of quality control to ensure the firm complies with professional standards and reports issued are appropriate in the circumstances.

Policies and procedures should be established which address:

- Leadership responsibilities for quality within the firm
- Relevant ethical requirements

- Acceptance and continuance of client relationships and specific engagements
- Human resources
- Engagement performance
- Monitoring.

Leadership

The engagement partner takes overall responsibility for the overall quality of the engagement and shall ensure:

- Compliance with ethical requirements during the engagement.
- Appropriate acceptance and continuance procedures have been performed.
- The engagement team and auditor's experts used have the appropriate competence and capabilities.
- Reviews have been performed in accordance with the firm's review policies.
- Sufficient appropriate evidence has been obtained to support the audit conclusion through a review of the documentation and discussion with the audit team.
- Appropriate consultation on difficult or contentious matters has been undertaken.

Relevant ethical requirements

The firm should ensure compliance with the requirements of the ACCA Code of Ethics. This is covered in Chapter 3.

Acceptance and continuance of client relationships

The firm should ensure only clients and work of an acceptable level of risk are accepted. This requires consideration of:

- Integrity of management.
- Competence of the engagement team.
- Compliance with ethical requirements.
- Significant matters that have arisen during the current or previous audit engagement and their implications for continuing the relationship.

Human resources

The engagement partner should ensure that the engagement team collectively have the competence and capabilities to perform the audit in accordance with professional standards. This includes knowledge of professional standards, knowledge of relevant industries in which the client operates, the ability to apply judgment and an understanding of the firm's quality control policies and procedures.

Engagement performance

Engagement performance comprises direction, supervision and review of the engagement.

Direction involves informing team members of:

- their responsibilities
- objectives of the work to be performed
- the nature of the business
- risks
- problems that may arise
- the detailed approach to the performance of the engagement.

Supervision includes:

- Tracking the progress of the audit
- Considering the competence of the team
- Addressing significant matters arising and modifying the planned approach accordingly
- Identifying matters for consultation. Consultation may be required where the firm lacks appropriate internal expertise.

Review responsibilities include consideration of whether:

- The work has been performed in accordance with professional standards
- Appropriate consultations have taken place
- The work performed supports the conclusions reached
- The evidence obtained is sufficient and appropriate to support the auditor's report.

The engagement partner should perform a review of critical areas of judgment, significant risks and other areas of importance throughout the audit. The extent and timing of the partner's reviews should be documented.

Engagement Quality Control Review

An Engagement Quality Control Review (EQCR) shall be performed for listed entities, entities where an EQCR is required as a safeguard for an ethical threat, and other high risk engagements.

An EQCR includes:

- Discussion of significant matters with the engagement partner.
- Review of the financial statements and proposed auditor's report.
- Review of selected audit documentation relating to significant judgments and conclusions reached.
- Evaluation of conclusions reached in forming the audit opinion.

For listed entity audits, the EQCR should also consider:

- Independence of the engagement team.
- Whether appropriate consultation has taken place on contentious matters or differences of opinion.
- Whether documentation reflects the work performed in relation to significant judgments.

Note: An engagement quality control reviewer may also be referred to as an independent review partner.

Monitoring

The firm should have a monitoring process in place to ensure the firm's policies and procedures are relevant, adequate and operating effectively. This is achieved in two ways:

(1) Pre-issuance/hot review

(2) Post-issuance/cold review

	Pre-issuance/hot review	Post-issuance/cold review
Timing	Before the audit report is signed	After the audit report has been signed
Objective	To ensure the appropriate audit report is issued	To ensure the firm's quality control procedures are working effectively
Which clients	All high risk clients and listed clients	A selection of completed audit files

Matters considered	Focus will be on judgmental areas such as: • Materiality • Independence • Matters requiring consultation • Uncorrected misstatements • Significant risks and responses • Audit opinion	The reviewer will ensure working papers are: • On file • Completed • Signed as completed • Reviewed • Demonstrate sufficient appropriate evidence has been obtained • Demonstrate all matters were resolved before issuing the audit report
Conducted by	Independent partner of suitable experience, expertise and authority	Suitably senior person within the firm, the firm's own compliance department or an external consultant
Outcome	If issues are identified the EQCR can discuss these with the engagement partner and ensure the appropriate opinion is then issued	If issues are identified the firm may decide to: • Provide more training to staff • Update and improve their policies and procedures • Arrange additional quality control reviews • Take disciplinary action against individuals found not to be following procedure on a consistent basis

8 Audit documentation

Purposes of audit documentation

ISA 230 *Audit Documentation,* requires auditors to prepare and retain written documentation that:

- Provides a sufficient appropriate record of the auditor's basis for the audit report.

- Provides evidence that the audit was planned and performed in accordance with ISAs and applicable legal and regulatory requirements.
- Assists the engagement team to plan and perform the audit.
- Assists members of the engagement team responsible for supervision to direct, supervise and review the audit work.
- Enables the engagement team to be accountable for its work.
- Retains a record of matters of continuing significance to future audits.

Documentation should be sufficient to enable an experienced auditor, with no previous connection to the audit, to understand:

- the nature, timing and extent of audit procedures performed
- the results of the procedures performed and the evidence obtained
- the significant matters arising during the course of the audit and the conclusions reached thereon, and significant professional judgments made in reaching those conclusions.

Documentation is retained in an audit file, which should be completed in a timely fashion after the date of the audit report (normally not more than 60 days after) and retained for the period required by national regulatory requirements (this is normally five years from the date of the audit report).

Audit documentation should prove that the auditor has complied with professional and ethical standards and therefore the work has been performed to the required standard. If legal action is taken against the auditor, the audit files will provide the auditor's defence in court that they have not been negligent in their duties.

Illustration 1: Wimble & Co working paper

Wimble & Co Audit and Accounting Practitioners: Working Paper

Client:	Murray Co	Reference:	RA1
Period end:	31/12/X4	Prepared by:	Rob Cash
Subject:	Risk Assessment	Date prepared:	Dec 1 20X4

Objective: To identify the risks of material misstatement in the financial statements of Murray Co for the year ended 31 December 20X4, in order to provide a basis for designing and performing audit procedures that respond to the assessed risks.

Work performed:	Discussion among the engagement team of the susceptibility of the financial statements to material misstatement: **RA1/1** A summary of the understanding of the entity and its environment obtained, detailing the key elements including internal control components, sources of information and risk assessment procedures performed: **RA/2** Analytical procedures performed: **RA/3**
Results:	The identified and assessed risks of material misstatement: **RA/4**
Conclusions:	The overall responses to address the risks of material misstatement: **RA/5**
Reviewed by:	*An Audit Manager*
Date reviewed:	*December 5 20X4*

Wimble & Co working paper

Features of Wimble & Co working paper

Name of client: identifies the client being audited.

Period-end date: identifies the period to which the audit work relates.

Subject: identifies the topic of the working paper such as the area of the financial statements being audited, or the overall purpose of the work.

Working paper reference: provides a clear reference to identify the working paper; RA1 is the first working paper in the risk assessment section.

Preparer: identifies the name of the audit team member who prepared the working paper; to enable any queries to be directed to the relevant person.

Date prepared: the date the audit work was performed; the end of time period to which issues were considered.

Objective: the aim of the work; explains the relevance of the work being performed (in relation to Financial Statement assertions where appropriate).

Work performed: the work done cross-referenced to supporting working papers, including details of the sources of information, and items selected for testing (where relevant).

Results of work performed: any significant issues identified, exceptions or other significant observations including whether further audit work is necessary.

Conclusions: key points (including whether the area is true and fair where relevant).

Reviewer: the name of the audit team member who reviewed the work; evidences review as required by the ISAs.

Date of review: this must be before the audit opinion is signed

Types of audit documentation

Audit documentation includes:

- Planning documentation:
  - overall audit strategy
  - audit plan
  - risk analysis
- Audit programmes
- Summary of significant matters
- Written representation from management
- Checklists
- Correspondence
- Copies of client records.

For large audits much of the knowledge of the business information may be kept on a permanent file and the audit plan may contain a summary or simply cross refer to the **permanent file**. Typical information on a permanent file includes:

- Names of management, those charged with governance, shareholders
- Systems information
- Background to the industry and the client's business
- Title deeds
- Directors' service agreements
- Copies of contract and agreements.

Example contents of a current audit file

The audit work for a specific period is kept on a **current file**.

Typically, there are at least three sections, as follows:

- planning
- performance
- completion.

Planning

The main element of this section is likely to be the Audit Planning Memorandum.

This document is the written audit plan and will be read by all members of the audit team before work starts. Its contents are likely to include:

- background information about the client, including recent performance
- changes since last year's audit (for recurring clients)
- key accounting policies
- important laws and regulations affecting the company
- client's trial balance (or draft Financial Statements)
- preliminary analytical procedures
- key audit risks
- overall audit strategy
- materiality assessment
- timetable of procedures
- deadlines
- staffing and a budget (hours to be worked x charge-out rates)
- locations to be visited.

Performance

Working papers are likely to consist of:

- Lead Schedule – showing total figures, which agree to the financial statements
- Back-up schedules – breakdowns of totals into relevant sub-totals

- Audit work programme detailing:
  - the objectives being tested
  - work completed
  - how sampled items selected
  - conclusions drawn
  - who did the work
  - date work completed
  - who reviewed it.

Completion

The completion (also known as review) stage of an audit has a number of standard components:

- Going concern review
- Subsequent events review
- Final analytical procedures
- Accounting standards (disclosure) checklist
- Written representation from management
- Summary of adjustments made since trial balance produced
- Summary of unadjusted errors
- Draft final financial statements
- Draft report to those charged with governance and management letter.

Security and retention of working papers

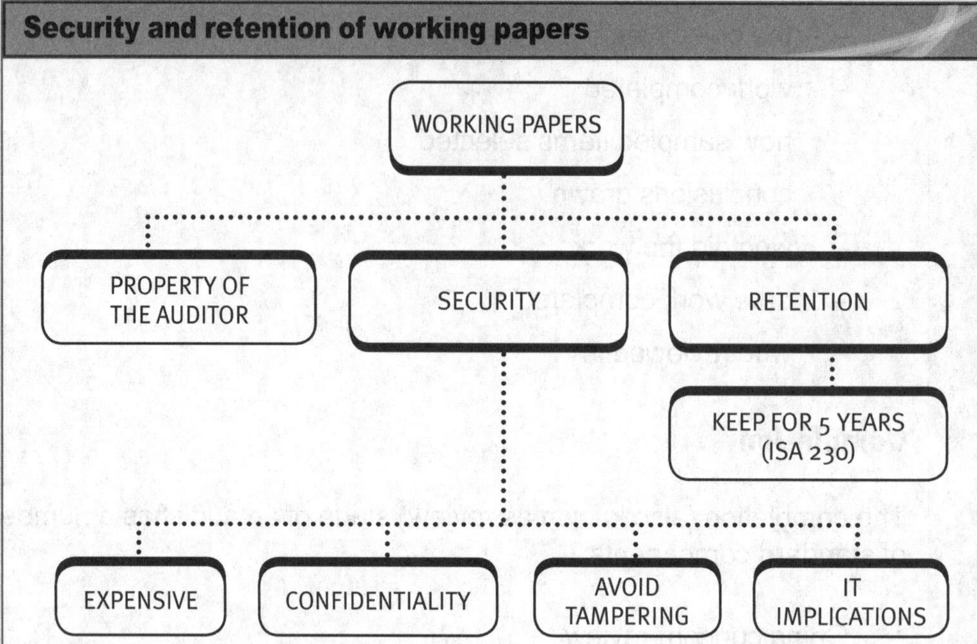

Who owns the working papers?

The auditor owns the audit working papers. This is important because:

- Access to the working papers is controlled by the auditor, not the client, which is an element in preserving the auditor's independence.
- In some circumstances care may need to be taken when copies of client generated schedules are incorporated into the file.

Security

Working papers must be kept secure.

- By its nature, audit evidence will comprise confidential, sensitive information. If the files are lost or stolen, the auditor's duty of confidentiality will be compromised.
- Audits are expensive. If the files are lost or stolen, the evidence they contain will need to be recreated, so the work will need to be done again. The auditors may be able to recover the costs from their insurers, but otherwise it will simply represent a loss to the firm.
- There have been cases of unscrupulous clients altering auditors' working papers to conceal frauds.

The implications of IT-based audit systems are also far reaching.

- By their nature, laptops are susceptible to theft, even though the thief may have no interest in the contents of the audit file. Nevertheless, all the problems associated with re-performing the audit and breaches of confidentiality remain.
- It is more difficult to be certain who created or amended computer based files than manual files – handwriting, signatures and dates have their uses – and this makes it harder to detect whether the files have been tampered with.

This means that the following precautions need to be taken.

- If files are left unattended at clients' premises – overnight or during lunch breaks – they should be securely locked away, or if this is impossible, taken home by the audit team.
- When files are left in a car, the same precautions should be taken as with any valuables.
- IT-based systems should be subject to passwords, encryption and backup procedures.

Retention

Audit files should be assembled in a timely fashion. This is, ordinarily, no longer than 60 days after the date of the auditor's report.

Once complete the files should be retained as long as required by national law. However, ISA 230 *Audit Documentation,* states that this period is, ordinarily, no shorter than five years from the date of the auditor's report. This should therefore be considered the minimum retention period.

All of this means that firms need to make arrangements for:

- secure storage of recent files
- archiving older files
- archiving and backup of IT based files.

Test your understanding 1

ISA 320 *Materiality in Planning and Performing an Audit* provides guidance on the concept of materiality in planning and performing an audit.

Required:

Define materiality and explain how the level of materiality is assessed.

(5 marks)

Test your understanding 2

You are an audit senior responsible for understanding the entity and its environment and assessing the risk of material misstatements for the audit of Rock Co for the year ending 31 December. Rock Co is a company listed on a stock exchange. Rock Co is engaged in the wholesale import, manufacture and distribution of basic cosmetics and toiletries for sale to a wide range of stores, under a variety of different brand names. You have worked on the audit of this client for several years as an audit junior.

Required:

(a) **Describe the information you will seek, and procedures you will perform in order to understand the entity and its environment and assess risk for the audit of Rock Co.**

(10 marks)

(b) You are now nearing the completion of the audit of Rock Co. Draft financial statements have been produced. You have been given the responsibility of performing a review of the audit files before they are passed to the audit manager and the audit partner for their review. You have been asked to concentrate on the proper completion of the audit working papers. Some of the audit working papers have been produced electronically but all of them have been printed out for you.

Required:

Describe the types of audit working papers you should expect to see in the audit files and the features of those working papers that show that they have been properly completed.

(10 marks)

(Total: 20 marks)

Test your understanding 3 – OT Case 1

You are the audit manager responsible for planning the audit of Rottnest Co. During the planning of the audit you have identified an increased risk of material misstatement due to fraud. The audit strategy and audit plan you have prepared for the audit reflects this increased risk.

(1) Which of the following statements regarding fraud is correct?

A The auditor may not detect all material fraud in the financial statements but this won't necessarily mean the auditor has been negligent due to the nature of fraud and the likelihood of concealment

B The auditor must detect all material fraud in the financial statements

C The auditor must detect every fraud in the financial statements

D The auditor is not responsible for detecting fraud as this is management's responsibility

(2) If material misstatement as a result of fraud is detected during the audit, and is not corrected by management, how will this be communicated to the shareholders?

A The auditor must send a letter to the shareholders informing them of the fraud

B The auditor must speak at the annual general meeting and specifically inform them

C The auditor will report it to the police and the police will notify the shareholders

D Through the audit report as the opinion will be modified

(3) Which of the following procedures must the auditor perform to respond to the risk of fraud?

(i) The auditor must obtain written representation from management confirming they have disclosed all known and suspected frauds to the auditor.

(ii) The auditor must incorporate an unpredictable element into the design of their audit procedures.

(iii) The auditor must test year end journal entries and estimates which may be used to manipulate the financial statements.

A (i) and (ii) only

B (i) and (iii) only

C (ii) and (iii) only

D (i), (ii) and (iii)

(4) The audit plan sets out the scope, direction and framework for the audit? True or false?

A True

B False

(5) Which matters will not be included in the audit strategy?

A Risk assessment and materiality

B Communications with the client

C Specific audit procedures to respond to the risks assessed

D The need for professional scepticism

Test your understanding 4 – OT Case 2

Your firm has recently been appointed auditor of Albany Co, a large company with sophisticated computer systems. The planning is shortly due to commence. It has been agreed with the client that an interim and final audit will be performed.

(1) Which of the following is not a benefit of planning the audit?

A It ensures the audit is performed efficiently and effectively

B It helps identify the resources to be allocated

C It ensures the financial statements will be correct

D It minimises the risk the auditor will issue an inappropriate opinion

(2) Which of the following is not part of the planning stage of the audit?

A Preliminary materiality assessment

B Risk assessment

C Developing the audit strategy

D Final analytical procedures

(3) When should the interim audit take place?

A After the year end before the audit report is signed

B Before the year end to avoid interfering with the client's year end procedures

C At the same time as the final audit

D After the audit report has been signed

(4) Which of the following will the auditor not perform at the interim audit?

A Obtaining written representation from management

B Tests of controls

C Transaction testing for transactions that have occurred to date

D Performing risk assessment procedures

(5) What are the main reasons for performing an interim audit?

(i) Increased fee income for the firm

(ii) To reduce time pressure at the final audit

(iii) To assess the level of control risk and determine the amount of substantive testing required at the final audit

A (i) and (ii) only

B (i) and (iii) only

C (ii) and (iii) only

D (i), (ii) and (iii)

Test your understanding 5 – OT Case 3

You are the partner within Mosaic Co. Your firm has an established reputation for performing high quality audits. Your firm has a quality control procedures document which is updated regularly. The procedures document is published in the employee handbook of which each employee receives a copy on joining the firm. The procedures are also available on your firm's intranet site so staff are able to access it at any time. The firm's procedures have been designed to ensure compliance with ISA 220 *Quality control for an audit of financial statements.*

(1) At the start of an audit, all audit team members are required to attend a planning meeting where they are informed of the nature of the client, the risks identified to date and any other issues of which they should be aware when performing the audit.

This is an example of

A Direction

B Consultation

C Review

D Supervision

(2) Which of the following is NOT an element of a quality control system?

A Human resources

B Engagement performance

C Engagement quality control review

D Monitoring

(3) Which of the following are primary reasons why a firm should perform audits to a high standard of quality?

(i) To maintain confidence in the audit profession

(ii) To ensure audit reports issued are appropriate

(iii) To avoid punishment

(iv) To ensure clients receive a competent and professional service

A (i) and (ii)

B (i), (iii) and (iv)

C (iii) and (iv)

D (i), (ii) and (iv)

(4) Which of the following should NOT perform an Engagement Quality Control Review?

A External consultant

B Engagement partner of the client subject to review

C Engagement partner of the audit firm not involved with the client subject to review

D Senior manager or director of the audit firm not involved with the client subject to review

(5) Which of the following statements regarding quality control is true?

A Where deficiencies in quality control procedures are identified the firm should take action such as providing additional training or increasing the frequency of quality control reviews.

B The firm only needs to act on quality control deficiencies identified by an external quality control review such as that performed by the ACCA.

C The firm should monitor its quality control procedures and policies on a regular basis to ensure they are working effectively.

D Every person within the audit firm has a responsibility to ensure quality control is adhered to.

9 Chapter summary

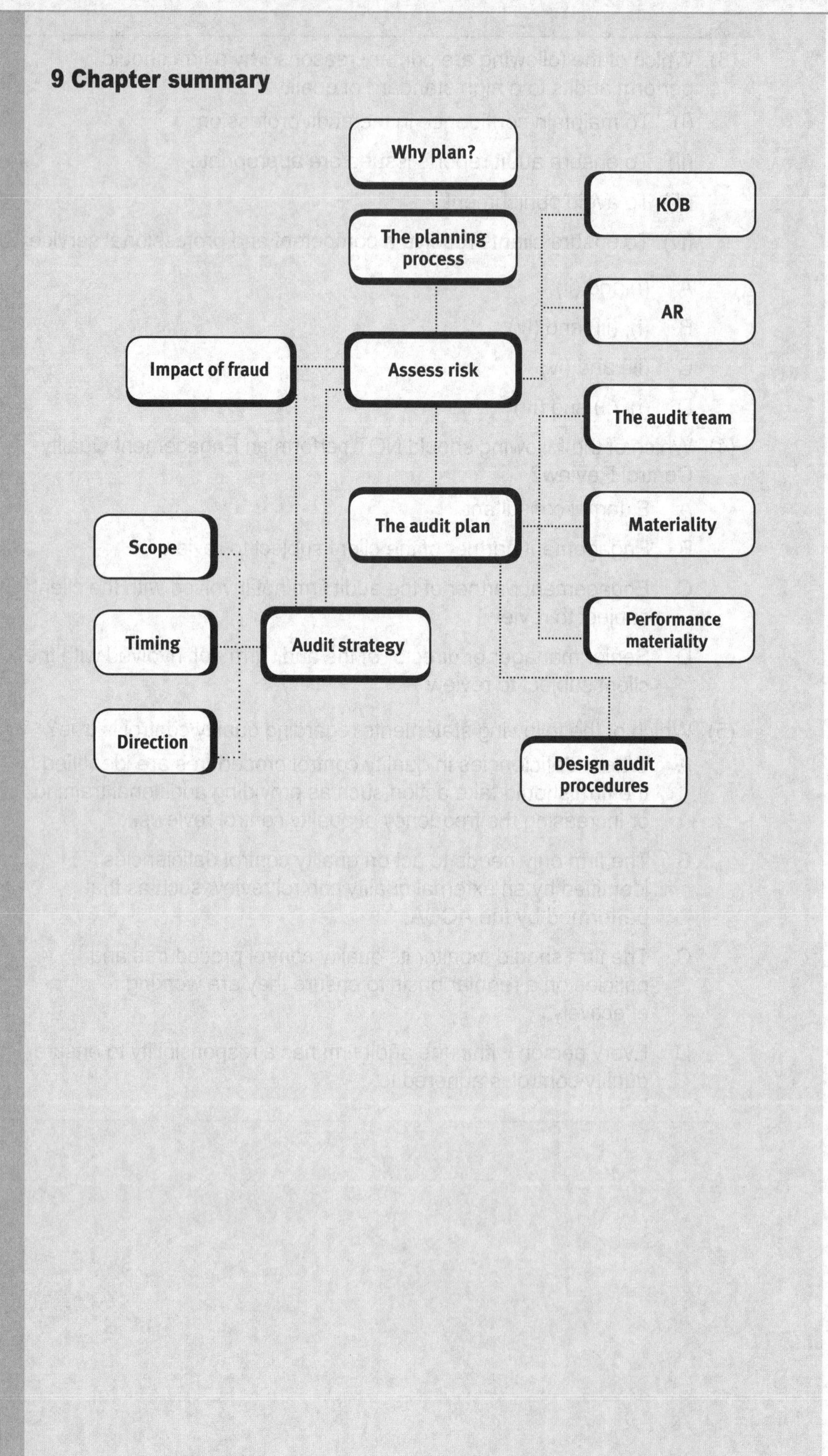

Test your understanding answers

Test your understanding 1

Materiality is defined as follows:

'Misstatements, including omissions, are considered to be material if they, individually or in aggregate, could reasonably be expected to influence the economic decisions of users taken on the basis of the financial statements.'

In assessing the level of materiality there are a number of areas that should be considered. Firstly the auditor must consider both the amount (quantity) and the nature (quality) of any misstatements, or a combination of both. The quantity of the misstatement refers to the relative size of it and the quality refers to an amount that might be low in value but due to its prominence could influence the user's decision, for example, directors' transactions.

In assessing materiality the auditor must consider that a number of errors each with a low value may when aggregated amount to a material misstatement.

The assessment of what is material is ultimately a matter of the auditors' professional judgment, and it is affected by the auditor's perception of the financial information needs of users of the financial statements.

In calculating materiality the auditor should also consider setting the performance materiality level. This is the amount set by the auditor, it is below materiality, and is used for particular transactions, account balances and disclosures.

Materiality is often calculated using benchmarks such as 5% of profit before tax or 1% of revenue. These values are useful as a starting point for assessing materiality.

Test your understanding 2

(a) **Information and procedures: understanding the entity and its environment and risk assessment for Rock Co**

(i) Understanding the entity and risk assessment is likely to involve a review of prior year risk assessments as a starting point and the identification of changes during the year from the information gathered that may alter that assessment.

(ii) Risk assessment procedures involve enquiries of management and others, analytical procedures and observation and inspection. Members of the engagement team should discuss the susceptibility of the financial statements to material misstatements.

(iii) Risk assessment also involves obtaining an understanding of the relevant industry, regulatory and other matters including the financial reporting framework, the nature of the entity, the application of accounting policies, the entity's objectives and related business risks, and its financial performance. This may involve:

(1) a review of prior year working papers noting any particular issues that arose warranting attention in the current year.

(2) discussions with the audit senior or manager working on Rock in prior years to establish any particular problem areas.

(3) discussions with Rock (and their other advisors such as banks and lawyers) to establish any particular problem areas.

(4) review of any third party information on the client such as press reports.

(5) a review of management accounts, any financial information provided to the stock exchange or draft financial statements that may be available to establish trends in the business.

(6) a review of any changes in stock exchange requirements.

(7) a review of systems documentation (either generated by Rock Co or held by the firm) to see if it needs updating.

(iv) Auditors should obtain an understanding of the control environment, the entity's process for identifying and dealing with business risk, information systems, control activities and monitoring of contents.

(v) Risks should be assessed at the financial statements level, and at the assertion level, and identify significant risks that require special audit consideration, and risks for which substantive procedures alone do not provide sufficient, appropriate audit evidence.

(vi) Analytical procedures are often used to highlight areas warranting particular audit attention. In the case of Rock Co, they are likely to focus on inventory which is likely to have a significant effect on profit (there may be slow moving or obsolete inventory that needs to be written down) and on property, plant and equipment which (as a manufacturer and distributor) is likely to be a significant item on the statement of financial position.

(vii) Risk assessment will facilitate the determination of materiality and tolerable error (calculations are normally based on revenue, profit and assets) that will be used in determining the sample sizes and in the evaluation of errors.

(b) **Types and features of audit working papers**

(i) Types of audit working papers include:

(1) systems documentation (flowcharts, systems manuals, narrative notes, checklists and questionnaires, etc.)

(2) constitutional documents

(3) agreements with banks and other providers of finance

(4) details of other advisors used by the entity such as lawyers

(5) regulatory documentation relating to the stock exchange listing

(6) audit planning documentation

(7) audit work programs

(8) working papers showing the work performed

(9) lead schedules showing summaries of work performed and conclusions on individual account areas and the amounts to be included in the financial statements

(10) trial balances, management accounts and financial statements

(11) standard working papers relating to the calculation of sample sizes, for example

(12) schedules of unadjusted differences

(13) schedules of review points

(14) letters of deficiency and written representation letters.

(ii) Features of audit working papers. All working papers (without exception) should show:

(1) By whom they were prepared and when.

(2) When they were reviewed and/or updated, and by whom, by means of signatures and dates – these may be electronic in the case of electronic working papers.

(3) Audit planning documentation should include the risk assessment which should be cross referenced to the audit program, and the audit program should be cross referenced to the audit working papers and vice versa.

(4) Working papers showing the work performed should be cross referenced to the audit program and the lead schedule on that particular section of the audit file, and should describe the nature of the work performed, the evidence obtained, and the conclusions reached.

(5) Each section of the audit file should have a lead schedule which should be cross referenced back to the relevant working papers.

(6) Trial balances should be cross referenced back to the relevant section of the audit file, and cross referenced forward to the financial statements.

(7) The financial statements should be cross referenced to the trial balance.

(8) Schedules of unadjusted differences should be cross referenced to the sections of the file to which they relate.

(9) Schedules of review points should all be 'cleared' to show that all outstanding matters have been dealt with.

Test your understanding 3 – OT Case 1

(1)	A	The auditor should plan and perform the audit to have a reasonable expectation of detecting material fraud and error. However, if a fraud is very well concealed, even a very thorough audit may not detect it.
(2)	D	Material misstatements are brought to the attention of the shareholders by modifying the audit opinion.
(3)	D	All three procedures must be performed to respond to the risk of fraud.
(4)	B	The scope, direction and framework are contained within the audit strategy.
(5)	C	Specific procedures are included in the audit plan.

Test your understanding 4 – OT Case 2

(1)	C	Financial statements cannot be verified as being correct due to the inclusion of estimates and judgments.
(2)	D	'Final' analytical procedures are performed at the completion stage of the audit.
(3)	B	The interim audit helps to develop the audit strategy. It should take place before the year end to avoid interfering with the client's year end procedures but should not be so early to be of little use.
(4)	A	Written representations are obtained at the end of the audit, just before the audit report is signed.
(5)	C	An interim audit may result in increased fees for the firm if a greater amount of work is performed. However, this is not a reason for performing an interim audit. The interim audit is a means of spreading the workload over a longer period to avoid time pressure.

Test your understanding 5 – OT Case 3

(1)	A	Briefing of the audit teams forms part of the direction of the audit.
(2)	C	Engagement quality control review is part of the engagement performance.
(3)	D	Quality is important for upholding the reputation of the profession and the firm in order to maintain investor confidence. Avoiding punishment is not the primary reason for ensuring a quality audit is performed.
(4)	B	An EQCR should be performed by someone independent of the engagement and someone of suitable authority such as a senior manager, director or partner.
(5)	B	The firm should perform its own quality control reviews and take action as necessary to ensure quality control procedures are followed.

chapter

6

Evidence

Chapter learning objectives

This chapter covers syllabus areas:

- C1a – The need to obtain an understanding of internal control relevant to the audit
- D1 – Financial statement assertions and audit evidence
- D2 – Audit procedures
- D3 – Audit sampling and other means of testing
- D5 – Computer assisted audit techniques
- D6 – The work of others

1 Audit evidence

In order for the auditor's opinion to be considered trustworthy auditors must come to their conclusions having completed a thorough examination of the books and records of their clients and they must document the procedures performed and evidence obtained, to support the conclusions reached.

The objective of the auditor, in terms of gathering evidence, is described in ISA 500 *Audit Evidence as:*

'to design and perform audit procedures in such a way to enable the auditor to obtain **sufficient appropriate audit evidence** to be able to draw reasonable conclusions on which to base the auditor's opinion.'

- **Sufficiency** relates to the **quantity** of evidence.
- **Appropriateness** relates to the **quality** or relevance and reliability of evidence.

Sufficient evidence

There needs to be 'enough' evidence to support the auditor's conclusion. This is a matter of professional judgment. When determining whether there is enough evidence the auditor must consider:

- the risk of material misstatement
- the materiality of the item
- the nature of accounting and internal control systems
- the results of controls tests
- the auditor's knowledge and experience of the business
- the size of a population being tested
- the size of the sample selected to test
- the reliability of the evidence obtained.

Sufficient evidence

Consider, for example, the audit of a bank balance:

Auditors will confirm year-end bank balances directly with the bank. This is a good source of evidence but on its own is not sufficient to give assurance regarding the completeness and final valuation of bank and cash amounts. The key reason is timing differences. The client may have received cash amounts or cheques before the end of the year, or may have paid out cheques before the end of the year, that have not yet cleared the bank account.

For this reason the auditor should also review and reperform the client's year-end bank reconciliation.

In combination these two pieces of evidence will be sufficient to give assurance over the bank balances.

Appropriate evidence

Appropriateness of evidence breaks down into two important concepts:

- reliability
- relevance.

Reliability

Auditors should always attempt to obtain evidence from the most trustworthy and dependable source possible. Evidence is considered more reliable when it is:

- obtained from an independent external source
- generated internally but subject to effective control
- obtained directly by the auditor
- in documentary form
- in original form.

Broadly speaking, the more reliable the evidence the less of it the auditor will need. However, if evidence is unreliable it will never be appropriate for the audit, no matter how much is gathered.

Relevance

To be relevant audit evidence has to address the objective/purpose of a procedure.

For example, when attending an inventory count, the auditor will:

- select a sample of items from physical inventory and trace them to inventory records to confirm the **completeness** of accounting records
- select a sample of items from inventory records and trace them to physical inventories to confirm the **existence** of inventory assets.

Whilst the procedures are perhaps similar in nature, their purpose (and relevance) is to test different **assertions** regarding inventory balances.

2 Financial statements assertions

The objective of audit testing is to assist the auditor in coming to a conclusion as to whether the financial statements are free from material misstatement.

For example:

Inventory

There are many ways inventory could be materially misstated:

- items could be missed out of inventory
- items from the next accounting period could be accidentally included
- it might not be valued at the lower of cost and net realisable value
- damaged or obsolete inventory might not be identified
- purchase cost may not be recorded accurately
- the inventory count may not be performed thoroughly.

For this reason auditors perform a range of tests on the significant classes of transaction, account balances and disclosures. These tests focus on what are known as **financial statements assertions**:

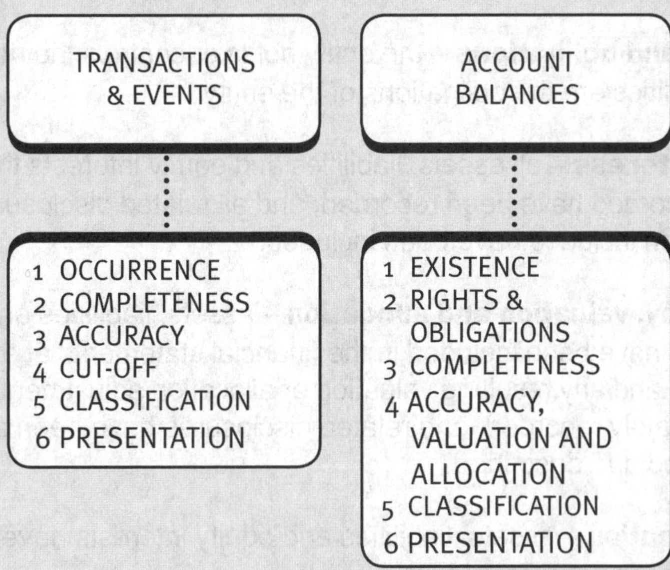

Assertions about classes of transactions and events, and related disclosures, for the period under audit

Occurrence – the transactions and events recorded and disclosed actually occurred and pertain to the entity.

Completeness – all transactions and events that should have been recorded have been recorded, and all related disclosures that should have been included have been included.

Accuracy – amounts and other data have been recorded appropriately and related disclosures have been appropriately measured and described.

Cut-off – transactions and events have been recorded in the correct accounting period.

Classification – transactions and events have been recorded in the proper accounts.

Presentation – transactions and events are appropriately aggregated or disaggregated and clearly described, and related disclosures are relevant and understandable in the context of the applicable financial reporting framework.

Assertions about account balances and related disclosures at the period end

Existence – assets, liabilities and equity interests exist.

Rights and obligations – the entity holds or controls the rights to assets and liabilities are the obligations of the entity.

Completeness – all assets, liabilities and equity interests that should have been recorded have been recorded, and all related disclosures that should have been included have been included.

Accuracy, valuation and allocation – assets, liabilities and equity interests have been included in the financial statements at appropriate amounts and any resulting valuation or allocation adjustments have been appropriately recorded, and related disclosures have been appropriately measured and described.

Classification – assets, liabilities and equity interests have been recorded in the proper accounts.

Presentation – account balances are appropriately aggregated or disaggregated and clearly described, and related disclosures are relevant and understandable in the context of the applicable financial reporting framework.

3 Sources of audit evidence

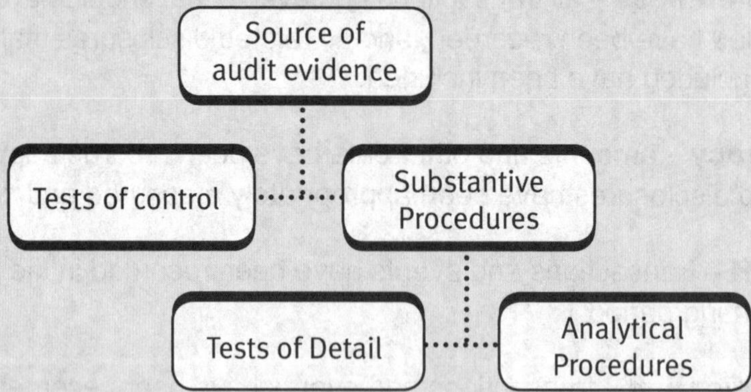

Auditors can obtain assurance from:

Tests of control: Tests of control are designed to evaluate the operating effectiveness of controls in preventing or detecting and correcting material misstatement.

Substantive procedures: Substantive procedures are designed to detect material misstatement at the assertion level.

Tests of controls

In order to design further audit procedures the auditor must assess the risk of material misstatement in the financial statements.

Remember: audit risk = inherent risk × **control risk** × detection risk

Internal controls are a vital component of this risk model, they are the mechanisms that clients design in an attempt to prevent, detect and correct misstatement. This is not only necessary for good financial reporting it is necessary to safeguard the assets of the shareholders and is a requirement of corporate governance.

The stronger the control system the lower the control risk and as a result, there is a lower risk of material misstatement in the financial statements.

In order to be able to rely on controls the auditor will need to:

- ascertain how the system operates
- document the system in audit working papers
- test the operation of the system
- assess the design and operating effectiveness of the control system
- determine the impact on the audit approach for specific classes of transactions, account balances and disclosures.

The focus of a test of control is not the monetary amount of a transaction. A test of control provides evidence of whether a control procedure has operated effectively. For example, inspecting an invoice for evidence of authorisation. It is irrelevant whether the invoice is for $100 or $1000 as it the control being tested, not the amount. Therefore, it could be said that a test of control provides indirect evidence over the financial statements. The auditor makes the assumption that if controls are working effectively there is less risk of material misstatement in the financial statements. However, the test of control itself does not test the figure within the financial statements, this is the purpose of a substantive procedure.

We will learn more about the systems themselves and tests of controls in the chapter 'Systems and controls'.

Substantive procedures

Substantive procedures consist of:

- **Tests of detail**: tests of detail to verify individual transactions and balances.
- **Substantive analytical procedures**: analytical procedures (as seen in the chapter 'Risk') involve the evaluation of financial information through analysis of plausible relationships among both financial and non-financial data.

Tests of detail v analytical procedures

A test of detail looks at the supporting evidence for an individual transaction such as inspection of a purchase invoice to verify the amount/date/classification of a specific purchase. If there are 5000 purchase invoices recorded during the accounting period, this one test of detail has only provided evidence for one of those transactions.

An analytical procedure would be used to assess the reasonableness of the purchases figure in total. For example, calculate the percentage change in purchases from last year and then compare this with the percentage change in revenue to see if they move in line with each other as expected.

The analytical procedure is not looking at the detail of any of the individual purchases but at the total figure. It is possible that there are a number of misstatements within the purchases population which would only be discovered by testing the detail as they may cancel each other out. An analytical procedure would not detect these misstatements.

Because of this, analytical procedures should only be used as the main source of substantive evidence where the internal controls have been found to be reliable as there is less chance of misstatements being present as the control system would have detected and corrected them.

Substantive analytical procedures

Analytical procedures as substantive tests

We have already come across analytical procedures as a significant component of risk assessment at the planning phase of an audit. Later in the text we will also see that they are a critical component of the completion of an audit. Here we consider their use as substantive procedures, i.e. procedures designed to detect material misstatement.

Analytical procedures are used to identify trends and understand relationships between sets of data. This in itself will not detect misstatement but will identify possible sources. As such, analytical procedures cannot be used in isolation and should be coupled with other, corroborative, forms of testing, such as enquiry of management.

When performing analytical procedures, auditors do not simply look at current figures in comparison to last year. Auditors may consider other points of comparison, such as budgets and industry data. Other techniques are also available, including:

- ratio analysis
- trend analysis
- proof in total, for example: an auditor might create an expectation of payroll costs for the year by taking last year's cost and inflating for pay rises and changes in staff numbers.

Analytical procedures are useful for assessing several assertions at once as the auditor is effectively auditing a whole accounting balance or class of transaction to see if it is reasonable.

They can be used to corroborate other audit evidence obtained, such as statements by management about changes in cost structures, such as energy savings.

By using analytical procedures the auditor may identify unusual items that can then be further investigated to ensure that a misstatement doesn't exist in the balance.

However, in order to use analytical procedures effectively the auditor needs to be able to create an expectation. It would be difficult to do this if operations changed significantly from the prior year. If the changes were planned, the auditor could use forecasts as a point of comparison. Although these are inherently unreliable due to the amount of estimates involved. In this circumstance it would be pointless comparing to prior years as the business would be too different to be able to conduct effective comparison.

It would also be difficult to use analytical procedures if a business had experienced a number of significant one-off events in the year as these would distort the year's figures making comparison to both prior years and budgets meaningless.

The suitability of analytical procedures as substantive tests

The suitability of this approach depends on four factors:

- the assertion/s under scrutiny
- the reliability of the data
- the degree of precision possible
- the amount of variation which is acceptable.

For example.

(1) Assertions under scrutiny

- – They should be suitable for the assertion being tested. Analytical procedures are clearly unsuitable for testing the existence of inventories. They are, however, suitable for assessing the value of inventory in terms of the need for allowances against old inventories, identified using the inventory holding period ratio.
- – Analytical procedures are more suitable for testing balances which are likely to be predictable over time and therefore relationships between data can be analysed to identify usual fluctuations.

(2) Reliability of data

- – If controls over financial data are weak, the data is likely to contain misstatement and is therefore not suitable as a basis for assessment.

(3) Precision required

- As analytical procedures are a high level approach to test a balance as a whole, if the auditor needs to test with precision, analytical procedures are unlikely to identify the misstatements.
- Precision will be improved if disaggregated information is obtained and analysed. For example, when performing analytical procedures over revenue, it may produce more reliable results if sales by month/customer/product/region are analysed rather than the revenue figure as a whole.

(4) Acceptable variation

- The amount of acceptable variation between the expected figure and the actual figure will impact whether analytical procedures provide sufficient appropriate evidence. If the level of variation from actual is higher than the level of variation the auditor is willing to accept, further procedures will be necessary to ensure the balance in the financial statements is not materially misstated.

In some circumstances the auditor may rely solely on substantive testing:

- The auditor may choose to rely solely on substantive testing where it is considered to be a more efficient or more effective way of obtaining audit evidence, e.g. for smaller organisations.
- The auditor may have to rely solely on substantive testing where the client's internal control system cannot be relied on.

The auditor must always carry out some substantive procedures on material items, and also carry out specific substantive procedures required by ISA 330 *The auditor's response to assessed risks.*

Required minimum substantive procedures

ISA 330 *The Auditor's Response to Assessed Risks* requires the auditor to carry out the following substantive procedures:

- Agreeing the financial statements to the underlying accounting records.
- Examination of material journals.
- Examination of other adjustments made in preparing the financial statements.

4 Types of audit procedures

ISA 500 identifies eight types of procedures that the auditor can adopt to obtain audit evidence.

In the chapter 'Procedures' we will look in detail at how these procedures are applied in specific circumstances.

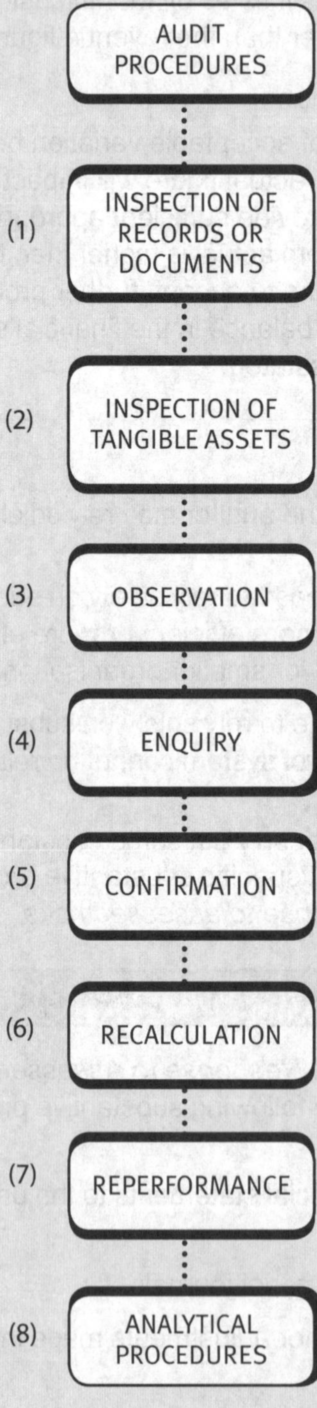

Explanation of techniques

Inspection of documents and records: examining records or documents, in paper or electronic form.

- May give evidence of rights and obligations, e.g. title deeds.
- May give evidence that a control is operating, e.g. invoices stamped paid or authorised for payment by an appropriate signature.
- May give evidence about cut-off, e.g. the dates on invoices, despatch notes, etc.
- Confirms sales values and purchases costs.

Inspection of tangible assets: physical examination of an asset.

- To obtain evidence of existence of that asset.
- May give evidence of valuation, e.g. evidence of damage indicating impairment of inventory or non-current assets.

Observation: looking at a process or procedure being performed by others.

- May provide evidence that a control is being operated, e.g. segregation of duties or a cheque signatory.
- Only provides evidence that the control was operating properly at the time of the observation. The auditor's presence may have had an influence on the operation of the control.
- Observation of a one-off event, e.g. an inventory count, may well give good evidence that the procedure was carried out effectively.

Enquiry: seeking information from knowledgeable persons, both financial and non-financial, within the entity or outside.

Whilst a major source of evidence, the results of enquiries will usually need to be corroborated in some way through other audit procedures. This is because responses generated by the audit client are considered to be of a low quality due to their inherent bias.

The answers to enquiries may themselves be corroborative evidence. In particular they may be used to corroborate the results of analytical procedures.

Written representations from management are part of overall enquiries. These involve obtaining written statements from management to confirm oral enquiries. These are considered further in the chapter 'Completion and review'.

External confirmation: obtaining a direct response (usually written) from an external, third party.

- Examples include:
  - circularisation of receivables
  - circularisation of payables where supplier statements are not available
  - confirmation of bank balances in a bank letter
  - confirmation of actual/potential penalties from legal advisers
  - confirmation of inventories held by third parties.
- May give good evidence of existence of balances, e.g. receivables confirmation.
- May not necessarily give reliable evidence of valuation, e.g. customers may confirm receivable amounts but, ultimately, be unable to pay in the future.

Recalculation: manually or electronically checking the arithmetical accuracy of documents, records, or the client's calculations, e.g. recalculation of the translation of a foreign currency transaction.

Reperformance: the auditor's independent execution of procedures or controls that were originally performed as part of the entity's internal control system, e.g. reperformance of a bank reconciliation.

5 Selecting items for testing

In accordance with ISA 500 *Audit Evidence*, the auditor has 3 options for selecting items to test:

(1) Select all items to test (100% testing)

This may be chosen where the population may be very small and it is easy for the auditor to test all items. Alternatively, if it is an area over which the auditor requires greater audit confidence, for example an area that is material by nature or is considered to be of significant risk, the auditor may decide to test all items within the population.

(2) Selecting specific items for testing

Items with specific characteristics may be chosen for testing such as:

- High value items within a population
- All items over a certain amount
- Items to obtain information

Although less than 100% of the population is being tested, this does not constitute sampling. As explained below, sampling requires all items in the population to have a chance of selection. In the categories above, only the items with the specific characteristics have a chance of selection.

(3) Sampling

The definition of sampling, as described in ISA 530 *Audit Sampling* is:

'The application of audit procedures to less than 100% of items within a population of audit relevance such that all sampling units have a chance of selection in order to provide the auditor with a reasonable basis on which to draw conclusions about the entire population.'

- When sampling, the auditor must choose a representative sample.
- If a sample is representative, the same conclusion will be drawn from that sample as would have been drawn had the whole population been tested.
- For a sample to representative, it must have the same characteristics as the other items in the population it was chosen from.

The need for sampling

It will usually be impossible to test every item in an accounting population because of the costs involved. Consider a manufacturer of fasteners (i.e. nuts, bolts, nails and screws); they will have many thousands, maybe millions, of items of inventory. It would simply be impossible to test the valuation of every single one due to the time and cost that would be involved.

It is also important to remember that auditors give reasonable **not** absolute assurance and are therefore not certifying that the financial statements are 100% accurate.

Auditors therefore need to understand the implications and effective use of **sampling**.

Statistical or non-statistical sampling

Statistical sampling means any approach to sampling that uses:

- random selection of samples; and
- probability theory to evaluate sample results.

Any approach that does not have both these characteristics is considered to be non-statistical sampling.

The approach taken is a matter of auditor judgment.

Designing a sample

When designing a sample the auditor has to consider:

- the purpose of the procedure
- the combination of procedures being performed
- the nature of evidence sought
- possible misstatement conditions.

The principal methods of sample selection are:

- **Random selection** – this can be achieved through the use of random number generators or tables.
- **Systematic selection** – where a constant sampling interval is used (e.g. every 50th balance) and the first item is selected randomly.
- **Monetary unit selection** – selecting items based upon monetary values (usually focusing on higher value items).
- **Haphazard selection** – auditor does not follow a structured technique but avoids bias or predictability.
- **Block selection** – this involves selecting a block of contiguous (i.e. next to each other) items from the population. This technique is used for cut-off testing.

When non-statistical methods (haphazard and block) are used the auditor uses judgment to select the items to be tested. Whilst this lends itself to auditor bias it does support the risk based approach, where the auditor focuses on those areas most susceptible to material misstatement.

Stratification

Stratification is the process of breaking down a population into smaller sub-populations. Each sub-population is a group of items (sampling units) which have similar characteristics.

The objective of stratification is to enable the auditor to reduce the variability of items within the sub-population and therefore allow sample sizes to be reduced without increasing sampling risk.

For example the auditor may stratify the population of revenue into three populations: revenue from Product A, revenue from Product B and revenue from Product C. The auditor may select a sample of revenue from Product A. The results of the testing of that sample can be extrapolated across the whole sub-population of revenue from Product A. A sample may be selected of revenue from Product B and again, the results of that testing can be extrapolated across that sub-population. Revenue from Product C may not be tested if it is considered immaterial.

Sampling risk

We saw in the chapter 'Risk' that sampling risk is a component of detection risk, the other component being non-sampling risk. Sampling risk arises from the possibility that the auditors' conclusion, based on a sample, may be different from the conclusion that would be reached if the entire population were subjected to the same audit procedure.

Auditors are faced with sampling risk in tests of controls and in substantive procedures. Sampling risk is essentially the risk that the auditor's sample from a population will not be representative.

In order to reduce sampling risk the auditor needs to increase the size of the sample selected.

Illustration 1: Murray Co sampling

Sampling

Murray Co deals with large retail customers, and therefore has a low number of large receivables balances on the receivables ledger. Given the low number of customers with a balance on Murray Co's receivables ledger, all balances would probably be selected for testing. However, for illustrative purposes the following shows how a sample of balances would be selected using systematic and Monetary Unit Sampling.

Credit and zero balances on the receivables ledger have been removed. The number of items to be sampled has been determined as 6. The customer list has been alphabetised.

Systematic Sampling

There are 19 customers with balances in the receivables ledger. The sampling interval is calculated by taking the total number of balances and dividing it by the sample size. The sampling interval (to the nearest whole number) is therefore 3.

The first item is chosen randomly; in this case item 10. Every third item after that is then also selected for testing until 6 items have been chosen.

$000

Customer Ref	Customer Name	Balance $	Item number	Sampling Item
A001	Anfield United Shop	176	1	
B002	The Beautiful Game	84	2	
B003	Beckham's	42	3	(5)
C001	Cheryl & Coleen Co	12	4	
D001	Dream Team	45	5	
E001	Escot Supermarket	235	6	(6)
G001	Golf is Us	211	7	
G002	Green Green Grass	61	8	
H001	HHA Sports	59	9	
J001	Jilberts	21	10	(1)
J002	James Smit Partnership	256	11	
J003	Jockeys	419	12	
O001	The Oval	92	13	(2)
P001	Pole Vaulters	76	14	
S001	Stayrose Supermarket	97	15	
T001	Trainers and More	93	16	(3)
W001	Wanderers	89	17	
W003	Walk Hike Run	4	18	
W004	Winners	31	19	(4)

Monetary Unit Sampling

Monetary Unit Sampling can utilise either the random or systematic selection method. This example illustrates the systematic selection method.

The cumulative balance is calculated.

The sampling interval is calculated by taking the total value on the ledger of $2,103,000 (to the nearest $000) and dividing by the sample size of 6. The sampling interval is therefore $351,000.

The first item is chosen randomly (a number between 1 and 2,103,000), in this case 233. Each item after that is selected by adding the sampling interval to the last value, until six items have been selected.

$000

Customer Ref	Customer Name	Balance	Cumulative	Sampling Item
A001	Anfield United Shop	176	176	
B002	The Beautiful Game	84	260	(1) $233
B003	Beckham's	42	302	
C001	Cheryl & Coleen Co	12	314	
D001	Dream Team	45	359	
E001	Escot Supermarket	235	594	(2) $584
G001	Golf is Us	211	805	
G002	Green Green Grass	61	866	
H001	HHA Sports	59	925	
J001	Jilberts	21	946	(3) $935
J002	James Smit Partnership	256	1,202	
J003	Jockeys	419	1,621	(4) $1,286
O001	The Oval	92	1,713	(5) $1,637
P001	Pole Vaulters	76	1,789	
S001	Stayrose Supermarket	97	1,886	
T001	Trainers and More	93	1,979	
W001	Wanderers	89	2,068	(6) $1,988
W003	Walk Hike Run	4	2,072	
W004	Winners	31	**2,103**	

Evaluating deviations and misstatements in a sample

Deviations

Any issues identified during a test of control are called **deviations**.

If the auditor tests a sample of 100 invoices for evidence of authorisation and 10 are found not to have been authorised, there is a deviation rate of 10%. There is no need to project this across the population as the deviation rate will still be 10%.

If the actual deviation rate exceeds the tolerable deviation rate (i.e. the rate the auditor is willing to accept), the risk of material misstatement is greater and more substantive procedures will be required.

Misstatements

Misstatements are differences between the amounts actually recorded and what should have been recorded. Misstatements are identified when performing substantive tests of detail.

The auditor must first consider the nature and cause of the misstatement. If the misstatement is a true error and isolated, no further procedures will be performed as the misstatement is not representative of further misstatements.

If the auditor believes the misstatement could be representative of further misstatements the auditor will project misstatements found in the sample to the population as a whole, and evaluate the results of the sample by considering tolerable misstatement.

Tolerable Misstatement is defined in ISA 530 *Audit Sampling as:*

"A monetary amount set by the auditor in respect of which the auditor seeks to obtain an appropriate level of assurance that the monetary amount set by the auditor is not exceeded by the actual misstatement in the population."

Tolerable misstatement is the practical application of performance materiality to an audit sample:

- If the total projected misstatement in the sample is less than tolerable misstatement then the auditor may be reasonably confident that the risk of material misstatement in the whole population is low and no further testing will be required.
- If the total projected misstatement in the sample exceeds tolerable misstatement the auditor will extend the sample in order to determine the total misstatement in the population.

Evaluating misstatements in a sample

A sample of $50,000 has been tested out of a population of $800,000. Misstatements of $2,000 were found. Tolerable misstatement has been set at $10,000.

The auditor needs to consider whether the misstatement is a true error and therefore isolated, or whether the misstatement is likely to be representative of further misstatements in the population.

If the misstatement is a true error, no further procedures will be necessary.

If it is expected that the misstatement is likely to be representative of further misstatements, the auditor should extrapolate the effect of the misstatement across the population to assess whether the projected misstatement is greater than tolerable misstatement.

Here, the auditor might expect that there are misstatements of $32,000 ($2,000/$50,000 × $800,000) in the population.

As the projected misstatement of $32,000 exceeds tolerable misstatement of $10,000, further audit testing will be required.

6 Computer assisted audit techniques (CAATs)

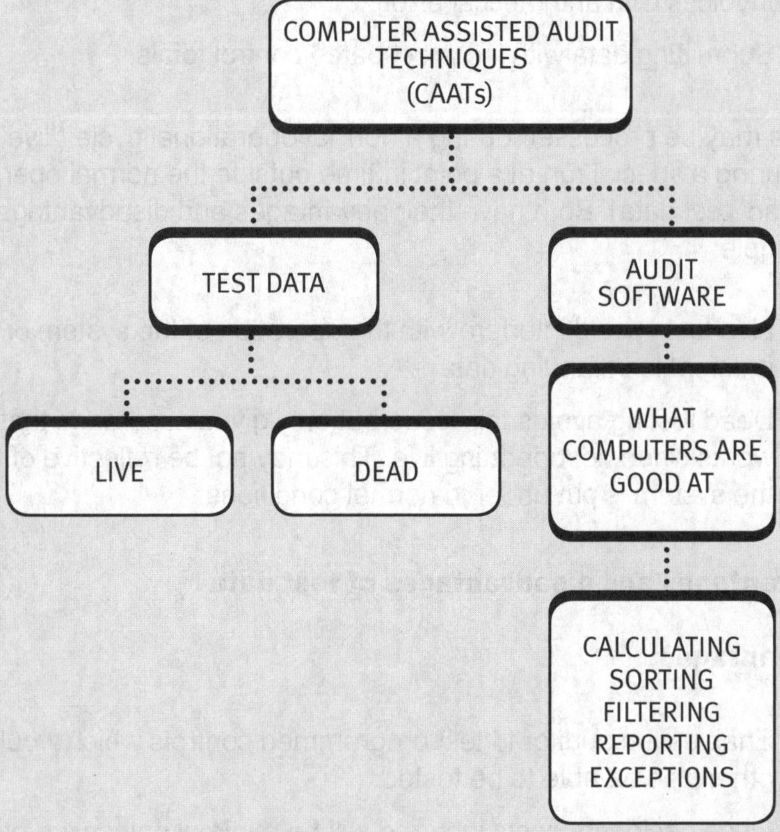

The use of computers as a tool to perform audit procedures is often referred to as a 'computer assisted audit techniques' or CAATs for short.

There are two broad categories of CAAT:

(1) Test data

(2) Audit software

Test data

Test data involves the auditor submitting 'dummy' data into the client's system to ensure that the system correctly processes it and that it prevents or detects and corrects misstatements. The objective of this is to test the operation of application controls within the system.

To be successful test data should include both data with errors built into it and data without errors. Examples of errors include:

- Codes that do not exist, e.g. customer, supplier and employee.
- Transactions above pre-determined limits, e.g. salaries above contracted amounts, credit above limits agreed with customer.
- Invoices with arithmetical errors.
- Submitting data with incorrect batch control totals.

Data may be processed during a normal operational cycle ('live' test data) or during a special run at a point in time outside the normal operational cycle ('dead' test data). Both have their advantages and disadvantages, for example:

- Live tests could interfere with the operation of the system or corrupt master files/standing data.
- Dead testing avoids this issue but only gives assurance that the system works when not operating live. This may not be reflective of the strains the system is put under in normal conditions.

Advantages and disadvantages of test data

Advantages

- Enables the auditor to test programmed controls which wouldn't otherwise be able to be tested.
- Once designed, costs incurred will be minimal unless the programmed controls are changed requiring the test data to be redesigned.

Disadvantages

- Risk of corrupting the client's systems.
- Requires time to be spent on the client's system if used in a live environment which may not be convenient for the client.

Audit software

Audit software is used to interrogate a client's system. It can be either packaged, off-the-shelf software or it can be purpose written to work on a client's system. The main advantage of these programs is that they can be used to scrutinise large volumes of data, which it would be inefficient to do manually. The programs can then present the results so that they can be investigated further.

Specific procedures they can perform include:

- extracting samples according to specified criteria, such as:
  - random
  - over a certain amount e.g. individually material balances or expenses
  - below a certain amount e.g. debit balances on a payables ledger or credit balances on a receivables ledger
  - at certain dates e.g. receivables or inventory over a certain age
- calculating ratios and select indicators that fail to meet certain pre-defined criteria (i.e. benchmarking)
- casting ledgers and schedules
- recalculation of amounts such as depreciation
- preparing reports (budget vs actual)
- stratification of data (such as invoices by customer or age)
- identifying changes to standing data e.g. employee or supplier bank details
- produce letters to send out to customers and suppliers.

These procedures can simplify the auditor's task by selecting samples for testing, identifying risk areas and by performing certain substantive procedures. The software does not, however, replace the need for the auditor's own procedures.

Advantages and disadvantages of audit software

Advantages

- Calculations and casting of reports will be quicker.
- More transactions can be tested with manual testing.
- The computer files are tested rather than printouts.
- Once set up, can be a cost effective means of testing.

Disadvantages

- Bespoke software (specific to one client) can be expensive to set up.
- Training of audit staff will be required incurring additional cost.
- The audit software may slow down or corrupt the client's systems.
- If errors are made in the design of the software, issues may go undetected by the auditor.

General advantages and disadvantages of CAATs

General advantages of CAATs

- Enables the auditor to test more items more quickly.
- The auditor is able to test the system rather than printouts.
- Obtain greater evidence as the results of CAATs can be compared with other tests to increase audit confidence.
- Perform audit tests more cost effectively.

Disadvantages of CAATs

- CAATs can be expensive and time consuming to set up.
- Client permission and cooperation may be difficult to obtain.
- Potential incompatibility with the client's computer system.
- The audit team may not have sufficient IT skills and knowledge to create the complex data extracts and programming required.
- The audit team may not have the knowledge or training needed to understand the results of the CAATs.
- Data may be corrupted or lost during the application of CAATs.

Other techniques

There are other forms of CAAT that are becoming increasingly common as computer technology develops, although the cost and sophistication involved currently limits their use to the larger accountancy firms with greater resources. These include:

Integrated test facilities – this involves the creation of dummy ledgers and records to which test data can be sent. This enables more frequent and efficient test data procedures to be performed live and the information can simply be ignored by the client when printing out their internal records; and

Embedded audit software – this requires a purpose written audit program to be embedded into the client's accounting system. The program will be designed to perform certain tasks (similar to audit software) with the advantage that it can be turned on and off at the auditor's wish throughout the accounting year. This will allow the auditor to gather information on certain transactions (perhaps material ones) for later testing and will also identify peculiarities that require attention during the final audit.

Auditing around the computer

This term means that the 'internal' software of the computer is not documented or audited by the auditor, but the inputs to the computer are agreed to the expected outputs to the computer.

Audit outcome

Increase the AUDIT RISK Why?

The actual computer files and programs are NOT TESTED.

Therefore no DIRECT evidence that the programs are working as documented

Where errors are found it may be difficult or even impossible to determine why those errors have occurred.

If the issues cannot be resolved, a modified audit report may needed.

7 Using the work of others

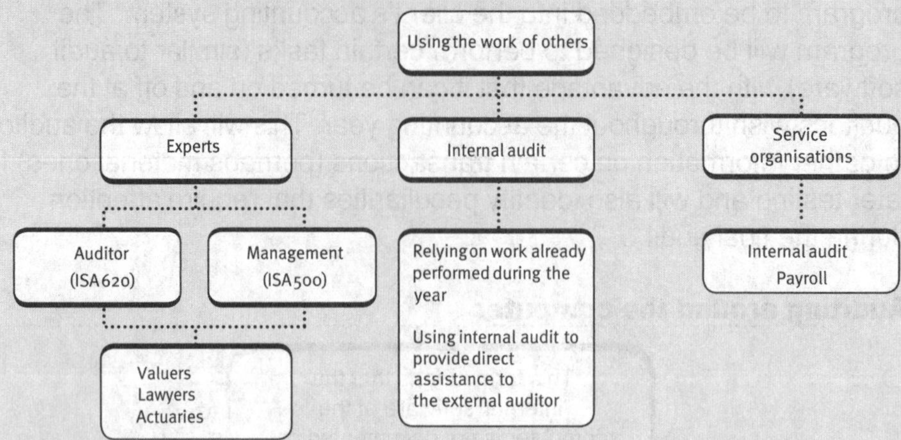

Using experts

- In certain circumstances auditors may need to rely on the work of, or consult parties not involved in the audit process.
- This may be where they lack technical knowledge and skills to gather evidence.
- Auditors may also choose to rely on the work of others because they find it effective and efficient to do so.

Examples:

- property valuations
- construction work in progress
- legal provisions
- assessment of oil reserves
- specialist inventory – livestock, jewellery
- actuarial valuations for pension schemes.

There are two types of expert an auditor may use:

(1) Management's expert – an employee of the client or someone engaged by the audit client who has expertise that is used to assist in the preparation of the financial statements.

(2) Auditor's expert – an employee of the audit firm or someone engaged by the audit firm to provide sufficient appropriate evidence.

ISA 500 *Audit Evidence* provides guidance on what the auditor should consider before relying on the work of management's expert. This guidance is very similar to that given in ISA 620 *Using the Work of an Auditor's Expert* which is given below.

Using an Auditor's Expert

ISA 620 *Using the Work of an Auditor's Expert* states that the auditor should obtain sufficient and appropriate evidence that the work of the expert is adequate for the purpose of the audit. This is likely where the auditor does not possess those skills themselves.

Competence, capability and objectivity

- The external auditor must assess the expert's competence, capability and objectivity before asking the expert to perform work.
- Competence and capability can be achieved by enquiring of the expert's qualifications, experience, membership of a professional body, published work.
- Objectivity can be assessed enquiring whether there are any business or personal relationships between the expert and the client.

Agreeing the work to be performed

The auditor should obtain an understanding of the field of expertise of the expert to enable the external auditor to determine the scope and objectives of the work.

Before any work is performed by the expert the auditor should agree in an engagement letter with the expert:

- The nature, scope and objectives of the expert's work.
- The roles and responsibilities of the auditor and the expert.
- The nature, timing and extent of communication between the two parties.
- The need for the expert to observe confidentiality.

Evaluating the work

Once the work has been completed the auditor must then assess it to ensure it is appropriate for the purposes of the audit. This involves consideration of:

- the consistency of the findings with other evidence
- the relevance and reasonableness of the assumptions and methods used by the expert
- the relevance, completeness and accuracy of the source data used.

If the work is not deemed adequate, further work must be agreed with the expert.

Relying on internal audit

An internal audit department forms part of the client's system of internal control. If this is an effective element of the control system it reduces control risk, and therefore reduces the need for the auditor to perform detailed substantive testing. This will need to be taken into account during the planning phase of the audit.

Additionally, auditors may be able to co-operate with a client's internal audit department and place reliance on their procedures in place of performing their own.

Types of work the external auditor may wish to rely on include:

- Tests of controls
- Risk assessment
- Fraud investigations
- Compliance with laws and regulations.

ISA 610 (Revised) *Using the Work of Internal Auditors* states that before relying on the work of internal audit, the external auditor must assess the effectiveness of the internal audit function and assess whether the work produced by the internal auditors is adequate for the purpose of the audit.

Evaluating the internal audit function

- The extent to which the internal audit function's **organisational status** and relevant policies and procedures support the **objectivity** of the internal auditors).
- The **competence** of the internal audit function.
- Whether the internal audit function applies a systematic and disciplined **approach**, including quality control.

If the auditor considers it appropriate to use the work of the internal auditors they then have to determine the areas and extent to which the work of the internal audit function can be used (by considering the nature and scope of work) and incorporate this into their planning to assess the impact on the nature, timing and extent of further audit procedures.

Evaluating the internal audit work

They also have to plan adequate time to review the work of the internal audit function to evaluate whether:

- the work was properly planned, performed, supervised, reviewed and documented
- sufficient appropriate evidence has been obtained
- the conclusions reached are appropriate in the circumstances
- the reports prepared are consistent with the work performed.

To evaluate the work adequately, the external auditor may reperform some of the procedures that the internal auditor has performed to ensure they reach the same conclusion.

The extent of the work to be performed on the internal auditors work will depend on the amount of judgment involved and the risk of material misstatement in that area.

When reviewing and reperforming some of the work of the internal auditor, the external auditor must consider whether their initial expectation of using the work of the internal auditor is still valid.

Using internal audit to provide direct assistance

For audits of financial statements with a year ending on or after 15 December 2014, external auditors can consider whether the internal auditor can provide direct assistance with gathering audit evidence under the supervision and review of the external auditor. The auditing standard provides guidance to aim to reduce the risk that the external auditor over uses the internal auditor.

The following considerations will be made:

- Direct assistance cannot be provided where laws and regulations prohibit such assistance.
- The competence and objectivity of the internal auditor. Where threats to objectivity are present, the significance of them and whether they can be managed to an acceptable level must be considered.
- The external auditor must not assign work to the internal auditor which involves significant judgement, a high risk of material misstatement or with which the internal auditor has been involved.
- The planned work must be communicated with those charged with governance so agreement can be made that the use of the internal auditor is not excessive.

Where it is agreed that the internal auditor can provide direct assistance:

- Management must agree in writing that the internal auditor can provide such assistance and that they will not intervene in that work.
- The internal auditors must provide written confirmation that they will keep the external auditor's information confidential.
- The external auditor will provide direction, supervision and review of the internal auditor's work.
- During the direction, supervision and review of the work, the external auditor should remain alert to the risk that the internal auditor is not objective or competent.

Documentation

The auditor should document:

- The evaluation of the internal auditor's objectivity and competence.
- The basis for the decision regarding the nature and extent of the work performed by the internal auditor.
- The name of the reviewer and the extent of the review of the internal auditor's work.
- The written agreement of management mentioned above.
- The working papers produced by the internal auditor.

Examples of work of the internal audit function that can be used by the external auditor include:

- Testing of the operating effectiveness of controls.
- Substantive procedures involving limited judgment.
- Observations of inventory counts.
- Tracing transactions through the information system relevant to financial reporting.
- Testing of compliance with regulatory requirements.

Note that the auditor is not required to rely on the work of internal audit. In some jurisdictions, the external auditor may be prohibited or restricted from using the work of the internal auditor by law.

Objectivity, competence and approach

When evaluating the competence of the internal audit function, the external auditor will consider:

- whether the resources of the internal audit function are appropriate and adequate for the size of the organisation and nature of its operations
- whether there are established policies for hiring, training and assigning internal auditors to internal audit engagements
- whether internal auditors have adequate technical training and proficiency, including relevant professional qualifications and experience
- whether the internal auditors have the required knowledge of the entity's financial reporting and the applicable financial reporting framework
- whether the internal audit function possesses the necessary skills (e.g. industry-specific knowledge) to perform work related to the entity's financial statements
- whether the internal auditors are members of relevant professional bodies that oblige them to comply with the relevant professional standards including continuing professional development.

When evaluating whether the internal audit function applies a systematic and disciplined approach, the external auditor will consider:

- whether there are adequate documented internal audit procedures or guidance
- whether the internal audit function has appropriate quality control procedures.

(ISA 610 (Revised) *Using the Work of Internal Auditors*)

Service organisations

ISA 402 *Audit considerations relating to an entity using a service organisation* deals with the auditor's responsibility to obtain sufficient appropriate evidence when a client outsources functions to service organisations.

The client may outsource certain functions to another company – a service organisation, e.g.

- internal audit
- receivables collection
- the entire finance function
- payroll.

Advantages from the auditor's point of view

- The independence of the service organisation may give increased reliability to the evidence obtained.
- Their specialist skills tend to make them more reliable at processing information.
- The auditor may be able to place a high degree of reliance on the reports they produce as a result (reduced control risk).

Disadvantages

- The auditor may not be able to obtain information from the service provider.
- The auditor may not be allowed to test controls at the service provider.
- This would lead to difficulties in assessing the accuracy and reliability of the information produced by the service provider.
- Ultimately this could lead to a lack of sufficient appropriate evidence and a modified audit report.

References to the work of others in the audit report

The auditor shall not refer to the work of others unless required by law or regulation. If such reference is required by law or regulation, the auditor's report shall indicate that the reference does not diminish their responsibility for the audit opinion.

ISA 402 Service organisations

ISA 402 *Audit Considerations Relating to an Entity Using a Service Organisation* provides guidance to auditors on the audit impact of outsourcing.

Objectives of the auditor in relation to the use of a service organisation

- Obtain an understanding of the service organisation sufficient to identify and assess the risks of material misstatement.
- Design and perform audit procedures responsive to those risks.

Obtaining an understanding of the service provided

- Nature of the services and their effect on internal controls.
- Nature and materiality of the transactions to the entity.
- Level of interaction between the activities of the service organisation and the entity.
- Nature of the relationship between the service organisation and the entity including contractual terms.

Sources of information for obtaining an understanding

- Obtaining a type 1 or type 2 report from the service organsation's auditor.
- Contacting the service organisation through the client.
- Visiting the service organisation.
- Using another auditor to perform tests of controls.

A Type 1 report provides a description of the design of the controls at the service organisation prepared by the management of the service organisation. It includes a report by the service auditor providing an opinion on the description of the system and the suitability of the controls.

A Type 2 report is a report on the description, design and operating effectiveness of controls at the service organisation. It contains a report prepared by management of the service organisation. It includes a report by the service auditor providing an opinion on the description of the system, the suitability of the controls, the effectiveness of the controls and a description of the tests of controls performed by the auditor.

If the auditor intends to use a report from a service auditor they should consider:

- the competence and independence of the service auditor
- the standards under which the report was issued.

Responding to assessed risks

If controls are expected to operate effectively:

- obtain a type 2 report if available
- perform tests of controls at the service organisation
- use another auditor to perform tests of controls.

When using a type 2 report, the auditor should consider

- whether the date covered by the report is appropriate for the audit
- whether the client has any complementary controls in place
- the time lapsed since the tests of controls were performed
- whether the tests of controls performed by the auditor are relevant to the financial statement assertions.

The auditor should enquire of the client whether the service organisation has reported any frauds to them or whether they are aware of any frauds.

Impact on the audit report

If sufficient appropriate evidence has not been obtained, a qualified or disclaimer of opinion will be issued.

The use of a service auditor is not mentioned in the audit report as the auditor is fully responsible for their opinion.

Test your understanding 1

ISA 500 *Audit Evidence* requires audit evidence to be reliable.

Required:

List FOUR factors that influence the reliability of audit evidence.

(4 marks)

Test your understanding 2

List and explain FOUR methods of selecting a sample of items to test from a population in accordance with ISA 530 *Audit Sampling*.

(4 marks)

Test your understanding 3

List and explain FOUR factors that will influence the auditor's judgment regarding the sufficiency of the evidence obtained.

(4 marks)

Test your understanding 4 – OT Case 1

During the audit, the auditor will use sampling. There are a variety of sampling methods available. Some sampling methods are statistical and some non-statistical. The auditor must use an appropriate method for the item being tested.

(1) You have identified a higher than expected deviation rate when performing tests of controls over purchases. Which of the following would be an appropriate response?

(i) Pick alternative items to test in place of those just tested and ignore the deviations.

(ii) Extend the sample size.

(iii) Perform more substantive procedures over purchases as tests of controls have not provided sufficient appropriate evidence.

A (i) and (ii) only

B (iii) only

C (ii) and (iii) only

D (i), (ii) and (iii)

(2) Which of the following statements is true?

A Random sampling is a method where the auditor picks the sample with no particular pattern

B Deviations must be extrapolated to determine the effect on the population

C Block sampling is where the auditor tests all items in a population

D Monetary unit sampling is a statistical method of sampling

(3) Which of the following constitutes sampling?

A Where less than 100% of the items in a population are tested and have an equal chance of selection

B Where less than 100% of the items in a population are tested and have a chance of selection

C Where items within a population with certain characteristics are chosen for testing

D Where every nth item in a population are chosen for testing

(4) The sampling method chosen must always be statistical. Is this statement true or false?

A True

B False

(5) A deviation occurs when a result differs from expectation during a test of control. Is this statement true or false?

A True

B False

Test your understanding 5 – OT Case 2

You are planning the audit of Wyndham Co. The company sells diamonds and other precious stones. You have decided to use the work of an auditor's expert to provide sufficient appropriate evidence over the valuation of inventory.

(1) Before appointing an auditor's expert, what factors must the auditor consider?

(i) Competence

(ii) Capability

(iii) Objectivity

(iv) Reliability of the source data

A (i), (ii) and (iii)

B (ii), (iii) and (iv)

C (i) (iii) and (iv) only

D All of them

(2) How can the auditor assess the competence of an auditor's expert?

(i) Obtain copies of professional certificates and make enquiries of the expert's experience.

(ii) Ask for confirmation from the expert of their independence.

(iii) Inspect the register of members of the relevant professional body for the name of the expert.

A (i) and (ii) only

B (ii) and (iii) only

C (i) and (iii) only

D All of them

(3) What must be agreed with the auditor's expert in writing before the work is performed?

(i) Responsibilities of each party

(ii) Inherent limitations of the audit

(iii) Deadline for the work

(iv) Scope and objectives

A All of them

B (i), (iii) and (iv) only

C (iii) and (ii) only

D (i), (ii) and (iv) only

(4) Which of the following statements is true in respect of the expert's work?

A The auditor can rely on expert's work and does not need to review it

B The auditor may choose not to review the expert's work if it is an area in which the auditor lacks knowledge or experience

C The auditor must review the assumptions and source data used by the expert to ensure they were reasonable and reliable

D The auditor will engage a second expert to review the work of the first to ensure sufficient appropriate evidence has been obtained

(5) Which of the following statements best describes a management's expert?

A A management's expert is an employee of the company

B A management's expert is someone appointed by the company to provide evidence for the auditor

C A management's expert is someone recommended by the auditor which management appoints to provide evidence for the audit

D A management's expert is someone appointed by the company to provide evidence for management which may be relied upon by the auditor

8 Chapter summary

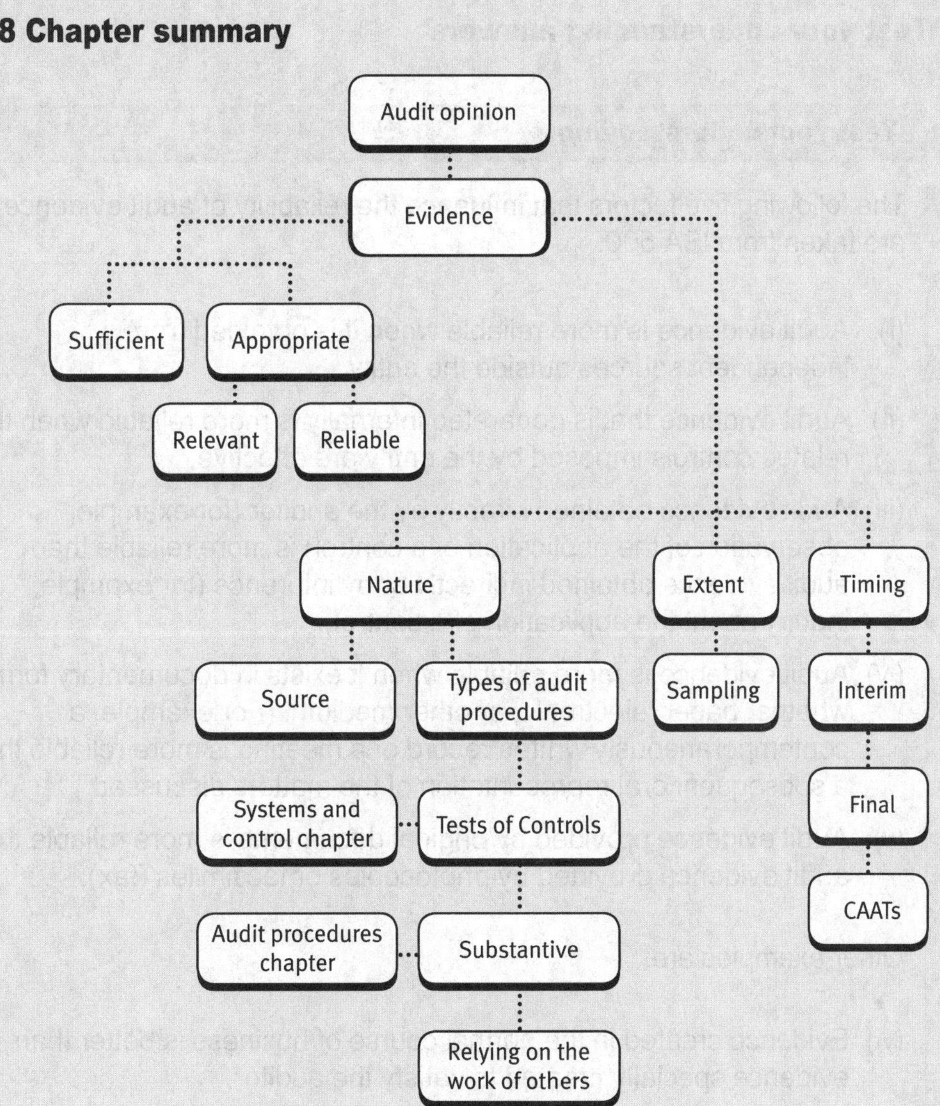

Test your understanding answers

Test your understanding 1

The following five factors that influence the reliability of audit evidence are taken from ISA 500:

(i) Audit evidence is more reliable when it is obtained from independent sources outside the entity.

(ii) Audit evidence that is generated internally is more reliable when the related controls imposed by the entity are effective.

(iii) Audit evidence obtained directly by the auditor (for example, observation of the application of a control) is more reliable than audit evidence obtained indirectly or by inference (for example, inquiry about the application of a control).

(iv) Audit evidence is more reliable when it exists in documentary form, whether paper, electronic, or other medium. (For example, a contemporaneously written record of a meeting is more reliable than a subsequent oral representation of the matters discussed.)

(v) Audit evidence provided by original documents is more reliable than audit evidence provided by photocopies or facsimiles (fax).

Other examples are:

(vi) Evidence created in the normal course of business is better than evidence specially created to satisfy the auditor.

(vii) The best-informed source of audit evidence will normally be management of the company (although management's lack of independence may reduce its value as a source of such evidence).

(viii) Evidence about the future is particularly difficult to obtain and is less reliable than evidence about past events.

Only four examples are required.

Test your understanding 2

Sampling methods

Methods of sampling in accordance with ISA 530:

- **Random** selection. Ensures each item in a population has an equal chance of selection, for example by using random number tables.
- **Systematic** selection. In which a number of sampling units in the population is divided by the sample size to give a sampling interval.
- **Haphazard** selection. The auditor selects the sample without following a structured technique – the auditor would avoid any conscious bias or predictability.
- **Sequence or block**. Involves selecting a block(s) of contiguous items from within a population.

Note: Only four sampling methods were asked for. Another method of sampling is:

- **Monetary Unit Sampling**. This selection method ensures that each individual $1 in the population has an equal chance of being selected.

Test your understanding 3

Sufficiency of evidence

- Assessment of risk at the financial statement level and/or the individual transaction level. As risk increases then more evidence is required.
- The materiality of the item. More evidence will normally be collected on material items whereas immaterial items may simply be reviewed to ensure they appear materially correct.
- The nature of the accounting and internal control systems. The auditor will place more reliance on good accounting and internal control systems limiting the amount of audit evidence required.
- The auditor's knowledge and experience of the business. Where the auditor has good past knowledge of the business and trusts the integrity of staff then less evidence will be required.
- The findings of audit procedures. Where findings from related audit procedures are satisfactory (e.g. tests of controls over revenue) then less substantive evidence will be collected.
- The source and reliability of the information. Where evidence is obtained from reliable sources (e.g. written evidence) then less evidence is required than if the source was unreliable (e.g. verbal evidence).

Test your understanding 4 – OT Case 1

(1)	C	Extend the sample size and perform more substantive tests. The auditor should never disregard deviations or misstatements identified during testing.
(2)	D	A describes haphazard sampling. Deviations are not extrapolated as the deviation rate will be the same across the population. Misstatements are extrapolated across the population. Block sampling is where items next to each other in the population are tested. If the auditor tests all items in the population the auditor is not using sampling.
(3)	B	Sampling is when each item in a population has a chance of selection. They do not need to have an equal chance.
(4)	B	False. Judgmental (non-statistical) methods are appropriate in the right circumstances e.g. if specific characteristics need to be tested.
(5)	A	True.

Test your understanding 5 – OT Case 2

(1)	A	Reliability of source data is evaluated after the expert has performed the work.
(2)	C	An independence confirmation from the expert would confirm objectivity but not competence.
(3)	B	Inherent limitations of an audit would not be communicated to the expert. This would be included in an audit engagement letter.
(4)	C	The auditor cannot just rely on the expert's work. They must review it to ensure it provides sufficient appropriate evidence and therefore must consider the assumptions and source data. If the auditor already had knowledge and experience in this area there would be no need to use an auditor's expert. If the auditor has evaluated the competence, capability and objectivity of the expert before using them, there should be no need to appoint a second expert to the review the first expert's work.
(5)	D	A management's expert is appointed by management to produce evidence to be used by management. If the evidence is reliable and relevant to the external audit, the auditor may choose to rely on that work.

chapter

7

Systems and controls

Chapter learning objectives

This chapter covers syllabus areas:

- C1 – Internal control systems
- C2 – The use and evaluation of internal control systems by auditors
- C3 – Tests of controls
- C4 – Communication on internal control

Detailed syllabus objectives are provided in the introduction section of the text book.

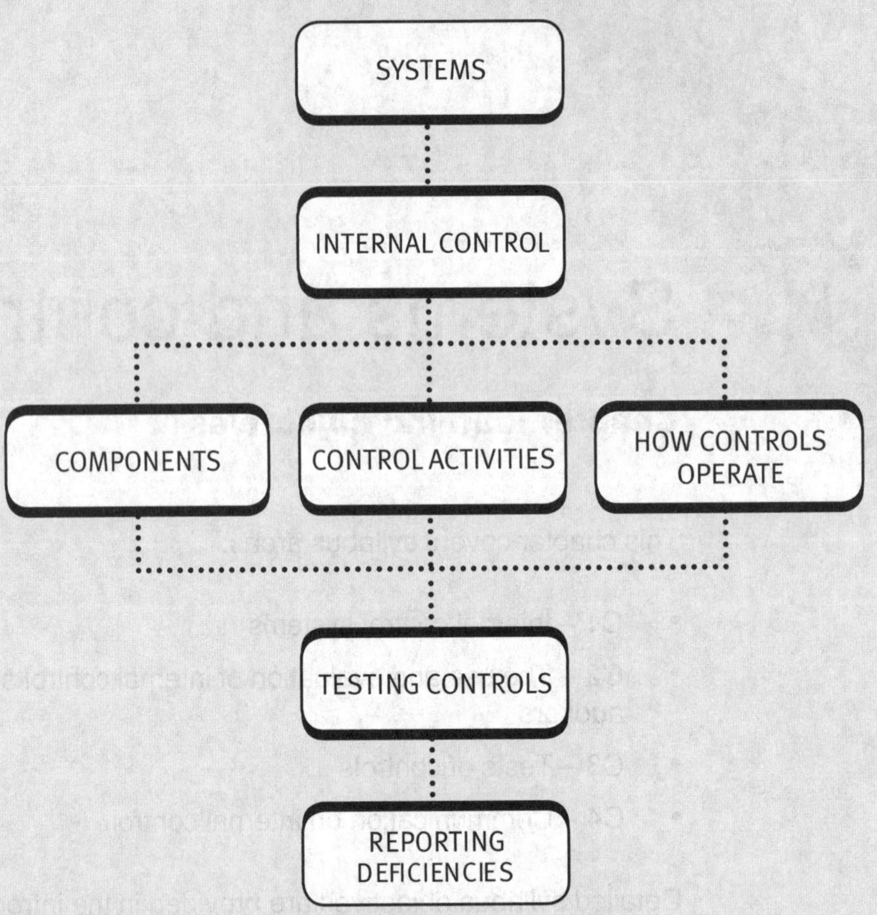

1 Effect of controls on the audit

This chapter considers the basic components of control systems and how the auditor fulfils their objectives for assessing control risk.

The auditor will ascertain the internal control system to assess whether it is likely to be reliable. If so, they will test the controls to ensure they are in place and working effectively.

Impact of tests of controls on the audit strategy and plan

The extent of substantive testing to be carried out will depend on the results of the tests of controls which will affect the auditor's assessment of the effectiveness of the internal control system and the auditor's assessment of control risk.

If control risk is deemed low:

- If tests of controls provide evidence that an effective control system is in place, this may allow the auditor to **place more reliance on internal controls** and evidence generated internally within the entity.
- Typically this increases the appropriateness of interim audit testing and allows the auditor to **reduce the quantity of detailed substantive procedures** performed at the final audit stage.
- The audit strategy and plan will be updated to reflect that fewer substantive procedures may be required or smaller sample sizes can be tested at the final audit stage.

If control risk is deemed high, the auditor should respond by:

- Increasing procedures conducted at and after the year-end.
- Increasing substantive procedures, in particular, tests of detail.
- Increasing the locations included in the audit scope.
- Placing less reliance on analytical procedures as the information produced by the client's systems is not reliable.
- Placing less reliance on written representations from management if the control environment generally is considered to be weak.
- Obtaining more evidence from external sources e.g. external confirmations from customers and suppliers.
- Updating the audit strategy and plan to reflect the additional testing required at the final audit stage.

Limitations of internal controls

The auditor can never eliminate the need for substantive procedures entirely because there are inherent limitations to the reliance that can be placed on internal control due to:

- Human error in the use of judgment.
- Ineffective controls.
- Collusion of staff in circumventing controls.
- The abuse of power by those with ultimate controlling responsibility (i.e. management override).
- Use of management judgement on the nature and extent of controls it chooses to implement.

As a result, the auditor must always perform substantive testing on material balances in the financial statements.

Control systems – basic principles

The auditor's main focus is on those systems relevant to the financial statements and, therefore, the audit. The basic objectives of these systems are to:

- Measure the effects of transactions and other relevant issues.
- Record those transactions and effects.
- Summarise them into a useable form.
- Publish those summaries to the relevant users of the information to assist decision making.

A simple system can be illustrated as follows:

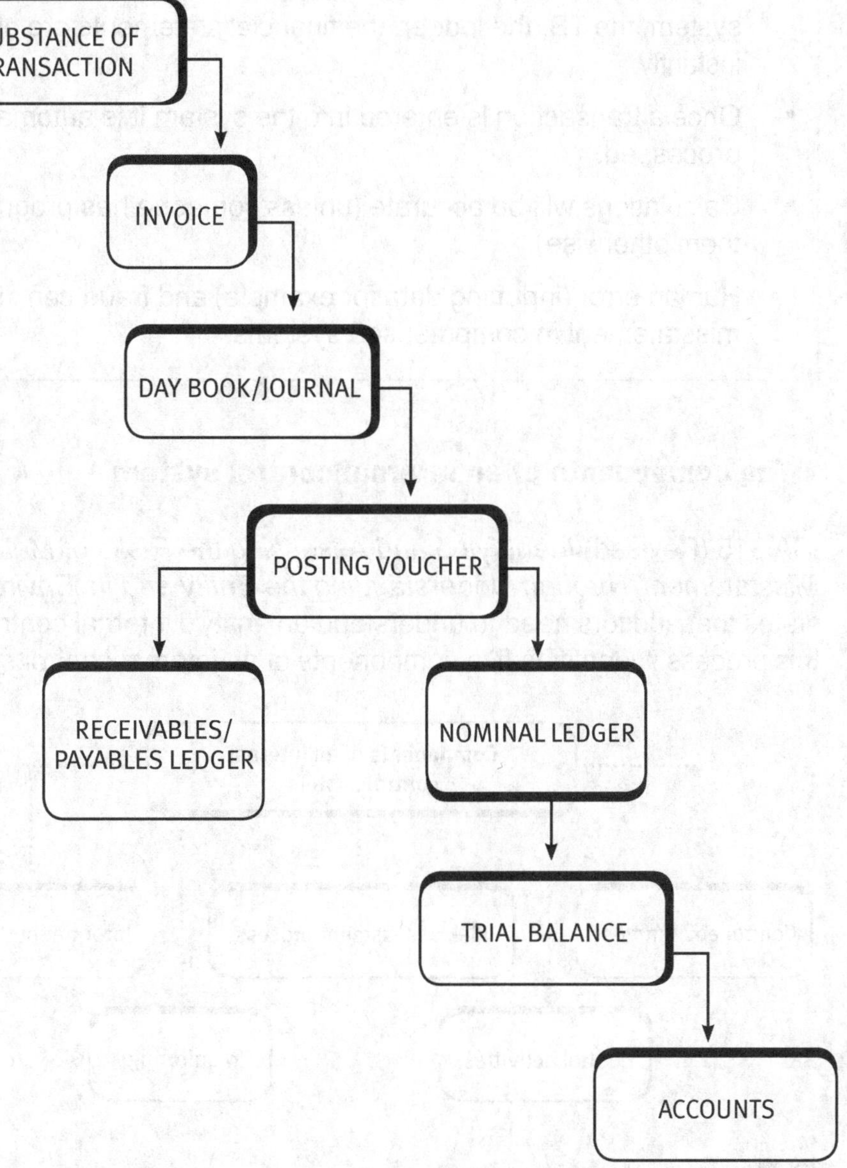

It should be noted that the above illustration represents a typical manual accounting system. These are rare nowadays due to the use of readily available and inexpensive accounting software. However, the basic principles of those systems are still the same and it is useful to understand how the flow of information in a system works.

Computerised systems

There are a number of things to understand about the impact of computerised accounting systems:

- The need to transfer information from one piece of paper to another is greatly reduced.

- The outputs from the system – the listings, trial balances, even the financial statements themselves – usually do not form part of a strict chronological sequence. So once an invoice is entered into the system, the TB, the ledger, the financial statements are all updated instantly.
- Once a transaction is entered into the system it is automatically processed.
- Calculations will be accurate (unless someone has programmed them otherwise).
- Human error (inputting data for example) and fraud can still lead to misstatement in computerised systems.

2 The components of an internal control system

ISA 315 (Revised) *Identifying and Assessing the Risks of Material Misstatement Through Understanding the Entity and its Environment,* states that auditors need to understand an entity's internal controls. To assist this process it identifies five components of an internal control system:

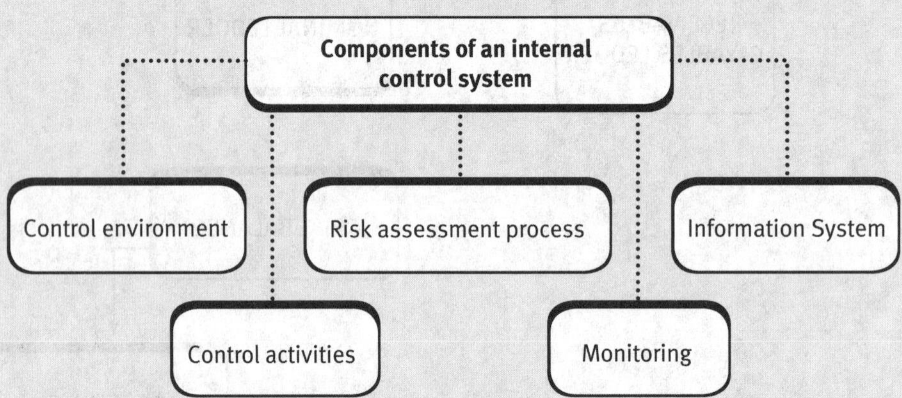

(i) The control environment

The control environment includes the **governance and management** function of an organisation.

It focuses largely on the **attitude, awareness and actions** of those responsible for designing, implementing and monitoring internal controls.

Elements of the control environment that are relevant when the auditor obtains an understanding include the following:

- Communication and enforcement of integrity and ethical values.
- Commitment to competence.
- Participation by those charged with governance.
- Management's philosophy and operating style.

- Organisational structure.
- Assignment of authority and responsibility.
- Human resource policies and practices.

Control environment

ISA 315 states that when assessing the control environment the auditor may also consider how management has responded to the findings and recommendations of the internal audit function regarding identified deficiencies in internal control relevant to the audit, including whether and how such responses have been implemented, and whether they have been subsequently evaluated by the internal audit function.

Evidence regarding the control environment is usually obtained through a mixture of enquiry and observation, although inspection of key internal documents (e.g. codes of conduct and organisation charts) is possible.

(ii) The risk assessment process

The risk assessment process forms the basis for how management determines the business risks to be managed, i.e. threats to the achievement of ongoing business objectives. These processes will vary hugely depending upon the nature, size and complexity of the organisation.

Threats to business objectives can lead to misstatement in the financial statements, e.g. non-compliance with laws and regulations may lead to fines and penalties, which require disclosure or provision in the financial statements.

If the client has robust procedures for assessing the business risks it faces, the risk of misstatement overall, will be lower.

(iii) The information system

The information system is all of the business processes relevant to financial reporting and communication. It includes the procedures within both information technology and manual systems.

The information system includes all of the procedures and records which are designed to:

- Initiate, record, process and report transactions.
- Maintain accountability for assets, liabilities and equity.
- Resolve incorrect processing of transactions.
- Process and account for system overrides.

- Transfer information to the general/nominal ledger.
- Capture information relevant to financial reporting for other events and conditions.
- Ensure information required to be disclosed is appropriately reported.

(iv) Control activities

The control activities include all policies and procedures designed to ensure that management directives are carried out throughout the organisation. Examples of specific control activities include those relating to:

- Authorisation.
- Performance review.
- Information processing.
- Physical controls.
- Segregation of duties.

Control activities

Examples of control activities include:

Authorisation – approval of transactions prior to being processed

- A manager signing off an employee's timesheet to confirm that the hours stated have been worked and can be paid. This should ensure the employee is not claiming for hours not worked.
- A manager signing a purchase order to confirm the order can be placed with the supplier. This should ensure that the goods are for a valid business use and the items are needed.

Performance review – to identify unusual differences between data

- Managers should compare actual spend against budgeted spend to detect unusual fluctuations. If actual spend is significantly higher than budget the department may have spent more than it should or it could indicate an error when processing the transactions.
- Management may compare the company's results with those of competitors as a benchmark.

Information processing – to ensure completeness and accuracy of processing

- Preparation of a bank reconciliation to ensure cash transactions have been recorded completely and accurately.
- Batch totals used when inputting data to ensure items are not omitted.

Physical controls – to prevent unauthorised access

- Restrictions on access to assets such as keeping cash in a safe to prevent theft.
- Password restrictions to prevent unauthorised access to computer files.

Segregation of duties – Assigning the responsibility for recording transactions, authorising transactions and maintaining custody of assets to different employees to prevent the risk of fraud and error.

- Warehouse staff should not be responsible for the inventory count as this would not detect if goods were being stolen by staff throughout the year.
- Employees who authorise transactions should not be the ones who originate the transaction.

IT controls

IT affects the way in which control activities are implemented. It is important that auditors assess how controls over IT maintain the integrity and security of information held. Such controls are normally divided into two categories:

- Application
- General

Application controls

Application controls are either manual or automated and typically operate at the business process level. Application controls relate to data integrity and ensure that only valid data is being processed and is being processed completely and accurately.

Examples include:

- Batch total checks (e.g. when entering invoices onto the system the system may give a batch total i.e. the number of invoices actually entered. The clerk entering the invoices can then double check that the correct number of invoices has been entered and none have been missed or entered twice).
- Sequence checks (to ensure the number sequence is complete and no items are missing).
- Matching master files to transaction records (e.g. sales invoice discounts to ensure the prices/discount levels being applied are correct).
- Arithmetic checks (to verify arithmetical accuracy).
- Range checks (to ensure that data stays within reasonable ranges).
- Existence checks (e.g. to check employees exist).
- Authorisation of transaction entries (to ensure the transaction is valid and should be processed).
- Exception reporting (the system may generate an exception report when something which isn't usual has occurred e.g. changes to bank details of employees which wouldn't be expected to change often).

General controls

General IT controls are policies and procedures that relate to many applications. They support the effective functioning of application controls by helping to ensure the continued proper operation of information systems. General controls tend to relate to access, control over program changes, infrastruture, environment and business continuity/disaster recovery.

E.g. controls over:

- Data centre and network operations e.g. not allowing non-company issued laptops to connect to the network.
- System software acquisition – tendering, testing, controls during installation, training.
- Program change and maintenance – testing, authorisation, restricted access.
- Access security – passwords, door locks, swipe cards.
- Business continuity/disaster recovery – backup procedures to enable data to be restored, back up power supply.

An effective IT system should include both application and general control procedures.

(v) Monitoring of controls

This is the client's process of **assessing the effectiveness of controls** over time and taking necessary remedial action. Clearly if a control is not implemented properly or is simply considered ineffective then misstatements may pass undetected into the financial statements.

Monitoring can be either ongoing or performed on a separate evaluation basis (or a combination of both). Either way, it needs to be effective for the system to work. Monitoring of internal controls is often the key role of internal auditors.

3 Ascertaining the systems

Procedures used to obtain evidence regarding the design and implementation of controls include:

- Enquiries of relevant personnel.
- Observing the application of controls.
- Tracing a transaction through the system to understand what happens (a walkthrough test).
- Inspecting documents, such as internal procedure manuals.

It should also be noted that enquiry alone is not sufficient to understand the nature and extent of controls.

Prior knowledge of client systems

In addition to this, auditors can also use their prior knowledge of the client and the operation of the systems in prior years. However, it must be noted, that auditors cannot simply rely on their systems knowledge from the prior year's audit; much can happen in a year and systems knowledge must be updated and the systems tested once more.

4 Documenting client systems

Possible ways of documenting systems include:

- **Narrative notes** – a written description of a system.
- **Flowchart** – diagrammatical representation of the system.

- **Organisation chart** – diagram showing reporting lines, roles and responsibilities.
- **Internal Control Questionnaire (ICQ)** – a list of controls given to the client to say whether or not those controls are in place.
- **Internal Control Evaluation Questionnaire (ICE)** – the client is asked what controls they have in place for a given control objective.

For example; an ICQ might ask a client: "does a supervisor authorise all weekly timesheets?" An ICE would ask "how does the company ensure that only hours worked are recorded on timesheets?"

The method adopted is a matter of auditor judgment.

Documentation Method	Advantages	Disadvantages
Narrative notes	• Simple to record • Facilitate understanding by all audit staff	• May be time consuming and cumbersome if the system is complex • May be more difficult to identify missing controls
Flow charts	• Easy to view the whole system in one diagram • Easy to spot missing controls due to the use of standard symbols	• May be difficult to amend as the whole diagram may need to be re-drawn • There is still a need for narrative notes to accompany the flow chart increasing the time involved to document the system fully
Internal control questionnaires (ICQs)	• Quick to prepare • Can ensure all controls are present	• Controls may be overstated as the client knows the answer the auditor is looking for is 'yes' • Unusual controls are unlikely to be included on a standard questionnaire and may not be identified • May contain a number of irrelevant controls

Internal control evaluations (ICEs)	• The client has to respond with the control they have in place rather than a yes/no answer which should mean controls are less likely to be overstated • Quick to prepare as a list of control objectives can be compiled and the client is asked what controls they have in place to address them	• Client may still overstate controls as they may say a control is in place for the control objective even if it is not • The checklist may contain control objectives not relevant to the client • Unusual risks and therefore objectives may not be identified

5 Testing the system

A test of control involves the auditor obtaining evidence that the client has implemented the controls they say they have and that they have worked effectively during the period.

Typical methods of controls testing include:

- Observation of control activities, e.g. observing the inventory count to ensure it is conducted effectively and in accordance with the instructions.
- Inspection of documents recording performance of the control, e.g. inspecting an order for evidence of authorisation.
- Computer assisted audit techniques (such as test data to ensure the programmed controls are working effectively. See the 'Evidence' chapter).

Designing valid tests of controls

To design a test of control the auditor must first identify the controls they want to test.

A control is an activity applied in addition to the normal processing of the system to ensure that the system has operated as it should.

Just because errors have not been made does not mean that controls have worked effectively. The person performing the processing may have not made any errors. There may have been no controls in place. A control would be an additional activity to ensure the person has not made any errors.

For example if the client claims to perform bank reconciliations the auditor should look at the file containing the reconciliations to verify that they are done and then reperform the reconciliation to ensure it has been done properly to test the effectiveness of the control. Simply performing the reconciliation and finding that it reconciles does not prove that the client has done the reconciliation themselves. Therefore, reperformance of the reconciliation on its own is not a valid test of control.

Similarly, performing a sequence check on a set of documents does not mean the client has performed a sequence check. It may just mean that no documents have gone missing. A sequence check is the control to ensure that no documents have gone missing.

6 Sales system

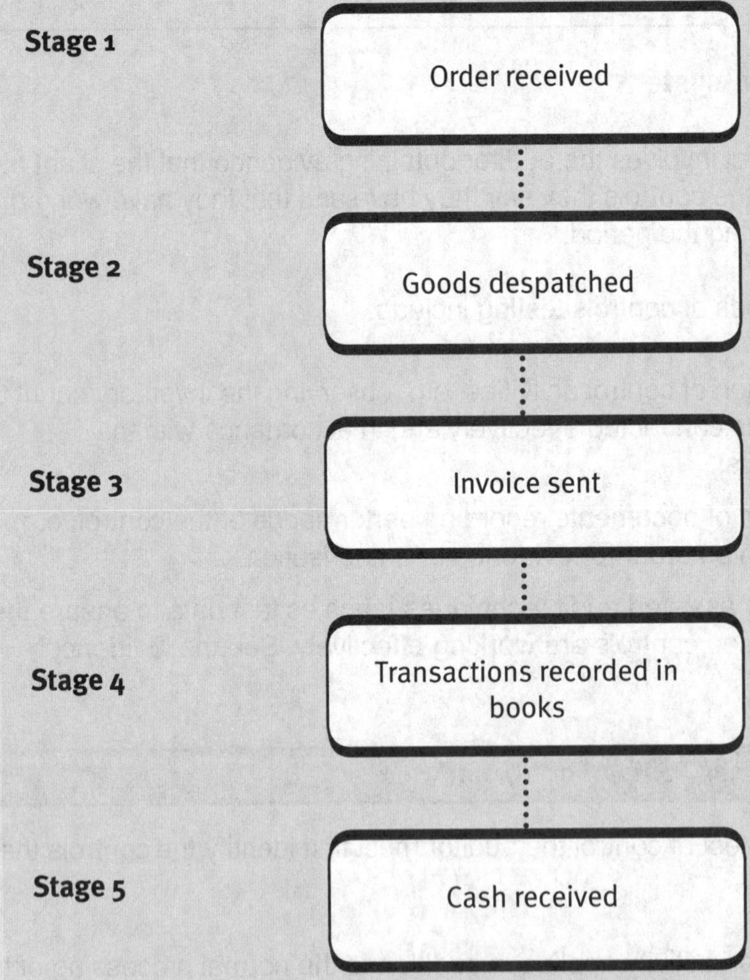

Objectives

A control objective looks at the risks within the system. Control activities will then be designed to address the objective (risk).

The objectives of controls in the sales system are to ensure that:

Stage	Objective
Ordering	• Goods are only supplied to customers who pay promptly and in full. • All orders are processed.
Despatch	• Orders are despatched promptly and in full to the correct customer. • All orders are despatched.
Invoicing	• All goods despatched are invoiced. • Invoices are raised accurately.
Recording	• Only valid sales are recorded. • All sales and related receivables are recorded and in the correct accounts. • Revenue is recorded in the period to which it relates. • Sales are recorded accurately and related receivables are recorded at an appropriate value.
Cash received	• Cash received is allocated against the correct customer and invoices to minimise disputes. • Overdue debts are followed up on a timely basis. • Irrecoverable debts identified and written off appropriately.

Test your understanding 1

Murray case study: Sales cycle

Ordering

For all new customers, a sales manager completes a credit application which is checked with a credit agency and a credit limit is entered onto the sales system by the credit controller. The sales system prompts sales managers to complete an annual credit check for existing customers, and the credit controller amends or approves existing credit limits for these customers. Approved customers are assigned with a unique customer account number.

Orders are placed with the sales team. The orders are entered onto the sales system by a sales assistant. The system automatically checks that the goods are available and that the order will not take the customer over their credit limit. The system generates two order confirmations, one of which is sent to the customer by mail/email confirming the goods ordered and likely despatch date, the other is retained on file.

Goods despatch

The warehouse receives the order electronically and goods despatch notes (GDNs) are generated automatically. A member of the warehouse team packs the goods from the GDN and a second member of the team double checks the goods packed to the GDN, signing the GDN to evidence the check.

Two copies of the GDN are sent with the goods ordered; one copy is retained by the customer and the other is signed by the customer and returned to Murray Co to confirm receipt of the goods and retained by the warehouse.

A copy of the GDN is sent to the sales team who update the system, confirming despatch of the goods. A weekly report is sent automatically to the sales manager, who follows-up any incomplete orders with the warehouse manager.

Invoicing

Once despatched, a copy of the GDN is sent to the accounts team at head office and a sequentially numbered sales invoice is raised from the GDN. Periodically a computer sequence check is performed for any missing sales invoice numbers.

When the invoice is sent to the customer, the system GDN is marked as 'invoiced'. A system report is reviewed by the senior accountant on a fortnightly basis for any GDNs that have not been invoiced. The report is printed and signed as evidence of review.

The system generates customer invoices using the company price list, which is updated quarterly. Discounts must be requested by a sales manager and authorised by the sales director to allow the accounts team to raise an invoice.

Recording transaction

The receivables ledger is reviewed for credit balances by the senior accountant on a monthly basis and the receivables ledger is reconciled with the receivables ledger control account on a monthly basis by the sales ledger manager and reviewed by the company accountant.

Monthly customer statements are sent to customers.

Cash receipt

Receipts are counted by the office assistant, recorded by the cashier in the cash book, and the sales ledger clerk is notified of the receipt. The sales ledger clerk agrees the amount received to the amount invoiced and marks the invoice as paid.

The credit controller reviews the aged receivables analysis on a fortnightly basis and investigates any old balances. Overdue debts are chased with a telephone call initially, followed by a copy invoice, and then a warning letter before the debt is passed to a debt collection agency.

Exercise:

Identify the controls in Murray Co's sales system and suggest how the auditor would test those controls.

Illustration 1: Murray Co goods despatch note

The key document in the sales cycle is the goods despatch note:

Murray Co — **Goods Despatch Note**

"*Supplying Equipment to the Sporting Nation*" — **Ref: AB123456MC**

www.murraysports.com — **Murray Company**

1 Murray Mound,
Wimbledon, London
WN1 2LN

Destination

Customer Ref: W004 — **Order Number:** ZY987654WS

Customer Name: Winners Co

Customer Address: 2 Edinburgh St, Dunblaine, Scotland DL2 2ES

Line	Product Number	Description	Quantity	Quality and quantity of goods checked and agreed
001	4378493729	Tennis racket	24	Yes
002	3257845743	Tennis balls (packs of 6)	6	Yes
003	4357849574	Tennis court net	3	Yes
004	3473895789	Tennis scoreboard	3	Yes
005	4574895743	Winner's trophy	1	Yes
006	3457435437	Runner-up trophy	1	Yes
007	4830998543	Participant's medal	24	Yes

Signed:

A Warehouse Packer

7 Purchase system

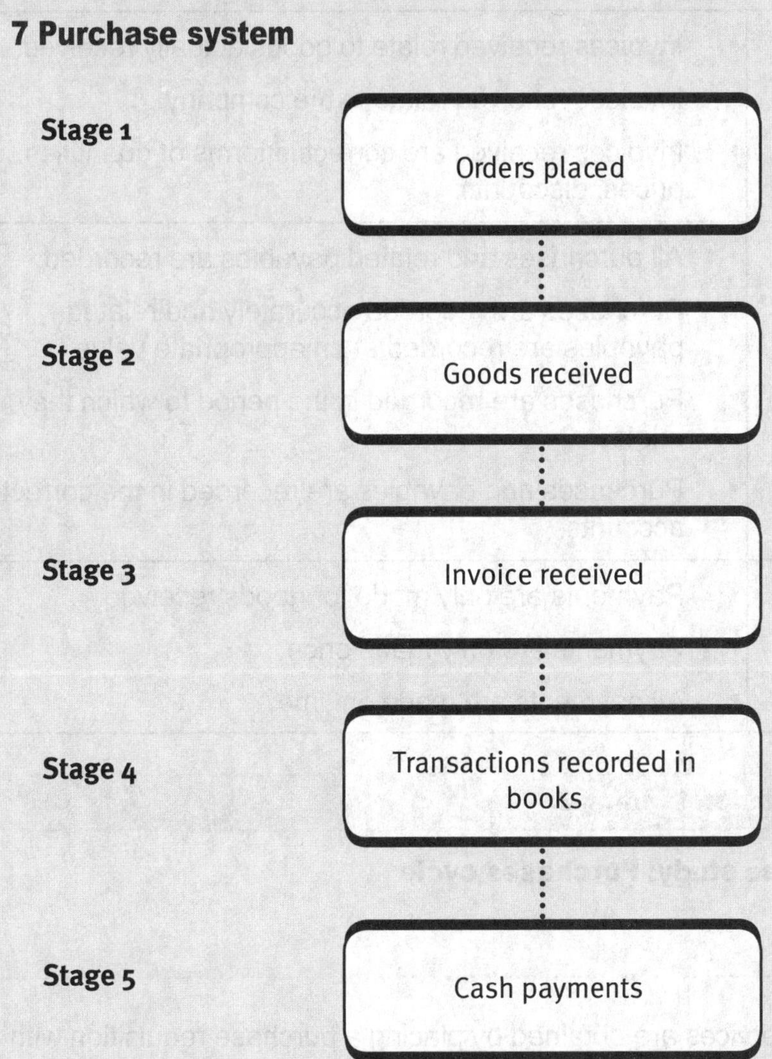

Objectives

A control objective looks at the risks within the system. Control activities will then be designed to address the objective (risk).

The objectives of controls in the purchases system are to ensure that:

Stage	Objective
Ordering	• All purchases are made with suppliers who have been checked for quality, reliability and pricing. • Purchases are only made for a valid business use. • Orders are placed taking consideration of delivery lead times to avoid disruption to the business.
Goods received	• Only goods ordered by the company are accepted. • Goods received are recorded promptly.

Invoice received	• Invoices received relate to goods actually received. • Invoices received relate to the company. • Invoices received are correct in terms of quantities, prices, discounts.
Recording	• All purchases and related payables are recorded. • Purchases are recorded accurately and related payables are recorded at an appropriate value. • Purchases are recorded in the period to which they relate. • Purchases and payables are recorded in the correct accounts.
Cash payments	• Payments are only made for goods received. • Payments are only made once. • All payments are made on time.

Test your understanding 2

Murray case study: Purchases cycle

Ordering

Goods or services are obtained by placing a purchase requisition with the centralised purchasing department. Requisitions are sequentially prenumbered, and the purchasing department perform a weekly sequence check. All requisitions must be authorised by an appropriate manager.

On receipt of a purchase requisition, a purchase officer agrees the manager's signature to the signatory list held on file and checks inventory levels where appropriate. Orders are placed with suppliers using sequentially prenumbered purchase orders.

Orders can only be placed with suppliers from the approved suppliers list. Suppliers can only be added to the approved suppliers list by the procurement team once the terms of the contract have been agreed, and references obtained. Written confirmation is requested for all orders placed, and the purchase officer agrees the quoted price against the agreed price list and ensures any bulk discounts to which Murray Co is entitled, have been honoured.

Goods receipt

Goods are received into the central warehouse. Goods are inspected for condition and quantity by a warehouse operative, and agreed to the purchase order before the supplier's delivery note is signed to accept the goods.

A sequentially pre-numbered goods received note (GRN) is prepared by the warehouse team manager, and grid-stamped. The grid stamp is signed by the warehouse operative to confirm that the goods have been inspected for condition and quantity and agreed to the purchase order.

The warehouse manager updates the inventory system on a daily basis from the prepared GRNs. The warehouse manager checks the sequence of purchase orders received on a weekly basis and informs the purchasing department of any missing orders so that they can be followed-up.

Invoicing

On receipt of an invoice by the head office accounts team, the invoice is matched to and filed with the relevant GRN, using the purchase order number marked on the invoice (if there is no purchase order number marked on the invoice, this must be obtained from the supplier). The invoice number is noted on the GRN grid-stamp. The invoice is also checked to the original purchase order to ensure the agreed prices and discounts have been honoured.

A monthly check of GRNs is made by the purchases ledger manager, to identify any GRNs for which no invoice has been received.

Recording transaction

The purchases ledger clerk enters invoices onto the system in batches. A batch control sheet is used, which details the number of invoices and the total value. These details are checked to the system batch report.

Each invoice is stamped as "recorded" once the details have been entered onto the system. The purchase ledger manager inspects the file of invoices on a monthly basis to ensure that all invoices have been recorded.

Suppliers are required to submit monthly supplier statements, which are reconciled to the suppliers ledger account by the purchases ledger manager. The purchase ledger is reconciled to the purchase ledger control account on a monthly basis by the purchase ledger manager, and reviewed by the company accountant.

Cash payment

The list of payments is sent to the company accountant, who agrees the details of each payment to the relevant invoice and signs each invoice to authorise payment and evidence the check. The list of payments is signed by the accountant once all invoices have been checked, and sent to the cashier's office for payment.

If any individual payment is for more than $25,000 or total payments are for more than $250,000 a second signatory is required. These payments must also be checked and signed by either the financial controller, or finance director.

Payments are made by the cashier's office by bank transfer. Invoices are stamped as "paid", and returned to the purchases ledger team who record the payment and file the invoices (separately from invoices not yet paid).

The purchase ledger manager checks GRNs on a monthly basis to ensure that invoices have been received and paid on a timely basis.

Exercise:

Identify the controls in Murray Co's purchases system and suggest how the auditor would test those controls.

Illustration 2: Murray Co goods received note

The key document in the purchases cycle is the goods received note:

Murray Co **Goods Received Note: A2012/123478**

Purchase Order number: MC/34324832809/RC

Date of receipt: 31st August 20X4

Time of receipt: 12:48pm

Description	**Quantity ordered**	**Quantity received**	**Quality of goods checked**
Vectran	75kg	75kg	Yes

Sign to confirm quantity and quality of goods checked: Warehouse Operative

Invoice number:

Problems with fraud

Fraud is specifically designed to mislead people. Consider the following example:

- A company only deals with suppliers on a list authorised by the Finance Director (FD).
- Payments to suppliers are made after the purchases clerk identifies the monthly payments to be made and prepares the cheques.
- The cheques are signed by the FD, who confirms the amounts paid and supplier names to supporting documentation.
- The cheques are countersigned by the Managing Director, who does not check the details but has a good knowledge of who the suppliers are.

This appears like a sensible combination of authorisation controls and segregation of duties.

However, now consider the implication if one of the suppliers is actually controlled by the FD. The supplier regularly overcharges and the purchases clerk is being bribed by the FD in return for their silence.

Of course, this is a potentially criminal scheme, but that is what a fraud is. The auditor, unfortunately, would place reliance on the control system and reduce substantive testing of purchases. It is for this reason that the auditor must always perform some substantive procedures and must always maintain an attitude of professional scepticism.

Non-current assets

Expenditure on non-current assets should be controlled in a similar way to other purchases. However, because of the significant amounts involved, additional controls will be in place.

Control objectives:

- Assets are only purchased if there is a business need.
- Assets are purchased at an appropriate price.
- The company can afford the capital expenditure proposed.
- Capital expenditure is appropriately treated in the accounting records.
- Capital expenditure is completely and accurately recorded in the accounting records.
- Assets are covered by adequate insurance to prevent loss to the company.
- Documents relating to assets are safeguarded from theft or damage.

Control	**Test of control**
Capex order should be requisitioned by an appropriate person.	Inspect the requisition for the signature of the person requisitioning the assets. Ensure this is a person of suitable authority by agreeing the name to a list of people authorised to make such requisitions.
Authorisation for purchase at a more senior level.	Inspect the purchase order for signature of appropriate senior person(s).

Several quotations obtained before purchase in order to obtain the best price.	Inspect the purchase requisition for the quotations to ensure they have been obtained.
Annual capital expenditure budget for each department.	Inspect the annual budget to ensure it is prepared and read board minutes for evidence that the budget has been approved by the board.
Regular review of revenue expenditure to ensure items of a capital nature have not been written off in error.	Inspect management accounts/revenue expenditure lists for evidence of review. Enquire of management how discrepancies are dealt with.
Annual reconciliation of the asset register to the physical assets held.	Inspect the reconciliation of the asset register and evidence of approval by a senior person to ensure the reconciliation has been performed correctly.
Maintaining an asset register, which would include cost, depreciation, location, responsible employee, insurance details, etc.	Inspect the asset register to ensure details expected to be recorded have been recorded to ensure good control is maintained over assets.
Adequate insurance cover.	Inspect insurance policies to ensure they are in place. Review the policies to ascertain the level of cover in place and compare this with the value of assets to ensure it is sufficient.
Secure, fire-proof storage of insurance documentation, ownership/purchase documentation, e.g. title deeds, vehicle registration documents, etc.	Inspect the storage facilities for important documentation to ensure it is appropriately secure and adequate back ups have been maintained in case of a fire or flood.

8 Payroll system

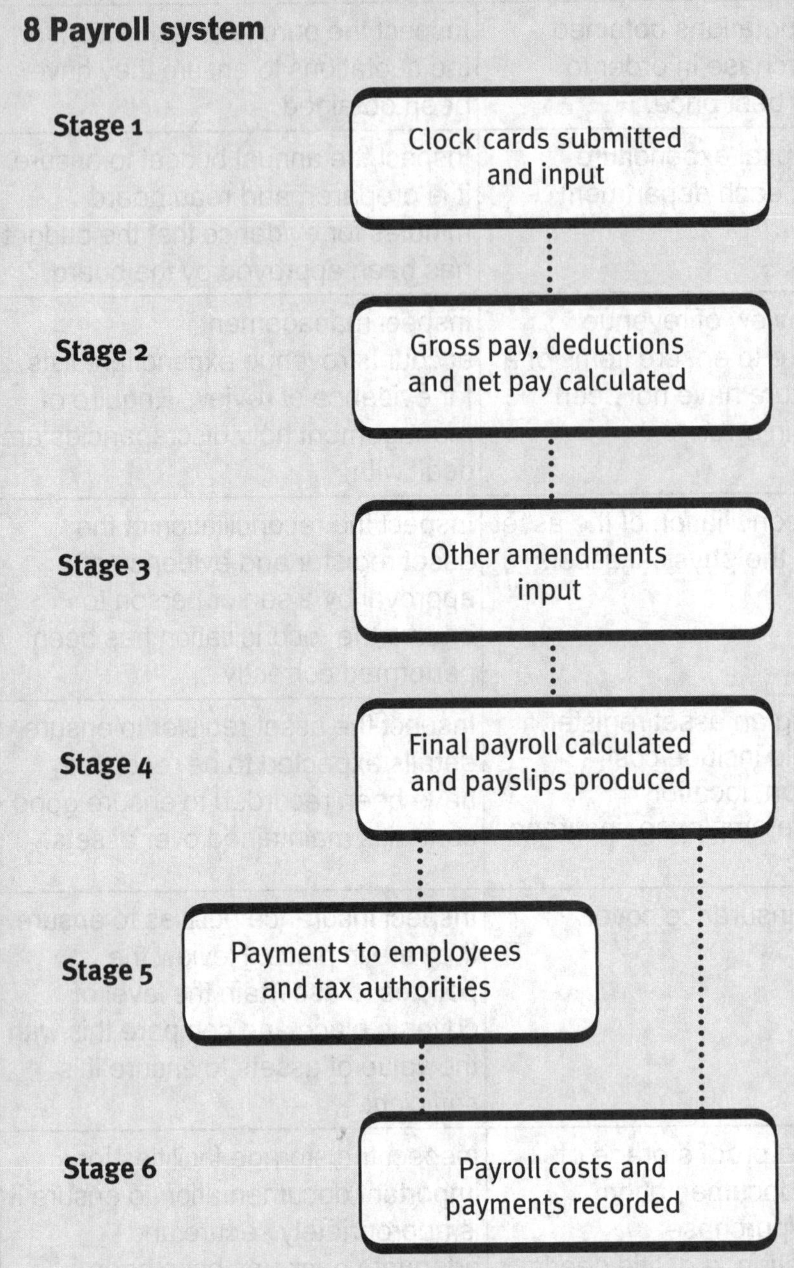

Objectives

A control objective looks at the risks within the system. Control activities will then be designed to address the objective (risk).

The objectives of controls in the payroll system are to ensure that:

Stage	Objective
Clock cards (or timesheets) submitted	• Employees are only paid for work actually done.
Payroll calculation	• Only genuine employees are paid. • Employees are paid at the correct rates of pay. • Gross pay is calculated and recorded accurately. • Net pay is calculated and recorded accurately.
Standing data amendments	• Standing data is kept up to date. • Access to standing data is restricted to prevent fraud or error occurring.
Recording	• All payroll amounts are recorded. • Payroll amounts are recorded accurately. • Payroll costs are recorded in the period to which they relate.
Payments to employees and tax authorities	• Correct amounts are paid to the employees and taxation authorities. • Payments are made on time. • Payments are only made to valid employees.

Test your understanding 3

Murray case study: Payroll cycle

Clock cards submitted and input

Murray Co employs a total of 300 people, 200 of these being workers who are paid weekly in cash. All workers are required to record their times of arrival and departure using a clock card which is inserted in a time recording clock. Use of the time recording clock is supervised by the relevant factory manager.

At weekly intervals the cards are collected and passed to the works office where the clerks total up the hours worked on each card and list the total hours worked (a 'hash' total). The cards and the add list are then passed to the wages clerk who enters the hours worked on the pre-printed payroll sheet (which already has the names printed on it), and agrees the add list total.

Gross pay, deductions and net pay calculated

The payroll sheets are then passed to the payroll manager who keeps the payroll records. He enters the rate of pay and calculates the gross pay. He also computes the tax deductions and employer's taxation, which he enters on the payroll along with the salaries and deductions for monthly paid workers. He passes the payrolls back to the wages clerk who calculates the net amount and totals all the columns on the payroll, and raises a payment list for monthly paid employees and payments to the tax authority.

Other amendments input

Leaver and joiner forms must be completed and authorised by the employee's immediate manager and the finance director at least one month before the amendment is required to the payroll. Other amendments to standing data, e.g. pay rises, are completed on a specific form for this purpose, and authorised in the same way.

A monthly report of amendments to standing data is sent to the finance director for review and authorisation.

Standing data files are sent to departmental managers on a quarterly basis for review.

Final payroll calculated and payslips produced

The completed payroll is then passed to the company accountant, who scans the payroll, compares the totals with the previous week, and initials the payroll. The company accountant raises a cheque requisition for the weekly paid workers, and signs the payment list for the monthly paid employees, which are then sent to the cashier's department. The payment list also shows payments to be made to the taxation authorities which the company accountant checks to last month's payroll records.

The payroll is returned to the payroll clerk who produces the payslips, and passes these to the cashier's department for processing.

Payments to employees and tax authorities

The cashier draws a cheque for the net amount of the payroll which is then signed by two directors. The cheque is given to a secure cash transit company who draw the money from the bank and deliver it under guard to the wages clerk. The cashier then puts the money into pay envelopes along with a pay slip for weekly paid workers.

The sealed envelopes and relevant clock cards are then used for payouts. Each worker obtains his money once he has identified himself and signed his clock card. Unclaimed wages are held for three weeks before being re-banked.

Monthly paid workers and the tax authorities are paid by bank transfer on the last day of each month, as per the payment list authorised by the company accountant.

Payroll costs and payments recorded

A copy of the payroll list is sent to the head office accounts team who record the payroll expense and payments made. Any unclaimed wages are notified by the wages office to the head office team on an anomalies list completed once all of the clock cards have been returned. The head office accounts team check the bank statements to ensure that this money has been re-banked.

Exercise:

Identify the controls in Murray Co's payroll system and suggest how the auditor would test those controls.

9 The Inventory System

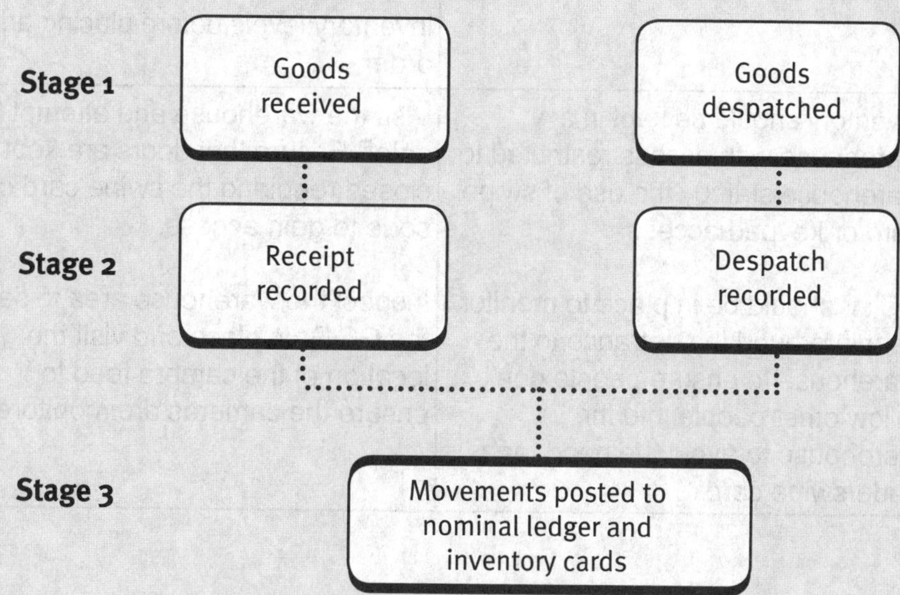

Objectives

The objectives of controls in the inventory system are to ensure that:

- Inventory levels meet the needs of production (raw materials and components) and customer demand (finished goods).
- Inventory levels are not excessive, preventing obsolescence and unnecessary storage costs.
- Inventory is safeguarded from theft, loss or damage.
- Inventory received and despatched is recorded on a timely basis.
- All inventory is recorded.
- Inventory should be recorded at the appropriate value (lower of cost and NRV).
- Only inventory owned by the company is recorded.

The inventory cycle

The majority of controls and tests of control for the inventory system appear within the revenue system (for goods despatched) and purchases system (for goods received). In addition to the controls mentioned in those sections, the following additional controls should be in place:

Control	Test of control
Inventory should be maintained at an appropriate level through the use of automatic ordering systems when inventory reaches a certain level or by checking inventory levels before orders are placed.	Use test data to place an order to reduce inventory of an item to below the re-order level and trace through the system to see if an order is automatically generated. Observe the ordering clerk checking inventory levels before placing an order.
Inventory should be kept in a warehouse with access restricted to warehouse staff by the use of swipe card or keypad access. CCTV should be in place to monitor people around the entrance to the warehouse to ensure people don't follow other people into the warehouse to avoid the need for a code/swipe card.	Visit the warehouse and attempt to enter. Ensure that doors are kept closed requiring the swipe card or code to gain access. Inspect the warehouse area to see the CCTV in place and visit the location of the camera feed to ensure the cameras are monitored.

Inventory should be kept in appropriate conditions e.g. temperature controlled environment for perishable items.	Visit the warehouse and inspect the conditions of storage. Inspect evidence of monitoring the conditions on a regular basis such as temperature logs.
Fire/smoke/heat detectors and sprinkler systems are in place to reduce the risk of damage caused by fire.	Inspect the warehouse to see the detectors and sprinkler systems are in place. Inspect certificates confirming they have been checked and tested on a regular basis.
Inventory is insured in case of theft or damage.	Inspect insurance policies to ensure they cover inventory, that adequate cover is in place by comparing against inventory value and that the policy has not lapsed.
Inventory movements should be recorded in the system promptly from the GRNs and GDNs and stamped to confirm they have been input to ensure the inventory system is up to date.	Inspect the GRNs and GDNs to see they have been stamped as entered into the system. Compare the date on the stamp to the date on the GRN/GDN to ensure it has been entered promptly.
Inventory counts should take place so that physical inventory quantities can be reconciled with the accounting system on a regular basis to ensure the records are up to date.	Obtain inventory counting instructions and review to ensure the count will be appropriately organised and controlled. Attend the inventory count to ensure the count is carried out in accordance with the instructions and perform test counts to ensure counts are carried out accurately.
Inventory should be reviewed during the count for damage or obsolescence and valued separately from the other inventory by making an allowance to write inventory down to NRV.	During the count, review the inventory to ensure damaged or obsolete items are separately identified.

See Chapter 8 Procedures for the detailed controls over inventory counts.

10 The cash cycle

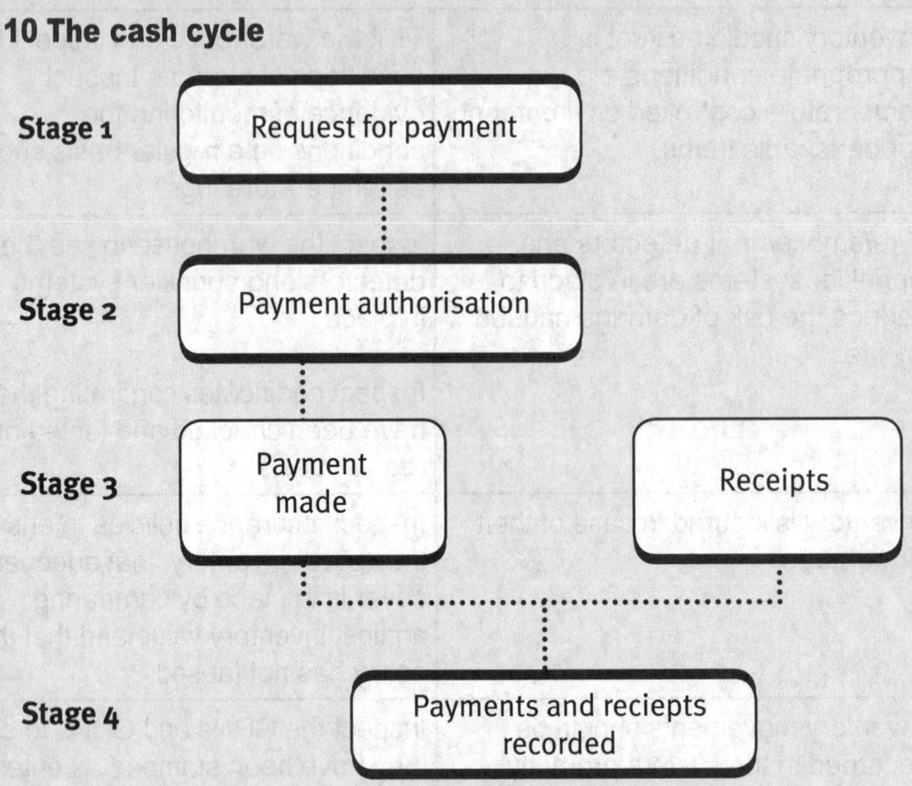

Objectives

The objectives of controls in the cash cycle are to ensure that:

- Petty cash levels are kept to a minimum, preventing theft.
- Payments can only be made for legitimate business expenditure.
- Cash can only be withdrawn for business purposes.
- Cash is safeguarded to prevent theft.
- Receipts are banked on a timely basis to prevent theft.
- Cash movements are recorded on a timely basis.

The cash cycle

The majority of controls within and tests of control for the cash cycle appear within the revenue system (for cash received) and purchases and payroll systems (for cash payments).

In addition, there should be adequate controls over access to cash and bank records, including:

Control	Test of control
An imprest system of petty cash is used and can only be used for items of expenditure less than $x. All other reimbursements must be made through an expense claim and processed as a bank payment.	In the presence of the client, count the petty cash to ascertain that the level is at the limit set. Inspect the petty cash vouchers to ensure amounts reimbursed are below the limit stated.
Petty cash reimbursements must be supported by an invoice to confirm the expenditure is business related before being authorised and paid.	Inspect the petty cash reimbursements for the supporting invoice and the signature of the person authorising the reimbursement.
Cash withdrawals must be authorised by a manager.	Inspect the withdrawal request for evidence of the manager's signature authorising the money can be taken out of the bank.
Cash and cheque books/stationery stored in a locked safe, with restricted access.	In the presence of the client, inspect where the cash and cheque books are stored to ensure they are secure e.g. within a safe. Enquire of management who has access to the safe to ensure this is restricted to people with suitable seniority.
Controls over bank transfers and online banking, e.g. secure passwords and PINs.	Enquire of management who has access to the online banking system. Inspect transactions in the banking system for the username of the person initiating and authorising transactions to ensure this is corroborates what has been said. Assess whether the person authorising the transactions is of suitable seniority.
Frequent banking of cash and cheques received.	Inspect the paying in books or bank statements to identify how frequently deposits are paid in to ensure this is adequate.

Regular bank reconciliations prepared and then reviewed by personnel of appropriate seniority.	Inspect the file of bank reconciliations to ensure they are performed regularly. Inspect the reconciliation for a manager's signature as evidence it has been reviewed and approved. Re-perform the reconciliation to ensure it has been carried out effectively.

11 Reporting to those charged with governance

ISA 265 *Communicating Deficiencies in Internal Control to Those Charged with Governance and Management* requires the auditor to communicate deficiencies in internal control to management. Significant deficiencies should be communicated in writing to those charged with governance.

The form, timing and addressees of this communication should be agreed at the start of the audit, as part of the terms of the engagement. This report, traditionally known as a management letter or report to management, is usually sent at the end of the audit process.

You may be required to identify and explain deficiencies from your analysis of the control system described in a scenario. You may also be asked to explain the consequence of the each deficiency and make a recommendation to overcome it:

Deficiency Clear description of what is wrong.

Consequence What could happen if the deficiency is not corrected. Focus on what matters to the client – the risk of lost profits, stolen assets, extra costs, errors in the accounts.

Recommendation This must deal with the specific deficiency you have observed. It must also provide greater benefits than the cost of implementation.

Try to specify exactly how the recommended control would operate including suggesting who should carry out the control procedures, and how frequently it should be performed.

When the auditor reports deficiencies, it should be made clear that:

- The report is not a comprehensive list of deficiencies, but only those that have come to light during normal audit procedures.
- The report is for the sole use of the company.
- No disclosure should be made to a third party without the written agreement of the auditor.
- No responsibility is assumed to any other parties.

If you are asked for a covering letter in the exam, you should include the above matters within it.

Management letter extract

Deficiency	Consequence	Recommendation
Purchase invoices were missing from the sequentially numbered invoice file.	There is a possibility that purchases and liabilities are not completely recorded. This could result in late payment of invoices which could cause damage to the company's relationship with the supplier resulting in removal of credit terms or discounts.	All invoices should be sequentially filed on receipt by the accounts department. Regular sequence checks should be made to ensure a complete record, with any missing items investigated (and copies requested if necessary).

Significant deficiencies

ISA 265 *Communicating Deficiencies in Internal Control to those Charged with Governance and Management* states that a significant deficiency in internal control is a deficiency or combination of deficiencies in internal control that, in the auditor's professional judgment, is of sufficient importance to merit the attention of those charged with governance.

Examples of matters the external auditor should consider in determining whether a deficiency in internal controls is significant include:

- The likelihood of the deficiencies leading to material misstatements in the financial statements in the future.
- The susceptibility to loss or fraud of the related asset or liability.

- The subjectivity and complexity of determining estimated amounts.
- The financial statement amounts exposed to the deficiencies.
- The volume of activity that has occurred or could occur in the account balance or class of transactions exposed to the deficiency or deficiencies.
- The importance of the controls to the financial reporting process.
- The cause and frequency of the exceptions detected as a result of the deficiencies in the controls.
- The interaction of the deficiency with other deficiencies in internal control.

Test your understanding 4

After performing tests of controls, the auditor is of the opinion that audit evidence is not sufficient to support the audit opinion; in other words many control errors were found.

Required:

Explain THREE actions that the auditor may now take in response to this problem.

(3 marks)

Test your understanding 5

Rhapsody Co supplies a wide range of garden and agricultural products to trade and domestic customers. The company has 11 divisions, with each division specialising in the sale of specific products, for example, seeds, garden furniture, agricultural fertilizers. The company has an internal audit department which provides audit reports to the audit committee on each division on a rotational basis.

Products in the seed division are offered for sale to domestic customers via an Internet site. Customers review the product list on the Internet and place orders for packets of seeds using specific product codes, along with their credit card details, onto Rhapsody Co's secure server. Order quantities are normally between one and three packets for each type of seed. Order details are transferred manually onto the company's internal inventory control and sales system and a two part packing list is printed in the seed warehouse. Each order and packing list is given a random alphabetical code based on the name of the employee inputting the order, the date and the products being ordered.

In the seed warehouse, the packets of seeds for each order are taken from specific bins and despatched to the customer with one copy of the packing list. The second copy of the packing list is sent to the accounts department where the inventory and sales computer is updated to show that the order has been despatched. The customer's credit card is then charged by the inventory control and sales computer. Bad debts in Rhapsody are currently 3% of the total sales.

Finally, the computer system checks that for each charge made to a customer's credit card account, the order details are on file to prove that the charge was made correctly. The order file is marked as completed confirming that the order has been despatched and payment obtained.

Required:

In respect of sales in the seeds division of Rhapsody Co:

(i) **explain FOUR deficiencies in the sales system**

(ii) **explain the possible effect of each deficiency; and**

(iii) **provide a recommendation to alleviate each deficiency.**

(12 marks)

Test your understanding 6

You are carrying out the audit of the purchases system of Spondon Furniture. The company has revenue of $10 million and all the shares are owned by Mr and Mrs Fisher, who are non-executive directors and are not involved in the day-to-day running of the company.

The bookkeeper maintains all the accounting records and prepares the annual financial statements.

The company uses a standard computerised accounting package.

You have determined that the purchases system operates as follows:

- When materials are required for production, the production manager sends a handwritten note to the buying manager. For orders of other items, the department manager or managing director sends handwritten notes to the buying manager. The buying manager finds a suitable supplier and raises a purchase order. The purchase order is signed by the managing director. Purchase orders are not issued for all goods and services received by the company.

- Materials for production are received by the goods received department, who issue a goods received note (GRN), and send a copy to the bookkeeper. There is no system for recording receipt of other goods and services.
- The bookkeeper receives the purchase invoice and matches it with the goods received note and purchase order (if available). The managing director authorises the invoice for posting to the purchase ledger.
- The bookkeeper analyses the invoice into relevant nominal ledger account codes and then posts it.
- At the end of each month, the bookkeeper prepares a list of payables to be paid. This is approved by the managing director.
- The bookkeeper prepares the cheques and remittances and posts the cheques to the purchase ledger and cashbook.
- The managing director signs the cheques and the bookkeeper sends the cheques and remittances to the payables.

Mr and Mrs Fisher are aware that there may be weaknesses in the above system and have asked for advice.

Explain the deficiencies in controls in Spondon's purchases system and suggest improvements to overcome the deficiencies.

(12 marks)

Test your understanding 7

(a) **Define 'tests of control' and explain why they are an important procedure in the statutory audit of any company.**

(2 marks)

You are an audit senior working at a medium sized firm of auditors. One of your clients is an exclusive hotel called 'Numero Uno' situated in the centre of Big City. As part of your audit procedures you are assessing the controls surrounding payroll. You have read last year's audit file and have obtained the following information:

The hotel employs both full and part time staff. Due to the nature of the business most of the work is done in shifts. All staff are paid on a monthly basis.

New members of staff are given an electronic photo identification card on the day they join by the personnel department. This card is used to 'clock in' and 'clock out' at the start and end of the shift to record the hours worked.

At the end of each week the information recorded on the system is sent automatically to the payroll department and also to the head of each of the three main operating divisions: Rooms, Food & Beverage and Corporate Events. Each division head must reply back to the payroll department by email to authorise the hours worked by their staff.

The payroll clerk collates all the authorised information and then inputs the hours worked into a standardised computerised payroll package. This system is password protected using an alphanumerical password that only the payroll clerk and the finance manager know.

Once the hours have been inputted, the calculations of gross pay and taxation are calculated automatically along with any other statutory deductions. At the end of the calculations a payroll report is produced and printed. The finance manager reviews the report and compares the data to last month to identify and follow up any unusual variances. When he is satisfied with the information he authorises the payroll run by signing the payroll report and the payroll clerk submits the data.

Payslips are sent to the home address of each employee and payment is made by bank transfer.

Required:

(b) **With reference to the scenario:**

(i) **Identify and explain FOUR STRENGTHS within the hotel's internal control system in respect of payroll.**

(4 marks)

(ii) **For each of the identified strengths, state a test of control the auditor could perform to assess if the controls are operating effectively.**

(4 marks)

Test your understanding 8 – OT Case 1

You are testing the controls over the payroll system of Bunbury Co. You have confirmed that the following controls have operated throughout the year:

- Sample check of payroll calculations by a payroll manager.
- Review of the payroll listing once prepared before details are entered into the banking system.
- Segregation of duties between calculation of monthly payroll and responsibility for changes to standing data.
- Each department manager receives a list of employees in their department for them to sign to confirm those employees should be paid.

(1) Which of the following is the main reason for the control of segregation of duties between calculation of payroll and responsibility for changes to standing data?

A Changes to standing data must be performed by a manager whereas payroll calculations can be performed by a payroll clerk

B If one person was responsible for both they would be more likely to make errors due to a high workload

C If one person was responsible for both they could increase their salary and make fraudulent payments to themselves

D Each individual role within an organisation must be carried out by different people

(2) Which of the following procedures would provide the most reliable evidence that the first control, payroll calculations are checked by a payroll manager, is working effectively?

A Enquiry with the payroll clerk performing the payroll calculation

B Enquiry with the payroll manager performing the check

C Recalculation of the payroll amounts by the auditor

D Inspection of the payroll report for evidence that a sample of payroll amounts are checked

(3) Which of the following is not a test of control?

A Inspection of employee contracts to confirm the salary the employee should be paid

B Inspection of payroll reports for evidence of authorisation by the manager

C Inspection of the list of employees for each department for evidence of the department manager's review

D Observation of the payroll function to confirm segregation of duties is in place

(4) Which of the following is a control objective relevant to the control that each department manager reviews the list of employees to be paid?

A To ensure payroll is accurately calculated

B To ensure only valid employees are paid

C To ensure employees are paid for the correct hours

D To ensure employees are paid at the correct salary

(5) Which of the following could be used by Bunbury Co to monitor the effectiveness of the company's controls?

A Internal audit assignments

B Performing bank reconciliations

C Authorisation of payments

D Segregation of duties

Test your understanding 9 – OT Case 2

You are performing the risk assessment for the audit of Kununurra Co, a client your firm has audited for the past two years. From your review of the previous year audit file you have found that no significant control deficiencies were identified. The systems are documented on the permanent audit file in the form of flow charts and narrative notes.

(1) Which of the following best describes the requirement of the auditor in respect of the controls documentation?

A The auditor must document the systems this year as they may have changed since last year

B The auditor may enquire whether the systems have changed since last year and if not no further work is necessary

C The auditor must perform procedures to ensure the systems work as documented on file e.g. by performing walkthrough tests

D No work is necessary on systems documentation unless the client informs the auditor that changes have occurred

(2) Which of the following best describes the auditor's approach in respect of reliance on internal controls?

A Tests of controls must be performed over material areas of the financial statements

B Tests of controls must be performed each year over the areas the auditor is hoping to place reliance

C Tests of controls are not necessary this year as no deficiencies were identified last year

D Tests of controls must be performed over all areas irrespective of whether the auditor is planning to place reliance on those controls

(3) A flow chart is a diagrammatic depiction of a system which is useful when the system is complicated or has many elements. Is this statement true or false?

A True

B False

(4) Which of the following would not be included in an internal control evaluation questionnaire?

A How does the company ensure sales are only made to creditworthy customers?

B How does the company ensure that purchases are only made for a valid business use?

C How does the company ensure that all purchases are recorded?

D Is access to the warehouse restricted to authorised personnel only?

(5) Internal controls should be monitored on an on-going basis to ensure they are working effectively, are adequate and relevant. Which of the following will not monitor the internal controls of a company?

A Management

B Consultancy firm hired by management to evaluate the controls

C Internal auditor

D External auditor

12 Chapter summary

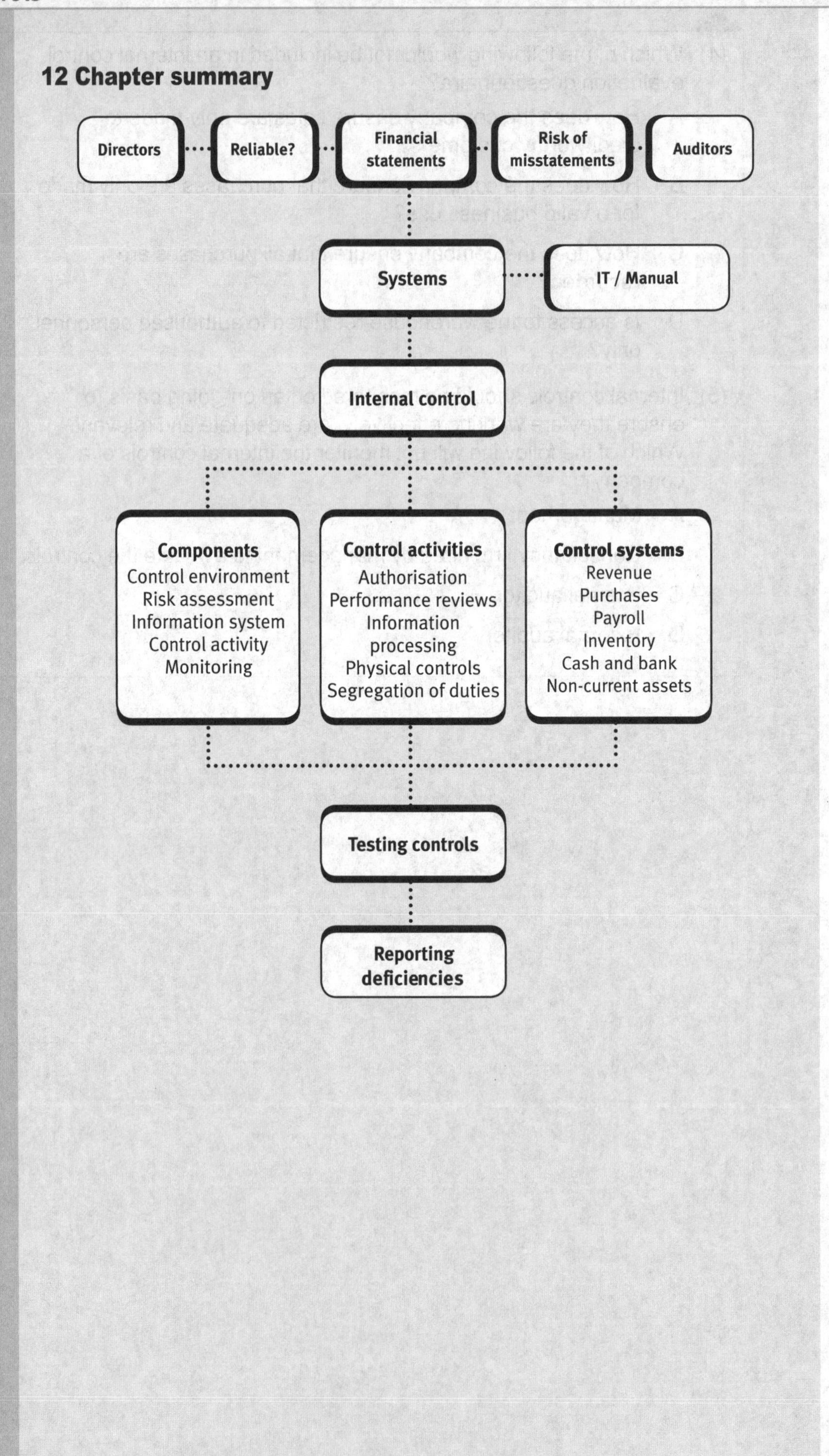

Test your understanding answers

Test your understanding 1

Ordering

Control	Test of control
Credit checks, setting of credit limits, and checks that an order will not take a customer over their credit limit: ensures that sales are only made to customers that are likely to make a full and prompt payment, reducing the risk of bad debts.	Inspect a sample of new and existing customer's files to ensure a recent, satisfactory credit check has been obtained. Review the customer's file and ensure that credit reports are obtained on a regular basis e.g. annually by looking at the dates on the reports. Inspect the customer's account to ensure that credit limits have been put in place. Try to enter an order into the system that will take the customer over their credit limit. The system should reject it.
Checking that the goods are available: ensures that orders can be honoured and despatched promptly. Goods not despatched promptly can result in complaints from customers.	With the client's permission, attempt to enter an order for goods that are known to be out of stock. The system should reject the order. Where orders are taken when the goods are out of stock, review the unfulfilled orders file or evidence of review such as a log in the file detailing when it was last reviewed. This ensure it is checked frequently so that orders are fulfilled as soon as possible.
Written confirmation of the order: ensures that orders are recorded accurately and that customers receive the goods they ordered.	Select a sample of sales made and inspect a copy of the written order retained on file to ensure the order was confirmed in writing to minimise the risk of discrepancies.

Approved customers are assigned with a unique customer account number: to ensure that sales are only made to customers that have been approved for credit, therefore minimising bad debts.	With the client's permission, attempt to enter an order for a fictitious customer account number. The system should reject the order.

Goods despatch

Control	**Test of control**
Order received electronically by warehouse and automatic generation of GDN: eliminates risk of human error/oversight ensuring that all orders are fulfilled.	Input a fictitious order into the system and trace it through to the despatch system to ensure the GDN is automatically generated.
Second member of warehouse team checks the goods packed, signing the GDN to evidence the check: segregation of duties reduces the risk of misappropriation of assets.	Visit a warehouse and observe the goods despatch process to assess whether all goods are double checked against the goods despatch note (GDN) prior to signing and sending out. Inspect the GDN for evidence of the signature to confirm the physical goods have been checked GDN and the GDN has been checked against the order prior to despatch.
Customers sign GDN and return to Murray Co: helps to ensure that customers pay in full as proof of delivery and acceptance of goods is obtained.	Inspect a sample of GDNs retained by the warehouse to ensure they are signed by customers as evidence of checking the goods and retained in the warehouse in case of disputes.
Weekly report to sales manager: monitors despatch of goods to ensure that all orders are fulfilled.	Inspect the weekly sales report for the sales manager's signature as evidence of his review. Enquire of the manager what actions are taken where orders have not been fulfilled.

Invoicing

Control	Test of control
The invoice is checked to the GDN: the invoice is raised from the GDN and not the original order, as there may have been a problem meaning that the order was not fulfilled.	Inspect the GDNs for evidence of being matched to invoices. Agree the details on both to ensure the control has been effective.
Sequentially numbered sales invoice and computer sequence check: to ensure that all invoices are processed – if any invoice in the sequence is missing it can be traced.	Review the last system generated sequence check of sales invoices to identify any omissions. Review the report produced by the system and inspect for evidence of a manager's review to confirm the sequence is complete and the report has been reviewed.
System GDN marked as 'invoiced': to prevent the customer being invoiced twice.	Inspect the GDNs to make sure they have been marked 'invoiced'.
System report reviewed by the senior accountant: to ensure that all goods are invoiced.	Inspect the file of GDNs with no invoice system reports for evidence of completion on a fortnightly basis such as a manager's signature.
Company price list: to ensure that customers are charged the correct price.	Inspect the price list for approval by the directors. Obtain a copy of the current price list and agree for a sample of invoices that relevant/current prices have been used. Agree the prices in the system to the approved price list. Enquire of management who has authority to amend standing data such as prices in the system to ensure only persons of suitable authority have access. Try to input a change to the prices in the system using a user ID of a clerk to ensure that the system does not allow access to this standing data.

Discounts must be requested by a sales manager and authorised by the sales director: segregation of duties and authorisation prevents fraud and unauthorised discounts.	With the client's permission, attempt to process an invoice with a sales discount without authorisation from the sales director. The system should reject the invoice. Inspect sales orders with discounts given for evidence of the sales director's signature authorising the discount.

Recording transaction

Control	**Test of control**
Review of receivables ledger for credit balances*:* identifies overpayments which may be caused by goods invoiced where no sale was recorded.	Inspect the receivables ledger for evidence of monthly review for credit balances such as a manager's signature.
Receivables ledger reconciliation: ensures that debts and receipts recorded in individual customer ledgers have also been recorded in the accounts (and visa versa). Segregation of duties monitors performance of controls and prevents fraud.	Inspect the receivables ledger reconciliations for evidence of performance on a monthly basis. Inspect the reconciliations for the manager's signature as evidence of review. Re-perform the reconciliation to ensure it has been carried out effectively.
Monthly customer statements sent to customers*:* enables customers to identify misrecorded invoices and receipts and notify the company.	For a sample of customers with outstanding balances, inspect copies of monthly statements sent out to confirm statements are in fact issued.

Cash receipt

Control	**Test of control**
Receipts are counted by the office assistant, recorded by the cashier, and the sales ledger clerk agrees the amount received to the amount invoiced: Segregation of duties prevents fraud.	Observe the cash receipt process to assess the adequacy of segregation of duties.
The invoice is marked as paid: ensures that customers are not chased for debts they have paid.	For a sample of cash receipts, inspect the relevant invoice to ensure it has been marked as paid.
The credit controller reviews the aged receivables to identify old balances which require investigation.	Inspect the aged receivables analysis for evidence of fortnightly review such as a manager's signature.
Credit control procedures are then followed: to ensure full and prompt payment by customers.	Inspect records of contact made with customers who have overdue debts, to ensure compliance with credit control procedures. E.g. notes of telephone calls, copies of letters sent.

Test your understanding 2

Ordering

Control	Test of control
Centralised purchasing department: ensures that purchasing is cost effective and only necessary goods and services are procured.	Inspect organisation chart to verify that a centralised purchasing department is in place. Enquire of the purchasing director whether all purchases must go through the department or if some purchases are made within individual departments to assess the effectiveness of the control. Inspect a sample of purchase orders to ensure they have been generated by the central purchasing department.
Sequentially prenumbered requisitions and sequence check performed by the purchasing department: ensures that all requisitions are fulfilled, preventing stock outs/manufacturing delays.	Enquire of the staff responsible for the sequence check what they do to evidence the control e.g. a log in the file with a signature to confirm the sequence check has been performed for that week. Inspect the log and ensure it is completed weekly and is up to date. Inspect the log for a signature to confirm the check has been performed.
Requisitions are authorised and manager's signature agreed: ensures only necessary goods and services are procured.	Inspect a sample of requisitions for the signature of an appropriate manager.
Inventory levels are checked prior to ordering: ensures only necessary goods and services are procured.	Inspect a sample of requisitions for evidence of inventory levels having been checked first, such as a signature. Observe the ordering process to see the ordering clerk checking inventory levels first.

Sequentially prenumbered purchase orders and weekly check by warehouse manager: to ensure that all goods and services ordered are received so any missing purchase orders can be followed-up.	Review purchase order for evidence of the purchasing department's weekly sequence check such as a signature to confirm it has been performed.
Approved suppliers list: gives assurance about the quality of goods and services and reliability of the suppliers.	For a sample of purchase orders placed, agree the supplier name to the approved suppliers list. Attempt to place an order with an unapproved supplier. The system should not allow it to proceed.
Written confirmation for all orders: ensures all and only necessary goods and services are received.	For a sample of purchase requisitions, inspect the purchase order and written confirmation from the supplier.
Price agreed to price list and for discounts: ensures that the correct prices are being charged by the supplier and discounts are being obtained.	Inspect a sample of purchase orders for evidence of prices having been agreed to price list such as a signature of the person checking. Select a sample of orders and agree to the authorised price list to test the effectiveness of the control.

Goods receipt

Control	**Test of control**
Goods received into the central warehouse: having one, secure delivery area prevents goods received being lost or stolen.	Visit a warehouse and inspect the delivery area for security of goods e.g. locked area, security guard, CCTV.
Goods are inspected for condition and quantity and agreed to the purchase order: prevents Murray Co from having to pay for unnecessary, or poor quality goods.	Observe the goods receipt process to ensure goods are inspected for condition and quantity before the supplier's delivery note is signed. Inspect the delivery note for a signature confirming the goods have been checked on arrival.
Sequentially pre-numbered goods received note (GRN) prepared by the warehouse team manager. The warehouse manager checks the sequence of PO's received weekly and informs the purchasing department of any missing orders.: sequential pre-numbering accompanied by a sequence check ensures that all GRNs are actioned avoiding the risk of goods not being available to fulfil customer orders when required.	Inspect evidence of the sequence check being performed such as a signature of the warehouse manager.
Grid-stamp: a grid stamp, is a grid that can be ink-stamped onto any document, with boxes for recording different information such as confirmation the goods have been inspected for condition and agreed to the PO.	Inspect a sample of GRNs to ensure grid-stamped and signed by the warehouse operative to confirm the goods have been inspected and agreed to the PO.
Inventory system updated on a daily basis by the warehouse manager: prevents unnecessary goods being ordered, ensures inventory levels are up-to-date when checked before acceptance of customer orders.	Inspect a sample of GRNs for the previous day to ensure the inventory system has been updated for them.

Invoicing

Control	Test of control
The invoice is matched to the GRN: by matching the invoice to the GRN and not the original order it ensures that only goods that have been received are paid for.	Inspect a sample of invoices and ensure filed with the relevant GRN, and the invoice number is written on the GRN.
Using the purchase order number marked on the invoice: when placing an order, the supplier will be given the purchase order number. This allows the purchase to be matched to the relevant GRN and requisition.	Inspect the invoice for the PO number and that it is matched to the relating GRN and requisition.
The invoice number is noted on the GRN grid stamp, and a monthly check of GRNs with no invoice: this prevents the goods received being invoiced twice, and ensures that all liabilities are recorded.	Review the GRN for the grid stamp. Inspect evidence of signature to confirm the monthly check has been carried out by the purchase ledger manager.

Recording transaction

Control	Test of control
Batch controls: the system will notify the clerk inputting the data of how many invoices have been input. This will be checked to the physical number of invoices and will highlight if too many or too few invoices have been entered.	Inspect a sample of batch control sheets for evidence of completion and agreement to the batch system report.
Invoice stamped as "recorded" and checks to ensure all invoices recorded: Prevents under or overstatement of trade payables.	Select a sample of invoices recorded on the system and inspect them to ensure they are marked as "recorded".
Supplier statement reconciliations: enables misrecorded purchases, payments and liabilities to be identified and corrected.	For a sample of suppliers, inspect the monthly supplier statements received for evidence of the reconciliation being performed. Reperform the reconciliation to confirm it has been reconciled correctly to test the effectiveness of the control.

Control account reconciliation: ensures that credits and payments recorded in individual supplier ledgers have also been recorded in the accounts (and vice versa). Segregation of duties monitors performance of controls and prevents fraud.	Inspect the purchases ledger reconciliations for evidence of performance and review on a monthly basis. Re-perform the reconciliation to ensure it has been carried out effectively.

Cash payment

Control	Test of control
The company accountant checks and authorises payments: payments should only be authorised by a senior member of the finance department to prevent error or fraud.	For a sample of payments made, inspect the payment list for evidence of the company accountant's review and authorisation.
Individual payments of more than $25,000, or total payments of more than $250,000 require a second signatory: a second signatory prevents fraud on unusual transactions.	Inspect a sample of invoices > $25,000 for evidence of a second signatory and agree that the signature is of someone with authority to authorise such amounts.
Payments are made by the cashier's office and recorded by the purchases ledger team: segregation of duties prevents fraud.	Observe the process of payments from the cashiers office to ensure segregation of duties is in place.
Invoices are stamped as "paid" and filed separately from invoices not yet paid: this prevents invoices being paid twice.	Inspect the file of paid invoices and ensure kept separate from invoices not yet paid. Inspect them stamped as 'Paid'.
GRNs are checked on a monthly basis: to ensure that suppliers are paid on a timely basis, which ensures that early settlement discounts available are obtained, and supplier goodwill is maintained.	Review evidence of the purchase ledger manager's monthly invoice review such as a signature.

Test your understanding 3

Clock cards submitted and input

Control	**Test of control**
Clock card to record time and supervision of clock card use: ensures that only genuine employees are paid, for work done.	Observe the use and supervision of clocking in and out procedures to ensure that employees are not able to clock in for other people.
Hash total and agreement of the total: segregation of duties by performing and checking the procedure reduces the risk of human error.	Observe the process of the clerks totalling the hours and passing the list to the wages clerk to confirm segregation of duties is in place. Inspect a sample of payroll sheets for the clerk's signature as evidence they have checked the add list total.
Pre-printed payroll sheet: ensures that only genuine employees are paid.	Inspect a sample of payroll sheets to ensure employee's names are pre-printed. Enquire of the manager how often the list is checked to make sure the list is up to date. For recent changes made to the standing data e.g. leavers or joiners, inspect the notification for the change and authorisation of an appropriate senior person confirming the change can be made. Inspect the details in the payroll system to ensure the changes were processed in accordance with the instruction.

Gross pay, deductions and net pay calculated

Control	Test of control
Payroll sheets are kept by the payroll manager: payroll data is sensitive information; a responsible individual must therefore be responsible for payroll documentation; segregation of duties prevents fraud.	Enquire of the payroll manager where the payroll sheets are kept and inspect them to ensure they are kept secure. For computer payroll files, attempt to access the files with a user ID of someone other than the manager. The file should not allow access.
Calculation of pay and taxation: it is essential that these calculations are performed correctly; a responsible individual must therefore be responsible for the main calculations; segregation of duties between calculation of gross pay and deductions, and net pay prevents error and fraud.	Review a sample of calculations of gross pay, tax deductions and net pay to ensure the appropriate rates of pay, and tax deductions are being used. Inspect the payroll listing for evidence of a manager's approval signature confirming the calculations are correct and payment can be made.

Other amendments input

Control	Test of control
Completion and authorisation of standing data forms such: ensures that only genuine employees are paid, at authorised rates of pay.	Select a sample of employees with payrises or other amendments from human resources records and inspect the system details to ensure that the relevant payroll form has been completed and authorised on a timely basis.
Use of specific forms such as for starters and leavers: prevents errors in processing information.	Select a sample of leavers and joiners from human resources records and trace the changes to the system to ensure that payroll forms have been completed and authorised on a timely basis.

Monthly review of standing data amendments and quarterly review of standing data files: ensures that any unauthorised amendments to standing data are identified and resolved.	Select a sample of amendments made to standing data and trace to the monthly report authorised by the finance director, and the relevant amendment form. Inspect the standing data files sent to departmental managers for evidence of review. For any anomalies identified by departmental managers, enquire of and corroborate the reasons for the anomaly and what action was taken to resolve the issue.

Final payroll calculated and payslips produced

Control	Test of control
Company accountants review of payroll: ensures that any anomalies can be identified and resolved; payroll is a significant cost for most companies and it is important that a responsible individual, independent of preparation of payroll undertakes this role.	Inspect the weekly payroll for the company accountant's signature to confirm the review has been performed.
The company accountant raises the cheque requisition and authorises the payment list, the cashier's department makes the relevant payments: segregation of duties prevents fraud and error.	For a sample of cheques raised for wages, inspect the cheque requisition to ensure completed by the company accountant. Inspect the monthly payment list for salaried employees for the company accountant's signature.

Payments to employees and tax authorities

Control	Test of control
Payroll cheque signed by two directors: this is likely to be a large amount of money and therefore requires authorisation by two senior personnel to prevent fraud and error.	Inspect the bank mandate to ensure it requires the signature of two directors for large cheques.
Cash is delivered by a secure transit company, under guard: due to the amount of cash likely to be needed to pay the weekly paid workers, it would not be appropriate for Murray Co staff to go to the bank to get the money themselves as this would threaten their personal safety.	Observe the cash being delivered by the security firm. Inspect invoices for services of the security firm to ensure the service is provided weekly.

Payroll costs and payments recorded

Control	Test of control
The head office accounts team record the payroll expense and payments and the wages office notify the team of unclaimed wages: segregation of duties prevents fraud and error.	Inspect the anomalies list to see it has been prepared. Enquire of the wages office and the head office team that his notification occurs on a weekly basis to corroborate the control works effectively.
Bank statements checked for deposit of unclaimed wages: prevents misappropriation.	Inspect the payroll list or bank statements for evidence that the bank statements are checked to ensure any unclaimed wages have been banked.

Test your understanding 4

The auditor could expand the amount of test of controls in that audit area. This may indicate that the control deficiency was not as bad as initially thought.

The problem could be raised with those charged with governance to ensure that they are aware of the problem.

The auditor could perform additional substantive procedures on the audit area. This action will help to quantify the extent of the error and makes the implicit assumption that the control system is not operating correctly.

If the matter is not resolved, then the auditor will also need to consider a modification to the audit report.

Test your understanding 5

Deficiency *(1 mark)*	**Potential effect** *(1 mark)*	**Recommendation** *(1 mark)*
Recording of orders		
Orders placed on the Internet site are transferred manually into the inventory and sales system. Manual transfer may result in error, for example, in recording order quantities or product codes.	Customers will be sent incorrect goods resulting in increased customer complaints.	The computer systems are amended so that order details are transferred directly between the two computer systems. This will remove manual transfer of details limiting the possibility of human error.
Control over orders and packing lists		
Each order/packing list is given a random alphabetical code. This type of code makes it difficult to check completeness of orders at any stage in the despatch and invoicing process.	Packing lists can be lost resulting either in goods not being despatched to the customer or the customer's credit card not being charged.	Orders/packing lists are controlled with a numeric sequence. At the end of each day, gaps in the sequence of packing lists returned to accounts are investigated.

Obtaining payment		
The customer's credit card is charged after despatch of goods to the customer, meaning that goods are already sent to the customer before payment is authorised.	Rhapsody Co will not be paid for the goods despatched where the credit company rejects the payment request. Given that customers are unlikely to return seeds, Rhapsody Co will automatically incur a bad debt.	Authorisation to charge the customer's credit card is obtained prior to despatch of goods to ensure Rhapsody Co is paid for all goods despatched.
Completeness of orders		
There is no overall check that all orders recorded on the inventory and sales system have actually been invoiced.	Entire orders may be overlooked and consequently sales and profit understated.	The computer is programmed to review the order file and orders where there is no corresponding invoice for an order, these should be flagged for subsequent investigation.

Test your understanding 6

Deficiency *(1 mark)*	**Recommendation** *(1 mark)*
(1) Hand written orders (with no numbering). Orders could be placed for goods not required. Orders could be lost and not placed. Therefore over spending or potential stock outs due to orders not being processed.	Have prenumbered orders which are authorised by a manager. A sequence check should be performed on a regular basis to ensure completeness.
(2) Purchase orders are not issued for all goods and services. Goods/services could be purchased that are not legitimate or required increasing costs for the company.	Purchase orders should be required for all goods. For services, a budget should be set and quotes obtained. Purchase orders should be authorised by someone other than the person requesting the goods to ensure they are for business use.

	Deficiency / Implication	Recommendation
(3)	No system for recording receipt of other goods and services. Failure to record goods received could lead to over-ordering as inventory levels will be inaccurate.	A goods received note should be completed and used to update the inventory records on a daily basis.
(4)	It doesn't state that the GRNs are checked to anything. Goods could be received that have not been ordered. Incorrect quantities could be received.	Agree the GRN to the purchase order to ensure the correct goods are being delivered.
(5)	There is no review of the bookkeeper's work e.g. posting of invoices into the nominal ledger. Errors could go undetected, therefore suppliers could be paid an incorrect amount.	A review of the nominal ledger postings by a manager should be performed on a regular basis.
(6)	A list of payables is given to the managing director without supporting documentation. The managing director will not know if payables are valid or correct therefore could be paying incorrect amounts.	The managing director should also review source documents before signing the list.
(7)	Lack of segregation of duties The managing director authorises invoices, approves payment and signs cheques. It is easy to process a purchase invoice to pay himself and this would go undetected.	Segregate duties by sharing the responsibility with another manager.

Test your understanding 7

(a) **Tests of control**

A test of control tests the operating effectiveness of controls in preventing, detecting or correcting material misstatements.

It is important for the external auditor to test controls to ensure their initial understanding obtained when assessing the control environment and internal controls is appropriate.

This will allow the auditor to identify and assess the risks of material misstatements in the financial statements and to determine to what extent to rely on the internal control system during the audit.

The auditor will then be able to design sufficient and appropriate substantive audit procedures to reduce detection risk, and therefore audit risk, to an acceptable level.

(b) **Payroll system strengths and tests of control**

Strengths in the control environment at the hotel in respect of payroll are set out below including the test of control to be performed by the auditor.

Strength (i)	**Explanation (i)**	**Test of control (ii)**
All staff are assigned a unique ID card by the personnel department to record hours worked.	Segregation of duties between allocating the cards and processing payroll will reduce the risk of the creation of 'ghost' employees' by the payroll department.	Ask a sample of employees to confirm who provided them with their unique ID card on joining the business. Inspect the ID cards for existence. Agree the employee details to HR records.
Hours worked are authorised by divisional heads.	There is a reduced risk that hours are overstated as the divisional head is more likely to identify errors or anomalies.	Inspect the email sent by the divisional head for a sample of months and agree to the employees hours recorded on the payroll system.

The payroll system is password protected with an alphanumerical password known only to the payroll clerk and finance manager.	The password is difficult to guess and therefore will reduce the risk of unauthorised access. There is a reduced risk that payroll data is manipulated.	The auditor should use test data and enter a 'dummy' password into the payroll system to ensure that access is not granted.
Payroll calculations are automatically calculated by the standardised payroll software.	There is a reduced risk of human error as the calculations are automatically generated using a standardised software package.	The auditor should recalculate a sample of employee's monthly pay from across the year and compare to the calculations on the payroll report for those months.
The finance manager reviews the payroll report and compares to last month before the final payroll is processed.	The comparison of data to the prior month should highlight any unusual movements that could be errors before the payroll is processed.	For a sample of months, inspect the payroll reports for evidence of the finance manager's signature confirming that the review has been performed.
Payslips are sent to the home address of each employee.	This should reduce the risk that payslips are misplaced or manipulated. It would also reduce the risk of a confidentiality breach.	Ask a sample of employees to confirm they receive their monthly payslips via post to their home address.
Payments are sent by bank transfer to each employee.	This will reduce the risk of payments being stolen or handed to the wrong employee.	Inspect the bank statements to identify payments made to a sample of employees on the payroll report for one month.

Test your understanding 8 – OT Case 1

(1)	C	Segregation of duties helps to prevent fraud.
(2)	D	Enquiry is not the most reliable form of evidence as the clerk or the manager could say what they think the auditor wants to hear. Recalculation of payroll by the auditor is a substantive test and does not confirm the manager has performed the necessary checks.
(3)	A	Inspection of employee contracts to confirm salary details is a substantive procedure.
(4)	B	The department manager would identify if any fictitious employees or employees who had left the company were included on the list and could notify the payroll department before any invalid payments were made.
(5)	A	Internal audit can monitor the effectiveness of controls by regularly testing them. B, C and D are all examples of control activities that would be tested for effectiveness.

Test your understanding 9 – OT Case 2

(1)	C	The auditor must ensure the systems documentation held on file is still correct. This can be achieved through a combination of enquiry and walkthrough tests but enquiry alone is not sufficient appropriate evidence.
(2)	B	Tests of controls are only performed when the auditor is planning to place reliance on those controls. If the auditor has decided that substantive testing is more efficient for a specific balance it is not necessary to test the controls over that area. Reliance cannot be placed on the results of tests of controls performed in previous years as the auditor would need to confirm they had worked effectively in the current year.
(3)	A	True.
(4)	D	An internal control questionnaire asks the client to respond with the control in place that addresses the risk. Restricted access as given in answer D is a control. This question would be included in an internal control questionnaire rather than an evaluation questionnaire.
(5)	D	The external auditor should not monitor the controls as this requires on-going involvement in the company on a regular basis. Whilst the external auditor may test the controls and identify deficiencies, this does not constitute monitoring. Management are ultimately responsible for the internal controls including assessing whether they are effective and whether any improvements are required. They may utilise an external consultant or internal audit function to help them fulfil this responsibility.

chapter

8

Procedures

Chapter learning objectives

This chapter covers syllabus areas:

- D2 – Audit procedures
- D4 – The audit of specific items
- D7 – Not-for-profit organisations

Detailed syllabus objectives are provided in the introduction section of the text book.

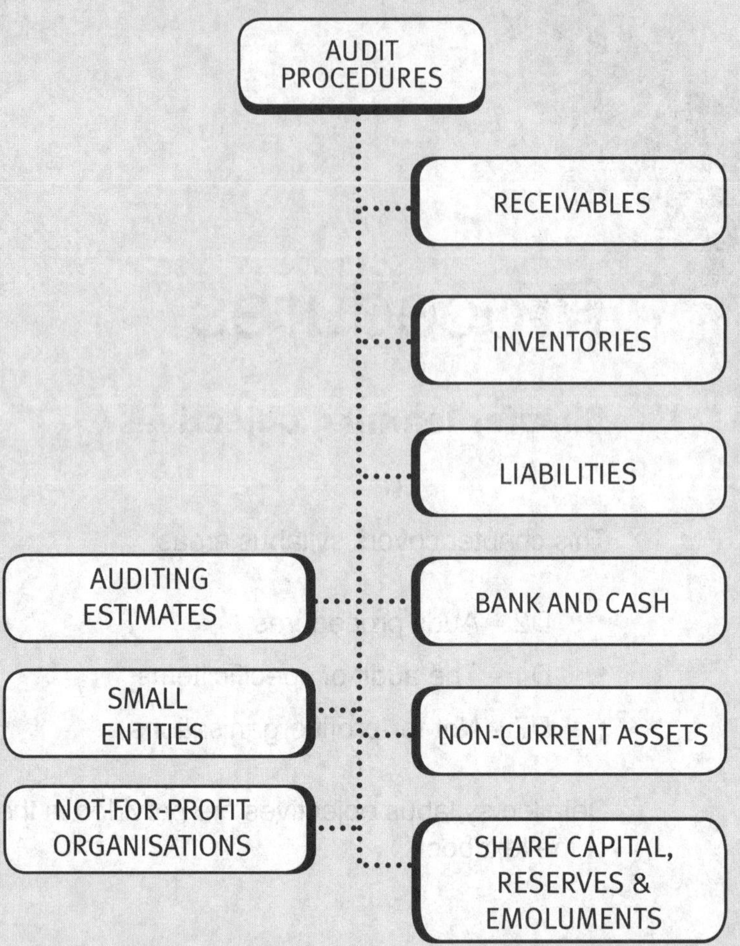

We dealt with the principles of audit evidence in an earlier chapter. This chapter deals with the **application** of those principles.

Audit procedures must be designed to respond to the specific risks of material misstatement identified for each individual client. In the exam, you should make your answers specific to the scenario. It is highly likely the scenario focuses on a specific risk such as valuation of inventory, recoverability of receivables, etc. Therefore audit procedures must focus on these features rather than general audit procedures over inventory or receivables.

This chapter is a starting point to help you familiarise yourself with the basic auditing techniques to allow you to apply them to questions. It is not an exhaustive summary of all audit procedures. Each section starts with the key assertions. These are the assertions most likely to be at risk, however, the auditor must obtain assurance over all relevant assertions.

1 Directional testing

The concept of directional testing derives from the principle of double-entry bookkeeping, i.e. for every debit there should be a corresponding credit; therefore any misstatement of a debit entry will also result in a misstatement of a credit entry.

Auditors primarily test debit entries for overstatement (assets and expenses) and credit entries for understatement (liabilities and income), indirectly testing the corresponding entries at the same time.

- All accounts are then tested for both understatement and overstatement; e.g. directly testing payables for understatement also indirectly tests expenses/cost of sales for understatement.
  - Testing for understatement tests completeness; testing for overstatement tests valuation, existence, rights and obligations, and occurrence.

2 Bank and cash

The key assertions for bank and cash are existence and valuation.

Bank and cash is a good example of where the reliability of the evidence available means that only a small quantity of evidence is needed. The auditor relies mainly on just two key pieces of evidence: the bank confirmation letter and the bank reconciliation.

- Obtain the company's bank reconciliation and cast to ensure arithmetical accuracy. Agree the cash book figure to the financial statements: **accuracy & valuation.**
- Obtain a bank confirmation letter from the company's bankers: **existence, rights & obligations**.
- Agree the balance per the cash book on the reconciliation to the year end cash book: **accuracy & valuation**.
- Agree the balance per the bank statement to an original year end bank statement and also to the bank confirmation letter: **accuracy & valuation.**
- Trace all of the outstanding lodgements to the pre year-end cash book, post year-end bank statement and also to paying-in-book pre year-end: **accuracy & valuation, existence.**
- Trace all unpresented cheques through to a pre year end cash book and post year-end statement. For any unusual amounts or significant delays obtain explanations from management: **accuracy & valuation, completeness**.
- Examine any old unpresented cheques to assess if they need to be written back into the purchase ledger as they are no longer valid to be presented: **accuracy & valuation, completeness**.
- Examine the bank confirmation letter for details of any security provided by the company or any legal right of set-off as this may require disclosure: **presentation**.

- Review the cash book and bank statements for any unusual items or large transfers around the year end, as this could be evidence of window dressing: **completeness, existence**.
- Count the petty cash in the cash tin at the year end and agree the total to the balance included in the financial statements: **accuracy & valuation, existence.**

Illustration 1: Murray Co bank reconciliation

Bank reconciliation as at 31 December 20X4

	$
Balance per cash book	(180,345.22)
Add Unpresented cheques	2,223.46
Less Outstanding lodgements	(1,600.34)
Difference	1.34
Balance per bank statement	(179,720.76)

Illustration 2: Murray Co bank confirmation letter

Wimble & Co
14 The Grove
Kingston
KI4 6AP

Manager (Audit Confirmations)
National Bank Anytown Branch
High Street, Anytown, AT1 1HS

14 December 20X4

Dear Sir,

Re: Murray Co

In accordance with the agreed practice for provision of information to auditors, please forward information on our mutual client as detailed below on behalf of the bank, its branches and subsidiaries. This request and your response will not create any contractual or other duty with us.

Company name: Murray Co

Main account number: 01789311

Sort code: 4-83-12

Information required

- Standard **x**
- Trade finance **x**
- Derivative and commodity trading
- Custodian arrangements
- Other information (see attached)

Audit confirmation date: 31/12/X4

The Authority to Disclose Information signed by your customer is already held by you. This is dated 30/11/X4. Please advise us if this Authority is insufficient for you to provide full disclosure of the information requested.

The contact name is: Don Henman (Audit Partner)
Telephone: 01234 123456

Yours Faithfully,

Wimble & Co

Wimble & Co

Murray Co bank confirmation letter

The bank confirmation letter provides direct confirmation of bank balances from the bank: it is third party, independent, written evidence and therefore very reliable. The format of the letter is usually standard and agreed between the bank and auditor.

The letter should be sent a minimum of two weeks before the client's year end. The letter should include enough information to allow the bank to trace the client. The bank should then forward on all details on all balances for the client; this will ensure completeness.

Permission must have been given by the client for the bank to release this information to the auditors, as they too have a duty of confidentiality to their clients. In some jurisdictions such disclosures are illegal, and so bank confirmation letters cannot be used as audit evidence.

Cash counts

Where cash in hand is material, or when fraud is suspected, a cash count should be arranged to verify existence.

The auditor should make sure that all cash balances are counted at the same time to avoid manipulation of the balances between different sites.

The auditor should always be accompanied by a member of the client staff to avoid any allegations of theft by the auditor.

The details of the cash counts should be recorded such as the locations counted, the amount counted at each location, the client staff present as well as the auditor performing the tests and the date performed.

Non-current liabilities

The key assertion for liabilities is completeness. With non-current liabilities allocation must also be assessed as there is a need to split the liability into its current and non-current elements.

The bank confirmation letter will provide details of loans held, the amounts outstanding, accrued interest and any security provided in relation to those loans. Additional procedures that the auditor will need to perform in relation to loan payables include:

- Obtain a breakdown of all loans outstanding at the year end, cast to verify arithmetical accuracy and agree the total to the financial statements: **completeness.**
- Agree the balance outstanding to the bank confirmation letter: **accuracy & valuation, rights & obligations**.
- Inspect bank confirmation letters for any loans listed that have not been included in the financial statements: **completeness**.
- Inspect financial statements for disclosures of interest rates, and the split of the loan between current and non-current: **allocation, classification, presentation**.
- Inspect the loan agreement for restrictive covenants (terms) and determine the effect of any loan covenant breaches: **allocation, classification, presentation**. [If loan covenants have been breached the loan may become repayable immediately and should therefore be included as a current liability].
- Inspect the cash book for loan repayments made: **existence, accuracy & valuation**.
- Recalculate the interest charge and any interest accrual in accordance with terms within the loan agreement, to ensure mathematical accuracy: **accuracy** of finance costs in the statement of profit or loss, **completeness** of accruals.

3 Non-current assets

The key assertions for non current assets are existence, valuation, completeness and rights and obligations.

Auditing tangible non-current assets requires the auditor to obtain sufficient appropriate evidence over many areas:

- existing assets
- additions

- disposals and the related profit/loss in the statement of profit or loss
- depreciation
- revaluations
- related disclosures (the property, plant and equipment note, depreciation policies, useful economic lives, revaluations and assets held under finance leases).

Illustration 3: Murray Co property plant and equipment

Non-current assets: property, plant and equipment note

	Land & buildings	**Fixtures, fittings & equipment**	**Motor vehicles**	**Total**
	$000	$000	$000	$000
Cost at 1 January 20X4	3,000	2,525	375	5,900
Additions	–	1,050	75	1,125
Disposals	–	(300)	–	(300)
Cost at 31 December 20X4	3,000	3,275	450	6,725
Accumulated depreciation at 1 January 20X4	386	489	125	1,000
Charge for the year	97	338	56	499
Disposals	–	(116)	–	(124)
Accumulated depreciation at 31 December 20X4	483	711	181	1,375
Carrying value at 31 December 20X4	2,517	2,564	269	5,350
Carrying value at 31 December 20X3	2,614	2,036	250	4,900

Procedures

- Obtain the non-current asset register, cast and agree the totals to the financial statements: verifies **completeness, classification, presentation**.
- Select a sample of assets from the non-current asset register and physically inspect them: verifies **existence**.
- Select a sample of assets visible at the client's premises and inspect the asset register to ensure they are included: verifies **completeness**.
- Cast the non-current asset register totals and sub-totals to ensure arithmetical accuracy: verifies **valuation**.
- Inspect assets for condition and usage to identify signs of impairment: verifies **valuation**.
- For revalued assets, inspect the valuer's report and agree the amount stated to the amount included in the general ledger and the financial statements: verifies **valuation**; and ensure that all assets in the same class have been revalued.
- Select a sample of additions and agree the cost to supplier invoice: verifies **valuation**.
- Obtain a list of additions and inspect the description to confirm that they relate to capital expenditure items rather than repairs and maintenance: verifies **existence.**
- Inspect the repairs and maintenance account in the general ledger for items of a capital nature: verifies **completeness**.
- Inspect supplier invoices (for equipment), title deeds (for property), and registration documents (for motor vehicles) to ensure they are in the name of the client: verifies: **rights and obligations**.
- If assets have been constructed by the client, obtain an analysis of the costs incurred, cast for arithmetical accuracy and agree a sample of costs to supporting documentation (e.g. payroll, material invoices): verifies **valuation**.

Disposals

- Obtain a breakdown of disposals, cast the list and agree all assets removed from the non-current asset register: verifies **existence**.
- Select a sample of disposals and agree sale proceeds to supporting documentation such as sundry sales invoices: verifies **accuracy of profit on disposal**.
- Recalculate the profit/loss on disposal and agree to the statement of profit or loss: verifies **accuracy of profit on disposal.**

Depreciation

- Inspect the capital expenditure budgets for the next few years to assess the appropriateness of the useful economic lives in light of plans to replace assets: **valuation.**
- Recalculate the depreciation charge for a sample of assets to verify arithmetical accuracy: **accuracy, valuation**.
- Inspect the financial statement disclosure of the depreciation charges and policies in the draft financial statements and compare to the prior year to ensure consistency: **presentation**.
- Recalculate the depreciation charge for revalued assets to ensure the charge is based on the new carrying value: **accuracy, valuation.**
- Review profits and losses on disposal of assets disposed of in the year, to assess the reasonableness of the depreciation policies (if depreciation policies are reasonable, there should not be a significant profit or loss): **valuation.**
- Compare depreciation rates to companies with the same type of assets to assess reasonableness: **valuation.**
- Perform a proof in total calculation for the depreciation charged for each category of assets, discuss with management if significant fluctuations arise: **completeness, valuation**. **(Analytical procedure)**

Illustration 4: Depreciation proof-in-total

The depreciation charge for fixtures and fittings for the year ending 31 December 20X4 included in the draft financial statements of Murray Co is $338,000 (to the nearest $000).

Murray Co's depreciation policy is to depreciate fixtures and fittings using the straight line method. The useful economic life for fixtures and fittings is ten years.

Exercise:

Create an expectation of what total depreciation for fixtures and fittings should be for year ending 31 December 20X4.

Solution

The total cost of fixtures and fittings in the draft financial statements of Murray Co is $3,275,000 (to the nearest $000).

We can set an **expectation for total depreciation for fixtures and fittings for the year ending 31 December 20X4** as $3,275,000/10: **$328,000** (to the nearest $000).

The **difference** ($10,000) is only **3%** more than our expectation, and we can therefore conclude that depreciation is materially correct.

Intangible non-current assets

Remember that the auditor's role is to obtain sufficient appropriate evidence that the financial statements conform in all material respects with the relevant financial reporting framework. For this reason, you will need to have a good understanding of the basic International Financial Reporting Standards.

Development costs

The key assertion for development costs is existence. Development costs should only be capitalised as an intangible asset if the recognition criteria of IAS 38 *Intangible Assets* have been met. **Note:** The audit procedures suggested below focus on obtaining evidence that the treatment of the relevant item conforms with these requirements.

- Obtain a breakdown of costs capitalised, cast for mathematical accuracy and agree to the amount included in the financial statements: verifies **valuation**.
- For a sample of costs, agree to invoices or timesheets: verifies **valuation**.
- Inspect board minutes for any discussions relating to the intended sale or use of the asset: verifies **existence**.
- Discuss the details of the project with management, to evaluate compliance with IAS 38 criteria: verifies **existence**.
- Inspect project plans and other documentation, to evaluate compliance with IAS 38 criteria: verifies **existence**.
- Inspect budgets to confirm financial feasibility: verifies **existence**.

Other intangible assets

- Inspect purchase documentation for purchased intangible assets: verifies **existence, rights and obligations** and **valuation**.
- Inspect specialist valuer's report and agree the amount stated to the amount included in the general ledger and the financial statements: verifies **valuation.**

Note: Audit procedures for amortisation are similar to those for depreciation.

4 Inventory

The key assertions for inventory are existence, valuation, completeness and rights and obligations.

The main source of evidence for inventory, is normally the year-end inventory count (although some clients may use perpetual or continuous inventory counting, throughout the year).

ISA 501 *Audit evidence – specific considerations for selected items* requires the auditor to:

- attend the physical inventory count (unless impracticable), if inventory is material to the financial statements; and
- perform procedures on the final inventory records to determine whether they accurately reflect the count results.

Attendance at the inventory count is required to:

- Evaluate management's instructions and procedures for the inventory count.
- Observe the performance of the count.
- Inspect the inventory.
- Perform test counts.

The inventory count is the responsibility of the client. **The auditor does not perform the count**. The auditor attends the count to help obtain sufficient appropriate evidence to form an opinion as to whether inventory is free from material misstatement.

In order to obtain sufficient appropriate evidence, the auditor must perform procedures before, during and after the inventory count during the final audit.

Before inventory count

- Contact client to obtain a copy of the inventory count instructions, to understand how the count will be conducted and assess the effectiveness of the count process.
- Inspect prior year working papers to understand the inventory count process and identify any issues that would need to be taken into account this year.
- Book audit staff to attend the inventory counts.
- Ascertain whether any inventory is held by third parties, and if applicable determine how to gather sufficient appropriate evidence.
- Consider the need for using an expert to assist in valuing the inventory being counted.
- Send a letter requesting direct confirmation of inventory balances held at year end from any third party warehouse providers used regarding quantities and condition.

Illustration 5: Murray Co inventory count instructions

(1) A finance manager must manage the inventory count.

(2) No goods are to be received or despatched during the inventory count.

(3) Each team will consist of two members of staff from the finance department.

(4) The teams will be allocated a team number and will be provided with a map of the warehouse. Each area of the warehouse is marked on the map with the number of the team that is to count inventory in that area. The warehouse manager will be in attendance to ensure that each team is clear about which area they are counting, before it is counted.

(5) One person must count the items. The second person will record the count and item information on the inventory tag. A description of the item, the inventory reference number (located on the inventory), quantity, unit of measure, location and team number should be noted on the tag.

(6) The tag will be taped to the shelf where the item is located. The tags are sequentially prenumbered; please use them in order.

(7) If you make a mistake on the tab do not use the tab, cross out the information, note the number of the replacement tag on the reverse of the unusable tag and hand to the Finance Manager at the end of the count, so that the sequence can be checked.

(8) Any damaged or obsolete items will be moved to a designated area. After the count, an assessment of the goods will be made by the finance manager with advice from a sales manager and the warehouse manager, to determine the allowance appropriate for the condition of the items.

(9) Once the first count is complete, a second count will take place, with each team counting an area that they were not responsible for on the first count (again according to the warehouse map).

(10) One person will count the item. The second person will sign the inventory tag to agree the details completed by the first team, and note the team number on the tag. Any discrepancies should be notified to the Finance Director immediately. The details noted on the inventory tag, including the inventory tag number must then be transferred to the inventory count sheets. The inventory count sheets are pre-printed with a description of the item and the inventory reference number (but not the quantities) and sequentially numbered.

(11) After the count, the inventory count sheets are compared to the inventory records by the finance manager any adjustments investigated and records updated by another finance manager (not involved in the count).

Exercise:

Discuss the reasons for each of the processes described on Murray Co's inventory count instructions.

Solution: Murray Co inventory count instructions

The reasons for each of the processes within the inventory count instructions include:

(1) A suitably trained and senior individual should be responsible for the count to ensure that any issues can be resolved on a timely basis. This needs to be someone other than the warehouse manager to ensure segregation of duties.

(2) Inventory records could be misstated if product lines are missed or double counted due to movements in the warehouse.

(3) Segregation of duties between those who have day-to-day responsibility for inventory and those who are checking it prevents errors and fraud being hidden by the warehouse team.

(4) Providing clear instructions for which team is to count what inventory ensures that all inventory is counted, and prevents double-counting.

(5) Segregation of duties within the team prevents errors and fraud.

(6) Pre-numbering the inventory tags will ensure that all inventory counted is detailed on the inventory count sheet.

(7) A sequence check will ensure that all inventory tags have been accounted for.

(8) Damaged or obsolete goods should be written down or provided against to ensure that they are stated at the lower of cost and NRV. A suitably trained member of the finance team should perform this assessment to ensure the valuation is appropriate.

(9) Counting the lines twice helps to ensure completeness and accuracy of the counts, and that any adjustments made are appropriate.

(10) The inventory count sheets should not have the quantities pre-printed to prevent the count team simply agreeing with the quantities, making counting errors more likely.

(11) The year-end inventory balance of Murray Co will be based on the records maintained. Therefore, the records must be complete, accurate and valid. It is important that an authorised individual who is independent of the count process and the warehouse can amend records.

During inventory count

Tests of controls

- Observe the count to ensure that the inventory count instructions are being followed. For example:
  - Non-warehouse staff performing and managing the count.
  - Sections of inventory being tagged or marked as counted to prevent double counting.
  - Counts sheets written in pen rather than pencil.
  - No movements of inventory during the count.
  - Sequentially numbered count sheets and a sequence check performed once the count is complete.
  - Teams of two people performing the count.
  - Count sheets show the description of the goods but do not show the quantities expected to be counted.
  - Damaged/obsolete items must be separately identified so they can be valued appropriately.
- See illustration of Murray Co inventory count instructions for more examples.

Substantive procedures

- Select a sample of items from the inventory count sheets and physically inspect the items in the warehouse: verifies **existence**.
- Select a sample of physical items from the warehouse and trace to the inventory count sheets to ensure that they are recorded accurately: verifies **completeness**.
- Enquire of management whether goods held on behalf of third parties are segregated and recorded separately: verifies **rights and obligations**.
- Inspect the inventory being counted for evidence of damage or obsolescence that may affect the net realisable value: verifies **valuation.**
- Record details of the last deliveries prior to the year end. This information will be used in final audit procedures to ensure that no further amendments have been made thereby overstating or understating inventory: verifies **completeness & existence**.
- Obtain copies of inventory count sheets at the end of the inventory count, ready for checking against final inventory listing after the inventory count: verifies **completeness** and **existence**.
- Attend the inventory count (if one is to be performed) at the third party warehouses: verifies **completeness** and **existence**.

After inventory count: final audit procedures

- Trace the items counted during the inventory count to the final inventory list to ensure it is the same as the one used at the year-end and to ensure that any errors identified during counting procedures have been rectified: verifies **completeness, presentation**.
- Cast the list (showing inventory categorised between finished goods, WIP and raw materials) to ensure arithmetical accuracy and agree totals to financial statement disclosures: verifies **completeness, classification**.
- Inspect purchase invoices for a sample of inventory items to agree their cost to verify **valuation**.
- Inspect purchase invoices for the name of the client to verify **rights**.
- Inspect post-year-end sales invoices for a sample of inventory items to determine if the net realisable value is reasonable. This will also assist in determining if inventory is held at the lower of cost and net realisable value: verifies **valuation**.
- Inspect the ageing of inventory items to identify old/slow-moving amounts that may require an allowance, and discuss these with management: verifies **valuation**.

- Recalculate work-in-progress and finished goods valuations using payroll records for labour costs and utility bills for overhead absorption: verifies **valuation.**
- Trace the good received immediately prior to the year-end to year-end payables and inventory balances: verifies **completeness & existence**.
- Trace goods despatched immediately prior to year-end to the nominal ledgers to ensure the items are not included in inventory and revenue (and receivable where relevant) has been recorded: verifies **completeness & existence**.
- Calculate inventory turnover/days ratio and compare this to prior year, to assess whether inventory is being held longer and therefore requires an allowance to bring the value down to the lower of cost and NRV: verifies **valuation. (Analytical procedure)**
- Calculate gross profit margin and compare this to prior year, investigate any significant differences that may highlight an error in costs of sales and closing inventory: verifies **valuation. (Analytical procedure)**

Inventory held by third parties

- Where a third party holds inventory on behalf of the client, obtain external confirmation from the third party of the quantity and condition of the goods to confirm **rights and valuation**.
- If the goods held by the third party are material the auditor should attend the inventory count to verify **existence** of the inventory.
- The auditor can also obtain a report from the third party's auditors confirming the reliability of the internal controls at the third party.

Standard costs

- Obtain the breakdown of the standard cost calculation and agree a sample of costs to invoices.
- Enquire of management the basis for the standard costs and how often they are updated to reflect current costs.
- Inspect the variance account and assess the level of variance for reasonableness. Discuss with management any significant variances arising.

Inventory count: cut-off procedures

The inventory count(s) will be affected by goods despatched and goods received.

During the count inventory movements should preferably stop to enable the count to be conducted without being affected by deliveries.

For some organisations this won't be possible as they may operate production and deliveries 24 hours a day.

In these types of organisations the client should move the items requiring despatch to a different location to that being counted prior to the count taking place. Any deliveries of goods should be made to a different location while the count is on-going to enable the count to be conducted without movement of items.

A separate count can then be performed on the items delivered during the count and these can be added to the warehouse items counted.

By having such controls in place, the completeness and existence of inventory at the count date can be verified as well as the cut-off assertion for purchases and sales.

Continuous/perpetual inventory systems

The procedures suggested above apply to all inventory counts, whether carried out as a one-off year-end count or where inventory is counted on a rolling basis throughout the year. The objective is the same:

- To identify whether the client's inventory system reliably records, measures and reports inventory balances.

Where the client uses a continuous counting system, lines of inventory are counted periodically (say monthly) throughout the year so that by the end of the year all lines have been counted.

Where the client uses a perpetual system the auditor should:

- Attend at least one count to ensure that adequate controls are applied during the counts (in the same way as for a year end count).
- Inspect the number and value of adjustments made as a result of the count. If significant adjustments are required each month, this would indicate that the system figures for inventory cannot be relied on at the year end and a full count will be required.

- If the system balance for inventory is deemed reliable as a result of these procedures, further procedures to verify cutoff, valuation and rights will still be required.
- The auditor should still inspect GRNs and GDNs around the year end to confirm correct cutoff.
- NRV testing and comparison of inventory days with prior year will be performed to identify issues with valuation.
- Inspection of purchase invoices for the name of the client will enable rights to be confirmed.

Advantages and disadvantages of perpetual counts

Advantages

- Reduces time constraints for the auditor, and enables them to attend counts relating to lines at greater risk of material misstatement.
- Slow moving and damaged inventory is identified and adjusted for in the client's records on a continuous basis meaning the year-end valuation should therefore be more accurate.

Disadvantages

- The auditor will need to obtain sufficient appropriate evidence that the system operates effectively at all times, not just at the time of the count.
- Additional procedures will be necessary to ensure that the amount included for inventory in the financial statements is appropriate, particularly with regard to cut-off and year-end allowances.

5 Receivables

The focus of testing for receivables is valuation and existence. **Note** the effect of directional testing, e.g. directly testing receivables for overstatement also indirectly tests revenue for overstatement (Dr: Receivables, Cr: Revenue).

- Obtain an aged receivables listing, cast it and agree the total to the financial statements: verifies **accuracy** and **presentation**.
- Agree the sales ledger control account with the sales ledger list of balances: verifies **completeness** and **existence**.

- Select a sample of year-end receivable balances and agree back to valid supporting documentation of GDN and sales order: verifies **existence**.
- Inspect after date cash receipts and follow through to pre-year-end receivable balances: verifies **valuation, rights and obligations** and **existence**.
- Select a sample of goods despatched notes (GDN) before and just after the year end and follow through to the sales invoice to ensure they are recorded in the correct accounting period: verifies **completeness** and **existence** (**cut-off** of revenue).
- Perform a positive receivables circularisation of a representative sample of Murray Co's year-end balances, for any non-replies, with Murray Co's permission, send a reminder letter to follow-up: verifies **existence** and **rights and obligations**.
- Inspect the **aged receivables report** to identify any slow moving balances, discuss these with the credit control manager to assess whether an allowance or write down is necessary: verifies **valuation** and **allocation**.
- Inspect customer correspondence in respect of any slow moving/aged balances to assess whether there are any invoices in dispute: verifies **existence** and **rights and obligations**.
- Inspect board minutes of Murray Co to assess whether there are any material disputed receivables that may require write off: verifies **existence** and **rights and obligations**.
- Inspect the sales ledger for any credit balances and discuss with management whether these should be reclassified as payables: verifies **existence of receivables** and **completeness of payables, classification**.
- Inspect a sample of post year-end credit notes to identify any that relate to pre-year-end transactions to ensure that they have not been included in receivables: verifies **existence** (**occurrence** of revenue).
- Calculate average receivable days and compare this to prior year, investigate any significant differences: verifies **completeness** and **valuation**. **(Analytical procedure)**

e.g

Illustration 6: Murray Co positive confirmation letter

Customer Co

Customer's address

7 January 20X5

Dear Sirs

As part of their normal audit procedures we have been requested by our auditors, Wimble & Co, to ask you to confirm the balance on your account with us at 31 December 20X4, our year end.

The balance on your account, as shown by our records, is shown below. After comparing this with your records will you please be kind enough to sign the confirmation and return a copy to the auditor in the prepaid envelope enclosed. If the balance is not in agreement with your records, will you please note the items making up the difference in the space provided.

Please note that this request is made for audit purposes only and has no further significance.

Your kind co-operation in this matter will be greatly appreciated.

Yours faithfully

Chief Accountant

Murray Co

Wimble & Co address

Dear Sirs

We confirm that, except as noted below^{x}, a balance of $XX was owing by us to Murray & Co at 31 December 20X4.

(*space for customer's signature*)

^{x}Details of differences:

Murray Co confirmation letters

A **positive** receivables circularisation requires customers to respond whether or not the balance is correct. A negative receivables circularisation requests customers to respond only if they disagree with the balance and is only suitable if the risk of material misstatement is low.

"7th January 20X5": The confirmation letter should be **sent as soon as possible after the year end**, to increase the chance of an accurate and timely response.

"As part of their normal audit procedures, we have been requested by our auditors to confirm the balance on your account with us at 31st December 20X4... please be kind enough to sign the confirmation and return a copy to the auditor...": It is the **client** who **writes to their customers** requesting the information but the **response** must be **sent directly to the auditors** to reduce the risk of the client interfering with any response.

"...*in the prepaid envelope enclosed":* By making it as easy as possible to respond increase the chance that sufficient customers will confirm balances for it to be a valid audit test.

"*If the balance is not in agreement with your records, will you please note the items making up the difference in the space provided*": Requesting the customer to complete the reconciliation increases the reliance the auditor can place on this evidence (although the auditor will review the reconciliation and investigate any unreconciled differences or disagreements).

Positive receivables circularisations are considered to be a reliable source of evidence because they are written and original from a third party external source.

Illustration 7: Murray Co aged receivables analysis

Aged receivables analysis at 31 December 20X4 ($000)

Ref	**Customer Name**	**Total**	**Current**	**30-60 days**	**60-90 days**	**90-120 days**	**120 days**
A001	Anfield United Shop	**176**	95	76	5	0	0
B001	Bibs and Balls	**0**	0	(24)	0	24	0

B002	The Beautiful Game	**84**	62	0	20	0	2
B003	Beckham's	**42**	32	10	0	0	0
C001	Cheryl & Coleen Co	**12**	12	0	0	0	0
D001	Dream Team	**45**	0	31	14	0	0
E001	Escot Supermarket	**235**	97	65	0	0	73
G001	Golf is Us	**211**	0	0	0	100	111
G002	Green Green Grass	**61**	50	11	0	0	0
H001	HHA Sports	**59**	40	0	19	0	0
J001	Jilberts	**21**	11	10	0	0	0
J002	James Smit Partnership	**256**	73	102	34	45	2
J003	Jockeys	**419**	278	120	21	0	0
O001	The Oval	**92**	48	44	0	0	0
P001	Pole Vaulters	**76**	0	0	76	0	0
P002	Polo Polo	**0**	0	0	0	0	0
S001	Stayrose Supermarket	**97**	24	23	23	27	0
T001	Trainers and More	**93**	73	20	0	0	0
T002	Tike Co	**(54)**	0	0	0	0	(54)
W001	Wanderers	**89**	60	29	0	0	0
W002	Whistlers	**(9)**	645	(654)	0	0	0
W003	Walk Hike Run	**4**	0	0	0	0	4
W004	Winners	**31**	21	10	0	0	0
Total		**2,040**	**1,621**	**(127)**	**212**	**196**	**138**

Exercise:

Identify, with reasons, four trade receivables balances from the aged receivables analysis that should be selected for further testing.

Solution: Murray Co aged receivables analysis

Jockeys: the outstanding balance is over 20% of the total receivables balance at the year end and is therefore material.

Golf is Us: this large and old balance may require write off, or a specific allowance made if the recoverability of the amount is in doubt (similarly for Escot supermarket).

Tike & Co: the large and old credit balance on the listing suggests that an error may have been made. A payment from another customer may have been misallocated to this account or the client may have overpaid an invoice, or paid an invoice twice in error. It may be appropriate to reclassify this balance, along with the balance for Whistlers, as a trade payable.

Whistlers: although the amount is small, the credit balance appears to be due to a difference between a recent large payment and the outstanding balance. This error may indicate other potential errors, and requires further investigation.

There are other balances that could be identified and justified for similar reasons to the above.

ISA 505 External confirmations

Note: ISA 505 *External confirmations* requires the auditor to maintain control over external confirmation requests when using external confirmations as a source of audit evidence.

This can be achieved by:

- the auditor preparing the confirmation letters and determine the information to be requested and the information that should be included in the request.
- the auditor selecting the sample of external parties to obtain confirmation from.
- the auditor sending the requests to the confirming party.

Prepayments

Prepayments are services or goods for which a company has paid in advance.

- Inspect bank statements to ensure payment has been made: verifies **existence**.
- Inspect invoices to ensure payment relates to goods or services not yet received: verifies **existence**.
- Recalculate the amount prepaid to confirm mathematical accuracy: verifies **valuation**.
- Compare prepayments with the prior year to identify any missing items or any new prepayments which require further testing: verifies **existence**, **valuation**, and **completeness**. **(Analytical procedure)**

6 Payables and accruals

The focus of testing for liabilities is completeness. Note the effect of directional testing, e.g. directly testing payables for understatement also indirectly tests cost of sales for understatement (Dr: Payables, Cr: Purchases).

- Obtain a listing of trade payables from the purchase ledger, cast to verify arithmetical accuracy and agree to the general ledger and the financial statements: verifies **completeness, classification, presentation**.
- Reconcile the total of purchase ledger accounts with the purchase ledger control account: verifies **completeness**.
- Obtain supplier statements and reconcile these to the purchase ledger balances. Investigate any reconciling items: verifies **existence, completeness, obligations and valuation**.
- Inspect after date payments, if they relate to the current year then follow through to the purchase ledger or accrual listing: verifies **completeness**.
- Inspect invoices received after the year end to ensure no further items need to be accrued: verifies **completeness**.
- Enquire of management their process for identifying goods received but not invoiced or logged in the purchase ledger and ensure that it is reasonable: verifies **completeness**.
- Select a sample of goods received notes before the year-end and follow through to inclusion in the year-end payables balance: verifies **completeness of payables** and **cut-off of purchases**.

- Select a sample of payable balances and perform a trade payables' circularisation, follow up any non-replies and any reconciling items between balance confirmed and trade payables' balance: verifies **completeness** and **existence**.
- Insect the purchase ledger for any debit balances, for any significant amounts discuss with management and consider reclassification as current assets: verifies **valuation** of payables and **completeness of receivables, classification**.
- Compare the list of trade payables and accruals against the prior year list to identify any significant omissions: verifies **completeness**. **(Analytical procedure)**
- Calculate the trade payable days and compare to prior years, investigate any significant differences: verifies **completeness** and **valuation**. **(Analytical procedure)**
- Obtain the list of accruals from the client, cast it to confirm mathematical accuracy and agree to the general ledger and the financial statements: verifies **completeness, classification**.
- Recalculate a sample of accrued costs by reference to contracts and payment schedules (e.g. loan interest): verifies **valuation** (**accuracy** of purchases and other expenses).
- Inspect invoices received post year end to confirm the actual amount and assess whether the accrual is reasonable: verifies **valuation**.
- Compare the accruals this year to last year to identify any missing items or unusual fluctuation in amount and discuss this with management: verifies **completeness and valuation. (Analytical procedure)**

Illustration 8: Murray Co supplier statement

Murray Co's trade payable balance at 31 December 20X4 is $1,400,000 (to the nearest $000). The total balance has already been agreed to the purchase ledger which shows that trade payables consists of fifteen suppliers.

A junior member of the audit team, Rob Cash, has been checking five of these balances by reconciling suppliers' statements to the balances on the purchase ledger. He is unable to reconcile a material balance, relating to Racket Co, who supply Vectran material to Murray Co, for stringing tennis rackets. He has asked for your assistance, and your suggestions on the audit work which should be carried out on the differences.

The balance of Racket Co on Murray Co's purchase ledger is shown below:

Purchase ledger Supplier: Racket Co

Date	Type	Reference	Status	Dr ($)	Cr ($)	Balance ($)
10.10	Invoice	6004	Paid 1		21,300	
18.10	Invoice	6042	Paid 1		15,250	
23.10	Invoice	6057	Paid 1		26,340	
04.11	Invoice	6080	Paid 2		35,720	
15.11	Invoice	6107	Paid 2		16,320	
26.11	Invoice	6154	Paid 2		9,240	
31.11	Payment	Cheque	Alloc 1	61,630		
	Discount		Alloc 1	1,260		
14.12	Invoice	6285			21,560	
21.12	Invoice	6328			38,240	
31.12	Payment	Cheque	Alloc 2	60,050		
	Discount		Alloc 2	1,230		
31.12	**Balance**					**59,800**

Racket Co have sent the following supplier statement:

Date	Type	Reference	Status	Dr ($)	Cr ($)	Balance ($)
07.10	Invoice	6004		21,300		
16.10	Invoice	6042		15,250		
22.10	Invoice	6057		26,340		
02.11	Invoice	6080		37,520		
13.11	Invoice	6107		16,320		
22.11	Invoice	6154		9,240		
10.12	Receipt	Cheque			61,630	
04.12	Invoice	6210		47,350		
12.12	Invoice	6285		21,560		
18.12	Invoice	6328		38,240		
28.12	Invoice	6355		62,980		
31.12	**Balance**					**234,470**

Racket Co's terms of trade with Murray Co allow a 2% cash discount on invoices where Racket Co receives a cheque from the customer by the end of the month following the date of the invoice (i.e. a 2% discount will be given on November invoices paid and received by 31 December).

On Murray Co's purchase ledger, under 'Status' the cash and discount marked 'Alloc 1' pay invoices marked 'Paid 1' (similarly for 'Alloc 2' and 'Paid 2').

Murray Co's goods received department checks the goods when they arrive and issues a goods received note (GRN). A copy of the GRN and the supplier's advice note is sent to the purchases accounting department.

Exercise:

(a) **Prepare a statement reconciling the balance on Murray Co's purchase ledger to the balance on Racket Co's supplier's statement.**

(b) **Describe the audit work you will carry out on each of the reconciling items you have determined in your answer to part (a) above, in order to determine the balance which should be included in the financial statements.**

Case Study Solution: Murray Co supplier statement

Many companies send out monthly statements of account as part of their credit control procedures. It is likely that audit clients will receive a number of these statements from suppliers at the year-end. These can be reconciled to their own payables control account to ensure that their records are correct. This is known as a supplier statement reconciliation and is an important source of audit evidence.

There are a two reasons why there may be a variance, including:

- **Timing differences**, e.g. invoices sent by the supplier but not yet received by the customer; payments sent by the customer but not yet received by the supplier; returns and credit notes not yet appearing on the supplier's statement; or
- **Errors**.

(a) **Reconciliation of purchase ledger balance to balance on supplier's statement:**

		$	$
	Balance per purchase ledger:		**59,800**
	Differences:		
(i)	31.11: Discount not allowed by supplier	1,260	
(ii)	04.11: Transposition error, invoice 6080	1,800	
(iii)	04.12: Invoice 6210 not on purchase ledger	47,350	
(iv)	28.12: Invoice 6355 not on purchase ledger	62,980	
(v)	31.12: Cash in transit	60,050	
(vi)	Discount not allowed	1,230	
			174,670
	Balance per supplier's statement:		**234,470**

(b) **Audit work**

(i) The date of the cash payment for the October invoices suggests that Racket Co will not have received the cheque for $61,630 until after the 30 November and so Murray Co may not be entitled to the 2% cash discount. The entry in Murray Co's ledger suggest the cheque was posted on 30 November however this is not conclusive evidence that the cheque was actually sent to Racket Co on this date.

– The auditor should enquire with Murray Co's purchase ledger controller about this item, and inspect correspondence with Racket Co to establish entitlement to the discount.

– If Murray Co is obliged to pay the 2% disallowed discount, this should be added to the purchase ledger balance.

– If Racket Co will allow the discount, there is no need to make any adjustments to the purchase ledger balance.

(ii) The apparent transposition error on invoice 6080 would be checked by inspecting the invoice.

- If the invoice shows $37,520, then an additional payable of $1,800 should be added at the year-end to correct this error.
- No adjustment will be necessary if Murray Co's figure is correct.

(iii) It appears that invoice 6210 for $47,350 has not been included on Murray Co's purchase ledger.

- The auditor should enquire with the warehouse manager whether these goods have been received.
- Inspect the GRNs around the expected delivery date in order to identify the relevant GRN.
- Inspect correspondence with Racket Co for discussions relating to a dispute regarding these goods (if relevant).
- If the goods have been received, the purchase invoices file should be inspected to identify if there is a related purchase invoice.
- If there is a purchase invoice, enquire with the purchases department why the invoice has not been posted to the purchase ledger. This may be because of a dispute (e.g. an incorrect price, the wrong quantity or a fault with the goods).
- If the goods relating to this invoice are in inventory (or have been sold) a purchase accrual should be made for this item (note that the actual quantity of goods received should be accrued for) and correspondence relating to this invoice with Racket Co should be inspected to assess what payment has been agreed.
- If the goods have not been received, no adjustment needs to be made (but a copy of correspondence disputing the delivery/invoice should be placed on file as evidence).

(iv) The appropriate treatment of invoice 6355 depends on whether or not Murray Co received the goods before the year-end. The auditor should:

- Inspect the GRN for the date to determine if the goods were received before the year-end.
- If the date is before the year-end, then Murray Co should include a purchase accrual at the year-end for this invoice.

(v) The cheque on 31 December appears to be cash in transit. The auditor should:

– Inspect Murray Co's bank statement to confirm that the cheque was cleared by the bank after the year-end.

– If the cheque cleared within one week of the year-end (with most other cheques issued immediately before the year-end) then this is validly cash in transit.

– If most cheques issued immediately before the year-end take more than a week to clear, this indicates window-dressing of the financial statements (i.e. the cheques were actually sent out after the year-end), in which case the amounts should Cr back to trade payables and Dr back to cash.

(vi) If, as appears likely, the cheque for $60,050 is not received by Racket Co until sometime after the year-end, then the discount of $1,230 may be disallowed. If this discount is disallowed, it should be added to payables at the year-end (see (i) above).

7 Provisions

IAS 37 *Provisions, Contingent Liabilities and Contingent Assets* requires an entity to recognise a provision if: a present obligation has arisen as a result of a past event; payment is probable ('more likely than not'); and the amount can be estimated reliably. If payment is only possible, a contingent liability must be disclosed in the notes to the financial statements.

As such, audit testing will focus on whether an obligation exists and whether the provision is valued appropriately. Completeness is also a key assertion as the company may understate liabilities to improve their financial position.

- Obtain a breakdown of the items to be provided for, cast it and agree the figure to the financial statements: verifies **accuracy** and **presentation**.
- Enquire with the directors or inspect relevant supporting documentation to **confirm** that a **present obligation** exists at the year end: verifies **rights and obligations.**
- Inspect relevant board minutes to ascertain whether **payment is probable:** verifies **existence.**

- Recalculate the provision and agree components of the calculation to supporting documentation: verifies **completeness**.
- Inspect post year-end bank statements to identify whether any payments have been made, compare actual payments to the amounts provided to assess whether the provision is reasonable: verifies **valuation**.
- Obtain confirmation from client's lawyer about the likely outcome and chances of payment (e.g. for a legal provision): verifies **existence** and **rights and obligations.**
- Inspect correspondence received from the lawyer regarding the legal provision to assess whether a provision should be recognised and if so, whether the amount of the provision is adequate: verifies **valuation** and **completeness**.
- Inspect the financial statement disclosure of the provision to ensure compliance with IAS 37 *Provisions, Contingent Liabilities and Contingent Assets*: verifies **presentation**.
- Obtain a written representation from management that they believe the provision is valued appropriately and is complete: verifies **valuation** and **completeness**.

Note: ISA 501 *Audit evidence – special considerations for selected items* requires the auditor to design and perform audit procedures in order to identify litigation and claims involving the entity which may give rise to a risk of material misstatement.

Illustration 9: Murray Co provision

The statement of financial position shows that Murray Co has $240,000 provisions for the year ended 31 December 20X4. The majority of the provision relates to provisions for warranties ($200,000). However, $40,000 of the provision relates to a claim made by an ex-employee of Murray Co who is claiming for unfair dismissal.

The audit plan includes the following audit procedures in relation to this provision:

- Enquire with the directors when the employee was dismissed in order to confirm that a present obligation exists at the year end.
- Inspect correspondence with the employee to verify that the employee was dismissed before the year end.
- Inspect relevant board minutes to ascertain whether it is probable that the payment will be made to the employee.
- Enquire with the solicitors on the merits of the unfair dismissal case and the likely payment.
- Obtain a breakdown of the costs to be provided for and cast it to ensure completeness.

- Recalculate the provision to confirm completeness and agree components of the calculation to supporting documentation, e.g. fee estimate from Murray Co's solicitors, claim received from ex-employee.
- Inspect post year-end bank statements to identify whether any payments have been made to the solicitors or ex-employee, compare actual payments to the amounts provided to assess whether the provision is reasonable.
- Obtain a written representation from management to confirm the adequacy and reasonableness of the provision.
- Inspect the financial statement disclosure of the provision to ensure compliance with IAS 37 *Provisions, Contingent Liabilities and Contingent Assets.*

8 Accounting estimates

There are many accounting estimates in the financial statements, e.g. allowances for receivables, expected life of property, plant and equipment, valuation of provisions etc. Accounting estimates are inherently risky because they are about the future, cannot be 'right', and are often not supported by documentary evidence.

ISA 540 *Auditing accounting estimates* requires the auditor to:

- Obtain an understanding of how management identify those transactions, events or conditions that give rise to the need for an estimate.

For each estimate in the financial statements, the auditor must also:

- Enquire of management how the accounting estimate is made and the data on which it is based.
- Determine whether events occurring up to the date of the auditor's report (after the reporting period) provide audit evidence regarding the accounting estimate.
- Review the method of measurement used and assess the reasonableness of assumptions made.
- Test the operating effectiveness of the controls over how management made the accounting estimate.
- Develop an expectation of the possible estimate (point estimate) or a range of amounts to evaluate management's estimate.
- Review the judgments and decisions made by management in the making of accounting estimates to identify whether there are any indicators of management bias.

- Evaluate overall whether the accounting estimates in the financial statements are either reasonable or misstated.
- Obtain sufficient appropriate audit evidence about whether the disclosures in the financial statements related to accounting estimates and estimation uncertainty (e.g. contingent liabilities) are reasonable.
- Obtain written representations from management and, where appropriate, those charged with governance whether they believe significant assumptions used in making accounting estimates are reasonable.

9 Share capital, reserves and director's remuneration

Each of the following areas are material by nature.

Share capital

- Agree authorised share capital and nominal value disclosures to underlying shareholding agreements/statutory constitution documents.
- Inspect cash book for evidence of cash receipts from share issues and ensure amounts not yet received are correctly disclosed as share capital called-up not paid in the financial statements.
- Inspect board minutes to verify issue of share capital during the year.

Dividends

- Inspect board minutes to agree dividends declared before the year-end.
- Inspect bank statements to agree dividends paid before the year-end.
- Inspect dividend warrants to agree dividend payment.

Director's emoluments

- Obtain and cast a schedule of director's remuneration split between wages, bonuses, benefits, pension contributions and other remuneration, and agree to financial statement disclosures.
- Inspect payroll records and agree wages, bonuses, and pension contributions.
- Inspect bank statements to verify the amounts actually paid to directors.
- Inspect board minutes for discussion and approval of directors' bonus announcements or other additional remuneration.
- Obtain a written representation from directors that they have disclosed director's remuneration to the auditor.

Reserves

- Agree opening reserves to prior-year closing reserves and reconcile movements.
- Agree movements in reserves to supporting documentation (e.g. revaluation reserve movements to the independent valuers report).

10 Statement of profit or loss

Remember directional testing. The majority of transactions and events in the statement of profit or loss are audited indirectly through the direct tests performed on the corresponding debits or credits in the statement of financial position. However, the auditor will normally perform **substantive analytical procedures** on these areas and some specific additional procedures, such as those suggested below.

Payroll

- Agree the total wages and salaries expense per the payroll system to the general ledger and the financial statements: verifies **completeness** and **presentation.**
- Cast the monthly payroll listings to verify the accuracy of the payroll expense: verifies **accuracy.**
- Recalculate the gross and net pay for a sample of employees, and agree to the payroll records: verifies **accuracy.**
- Re-perform calculation of statutory deductions to confirm whether correct deductions for this year have been included within the payroll expense: verifies **accuracy.**
- Select a sample of joiners and leavers, agree their start/leaving date to supporting documentation, recalculate that their first/last pay packet was accurately calculated and recorded: verifies **completeness, occurrence, accuracy.**
- For salaries, agree the total net pay per the payroll records to the bank transfer listing of payments and to the cashbook: verifies **occurrence.**
- For wages, agree the total cash withdrawn for wage payments equates to the weekly wages paid plus any surplus cash subsequently banked: verifies **completeness, occurrence.**
- Agree the year-end tax liabilities to the payroll records, and subsequent payment to the post year-end cash book: verifies **occurrence.**
- Agree the individual wages and salaries per the payroll to the personnel records and records of hours worked per clocking in cards: verifies **accuracy.**

Analytical procedures

- Perform a proof in total of total wages and salaries, incorporating joiners and leavers and the pay increase. Compare this to the actual wages and salaries in the financial statements and investigate any significant differences: verifies **completeness, accuracy.**
- Compare the payroll figure for this year to last year to identify any unusual fluctuations and discuss them with management: verifies **completeness, accuracy.**

Case study: Murray Co payroll proof in total

Total payroll for the year ending 31 December 20X3 was $1,220,000 (to the nearest $000). At this time Murray Co had 34 employees.

Total payroll for the year ending 31 December 20X4 included in the draft financial statements of Murray Co is $1,312,000 (to the nearest $000). Murray Co now has 37 employees.

All employees received a 5% pay rise on 31 March 20X4.

Exercise:

Create an expectation of what total payroll will be for year ending 31 December 20X4.

Solution

The average salary per employee in 20X3 was $35,882 ($1,220,000/34). We know that all employees received a payrise for 9 months of 20X2 of 5%. The average value of this payrise is therefore $1,346 per employee in 20X4 (5%×9/12×$35,882).

The average salary for 20X4 should therefore equal $37,228 ($35,882+$1,346).

We can set an **expectation for total payroll for the year ending 31 December 20X4** as 37×$37,228: **$1,377,000** (to the nearest $000).

The **difference** ($65,000) is **less than 5%** more than our expectation, and we can therefore conclude that the payroll cost is materially correct.

Revenue

- Inspect a sample of GDNs before and after the year end and ensure they have been recorded in the correct period: verifies **cutoff**.
- Recalculate discounts and sales tax applied for a sample of large sales invoices: verifies **accuracy**.
- Select a sample of customer orders and agree these to the despatch notes and sales invoices through to inclusion in the sales day book: verifies **completeness**.
- Inspect credit notes issued after the year end, trace to GDN and invoice and ensure the sale has been reversed: verifies **occurrence**.

Analytical procedures

- Compare revenue against prior year and investigate any significant fluctuations: verifies **occurrence, accuracy and completeness.**
- Compare revenue with budget/forecast and investigate any significant fluctuations: verifies **occurrence, accuracy and completeness.**
- Calculate the gross profit margin and compare to prior year. Investigate any significant differences: verifies **occurrence, accuracy and completeness**.

Purchases and other expenses

- Inspect GRNs before and after the year end and ensure they have been recorded in the correct period: verifies **cutoff**.
- Recalculate discounts and sales tax applied for a sample of large purchase invoices: verifies **accuracy**.
- Select a sample of purchase orders and agree these to the GRNs and purchase invoices through to inclusion in the purchases day book: verifies **completeness**.

Analytical procedures

- Compare expenses for each category year on year and investigate any significant fluctuations: verifies **accuracy, completeness and occurrence**.
- Compare expenses against budget and investigate any significant fluctuations.

- Calculate gross profit margin and compare with prior year to identify any possible misstatement of purchases. Discuss any significant movement with management: verifies **accuracy, completeness and occurrence**.
- Calculate operating profit margin and compare with prior year. Investigate any significant fluctuations: verifies **accuracy, completeness and occurrence.**
- Inspect purchase invoices for a sample of purchases/expenses in the ledger for the amount, name of the client and description of the goods: verifies **accuracy, occurrence and classification**.

Smaller entities

The characteristics of smaller commercial entities can lead to both advantages and disadvantages:

- **Lower risk**: Smaller entities may well be engaged in activity that is relatively simple and therefore lower risk. However, this will not be true for small – often one person businesses – where there is a high level of expertise in a particular field, e.g. consultancy businesses, creative businesses, the financial sector.
- **Direct control by owner managers** can be a strength because they know what is going on and have the ability to exercise real control. However, they are also in a strong position to manipulate the figures or put private transactions 'through the books'.
- **Simpler systems**: Smaller entities are less likely to have sophisticated IT systems, but pure, manual systems are becoming increasingly rare. This is good news in that many of the bookkeeping errors associated with smaller entities may now be less prevalent. However, a system is only as good as the person operating it.

Evidence implications

- The normal rules concerning the relationship between risk and the quality and quantity of evidence apply irrespective of the size of the entity.
- The quantity of evidence may well be less than for a larger organisation.
- It may be more efficient to carry out 100% testing in a smaller organisation.

Problems

- **Management override** – Smaller entities will have a key director or manager who will have significant power and authority. This could mean that controls are lacking in the first place or they are easy to override.
- **No segregation of duties** – Smaller entities tend to have a limited number of accounts clerks who process information. To overcome this the directors should authorise and review all work performed.
- **Less formal approach** – Smaller entities tend to have simple systems and very few controls due to the trust and the lack of complexity. It is therefore difficult to test the reliability of systems and substantive testing tends to be used more.

Not-for-profit organisations

Not for profit (NFP) organisations include charities and public sector entities. Below are some important differences between NFP and privately owned companies.

- Profit maximisation is not their main objective. Objectives will be either social or philanthropic.
- There are no shareholders.
- They will not distribute dividends.

Financial statements

NFP organisations such as charities which are not established as charitable companies will need to prepare:

- A statement of financial activities – showing income and expenditure similar to a statement of profit or loss but as the organisation does not exist to make a profit, any additional income over expenditure is known as a surplus and any expenditure in excess of income is a deficit.
- A balance sheet – the same as a statement of financial position showing assets and liabilities.
- A cash flow statement.
- Notes to the financial statements.

Audit risks

Control risk

Some NFP entities, particularly small charities, may have weaker control systems due to:

- being controlled by trustees who usually only work on a part time basis and are volunteers. They may not devote sufficient time to adequately oversee the strategic direction of the organisation.
- a lack of segregation of duties, as the organisation may not employ many staff in order to keep overheads down.
- the use of volunteers, who are likely to be unqualified and have little awareness of the importance of controls.
- the use of less formalised systems and controls.

Income

Significantly, with many charities, much of the income received is by way of donation. Some of these transactions will not be accompanied by invoices, orders or despatch notes. For cash donations in particular there is a greater risk of theft.

NFPs may apply for grant income which will only be provided if certain criteria are met otherwise the money may have to be repaid. There is a risk that grant income may have to be repaid if the organisation does not use the money for its intended purpose.

Restricted funds

Some donations are given with clauses stating the money must be used for a particular reason. For example, money may be donated to a hospital for them to purchase a specific piece of equipment or to be used by a specific department. These restricted funds must be shown separately in the balance sheet and the auditor must review donations to ensure that restricted funds are shown as such.

Going concern

Assessing the going concern of a NFP entity may also be more difficult, particularly for charities who are reliant on voluntary donations. Many issues, such as the state of the economy, could impact on their ability to generate income in the short term. Trends can also have an effect. For example charities raising money for medical research such as cancer and heart disease are seeing higher numbers of donations whereas charities such as animal protection are seeing a decline in income.

Complexity of regulations

NFPs may have complex internal and external regulations governing their activities, reporting requirements and taxation system. This will mean the audit team should have knowledge of these regulations and experience of auditing this type of specialised entity in order to be able to perform the audit with sufficient competence and due care.

Other planning activities

In addition to the specific audit risks that need to be considered at the risk assessment stage, the same planning activities are required as for the audit of a company. Differences that will require consideration are:

- Materiality assessment may be lower to address the higher risk and therefore more testing.
- The choice of audit team staff should include staff with experience of this type of entity and knowledge of the regulations and financial reporting requirements.

Audit testing

Sufficient appropriate evidence will still need to be obtained through either a mixture of tests of controls and substantive procedures or just substantive procedures if the controls are ineffective or not in place.

Procedures will still involve enquiries, inspection, analytical procedures, etc.

Testing tends to concentrate on substantive procedures where control systems are lacking.

Reporting

If sufficient appropriate evidence is not obtained with respect to the above matters as well as the usual risks of material misstatement faced by any organisation, the auditor will have to modify their audit report.

Other reporting responsibilities

Quite often, the scope of the external audit of a NFP is much larger than that for a company.

Auditors of not for profit organisations may be required to perform additional assignments such as:

- Value for money audits – assessing whether the organisation is getting the most out of the money spent. These are discussed in more detail in the internal audit chapter.
- Regularity audits – ensuring the expenditure of the organisation is in accordance with the regulations/legislation governing it.
- Performance indicators – auditing the targets of the organisation that have to be reported to stakeholders such as waiting times in an A&E department. This is covered in the P7 syllabus.

Test your understanding 1

(a) **List and explain FOUR assertions from ISA 315 *Identifying and Assessing the Risk of Material Misstatement Through Understanding the Entity and its Environment* that relate to the recording of classes of transactions.**

(4 marks)

(b) **List FOUR assertions relevant to the audit of tangible non-current assets and state one audit procedure which provides appropriate evidence for each assertion.**

(4 marks)

Test your understanding 2

You are an audit senior working at a medium sized firm of auditors. One of your clients is an exclusive hotel called 'Numero Uno' situated in the centre of Big City.

Numero Uno prides itself on delivering a first class dining experience and is renowned for its standards of service and cooking that few restaurants in the country come close to. Its inventory therefore consists of the very best foods and beverages from across the globe.

Food products held in inventory are mostly fresh as the head chef will only work with the very best ingredients. Food inventory is stored in the kitchens and managed by the head chef himself.

The majority of beverages held at the hotel are expensive wines that have been sourced from exclusive vineyards. The hotel also stocks a wide range of spirits and mixers. All beverages are stored either in the hotel cellar or behind the bar. The cellar can only be accessed by the duty manager who holds the key. As part of your audit procedures you will attend the year end inventory count of the hotel's beverages.

Required:

(a) **Describe the audit procedures an auditor would conduct before and whilst attending the inventory count of the beverages in the hotel.**

(7 marks)

(b) **Identify and explain THREE financial statement assertions that are most relevant to inventory.**

(3 marks)

(c) **Apart from attending the inventory count, describe the substantive procedures an auditor would carry out to confirm the valuation of the wine and spirits held in inventory at the year end.**

(5 marks)

(Total: 15 marks)

Test your understanding 3

(a) **Describe the steps an auditor should take when conducting a trade receivables confirmation (circularisation) test.**

(4 marks)

(b) **Explain why a direct confirmation test may not provide sufficient appropriate audit evidence on its own.**

(3 marks)

You are the audit manager in charge of the audit of Builders Mate, a limited liability company. The company's year end is 31 March, and Builders Mate has been an audit client for three years. Builders Mate sells small tools, plant and equipment exclusively to the building trade. They have 12 warehouse style shops located throughout the country. Builders Mate does not manufacture any products themselves.

The audit fieldwork is due to commence in 3 weeks time and you are preparing the audit work programme for the trade receivables section of the audit. Extracts from the clients trial balance show the following information.

	$
Trade receivables control account	124,500
General trade receivables allowance	(2,490)
Specific trade receivables allowance	0

From your review of last year's audit file you have determined that last year there were 2 specific allowances of $5k and $2k as well as a 3% general allowance.

Initial conversations with the client indicate that there are no specific allowances that are to be made this year however they intend to reduce the general allowance from 3% to 2%.

You are aware that two of Builders Mate's major customers went into administration during the year and they are likely to be liquidated in the near future. Both of these customers owed material amounts at the year-end.

Required:

(c) **Describe substantive procedures the auditor should perform on the year-end trade receivables of Builders Mate.**

(9 marks)

(d) **Describe how audit software could facilitate the audit of trade receivables.**

(4 marks)

(Total: 20 marks)

Test your understanding 4

You are the auditor of BearsWorld, a limited liability company which manufactures and sells small cuddly toys by mail order. The company is managed by Mr Kyto and two assistants. Mr Kyto authorises important transactions such as wages and large orders, one assistant maintains the payables ledger and orders inventory and pays suppliers, and the other assistant receives customer orders and despatches cuddly toys. Due to other business commitments Mr Kyto only visits the office once per week.

At any time, about 100 different types of cuddly toys are available for sale. All sales are made cash with order – there are no receivables. Customers pay using credit cards and occasionally by sending cash. Revenue is over $5.2 million.

You are planning the audit of BearsWorld and are considering using some of the procedures for gathering audit evidence recommended by ISA 500 as follows:

(i) Analytical procedures

(ii) Inquiry

(iii) Inspection

(iv) Observation

(v) Re-calculation

Required:

(a) **For EACH of the above procedures:**

(i) **Explain its use in gathering audit evidence.**

(5 marks)

(ii) **Describe one example for the audit of BearsWorld.**

(5 marks)

(b) **Explain the limitations of each procedure for BearsWorld.**

(5 marks)

(c) **Explain FIVE key features of small companies such as BearsWorld and the impact these may have on your audit work.**

(5 marks)

(Total: 20 marks)

Test your understanding 5 – OT Case 1

You are auditing the revenue section of the financial statements of Ningaloo Co. Tests of controls have been performed and have been evaluated as effective. Substantive procedures have not yet been performed. During the risk assessment you identified that a performance related bonus has been introduced for salesmen who reach a target sales figure each quarter.

(1) Which of the following statements is correct?

A As controls are working effectively within Ningaloo Co the audit plan does not need to contain any substantive procedures as full reliance can be placed on the control system

B The auditor will perform the same level of substantive procedures as were performed in the prior year

C The level of substantive procedures may be reduced as a result of the controls being found to work effectively

D The level of substantive procedures should increase if controls are found to be working effectively

(2) 'Select a sample of goods despatched notes from just before and just after the year end and trace to the sales day book'. Which of the financial statement assertions does the described audit procedure help to confirm?

A Occurrence

B Completeness

C Cut-off

D Accuracy

(3) Which of the following statements is correct with regard to directional testing?

A A procedure that directly tests receivables for overstatement would indirectly test revenue for understatement

B A procedure that directly tests receivables for overstatement would indirectly test revenue for overstatement

C To test revenue for overstatement the auditor must choose a sample from outside of the accounting system, such as GDNS, and trace them into the accounting system

D To test revenue for understatement the auditor must choose a sample from within the accounting system and trace it to the GDN

(4) Which of the following is an analytical procedure that can be used to test revenue?

A Comparison of revenue in the current year to revenue in the prior year

B Review of credit notes issued post year end

C Inspection of a sample of goods despatch notes and sales invoices

D Recalculation of the sales day book

(5) Sales managers have recorded fictitious sales in order to earn a larger bonus. Which of the following assertions is affected by this?

A Existence

B Completeness

C Accuracy

D Occurrence

Test your understanding 6 – OT Case 2

You are performing procedures over the non-current assets balance for your client Leveque Co. The balance consists of motor vehicles, fixtures and fittings and land and buildings. Motor vehicles are replaced on a three year cycle. Fixtures and fittings are replaced as and when required. The company uses the following depreciation rates:

- Land and buildings – no depreciation is charged due to values increasing
- Fixtures and fittings – 10% straight line
- Motor vehicles – 20% straight line

(1) Which of the following best describes the audit risk resulting from the depreciation policy used for land and buildings?

A Land and buildings may not exist

B Land and buildings may not be completely recorded

C Land and buildings may be understated

D Land and buildings may be overstated

(2) Which of the following procedures provides the most reliable evidence to assess whether 10% straight line is an appropriate rate for fixtures and fittings?

A Enquire of the client whether the rate is appropriate and how they chose that rate

B Contact the supplier of the fixtures to ask how long the fixtures should last

C Review disposals of fixtures and fittings to identify how long they had been used by Leveque and whether any significant profit or loss on disposal arose

D Compare the rate with other audit clients of your firm

(3) Which of the following statements is true in respect of Leveque's motor vehicles?

A The depreciation rate is unreasonable as the company only uses the assets for three years therefore depreciation should be charged over three years

B Motor vehicles have a useful life of longer than five years therefore depreciation should be charged over a longer period

C The depreciation rate is reasonable

D The depreciation charge for motor vehicles is unlikely to be material therefore the rate used does not matter

(4) The audit plan includes a procedure to trace a sample of assets included in the non-current asset register to the physical asset. Which assertion is being tested?

A Existence

B Completeness

C Valuation

D Rights and obligations

(5) Which of the following procedures helps to confirm rights and obligations over non-current assets?

A Physical inspection of the assets

B Inspection of the fixtures and fittings invoice

C Inspection of a valuation report for land and buildings

D Written representation from management confirming ownership

Test your understanding 7 – OT Case 3

You are assigned to the audit team of Carnarvon Co performing testing over non-current assets.

(1) Which of the following is not an audit procedure from ISA 500 *Audit Evidence*?

A Inspection

B Enquiry

C Check

D Recalculate

(2) Which of the following audit procedures would confirm the existence of property, plant and equipment?

A Recalculation of depreciation using the company's accounting policy

B Physical inspection of a sample of assets listed on the non-current asset register

C Reconcile the schedule of property, plant and equipment with the general ledger

D Review the repairs and maintenance expense account in the statement of profit or loss for items of a capital nature.

(3) Which of the following is NOT a financial statement assertion relevant to your testing of non-current assets?

A Occurrence

B Completeness

C Rights and obligations

D Existence

(4) Which of the following issues would result in a misstatement in the non-current assets balance?

(i) An error in recording the cost of the asset

(ii) A misclassification between fixtures & fittings and motor vehicles

(iii) The depreciation charge has been correctly credited to accumulated depreciation but debited to the irrecoverable debt expense account

(iv) A purchase invoice not being recorded in the asset register

A (ii) and (iv)

B (i) and (iii)

C (ii) and (iii)

D (i) and (iv)

(5) When testing the assertion of rights and obligations over land and buildings, which of the following would provide the most reliable evidence?

A Inspection of the insurance policy

B Physical inspection of the land and buildings

C Inspection of the title deeds

D Inspection of the non-current asset register

11 Chapter summary

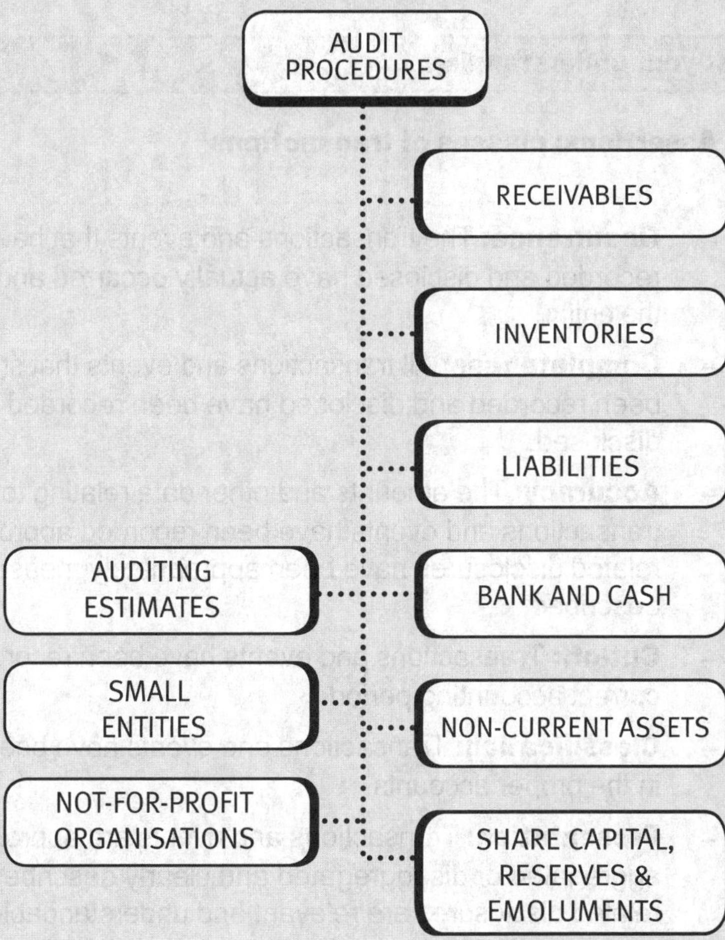

Test your understanding answers

Test your understanding 1

(a) **Assertions: classes of transactions**

- **Occurrence:** The transactions and events that have been recorded and disclosed have actually occurred and pertain to the entity.
- **Completeness:** All transactions and events that should have been recorded and disclosed have been recorded and disclosed.
- **Accuracy:** The amounts and other data relating to recorded transactions and events have been recorded appropriately and related disclosures have been appropriately measured and described.
- **Cut-off:** Transactions and events have been recorded in the correct accounting period.
- **Classification:** Transactions and events have been recorded in the proper accounts.
- **Presentation:** Transactions and events are appropriately aggregated or disaggregated and clearly described, and related disclosures are relevant and understandable in the context of the applicable financial reporting framework.

Note: Only four assertions were required.

(b) **Tangible non-current assets: assertions**

- **Completeness**: Agree a sample of assets physically verified on the premises back to the asset register to ensure that all non-current assets are recorded.
- **Existence**: Physically inspect a sample of assets included on the non-current asset register to verify existence.
- **Accuracy**, **valuation and allocation**: Recalculate the depreciation charge to ensure arithmetical accuracy.
- **Rights and obligations**: Inspect appropriate document of ownership for example, a purchase invoice, for the client's name to confirm the entity owns or controls the asset.
- **Classification/Presentation:** Inspect the non-current asset disclosure note in the financial statements and agree the figures to the non-current asset register to ensure assets are properly disclosed under the correct headings as required by IAS 16 *Property, plant and equipment*.

Test your understanding 2

(a) **Procedures before the count**

- Inspect prior year working papers to understand the inventory count process and identify any issues that would need to be taken into account this year.
- Contact Numero Uno (client) to obtain inventory count instructions for this year to understand how the count will be conducted and assess the effectiveness of the count process.
- Book audit staff to attend the inventory count.
- Ascertain whether any inventory is held by third parties determine how to gather sufficient appropriate evidence e.g. by visiting the premises or requesting an external confirmation.
- Consider the need for using an expert to assist in valuing the inventory being counted. There may be some speciality wines and spirits that require expert valuation.

During the count

- Observe the count to ensure that the instructions are being followed.
- Inspect the bottles being counted for evidence of damage or obsolescence that may affect the net realisable value and hence overall valuation of inventory.
- Select a sample of beverages from the inventory count sheets and physically observe the items in the cellar or bar to confirm they exist.
- Select a sample of physical beverages from the cellar or bar and trace to the inventory count sheets to ensure that they are recorded accurately and therefore that the records are complete.
- Record cut off information by obtaining details of the last deliveries prior to the year end. This information will be used in final audit procedures to ensure that no further amendments have been made thereby overstating or understating inventory.

(b) **Inventory assertions**

Identify	**Explain**
Existence	To confirm whether the inventory recorded actually exists.
Rights and obligations	To confirm whether the company owners or controls the asset and therefore has the right to record the inventories in its financial statements.
Completeness	To confirm if all inventory balances have been recorded.
Accuracy, valuation and allocation	To assess whether all inventories are valued appropriately (i.e. at the lower of cost and net realisable value and net of any provisions for damaged and slow moving goods).
Cut-off	To ensure that all inventory movements around the year-end are recorded in the correct period.
Presentation	To ensure inventory is disclosed properly in the financial statements as raw materials, work in progress and finished goods.

(c) **Substantive procedures**

- Trace the items counted during the inventory count to the final inventory list to ensure it is the same as the one used at the year-end and to ensure that any errors identified during counting procedures have been rectified.
- Inspect purchases invoices for a sample of beverages to agree their cost, ensuring that the description of goods on the invoice matches the beverage.
- For beverages sold to customers after the year end, inspect a sample of restaurant bills/invoices back to the final inventory records ensuring that the sales value exceeds the cost. Where sales value is less than cost, ensure that the beverage is stated at the realisable value.
- For high value items such as Champagne, vintage wine and exotic spirits use an expert valuer to review the net realisable value of a sample of items to ensure the value is reasonable.
- Inventory noted during the count as possibly obsolete or damaged should be traced to the inventory records to ensure the valuation has been adjusted to take this into account. The expert valuer may provide assistance with these valuations.

Test your understanding 3

(a) **Trade receivables circularisation**

Several steps should be performed by an auditor when performing a trade receivables circularisation audit test:

- Audit client approval should be obtained in advance to perform the direct confirmation test of trade receivables.
- Obtain a list of receivables balances, and cast it.
- Select a suitable sample from the list of receivables balances using an appropriate sampling technique.
- The confirmation letter should be designed and prepared for each receivable ensuring the contact details are correct and return details clearly state that the reply should be made direct to the auditor.
- A business reply envelope, addressed to the auditor, could be included for this purpose.
- The letter should be printed on client-headed paper and signed by the client, and then passed to the auditor.
- The sending of letters, including any follow-up requests, should be controlled and performed by the auditor to ensure the integrity of the test.
- Replies should be matched or reconciled to the audit client's receivables accounting records.
- Alternative audit procedures will be required for all non-responses to the confirmation letter.

(b) **Sufficiency of the evidence from a direct confirmation test**

Several factors influence the sufficiency of evidence gathered during a direct confirmation of trade receivables and other evidence may be required by an auditor to form an opinion in this area:

- There is often a low response rate from trade receivables meaning that other audit procedures will be required for these balances.
- The type of confirmation letter, whether a positive or negative confirmation request, will influence the sufficiency of evidence gathered. Negative confirmations provide less persuasive audit evidence than positive confirmations and it is unlikely that a negative confirmation will provide sufficient evidence on its own.
- The reliability of the responses to the confirmation requests may be in doubt for example if there is a risk of fraud being perpetrated.

- Mistakes and errors may be present in the accounting records of the trade receivables confirming the balance outstanding.
- Customers may agree with balances containing errors in their favour.

(c) **Substantive procedures for trade receivables**

- Obtain the receivables listing, cast it to verify arithmetical accuracy and agree the total to the financial statements.
- Confirm the trade receivables control account balance matches the sum of the individual trade receivables ledger accounts.
- For a sample goods dispatched notes around the year-end trace to the sales invoice and ledger accounts to ensure that the transactions have been recorded in the correct accounting period.
- Select a sample of individual trade receivables and perform a direct confirmation test using a positive confirmation letter.
- For non-responses to the direct confirmation test confirm cash has been received post year-end for the outstanding amounts.
- Cash receipts recorded in the trade receivables ledger account should be traced and agreed to their remittance advice as well as the cash book and bank statements.
- Recalculate the general allowance based on the 2% figure to ensure arithmetical accuracy.
- Discuss with the Builders Mate management why the general allowance has reduced from 3% to 2% and assess the reasonableness of the explanations provided and the reason for not making specific allowances for the two customers in administration who owe material amounts at the year-end.
- Inspect the aged receivables analysis to identify aged debts that may require a specific allowance. Discuss with management any such balances and ensure specific allowances are made if appropriate.
- Trace and confirm that the specific allowances made in the prior year were either written off or the cash was recovered in the current accounting period.
- Consider and discuss with management the potential implications of failing to make specific allowances on the audit opinion.
- Compare a sample of individual trade receivables to their prior year balance and investigate any unusual or unexpected changes between the balances.

(d) **Audit software**

Audit software can be used to improve the effectiveness and efficiency of the audit process of trade receivables.

- Audit software can be used to prepare an aged receivables analysis and to identify potential irrecoverable debts using a range of criteria set by the auditor.
- It can analyse the receivables ledger for credit balances or negative balances.
- Audit software will be more efficient and accurate at casting and recalculating figures, totals and balances such as the general allowance or casting of the receivables ledgers.
- It could also select a sample for testing and prepare direct confirmation letters.

Test your understanding 4

(a) Audit procedures

(i) *Analytical procedures* consist of evaluations of financial information made by a study of plausible relationships among both financial and non-financial data.

Inquiry means to seek relevant information from sources, both financial and non-financial, either inside or outside the company being audited. Evidence may be obtained orally or in writing.

Inspection is the physical review or examination of records, documents and tangible assets. It may include examination of records for evidence of controls in the form of a compliance test.

Observation involves looking at a process or procedure as it is being performed to ensure that the process actually works as documented.

Re-calculation means the checking of the mathematical accuracy of documents or records.

(ii) *Analytical procedures*

Compare revenue year on year to try to identify whether income has been understated, possibly by cash being taken prior to banking. There is no control over the opening of post so cash could be withdrawn by one assistant, and the deficit made up by a fraud on customers.

Inquiry

Obtain statements from suppliers to check the completeness of liabilities at the end of the year. As there is no control over purchases, invoices could have been misplaced resulting in a lower purchases and trade payables figure.

Inspection

The assets of the company, namely cuddly toys in inventory at the end of the year, can be inspected to ensure all inventory is recorded and that the toys are saleable in their current condition.

Observation

Procedures such as the opening of the post and recording of customer orders can be observed to ensure that the administrator is recording all orders in the sales day book and cash book.

Recalculation

Recalculating the cash book to confirm that the total amount of cash recorded is accurate and can be included in the revenue figure (cash receipts should equal revenue as there are no receivables).

(b) *Analytical procedures*

This method of collecting evidence will be useful in BearsWorld because it will help to identify unusual changes in income and expenditure. As BearsWorld is a relatively small company, monitoring gross profit will show relatively small changes in sales margin or purchasing costs. Decisions by Mr Kyto to amend margins can therefore be traced into the actual sales made.

However, the technique may be limited in its application because it will not detect errors or omissions made consistently year on year. If either assistant is defrauding the company (for example by removing cash) each year, then analytical procedures will not detect this.

Enquiry

Enquiry evidence will be very useful in the audit of BearsWorld, especially where this is derived from third parties. Third party evidence is generally more reliable than client originated evidence as there is a decreased likelihood of bias. Trade payables can therefore be verified using supplier statement reconciliations. A review of any customer complaints file (if these letters are kept) will also help to identify any orders that have not been despatched.

External inquiry evidence will be less useful in the audit of sales and receivables because goods are paid for prior to despatch – there are no receivables. Internal evidence will be available from Mr Kyto and the assistant; however the lack of segregation of duties means that this may not be so reliable.

Inspection

Inspection of documents within BearsWorld will be useful, particularly regarding checking whether expenses are bona fide. All purchase invoices, for example, should be addressed to BearsWorld and relate to purchases expected from that company, e.g. cuddly toys for resale, office expenses, etc.

Inspection of documents can take a long time; however, given the poor internal control system within BearsWorld, the auditor may have no choice but to use this method of gathering evidence.

The fact that an invoice is addressed to the company does not confirm completeness of recording so inspection of the cash book for unusual payments verified by checking the purchase invoice will also be required. Additional substantive testing would also be required due to poor controls.

Observation

Observation may be useful because it will show how the assistants check documents. However, no information is provided on any internal controls within BearsWorld so simply viewing how documents are checked without any evidence of checking has limited benefit.

Observation tests will be of limited usefulness because the assistants may act differently when an auditor is present. The same problem will apply to any observation checking carried out by Mr Kyto.

Recalculation

Recalculation evidence is very useful for checking additions on invoices, balancing of control accounts, etc. This means that the arithmetical accuracy of the books and records in BearsWorld can be confirmed.

The main weakness of recalculation checking is that calculations can only be carried out on figures that have been recorded. If there are any omissions then checks cannot be carried out.

(c) **Features of small companies**

Feature	Effect on audit
Concentration of ownership and management in one/few people.	There is likely to be more supervision, since the owner will want to protect his investment. But there is an increased risk of fraud by the owner as he may not distinguish between personal/business assets.
Less complicated business activities.	Easier for auditor to gain an understanding of the business and assess risk.
Less sophisticated accounting systems.	Auditor unlikely to use CAATs.
Limited internal controls as less segregation of duties and management can override.	Unlikely to rely on controls. Likely to perform extensive substantive testing.
Unlikely to have a qualified accountant.	Audit firm is likely to prepare the financial statements prior to the audit. This means they should be prepared with due care, but the auditor must be careful to check just as thoroughly as if the accounts had been prepared by someone else. Different staff should be used for the audit and the accounts preparation to safeguard against the self review threat.

Test your understanding 5 – OT Case 1

(1)	C	Substantive procedures must be performed on all material balances even if controls are working effectively. This is due to the inherent limitations of controls. However, the level may be reduced if controls are found to be effective.
(2)	C	Selecting transactions around the year end tests the assertion of cut-off.
(3)	B	If the receivable was overstated the related sale would also be overstated. To test for overstatement the auditor must choose a sample from within the accounting system and trace it back to supporting documentation.
(4)	A	B, C and D are all substantive tests of detail as they focus attention on individual sales transactions. Comparison of sales in the current year to the prior year is an analytical procedure as it is focused on identifying unusual trends or fluctuations that appear unusual which may indicate misstatement.
(5)	D	Occurrence. The transaction will not have occurred if it is fictitious. Existence is not relevant to the statement of profit or loss.

Test your understanding 6 – OT Case 2

(1)	D	Depreciation affects the valuation assertion therefore A and B are incorrect. If depreciation has not been charged the assets will be overvalued therefore overstated.
(2)	C	Enquiry is not the most reliable form of evidence and should be corroborated with other procedures. The auditor would not contact the supplier and this would not provide evidence of the useful life of the fixtures to Leveque. Comparison with other clients is only useful if those clients are in the same type of industry and using the same type of assets in the same manner as Leveque.
(3)	A	The depreciation rate should match the usage of the asset by the company therefore the rate should be based on 3 years not 5 years. As no figures are given for the motor vehicles it cannot be said that depreciation will be immaterial.
(4)	A	Testing from the ledger to the source addresses the assertion of existence.
(5)	B	Physical inspection verifies existence. A valuation certificate verifies the valuation of the land and buildings. Neither of these procedures confirms the assets are owned or controlled by Leveque. Written confirmation is not a reliable form of evidence for the assertion of rights and obligations as better procedures can be performed. The purchase invoice for fixtures and fittings should contain the name of the client which would help verify rights and obligations.

Test your understanding 7 – OT Case 3

(1)	C	Check is not a valid procedure. Every procedure 'checks' something. The auditor can check through inspection, enquiry, observation, etc.
(2)	B	A tests the accuracy of a depreciation charge. C and D test the completeness of PPE. B confirms existence.
(3)	A	Occurrence is an assertion relevant to the statement of profit or loss, not the statement of financial position.
(4)	D	A misclassification between motor vehicles and fixtures & fittings will not affect the overall non-current assets balance. The depreciation charge has been correctly credited to accumulated depreciation therefore the asset's carrying value will be correctly calculated. The mis-posting to irrecoverable debt expense will mean the classification of the expense in the statement of profit or loss is incorrect. An error recording the cost of the asset will mean asset is misstated. If the purchase invoice relating to the asset is not recorded, assets will be understated.
(5)	C	The other 3 procedures do not confirm the client owns or controls the assets. The title deeds in the client's name will confirm ownership.

chapter

9

Completion and review

Chapter learning objectives

This chapter covers syllabus areas:

- E1 – Subsequent events
- E2 – Going concern
- E3 – Written representations
- E4 – Audit finalisation and the final review

Detailed syllabus objectives are provided in the introduction section of the text book.

1 Introduction

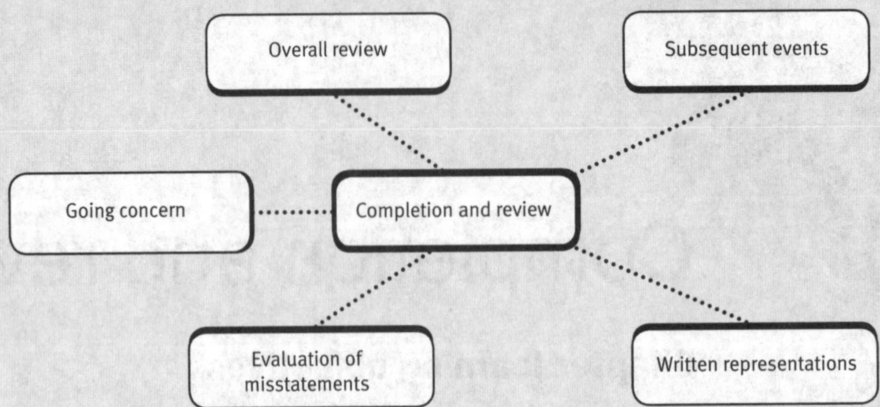

After the auditor has completed their substantive testing there are still many procedures that need to be performed before they can sign the audit report. These include:

- Subsequent events review
- Going concern review
- Obtaining written representations
- Overall review
- Evaluation of misstatements.

2 ISA 560 Subsequent events

Purpose

ISA 560 *Subsequent Events* requires the auditor to obtain sufficient appropriate evidence that events occurring between the date of the financial statements and the date of the auditor's report have been appropriately accounted for in accordance with IAS 10 *Events After the Reporting Period*.

The auditor must respond appropriately to facts that become known after the date of the auditor's report which may have caused them to amend their report if they were known at the date of the report.

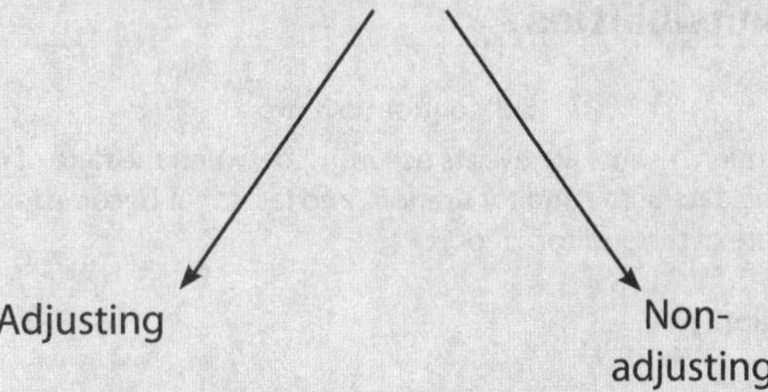

- **Adjusting** – events providing additional evidence relating to conditions existing at the reporting date they require **adjustment** in the financial statements.

- **Non-adjusting** – events concerning conditions which arose after the reporting date, but which may be of such materiality that **disclosure** is required to ensure that the financial statements are not misleading.

Examples

✓ Trade receivables going bad
✓ Credit notes relating to sales made before the reporting date
✓ Inventory at the year end sold lower than cost

Examples

✓ Take over
✓ Legal issues after the year end
✓ A fire after the year end

If a non-adjusting event impacts the going concern assumption, the event becomes an adjusting event as the going concern basis of preparation may no longer be appropriate.

For example, if the non-adjusting event is a fire which destroys the premises and inventory and adequate insurance is not in place, the company may not be able to replace the plant and equipment or inventory it needs to trade. It may not be able to buy or lease premises from which to operate. In this case, the financial statements would have to be prepared on a break up basis.

Auditor responsibilities

Subsequent events

Definition: Subsequent events are events occurring between the date of the financial statements and the date of the auditor's report, and facts that become known to the auditor after the date of the auditor's report

Auditors responsibility

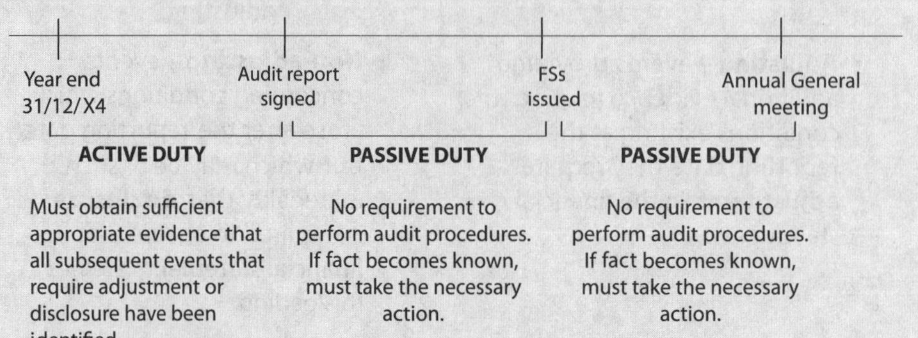

Between the date of the financial statements and the date of the auditor's report

- The auditor must perform audit procedures to ensure the client has complied with the correct accounting treatment of IAS 10.
- If material adjusting events are not adjusted for, or material non-adjusting events are not disclosed, the auditor will ask management to make the necessary amendments to the financial statements.
- A written representation from management should be obtained stating that all events requiring adjustment or disclosure have been adjusted or disclosed.
- If management refuse to amend the financial statements, the auditor should consider the implication for their audit report.
- If the matter is material, the audit report should be modified with either a qualified or adverse opinion depending on whether the matter is material or material and pervasive.

Between the date of the auditor's report and the date the financial statements are issued

- The auditor is under no obligation to perform audit procedures after the audit report has been issued, however, if they become aware of a fact which would cause them to issue a modified report, they must take action.
- The auditor should discuss the matter with management and consider if the financial statements require amendment.

- Request management to make the necessary amendments.
- Perform audit procedures on those amendments to ensure they have been put through correctly.
- Issue a new auditor's report.
- If management does not amend the financial statements and the audit report has not yet been issued to the client, the auditor can still modify the opinion.
- If the audit report has been provided to the client, the auditor shall notify management and those charged with governance not to issue the financial statements before the amendments are made.
- If the client issues the financial statements despite being requested not to by the auditor, the auditor shall take action to prevent reliance on the auditor's report.

After the financial statements are issued

- The auditor is under no obligation to perform audit procedures after the financial statements have been issued, however, if they become aware of a fact which would have caused them to modify their report, they must take action.
- The auditor should discuss the matter with management and consider if the financial statements require amendment.
- Request management to make the necessary amendments. Management must also take the necessary actions to ensure anyone who is in receipt of the previously issued financial statements is informed.
- The auditor should perform audit procedures on the amendments to ensure they have been put through correctly.
- Issue a new auditor's report including an emphasis of matter paragraph to draw attention to the fact that the financial statements and audit report have been reissued.
- If management refuses to recall and amend the financial statements, the auditor shall take action to prevent reliance on the auditor's report.

Audit procedures

- Enquiring of directors if they are aware of any subsequent events that require adjustment in the financial statements.
- Enquiring into management's procedures for the identification of subsequent events.
- Inspection of minutes of members' and directors' meetings.
- Reviewing accounting records including budgets, forecasts and interim information.
- Obtaining written representation from management that all subsequent events have been considered in the preparation of the financial statements.
- Inspection of correspondence with legal advisors.
- Enquiring of the progress with regards to reported provisions and contingencies.
- 'Normal' post reporting period work performed in order to verify year-end balances:
  - Inspecting after date receipts from receivables.
  - Inspecting the cash book for payments/receipts that were not accrued for at the year-end.
  - Inspecting the sales price of inventories.

Test your understanding 1

Murray case study: Subsequent events review for the year ended 31 December 20X4

(1) On 2 January 20X5, Golf is Us, a major customer of Murray Co, was placed into administration owing $211,000.

(2) On 3 January 20X5, the sales director left the company. The sales director is suing Murray Co for constructive dismissal. If successful, the claim amounts to $280,000.

(3) On 5 February 20X5 there was a fire at the premises of the third party warehouse provider, which destroyed all inventory held there. Approximately one half of Murray Co's inventory was stored in these premises. The total value of inventory stored at the premises was $1,054,000.

(4) The financial statements include a $40,000 provision for an unfair dismissal case brought by an ex-employee of Murray Co. On 7 February 20X5 a letter was received from the claimant's solicitors stating that they would be willing to settle out-of-court for $25,000. It is likely the company will agree to this.

Financial statement extracts	31 Dec 20X4	31 Dec 20X3
	$000	$000
Revenue	21,960	19,580
Total assets	9,697	7,288
Profit before tax	1,048	248

Exercise:

For each of the events above:

Discuss whether the financial statements require amendment.

3 Going concern

The going concern concept

Going concern is defined as the assumption that the entity will continue in business for the foreseeable future.

The period that management (and therefore the auditor) is required to consider is the period required by the applicable financial reporting framework or by law or regulation if longer. Generally the period is a minimum of twelve months from the year end. In some jurisdictions (e.g. the United Kingdom) the period is a minimum of twelve months from the date the financial statements are approved.

- Consideration of the foreseeable future involves making a judgment about future events, which are inherently uncertain.
- Uncertainty increases with time and judgments can only be made on the basis of information available at any point. Subsequent events can overturn that judgment.

The going concern concept – significance

Whether or not a company can be classed as a going concern affects how its financial statements are prepared.

- Financial statements are prepared on the basis that the reporting entity is a going concern.
- IAS1 *Presentation of financial statements*, states that an entity should prepare its financial statements on a going concern basis, unless
  - management intends to liquidate the entity or to cease trading or
  - the directors have no realistic alternative but to do so.

- Where the assumption is made that the company will cease trading, the financial statements are prepared using the **break-up or liquidation basis** under which:
  - the basis of preparation and the reason why the entity is not regarded as a going concern are disclosed.
  - assets are recorded at likely sale values.
  - inventory and receivables may need to be written down as inventory may be sold for a lower price or may be scrapped, and receivables may not pay if they know the company is ceasing to trade.
  - additional liabilities may arise (redundancy costs for staff, the costs of closing down facilities, etc.).

Responsibilities for going concern

Director's responsibilities in respect of going concern

- It is the directors' responsibility to assess the company's ability to continue as a going concern when they are preparing the financial statements.
- In order to do this the directors should prepare forecasts to help assess whether they are likely to be able to continue trading for the next 12 months as a minimum.
- If they are aware of any material uncertainties which may affect this assessment, IAS 1 requires them to disclose such uncertainties in the financial statements.
- When the directors are performing their assessment they should take into account a number of relevant factors such as:
  - current and expected profitability
  - debt repayment
  - sources (and potential sources) of financing.

Auditor's responsibilities in respect of going concern

ISA 570 (Revised) *Going Concern* states that the auditor shall:

- obtain sufficient appropriate evidence regarding the appropriateness of management's use of the going concern basis of accounting in the preparation of the financial statements.
- conclude on whether a material uncertainty exists about the entity's ability to continue as a going concern.
- report in accordance with ISA 570.

Indicators of going concern problems

Typical indicators and explanations of going concern problems include the following:

- Net current liabilities (or net liabilities overall): indicates an inability to meet debts as they fall due.
- Borrowing facilities not agreed or close to expiry of current agreement: lack of access to cash may make it difficult for a company to manage its operating cycle.
- Defaulted loan agreements: loans normally become repayable on default, the company may find it difficult to repay loan.
- Unplanned sales of non-current assets: indicates an inability to generate cash from other means and as non-current assets generate income, will cause a decline in income and therefore profits.
- Missing tax payments: results in fines and penalties, companies normally prioritise tax payments indicating a lack of working capital.
- Failure to pay the staff: indicates a significant lack of working capital.
- Negative cash flow: indicates overtrading.
- Inability to obtain credit from suppliers: suggests failure to pay suppliers on time and working capital problems.
- Major technology changes: inability or insufficient funds to keep up with changes in technology will result in loss of custom and obsolescence of inventory.
- Legal claims: successful legal claims may result in significant cash payments that can only be settled with liquidation.
- Loss of key staff: may result inability to trade.
- Over-reliance on a small number of products, staff, suppliers or customers: loss may result in inability to trade.
- Customers ceasing to trade or having cash flow difficulties: likely to become a bad debt and therefore payment won't be received.
- Emergence of a successful competitor: will impact revenue if customers switch.
- Uninsured/under-insured catastrophes: the company may not have enough cash to survive.
- Changes in laws and regulations: the cost of compliance may be more than the company can afford.

Audit procedures

Audit procedures to assess management's evaluation of going concern

- Evaluate management's assessment of going concern.
- Assess the same period that management have used in their assessment and if this is less than 12 months, ask management to extend their assessment.
- Consider whether management's assessment includes all relevant information.

Audit procedures to perform where there is doubt over going concern

- Analyse and discuss cash flow, profit and other relevant forecasts with management.
- Analyse and discuss the entity's latest available interim financial statements.
- Review the terms of debentures and loan agreements and determining whether any have been breached.
- Read minutes of the meetings of shareholders, the board of directors and important committees for reference to financing difficulties.
- Enquire of the entity's lawyer regarding the existence of litigation and claims and the reasonableness of management's assessments of their outcome and the estimate of their financial implications.
- Confirm the existence, legality and enforceability of arrangements to provide or maintain financial support with related and third parties and assessing the financial ability of such parties to provide additional funds.
- Review events after the period end to identify those that either mitigate or otherwise affect the entity's ability to continue as a going concern.
- Review correspondence with customers for evidence of any disputes that might impact recoverability of debts and affect future sales.
- Review correspondence with suppliers for evidence of issues regarding payments that might impact the company's ability to obtain supplies or credit.
- Review correspondence with the bank for indication that a bank loan or overdraft may be recalled.
- Obtain written representations from management regarding its plans for the future and how it plans to address the going concern issues.

Exam tip

Audit procedures should focus on cash flows rather than profits. A company can continue to trade as long as it can pay its debts when they fall due. Therefore identify procedures to obtain evidence about the amount of cash that is likely to be received and the amount of cash that it likely to be paid out and consider whether there is any indication of cash flow difficulties.

Disclosures

Where there is any significant doubt over the future of a company, the directors should include disclosure in the financial statements explaining:

- the principal events or conditions that cast significant doubt on the entity's ability to continue as a going concern and management's plans to deal with them.
- the company may be unable to realise its assets and discharge its liabilities in the normal course of business.

Where the directors have been unable to assess going concern in the usual way (e.g. for less than one year beyond the date on which they sign the financial statements), this fact should be disclosed.

Where the financial statements are prepared on a basis other than the going concern basis, the basis used should be disclosed.

Reporting implications

The auditor shall conclude on the appropriateness of management's use of the going concern basis.

The auditor should determine if in their judgment, based on the audit evidence obtained, a material uncertainty exists that may cast significant doubt on the entity's ability to continue as a going concern. If so, the auditor must determine whether management have made adequate disclosure of this uncertainty.

A material uncertainty exists when the magnitude of its potential impact and likelihood of occurrence is such that disclosure of the nature and implications of the uncertainty is necessary for the fair presentation of the financial statements and for the financial statements not to be misleading.

Examination of a cash flow forecast

One way of assessing the client's ability to continue as a going concern is to examine the **reasonableness of the assumptions** used to prepare the cash flow forecast.

The following procedures are typical of those that would be performed in the examination of a cash forecast. They are generic procedures. In the exam, remember to tailor the procedures to the scenario.

Procedures in the examination of a cash forecast would include:

- Agree the opening balance of the cash forecast is in agreement with the closing balance of the cash book, to ensure the opening balance of the forecast is accurate.
- Consider how reasonable company forecasts have been in the past by comparing past forecasts with actual outcomes. If forecasts have been reasonable in the past, this would make it more likely that the current forecast is reliable.
- Determine the assumptions that have been made in the preparation of the cash flow forecast. For example, if the company is operating in a poor economic climate, you would not expect cash flows from sales and realisation of receivables to increase, but either to decrease or remain stable. If costs are rising you would expect payments to increases in the cash forecasts.
- Agree the timing of receipts from realisation of receivables and payments to suppliers with credit periods and previous trade receivables and payables payment periods.
- Examine the company's detailed budgets for the forecast period and discuss any specific plans with the directors.
- Examine the assessment of the non-current assets required to meet production needs. Agree cash out flows for non-current assets to supplier quotations.
- For acquisitions of buildings, agree the timing and amount of cash out flows to completion date and consideration in sale and purchase agreement.
- Consider the adequacy of the increased working capital and the working capital cash flows included in the forecast.
- If relevant, inspect post year management accounts to compare the actual performance against the forecast figures.
- Recalculate and cast the cash flow forecast balances to verify arithmetical accuracy.
- Inspect board minutes for any other relevant issues which should be included within the forecast.

Test your understanding 2

Murray case study: Going concern review for the year ended 31 December 20X4

On 2 January 20X5, Golf is Us, a major customer of Murray Co, was placed into administration owing $211,000.

On 3 January 20X5, the sales director left the company and has yet to be replaced. The sales director is suing Murray Co for constructive dismissal.

On 5 January 20X5 there was a fire at the premises of the third party warehouse provider, which destroyed all inventory held there. Approximately one half of Murray Co's inventory was stored in these premises.

The assembly line for ergometers (rowing machines) was refurbished during the year at a cost of $1m. The additional $1.5m loan facility provided to Murray Co during the year is secured, in part, on the refurbished assembly line. The assembly line broke down during January, and six weeks later is still not working.

The company is seeking new funding through an initial public offering of shares in the company (i.e. listing on the stock exchange). In the event that the initial public offering does not proceed, this will require Murray Co's existing banking arrangements to be renegotiated and additional funding to be raised from either existing or new investors.

The financial statements of Murray Co show an overdraft at 31 December 20X4 of $180,000 (20X3: $120,000). The overdraft limit is $250,000. The cash flow forecast shows negative monthly cash flows for the next twelve months. As a result of cash shortages in February 20X5, a number of suppliers were paid late.

Exercise:

Using the information provided, explain the potential indicators that Murray Co is not a going concern.

4 Written representation letter

A **written representation** is: a written statement by management provided to the auditor to confirm certain matters or to support other audit evidence (ISA 580 *Written Representations*).

The purpose of obtaining this form of evidence is:

- to obtain evidence that management, and those charged with governance, have fulfilled their responsibility (as agreed and acknowledged in the terms of the audit engagement) for the preparation of the financial statements, including:
  - preparing the financial statements in accordance with an applicable financial reporting framework.
  - providing the auditor with all relevant information and access to records.
  - recording all transactions and reflecting them in the financial statements.
- to support other audit evidence relevant to the financial statements if determined necessary by the auditor or required by ISAs.

A representation to support other audit evidence may be appropriate where more reliable forms of evidence are not available, particularly in relation to matters requiring management judgment or knowledge restricted to management. Examples include:

- plans or intentions that may affect the carrying value of assets or liabilities.
- confirmation of values where there is a significant degree of estimation or judgment involved, e.g. provisions and contingent liabilities.
- formal confirmation of the directors' judgment on contentious issues, e.g. the value of assets where there is a risk of impairment.
- aspects of laws and regulations that may affect the financial statements, including compliance.

ISA 580 requires written representations to be in the form of a representation letter addressed to the auditor.

Note that written representations cannot substitute for more reliable evidence that should be available and do not constitute sufficient appropriate evidence on their own, about any of the matters with which they deal.

Written representations should only be sought to support other audit evidence.

In practice, the auditor will often draft the written representations letter but it must be printed on client headed paper and signed by the client.

The letter must be signed by an appropriate senior member of client management, with appropriate responsibilities for the financial statements and knowledge of the matters concerned. This would normally be the chief executive and chief financial officer.

The date of the written representation letter should be the same as the date the financial statements are authorised. It must be obtained (and signed) before the audit report is finalised.

Reliability of written representations

Written representations are client generated, and may be subject to bias. It is therefore a potentially unreliable form of audit evidence.

The auditor must consider the reliability of written representations in terms of:

- inconsistencies with other forms of evidence.
- concerns about the competence, integrity, ethical values or diligence of management.

If written representations are inconsistent with other evidence, the auditor must:

- consider the reliability of representations in general.
- reconsider their initial risk assessment.
- consider the need to perform further audit procedures.

If there are concerns about the competence, integrity, ethical values or diligence of management the auditor must:

- Consider whether the engagement can be conducted effectively.
- If they conclude that it cannot then they should withdraw from the engagement, where permitted by laws and regulations.
- If they are not permitted to withdraw they should consider the impact on the audit report – it is likely that this would lead to issue a disclaimer of opinion.

Steps if management refuse to provide written representations

Although possibly unreliable, written representations are a necessary and important source of evidence.

If management refuse to provide requested written representations, the auditor should:

- Discuss the matter with management to understand why they are refusing
- Re-evaluate the integrity of management and consider the effect that this may have on the reliability of other representations (oral or written) and audit evidence in general
- Consider the implication for the audit report.

If management refuses to provide written representations about their responsibilities, the auditor must issue a disclaimer of opinion.

Illustration 1: Murray Co written representation letter

Murray Co
1 Murray Mound, Wimbledon
London WN1 2LN

Wimble & Co
2 Court Lane, Wimbledon
London WN1 2LN

18 February 20X5

Dear Wimble & Co,

This written representation is provided in connection with your audit of the financial statements of Murray Company for the year ended December 31, 20X4 for the purpose of expressing an opinion as to whether the financial statements give a true and fair view in accordance with International Financial Reporting Standards.

We confirm that:

Financial Statements

- We have fulfilled our responsibilities, as set out in the terms of the audit engagement dated 25 November 20X4, for the preparation of the financial statements in accordance with International Financial Reporting Standards; in particular the financial statements give a true and fair view in accordance therewith.

- Significant assumptions used by us in making accounting estimates, including those measured at fair value, are reasonable. (ISA 540)
- All events subsequent to the date of the financial statements and for which International Financial Reporting Standards require adjustment or disclosure have been adjusted or disclosed. (ISA 560)
- The effects of uncorrected misstatements are immaterial, both individually and in the aggregate, to the financial statements as a whole. A list of the uncorrected misstatements is attached. (ISA 450)
- The basis and amount of the warranty provision are reasonable. (specific matter)

Information provided

- We have provided you with:
  - Access to all information of which we are aware that is relevant to the preparation of the financial statements, such as records, documentation and other matters.
  - Additional information that you have requested from us for the purpose of the audit.
  - Unrestricted access to persons within the entity from whom you determined it necessary to obtain audit evidence.
- All transactions have been recorded in the accounting records and are reflected in the financial statements.
- We have disclosed to you the results of our assessment of the risk that the financial statements may be materially misstated as a result of fraud. (ISA 240)
- We have disclosed to you all information in relation to fraud or suspected fraud that we are aware of and that affects the entity and involves:
  - Management
  - Employees who have significant roles in internal control; or
  - Others where the fraud could have a material effect on the financial statements. (ISA 240)
- We have disclosed to you all information in relation to allegations of fraud, or suspected fraud, affecting the entity's financial statements communicated by employees, former employees, analysts, regulators or others. (ISA 240)
- We have disclosed to you all known instances of non-compliance or suspected non-compliance with laws and regulations whose effects should be considered when preparing financial statements. (ISA 250)

- We have disclosed to your all information in relation to settlement of the unfair dismissal, including our intentions thereon. (specific matter)
- We have disclosed to you all information in relation to the constructive dismissal brought by the previous Sales Director, including our intention thereon. (specific matter)

Ed Perry

Edward Perry

Finance Director, Murray Co

Maria Williams

Maria Williams

Managing Director, Murray Co

5 Audit finalisation and final review

Overall review of financial statements

At the finalisation stage the auditor should perform the following procedures:

- Review the financial statements to ensure compliance with accounting standards and local legislation disclosure. This is sometimes done using a disclosure checklist.
- Review the disclosure of the accounting policies to ensure that they are in accordance with the accounting treatment adopted in the financial statements, and that they are sufficiently disclosed.
- Review the financial statements to ensure they are consistent with the auditor's knowledge of the business and the results of their audit work.
- Review the financial statements to assess whether they adequately reflect the information and explanations previously obtained and conclusions reached during the course of the audit.
- Perform analytical procedures, under ISA 520 *Analytical Procedures*; to corroborate conclusions formed during the audit and assist when forming an overall conclusion as to whether the financial statements are consistent with the auditor's understanding of the entity.
- Review the aggregate of uncorrected misstatements to assess whether a material misstatement arises; if so discuss with management with regards to a potential adjustment. See below.

As part of the overall review, the auditor should assess whether the audit evidence gathered by the team is sufficient and appropriate to support the audit opinion.

Overall review of evidence

What happens in the final review?

The overall review stage of the audit is the point at which the final decisions are taken:

OVERALL REVIEW

Financial statements ok?

- **Do the financial statements comply with the relevant reporting framework?**
  - Law.
  - Applicable accounting standards.
  - GAAP.
  - Other regulations (e.g. Stock Exchange listing requirements).
  - Does other information published with the financial statements (e.g. Directors' report, – Chairman's review) conflict with them in any way?

Audit evidence ok?

- **Does the evidence gathered in the course of the audit support the audit opinion?**
  - Was the audit plan followed?
  - Has sufficient, appropriate audit evidence been gathered?
  - Has the work been performed in accordance with professional standards and legal requirements?
  - What issues arose? What errors were found?
  - Have the matters been raised for future consideration?
  - Was the plan suitably modified to allow for changing circumstances?
  - Have necessary consultations taken place both within the firm and with outside experts?
  - Has the file been adequately reviewed at lower levels within the firm (e.g. by the senior and the manager)?
  - Have the necessary checklists been completed?
  - Work supports conclusions reached and is appropriately documented

Other completion procedures

- **Have the necessary completion procedures been carried out?**
  - Final analytical procedures.
  - Consideration of the firm's continued independence.
  - Second partner review (if appropriate).
  - Subsequent events review.
  - Going concern review.
  - Written representations obtained
  - Objectives of the engagement procedures have been achieved.

The review is carried out by the engagement partner who has ultimate responsibility for committing the audit firm when signing the audit report.

What is the purpose of a final review?

It is the responsibility of the engagement partner to perform a review of audit documentation (including a discussion with the engagement team) in order to satisfy themselves that sufficient appropriate evidence has been obtained to support any conclusions reached and, ultimately, the audit opinion. Considerations include, for example:

- Has work been performed in accordance with professional standards?
- Have the significant risks identified during planning been addressed?
- Are there any critical areas of judgment relating to difficult or contentious matters?
- Are there any significant matters for further consideration?

- Have appropriate consultations taken place or are more needed?
- Have the objectives of the engagement procedures been achieved?
- Does the work documented support the conclusions made?
- Is there a need to revise the nature, timing and extent of procedures?
- Is the evidence sufficient to support an opinion?

Reviews are also significant for a firm's appraisal system and development of staff. Additionally they are an important element of any monitoring system, implemented to identify and rectify deficiencies that could lead to poor quality work.

Appropriate review procedures are an integral part of an audit and are a requirement of ISA 220 *Quality Control for an Audit of Financial Statements.*

6 Evaluation of misstatements

The auditor must consider the effect of misstatements on both the audit procedures performed and ultimately, if uncorrected, on the financial statements as a whole.

Guidance on how this is performed is given in ISA 450 *Evaluation of Misstatements Identified During the Audit.*

In order to achieve this the auditor must:

- Accumulate a record of all identified misstatements, unless they are clearly trivial.
- Consider if the existence of such misstatements indicates that others may exist, which, when aggregated with other misstatements, could be considered material.
- If so, consider if the audit plan and strategy need to be revised.
- Assess the materiality of the matter (both quantitative and qualitative).
- Report all misstatements identified during the course of the audit to an appropriate level of **management** on a timely basis.
- Request that **all** misstatements are corrected.
- If management refuses to correct some or all of the misstatements the auditor should consider their reasons for refusal and take these into account when considering if the financial statements are free from material misstatement.

Evaluation of uncorrected misstatements

If management have failed to correct all of the misstatements reported to them, the auditor should:

- Revisit their assessment of materiality to determine whether it is still appropriate in the circumstances.
- Determine whether the uncorrected misstatements, either individually or in aggregate, are material to the financial statements as a whole. In so doing the auditor must consider both the size and nature of the misstatements.
- Report the uncorrected misstatements to **those charged with governance** and explain the effect this will have upon the audit opinion.
- Request a written representation from those charged with governance that they believe the effects of uncorrected misstatements are immaterial.

Once these procedures have been completed the auditor should then consider the impact of uncorrected misstatements on their audit report. The impact on the audit report is considered in the next chapter.

Evaluation of misstatements

You are at the completion stage of the audit of a client. The PBT for the year is $8mn and total assets are $35mn. The following matters have not been corrected by management and have been left for your attention:

(1) A major customer has gone into liquidation owing an amount of $200,000 which has not been written off.

(2) A provision required of $300,000 has not been recognised.

The bad debt of $200,000 represents 2.5% of PBT and 0.57% of total assets therefore is not material.

The provision of $300,000 represents 3.75% of PBT and 0.86% of total assets therefore is not material.

Cumulatively they have a bigger effect on the financial statements:

$500,000 represents 6.25% of PBT and 1.4% of total assets which is material. The two amounts will need to be adjusted to avoid a modified opinion.

The auditor should ask for both issues to be corrected in accordance with ISA 450.

Test your understanding 3

ISA 570 *Going Concern* provides guidance to auditors in respect of ensuring that an entity can continue as a going concern.

Required:

Explain the actions that an auditor should carry out to try and ascertain whether an entity is a going concern.

(5 marks)

Test your understanding 4

Smithson Co provides scientific services to a wide range of clients. Typical assignments range from testing food for illegal additives to providing forensic analysis on items used to commit crimes to assist law enforcement officers.

The annual audit is nearly complete. As audit senior you have reported to the engagement partner that Smithson is having some financial difficulties. Income has fallen due to the adverse effect of two high-profile court cases, following which a number of clients withdrew their contracts with Smithson. A senior employee then left Smithson, stating lack of investment in new analysis machines was increasing the risk of incorrect information being provided by the company. A cash flow forecast prepared internally shows Smithson requiring significant additional cash within the next 12 months to maintain even the current level of services.

Required:

(a) **Define 'going concern' and discuss the auditor's and directors responsibilities in respect of going concern.**

(5 marks)

(b) **State the audit procedures that may be carried out to try to determine whether or not Smithson Co is a going concern.**

(10 marks)

(c) **Explain the audit procedures the auditor may take where the auditor has decided that Smithson Co is unlikely to be a going concern.**

(5 marks)

(Total: 20 marks)

Test your understanding 5

Potterton is a listed company that manufactures body lotions under the 'ReallyCool' brand. The company's year end is 31 March 20X2, and today's date is 1 June 20X2. Draft profit before taxation is $4 million.

The audit is nearing completion, but two issues remain outstanding:

(1) On 27 May 20X2 a legal claim was made against the company on behalf of a teenager who suffered severe burns after using 'ReallyCool ExtraZingy Lotion' in July 20X1. Potterton is considering an out-of-court settlement of $100,000 per year for the remaining life of the claimant. However, no adjustment or disclosure has been made in the financial statements.

(2) At a Board Meeting on 30 April 20X2, the directors of Potterton proposed a dividend of $2 million. It is highly likely that the shareholders will approve the dividend at the Annual General Meeting on 3 September 20X2. The directors have recorded the dividend in the draft Statement of Changes in Equity for the year ended 31 March 20X2.

Required:

(a) **Explain whether the two outstanding issues are adjusting or non-adjusting events, in accordance with IAS 10 *Events after the Reporting Period*.**

(8 marks)

(b) **Explain appropriate audit procedures in order to reach a conclusion on the two outstanding issues.**

(5 marks)

(c) **Explain the likely impact on the audit opinion if the directors refuse to make any further adjustments or disclosures in the financial statements.**

(4 marks)

(Total: 17 marks)

Test your understanding 6

ISA 580 *Written Representations* provides guidance on the use of written representations as audit evidence.

Required:

(a) **List SIX items that could be included in a written representation.**

(3 marks)

(b) **List THREE reasons why auditors obtain written representations.**

(3 marks)

Test your understanding 7

(a) **Explain the purpose of a written representation.**

(5 marks)

(b) You are the manager in charge of the audit of Crighton-Ward, a public limited liability company which manufactures specialist cars and other motor vehicles for use in films. Audited revenue is $140 million with profit before tax of $7.5 million.

All audit work up to, but not including, the obtaining of written representations has been completed. A review of the audit file has disclosed the following outstanding points:

Lion's Roar

The company is facing a potential legal claim from the Lion's Roar company in respect of a defective vehicle that was supplied for one of their films. Lion's Roar maintains that the vehicle was not built strongly enough while the directors of Crighton-Ward argue that the specification was not sufficiently detailed. Dropping a vehicle 50 metres into a river and expecting it to continue to remain in working condition would be unusual, but this is what Lion's Roar expected. Solicitors are unable to determine liability at the present time. A claim for $4 million being the cost of a replacement vehicle and lost production time has been received by Crighton-Ward from Lions' Roar. The directors' opinion is that the claim is not justified.

Depreciation

Depreciation of specialist production equipment has been included in the financial statements at the amount of 10% pa based on reducing balance. The treatment is consistent with prior accounting periods (which received an unmodified auditor's report) and other companies in the same industry and sales of old equipment show negligible profit or loss on sale. The audit senior, who is new to the audit, feels that depreciation is being undercharged in the financial statements.

Required:

For each of the above matters:

(i) **discuss whether or not a paragraph is required in the written representation and**

(ii) **if appropriate, draft the paragraph for inclusion in the written representation.**

(10 marks)

(c) A suggested format for the written representation has been sent by the auditors to the directors of Crighton-Ward. The directors have stated that they will not sign the written representation this year on the grounds that they believe the additional evidence that it provides is not required by the auditor.

Required:

Discuss the actions the auditor may take as a result of the decision made by the directors not to sign the written representation.

(5 marks)

(Total: 20 marks)

Test your understanding 8 – OT Case 1

The audit of Leonora Co is nearly complete and you are performing your procedures in respect of going concern. During the audit you have identified several indicators that the company may not be able to continue as a going concern.

(1) Which of the following is correct in terms of responsibilities for going concern?

A The auditor chooses the basis of preparation for the financial statements.

B The client should make adequate disclosure of going concern uncertainties and the auditor should assess the adequacy of them.

C The auditor will make disclosure of going concern uncertainties in the financial statements.

D The auditor will notify the shareholders immediately of any going concern issues identified during the audit.

(2) State whether each of the following statements are true or false in respect of assessing the going concern status of Leonora Co?

A The auditor should prepare forecasts to assess whether Leonora Co are likely to be able to continue trading

B The directors of Leonora Co should prepare forecasts for a period of at least 12 months to assess whether the company is likely to be able to continue trading

C If the directors of Leonora Co prepare forecasts for a period of less than 12 months, the auditor should ask them to extend their assessment period

D If the directors of Leonora Co prepare forecasts for a period of less than 12 months, the auditor should extend the assessment period by preparing a forecast for the additional 6 months

(3) Which of the following is correct in respect of going concern?

A Financial statements must be prepared on the going concern basis for all companies.

B If there are material uncertainties regarding going concern, the financial statements must be prepared on the break up basis.

C Going concern means the company is no longer profitable.

D The directors of the company must disclose material uncertainties regarding going concern in the notes to the financial statements.

(4) Which of the following are indicators of going concern problems?

(i) Declining revenues

(ii) Significant outstanding receivables

(iii) Loan repayments due to be made

(iv) Declining current and quick ratios

A (i), (ii) and (iii) only

B (ii), (iii) and (iv) only

C All of them

D (iii) only

(5) Which of the following procedures is not appropriate for obtaining evidence regarding the going concern assumption?

A Obtain external confirmation from a customer regarding their outstanding balance.

B Examine cash flow forecasts.

C Discuss with management their plans for the future.

D Inspect correspondence with the bank regarding loan or overdraft facilities.

Test your understanding 9 – OT Case 2

You are currently performing subsequent events procedures for the audit of Kookynie Co. From a review of the board minutes you identify that a customer is suing the company for an injury they suffered on the client's premises on 5 February 20X0. The client's year end is 31 January 20X0. The directors are proposing amending the financial statements to include a provision for the amount of compensation they expect to have to pay to the customer. Legal advice received indicates that the claim is possible to succeed.

(1) Which of the following is correct with regard to subsequent events?

A The auditor must perform audit procedures to identify events occurring after the date of the financial statements up to the date the audit report is signed that could have an effect on the financial statements

B The auditor does not need to consider any events which occur after the date of the financial statements as it is outside of the reporting period

C The auditor has no responsibility after the audit report has been signed, even if they become aware of events occurring which means the opinion is now incorrect

D The auditor only needs to consider subsequent events that the directors have informed them about

(2) Which of the following statements is NOT correct in respect of subsequent events?

A The auditor must ensure the client has complied with IAS 10 *Events after the reporting period* when performing the audit of subsequent events

B The auditor must comply with IAS 10 *Events after the reporting period* when performing the audit of subsequent events

C The auditor must comply with ISA 560 Subsequent e*vents* when performing the audit of subsequent events

D Events after the reporting period may be adjusting or non-adjusting

(3) Which of the following is correct in respect of adjusting events?

A Adjusting events are those events which occur before the audit report has been signed

B Adjusting events are those which occur after the year end date

C Adjusting events are those which occur after the year end date and provide evidence of a condition existing at the year end date

D Adjusting events require disclosure in the notes to the financial statements

(4) In respect of the customer's claim, which of the following statements is true?

A If the claim was probable, a provision should be recognised in the financial statements dated 31 January 20X0

B The injury was caused after the year end therefore was not a condition in existence at the year end

C The injury was caused after the year end therefore has no impact on the financial statements being audited

D The claim is an adjusting event and the financial statements should reflect the claim

(5) Which of following procedures would be not be appropriate in respect of Kookynie Co's subsequent events review?

A Inspect correspondence from the lawyers regarding the likely outcome of the case and the estimate of compensation if the claim is successful

B Discuss with management the details of the accident giving rise to the claim

C Obtain written representation from management that all known subsequent events have been disclosed to the auditor and reflected in the financial statements.

D Telephone the lawyer to discuss further details of the case of which the client may not be aware

Test your understanding 10 – OT Case 3

You are completing the audit of Balladonia Co and you are waiting for the client to sign and return the written representation letter. The directors have expressed concern about signing the letter. They have stated that the auditor has been provided with all of the information they require and therefore do not understand why the representation letter is necessary.

(1) State whether each of the following statements is true or false in respect of written representations?

A As you have received all other information during the audit, the decision by management not to provide the written representation letter is not an issue that would affect the audit report

B A written representation is an important piece of evidence which the auditor must obtain

C A written representation does not need to be obtained if the wording would be the same as the previous year's written representation

D Failure by management to provide a written representation may cast doubt over management integrity

(2) Which of the following statements is false?

A Written representations include confirmation that management have fulfilled their responsibilities in respect of the financial statements and have provided the auditor will all records and information during the audit.

B Written representations should only be relied on where there is limited other evidence available such as matters of judgment or matters confined to management.

C The auditor would obtain a written representation regarding the reasonableness of a depreciation charge as this is an estimate.

D Failure to obtain a written representation would result in a disclaimer of opinion.

(3) What would be the auditor's first course of action after being informed that management are unwilling to provide the written representation?

A Discuss the matter with management and try to resolve the issue

B Discuss the matter with those charged with governance and try to resolve the issue

C Discuss the matter with the shareholders and try to resolve the issue

D Modify the audit opinion

Written representation is required from management to confirm they believe the effects of any uncorrected misstatements are immaterial.

(4) Which of the following best describes a misstatement?

A An error in the financial statements

B A fraud which has a material effect on the financial statements

C An omission of a balance from the financial statements

D A difference between what has been reported in the financial statements and what should have been reported in the financial statements

(5) During the audit of Balladonia Co you discovered misstatements totalling $20,000. Profit before tax is $570,000. What is the most appropriate course of action?

A Ignore the misstatements if they are deemed to be immaterial

B Modify the audit opinion as a result of misstatement

C Request the client to correct the misstatements

D Modify the audit report with an Emphasis of Matter paragraph to highlight that misstatements are present in the financial statements

7 Chapter summary

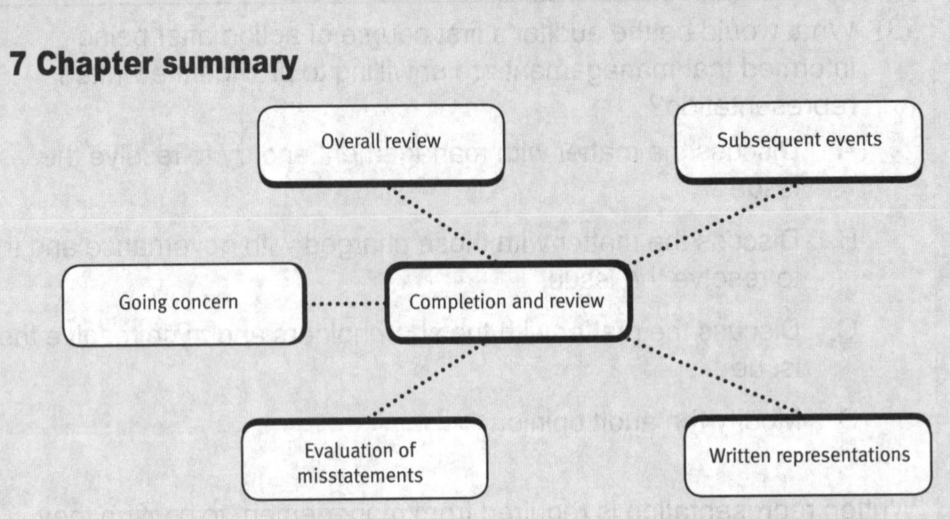

Test your understanding answers

Test your understanding 1

To determine whether or not the financial statements should be adjusted in respect of each of the events described, IAS 10 *Events After the Reporting Period* needs to be applied. If the event provides evidence of conditions that existed at the reporting date (an adjusting event), then an adjustment should be made. If the event provides evidence of conditions that arose after the reporting date (a non-adjusting event), no adjustment is required but a disclosure may be necessary if the event is material and non-disclosure would render the financial statements misleading.

The auditor will only compel the directors' to amend the financial statements for adjusting events if the adjustment is material. When assessing materiality in the exam, it is sufficient to calculate materiality in relation to each measure individually, using the lower end of the thresholds for prudence. If the item is material to one or more of the measures then it requires adjustment.

(1) Gold is Us was placed into administration after the year-end, which provides evidence of the recoverability of the receivables balance at the year end. Therefore this is an **adjusting event**. The total value of the balance is $211,000 which is 1% of revenue, 2% of total assets and 20% of profit, and is therefore **material**. The receivables balance should be written-off or an allowance for receivables created.

(2) The sales director left the company after the year-end and is suing for constructive dismissal, which is an event that arose after the reporting date. Therefore this is a **non-adjusting event**. The total value of the claim is $280,000, which is 1.3% of revenue, 2.9% of assets and 26.7% of profit before tax and is therefore material. This may also be considered material by nature. The nature of the event and any estimates of the financial impact should therefore be **disclosed**.

(3) A fire destroyed inventory after the year-end, which is therefore a **non-adjusting event** (as the inventory was not damaged at the year-end). The total value of inventory stored at the premises is $1,054,000, which is 5% of revenue, 11% of total assets and 101% of profit and is therefore **material** and the nature of the event and any estimates of the financial impact should be **disclosed**.

(4) After the year-end a letter was received offering to settle a claim for unfair dismissal out-of-court. This is an event that provides evidence of the valuation of the provision at the year-end and is therefore an **adjusting event**. The current provision is for $40,000 and the adjustment would therefore be $15,000. This is **not material** being 0.07% of revenue, 0.15% of total assets and 1.43% profit before tax. Therefore **no adjustment** is necessary.

Test your understanding 2

The following table explains the potential going concern indicators at Murray Co:

Indicator	Explanation
A major customer has been put into administration	Unless the customer can be replaced, this will result in significant loss of future revenues. The debt outstanding is unlikely to be paid resulting in a negative impact on cash flow.
The sales director left the company and has yet to be replaced.	Loss of a key director will impact on the company's sales. As Murray Co has already lost a major customer, without an experienced sales director to generate new sales the company will face significantly reduced sales and cash flows.
The sales director is suing Murray Co for constructive dismissal.	Murray Co will need to pay expensive legal costs in order to defend this litigation, squeezing cash flows even further. In addition, this may damage their reputation and make it difficult to recruit a suitable replacement or other key staff. Any compensation awarded to the sales director will mean further outflow of cash.

Murray Co is seeking new funding through an initial public offering of shares in the company.	If Murray Co does obtain new funding through listing, alternative finance will need to be obtained in order to continue to operate. This may not be easy to obtain given their other problems.
Murray Co is operating close to it's overdraft limit.	Murray Co is heavily dependent on a short-term source of finance, that is repayable on demand. It may be difficult to obtain further sources of finance if the overdraft reaches it limit.
The cash flow forecast shows negative monthly cash flows for the next twelve months.	If the company continues to have cash outflows then the overdraft will increase further and there may be no cash available to pay debts as they fall due.
A number of suppliers have been paid late.	If suppliers are paid late they may refuse to supply Murray Co with goods/components or impose 'cash on delivery' terms which will disrupt production, and delay sales to customers. This may cause them to lose customers altogether.
The loan facility is secured, in part, on the refurbished assembly line which has broken down.	The bank may withdraw the loan facility if the asset on which it is secured is significantly impaired. Murray Co do not have sufficient cash to repay the loan. Unless Murray Co can negotiate with the bank or raise alternative finance (or sell non-current assets), they will have no realistic alternative but to liquidate.
The assembly line broke down during January, and six weeks later is still not working.	If Murray Co cannot meet customer orders due to manufacturing problems, refunds may have to be given, customer goodwill may be lost along with future revenue, which will put further pressure on cash flows.
A fire at the premises of the third party warehouse provider, destroyed approximately one half of Murray Co's inventory.	If Murray Co cannot meet customer orders due to this lost revenue, refunds may have to be given, customer goodwill may be lost along with future revenue, which will put further pressure on cash flows. If the losses are not covered by insurance, this will significantly impact profit.

Test your understanding 3

Audit work: going concern

- Review management's plans for future actions based on its going concern assessment.
- Gather additional sufficient and appropriate audit evidence to confirm or dispel whether or not a material uncertainty exists regarding the going concern concept.
- Seek written representation from management regarding its plans for future action.
- Obtain information from company bankers regarding continuance of loan facilities.
- Review receivables ageing analysis to determine whether there is an increase in days, which may also indicate cash flow problems.

Test your understanding 4

(a) Going concern

"Going concern" means that the entity will continue in operational existence for the foreseeable future without the intention or the necessity of liquidation or otherwise ceasing trade. It is one of the fundamental accounting concepts used by auditors and stated in IAS 1 *Presentation of financial statements*.

The auditor's responsibility in respect of going concern is explained in ISA 570 *Going Concern*.

The ISA states: "When planning and performing audit procedures and in evaluating the results thereof, the auditor should consider the appropriateness of management's use of the going concern assumption in the preparation of the financial statements."

The auditor's responsibilities are:

(i) To carry out appropriate audit procedures that will identify whether or not an organisation can continue as a going concern.

(ii) To ensure that the organisation's management have been realistic in their use of the going concern assumption when preparing the financial statements.

(iii) To report to the members where they consider that the going concern assumption has been used inappropriately, for example; when the financial statements indicate that the organisation is a going concern but audit procedures indicate this may not be the case.

It is the directors' responsibility to prepare the financial statements on an appropriate basis, be that either the going concern or the break-up basis.

(b) Audit procedures regarding going concern

- Obtain a copy of the cash flow forecast and discuss the results of this with directors.
- Discuss with the directors their view of whether Smithson can continue as a going concern. Ask for their reasons and try and determine whether these are accurate.
- Enquire of the directors whether they have considered any other forms of finance for Smithson to make up the cash shortfall identified in the cash flow forecast.
- Obtain a copy of any interim financial statements of Smithson to determine the level of sales/income after the year-end and whether this matches the cash flow forecast.
- Enquire about the possible lack of capital investment within Smithson identified by the employee leaving. Review current levels of non-current assets with similar companies and review purchase policy with the directors.
- Consider the extent to which Smithson rely on the senior employee who recently left the company. Ask the HR department whether the employee will be replaced and, if so, how soon.
- Obtain a solicitor's letter and review to identify any legal claims against Smithson related to below standard services being provided to clients. Where possible, consider the financial impact on Smithson and whether insurance is available to mitigate any claims.

- Review Smithson's order book and client lists to try and determine the value of future orders compared to previous years.
- Review the bank letter to determine the extent of any bank loans and whether repayments due in the next 12 months can be made without further borrowing.
- Review other events after the end of the financial year and determine whether these have an impact on Smithson.
- Obtain a written representation confirming the directors' opinion that Smithson is a going concern.

(c) Audit procedures if Smithson is not considered to be a going concern

- Discuss the situation again with directors. Consider whether additional disclosures are required in the financial statements or whether the financial statements should be prepared on the break-up basis.
- Explain to the directors that if additional disclosure or restatement of the financial statements is not made then the auditor will have to modify the audit report and opinion.
- Consider how the audit report should be modified. Where the directors provide adequate disclosure of the going concern situation of Smithson, then a section should be included in the audit report headed 'Material Uncertainty Related to Going Concern' to draw attention to the going concern disclosures.
- Where the directors do not make adequate disclosure of the going concern situation then modify the audit opinion due to material misstatement from inadequate disclosure.
- The modification will be an 'except for' qualification or an adverse opinion depending on whether the issue is material or material and pervasive.
- The 'Basis for Opinion' section will be amended to 'Basis for Adverse Opinion' or 'Basis for Qualified Opinion' to explain the reason for the modified opinion.
- The Key Audit Matters section will reference the 'Basis for Adverse/Qualified Opinion' section.

Test your understanding 5

(a) **Analysis of events**

Legal claim: The legal claim is within the scope of IAS 10, because it was received on 27 May 20X2. This date is after the reporting date (31 March 20X2) but before the date that the financial statements will be authorised for issue. The legal claim is an adjusting event because it provides evidence of conditions existing at the end of the reporting period. As at 31 March 20X2, the claimant had purchased and used the product, and the damage to the claimant's skin had already occurred.

The legal claim is material, because, if the claimant lived for, say, another 40 years, the company would owe him/her $4 million. This is 100% of the current year draft profit before taxation.

Therefore profit should be reduced and liabilities increased by the expected value of the claim.

Proposed dividend: The proposed dividend is within the scope of IAS 10, because it was proposed after the reporting date (31 March 20X2) but before the date that the financial statements will be authorised for issue. The proposed dividend is a non-adjusting event because it is indicative of a condition that arose after the end of the reporting period. No liability for the dividend can exist until the shareholders approve the dividend.

The proposed dividend is material because it constitutes 50% ($2m/$4m x 100) of the company's profit before tax, as well as being material by nature.

Therefore the dividend should not be recognised in the financial statements for the year ended 31 March 20X2. However, the proposed dividend should be disclosed in a note to the financial statements.

(b) **Audit procedures**

Legal claim:

- Review legal correspondence in order to understand the likely outcome of the legal claim.
- Review customer correspondence/legal files in order to identify other similar claims which could give rise to additional liabilities.

- Discuss with production director the likely cause of the burns (e.g. allergy in user or inadequate printed instructions on product use) to determine the likelihood of any claim being successful in court.
- Review trade/consumer press to identify whether the claim might damage Reallycool's reputation which could impact future revenues or even create a going concern threat.
- Propose adjustment of the financial statements to the directors.

Proposed dividend:

- Inspect board minutes in order to confirm the amount of the proposed dividend.
- Propose an adjustment to the financial statements to remove the dividend from being recognised in the statement of changes in equity but ensure that the dividend proposal is disclosed within the notes.

(c) **Impact on audit opinion**

- The auditor must modify the audit opinion if the directors refuse to make the relevant adjustments in the financial statements requested by the auditors.
- Both the legal claim (which should have been recognised) and the proposed dividend (which should have been disclosed rather than recognised) are materially misstated.
- The auditor must express a qualified ('except for') opinion if they conclude that the misstatements are material, but not pervasive, to the financial statements.
- The auditor must express an adverse opinion if they conclude that misstatements are both material and pervasive to the financial statements.
- Given the size of the amounts involved, an adverse opinion may be appropriate in these circumstances.
- The 'Basis for Opinion' section will be amended to 'Basis for Adverse' or 'Basis for Qualified Opinion' to explain the reason for the modified opinion.
- The Key Audit Matters section will reference the 'Basis for Adverse/Qualified Opinion' section.

Test your understanding 6

(a)	No irregularities involving management or employees that could have a material effect on the financial statements.	½ mark
	All books of account and supporting documentation have been made available to the auditors.	½ mark
	Financial statements are free from material misstatements including omissions.	½ mark
	No non-compliance with any statute or regulatory authority.	½ mark
	No plans that will materially alter the carrying value or classification of assets or liabilities in the financial statements.	½ mark
	No plans to abandon any product lines that will result in any excess or obsolete inventory.	½ mark
	No events, unless already disclosed, after the end of the reporting period that need disclosure in the financial statements.	½ mark
(b)	Formal confirmation by management of their responsibilities.	1 mark
	Contentious matter where no other, better quality, evidence is available.	1 mark
	Required by ISA 580 and other ISAs.	1 mark

Test your understanding 7

(a) Written representations are a form of audit evidence. They are written by the company's directors and sent to the auditor, just before the audit report is signed.

Written representations are required for two reasons:

– First, so the directors can acknowledge their collective responsibility for the preparation of the financial statements and to confirm that they have approved those statements.

– Second, to confirm any matters, which are material to the financial statements where representations are crucial to obtaining sufficient and appropriate audit evidence.

In the latter situation, other forms of audit evidence are normally unavailable because knowledge of the facts is confined to management and the matter is one of judgment or opinion.

Obtaining written representations does not mean that other evidence does not have to be obtained. Audit evidence will still be collected and the representation will support that evidence. Any contradiction between sources of evidence should, as always, be investigated.

(b) *Lion's Roar*

The amount of the claim is material being 50% of profit before taxation.

There is also a lack of definitive supporting evidence for the claim. The two main pieces of evidence available are the claim from Lion's Roar itself and the legal advice from Crighton Ward's solicitors. However, any claim amount cannot be accurately determined because the dispute has not been settled.

The directors have stated that they believe the claim not to be justified, which is one possible outcome of the dispute. However, in order to obtain sufficient evidence to show how the treatment of the potential claim was decided for the financial statements, the auditor must obtain this opinion in writing. Reference must therefore be made to the claim in the written representation.

Paragraph for inclusion in the written representation: 'A legal claim against Crighton-Ward by Lion's Roar has been estimated at $4 million by Lion's Roar. However, the directors are of the opinion that the claim is not justified on the grounds of breach of product specification.

No provision has been made in the financial statements, although disclosure of the situation is adequate. No similar claims have been received or are expected to be received.'

Depreciation

This matter is unlikely to be included in the written representation because the auditor appears to have obtained sufficient evidence to confirm the accounting treatment. The lack of profit or loss on sale confirms that the depreciation charge is appropriate – large profits would indicate over-depreciation and large losses, under-depreciation. The amount also meets industry standards confirming that Crighton-Ward's accounting policy is acceptable. Including the point in the written representation is inappropriate because the matter is not crucial and does not appear to be based on judgment or opinion. The only opinion here appears to be that of the auditor – unless the 'feelings' can be turned into some appropriate audit evidence, the matter should be closed.

(c) Lack of written representation

The auditor may take the following actions:

- Discuss the situation with the directors to try and resolve the issue that the directors have raised.
- The auditor will need to explain the need for the written representation again (and note that the signing of the letter was mentioned in the engagement letter).
- Ascertain exact reasons why the directors will not sign the letter.
- Consider whether amendments can be made to the letter to incorporate the directors' concerns that will still provide the auditor with appropriate and sufficient audit evidence.
- The discussion must clearly explain the fact that if the auditor does not receive sufficient and appropriate audit evidence, then the audit report will have to be modified.
- The reason for the modification will be the auditor's inability to obtain sufficient appropriate evidence regarding the amounts and disclosures in the financial statements.
- A qualified 'except for' opinion or disclaimer of opinion will be required.

- The 'Basis for Opinion' section will be amended to 'Basis for Qualified Opinion' or 'Basis for Disclaimer of Opinion' to explain the reason for the modified opinion.
- The Key Audit Matters section will reference the 'Basis for Qualified/Disclaimer of Opinion' section.
- Even if the letter is subsequently signed, the auditor must still evaluate the reliability of the evidence.
- If, in the auditor's opinion, the letter no longer provides sufficient or reliable evidence, then a modification will be required.

Test your understanding 8 – OT Case 1

(1)	B	The directors (client) must make the disclosures in the financial statements. The auditor will audit them.
(2)	A – False	The auditor should review the forecasts prepared by the directors. The auditor should not prepare them.
	B – True	The directors (client) should prepare the forecasts in order to assist with their assessment of going concern in order to determine the appropriate basis on which to prepare the financial statements.
	C – True	The directors are required to consider at least a 12 month period for their going concern assessment. The auditor must ask them to extend their assessment if they fail to consider at least 12 months.
	D – False	The auditor should not extend the assessment or prepare the forecasts for the client.
(3)	D	The FS should be prepared on the break up basis if the company is not a going concern. If there are material uncertainties regarding going concern, these must be disclosed by the directors. A company may be profitable but not have the cash to pay its debts when they fall due.
(4)	C	All are indicators of going concern problems.
(5)	A	Obtaining external confirmation from a customer may confirm the balance owed but does not provide evidence that the money will be received.

Test your understanding 9 – OT Case 2

(1)	A	The auditor has an active duty up to the date the audit report is signed. If they become aware of events after this date, up to the date the FS are issued, they must take action.
(2)	B	IAS 10 refers to the accounting treatment the client should comply with. The auditor must comply with ISA 560 *Subsequent events*.
(3)	C	Adjusting events provide evidence of conditions existing at the year end.
(4)	B	As the injury was suffered after the year end it is a non-adjusting event. Therefore a provision is not required at 31 January 20X0. If it is material, disclosure should be made.
(5)	D	The auditor has no right to contact the lawyer in this manner. A lawyer confirmation letter may be sent with client permission. It would not be professional for the lawyer to discuss details of the case with the auditor that are not known to the client.

Test your understanding 10 – OT Case 3

(1)	A – False	Written representations are required by ISA 580. Without it the auditor does not have sufficient appropriate evidence and as such must modify the audit report.
	B – True	
	C – False	The written representation must be dated just before the date of the audit report. Even if the wording is the same, a written representation must be obtained each year.
	D – True	Management are informed in the engagement letter that written representations will be required. Failure to provide one indicates management are trying to conceal information from the auditor which casts doubt over their integrity.
(2)	C	Sufficient other evidence is available to assess the reasonableness of depreciation.
(3)	A	The first course of action would be to try and resolve the issue with management. If that failed the auditor could discuss the matter with those charged with governance. The shareholders would not be involved in this issue. The audit opinion would be modified if the issue could not be resolved with management or those charged with governance.
(4)	D	Errors, frauds and omissions are all types of misstatement. Therefore the best description of a misstatement is answer D. A difference between what should be reported and what has been reported can be caused by an error, fraud or omission.
(5)	C	Even if misstatements are immaterial they should not be ignored altogether. The client will be asked to correct them. There is no need to modify the audit report or opinion if they remain uncorrected provided the refusal to correct does not indicate the presence of other misstatements. An Emphasis of Matter paragraph is not appropriate in this situation. There is no need to communicate immaterial matters to the users of the financial statements.

chapter

10

Reporting

Chapter learning objectives

This chapter covers syllabus areas:

- E5 – Audit reports
- A3g – Communicating with those charged with governance

Detailed syllabus objectives are provided in the introduction section of the text book.

There have been significant changes to the format of the audit report which are effective for audits of financial statements for periods ending on or after 15 December 2015.

The new audit report is expected to have the following benefits:

- Enhanced communication between auditors, those charged with governance and users.
- Increased attention by management and those charged with governance to the new Key Audit Matters (KAM) section of the audit report.
- Increased professional scepticism over KAM.
- Increased audit quality or users' perception of audit quality.

1 The audit report

The objectives of an auditor, in accordance with ISA 700 (Revised) *Forming an Opinion and Reporting on Financial Statements,* are:

- to form an opinion on the financial statements based upon an evaluation of their conclusions drawn from audit evidence
- to express clearly that opinion through a written report.

The auditor forms an opinion on whether the financial statements are prepared, in all material respects, in accordance with the applicable financial reporting framework. In order to do that they must conclude whether they have obtained reasonable assurance about whether the financial statements as a whole are free from material misstatement (whether due to fraud or error).

In particular the auditor should evaluate whether:

- the financial statements adequately disclose the significant accounting policies
- the accounting policies selected are consistently applied and appropriate
- accounting estimates are reasonable
- information is relevant, reliable, comparable and understandable
- the financial statements provide adequate disclosures to enable the users to understand the effects of material transactions and events
- the terminology used is appropriate.

When the auditor concludes that the financial statements are prepared, in all material respects, in accordance with the applicable financial reporting framework they issue an **unmodified opinion** in the audit report.

If there are no other matters which the auditor wishes to draw to the attention of the users, they will issue an **unmodified report**.

2 Contents of an unmodified audit report

	Section	Purpose
1	Title	To clearly identify the report as an Independent Auditor's Report.
2	Addressee	To identify the intended user of the report.
3	Auditor's opinion	Provides the auditor's conclusion as to whether the financial statements give a true and fair view.
4	Basis for opinion	Provides a description of the professional standards applied during the audit to provide confidence to users that the report can be relied upon.
5	Key audit matters	To draw attention to any other significant matters of which the users should be aware to aid their understanding of the entity. (**Note:** This section is only compulsory for listed entities)
6	Other information	To clarify that management are responsible for the other information. The auditor's report does not cover the other information and the auditor's responsibility is only to read the other information and report in accordance with ISA 720.
7	Responsibilities of management	To clarify that management are responsible for preparing the financial statements and for the internal controls. Included to help minimise the expectations gap.

8	Auditor's responsibilities for the audit of the financial statements	To clarify that the auditor is responsible for expressing reasonable assurance as to whether the FS give a true and fair view and express that opinion in the audit report. The section also describes the auditor's responsibilities in respect of risk assessment, internal controls, going concern and accounting policies. Included to help minimise the expectations gap.
9	Other reporting responsibilities	To highlight any additional reporting responsibilities, if applicable. This may include responsibilities in some jurisdictions to report on the adequacy of accounting records, internal controls over financial reporting, or other information published with the financial statements.
10	Name of the engagement partner	To identify the person responsible for the audit opinion in case of any queries.
11	Signature	Shows the engagement partner or firm accountable for the opinion.
12	Auditor's address	To identify the specific office of the engagement partner in case of any queries.
13	Date	To identify the date up to which the audit work has been performed. Any information that comes to light after this date will not have been considered by the auditor when forming their opinion.

The illustration below is an example of the wording of an unmodified report, i.e. when the auditor concludes that the financial statements are prepared, in all material respects, in accordance with the applicable financial reporting framework. In essence, this is the report an auditor gives when there are no concerns about the financial statements prepared by management.

Illustration 1: Unmodified audit report

INDEPENDENT AUDITOR'S REPORT

To the Shareholders of Murray Company

Report on the Audit of the Financial Statements [sub-title is not included if there is no separate Report on Other Legal and Regulatory Requirements]

Opinion

We have audited the financial statements of the Murray Company (the Company), which comprise the statement of financial position as at 31 December, 20X4, and the statement of comprehensive income, statement of changes in equity and statement of cash flows for the year then ended, and notes to the financial statements, including a summary of significant accounting policies.

In our opinion, the accompanying financial statements present fairly, in all material respects, (or give a true and fair view of) the financial position of the Company as at December 31, 20X4, and its performance and its cash flows for the year then ended in accordance with International Financial Reporting Standards (IFRSs).

Basis for Opinion

We conducted our audit in accordance with International Standards on Auditing (ISAs). Our responsibilities under those standards are further described in the Auditor's Responsibilities for the Audit of the Financial Statements section of our report. We are independent of the Company in accordance with the ethical requirements that are relevant to our audit of the financial statements in [jurisdiction], and we have fulfilled our other ethical responsibilities in accordance with these requirements. We believe that the audit evidence we have obtained is sufficient and appropriate to provide a basis for our opinion.

Key Audit Matters

Key audit matters are those matters that, in our professional judgment, were of most significance in our audit of the financial statements of the current period. These matters were addressed in the context of our audit of the financial statements as a whole, and in forming our opinion thereon, and we do not provide a separate opinion on these matters.

[Description of each key audit matter in accordance with ISA 701]

Other information

Management is responsible for the other information. The other information comprises the Chairman's statement, but does not include the financial statements and the auditor's report thereon.

Our opinion on the financial statements does not cover the other information and we do not express any form of assurance conclusion thereon.

In connection with our audit of the financial statements, our responsibility is to read the other information and, in doing so, consider whether the other information is materially inconsistent with the financial statements or our knowledge obtained in the audit or otherwise appears to be materially misstated. If, based on the work we have performed, we conclude that there is a material misstatement of this information, we are required to report that fact. We have nothing to report in this regard.

Responsibilities of Management and Those Charged With Governance for the Financial Statements

Management is responsible for the preparation and fair presentation of these financial statements in accordance with International Financial Reporting Standards, and for such internal control as management determines is necessary to enable the preparation of financial statements that are free from material misstatement, whether due to fraud or error.

In preparing the financial statements, management is responsible for assessing the Company's ability to continue as a going concern, disclosing as applicable, matters related to going concern and using the going concern basis of accounting unless management either intends to liquidate the Company or to cease operations, or has no realistic alternative but to do so.

Those charged with governance are responsible for overseeing the Company's financial reporting process.

Auditor's Responsibilities for the Audit of the Financial Statements

Our objectives are to obtain reasonable assurance about whether the financial statements as a whole are free from material misstatement, whether due to fraud or error, and to issue an auditor's report that includes our opinion. Reasonable assurance is a high level of assurance, but is not a guarantee that an audit conducted in accordance with ISAs will always detect a material misstatement when it exists. Misstatements can arise from fraud or error and are considered material if, individually or in the aggregate, they could reasonably be expected to influence the economic decisions of users taken on the basis of these financial statements.

As part of an audit in accordance with ISAs, we exercise professional judgment and maintain professional scepticism throughout the audit. We also:

- Identify and assess the risks of material misstatement of the financial statements, whether due to fraud or error, design and perform audit procedures responsive to those risks, and obtain audit evidence that is sufficient and appropriate to provide a basis for our opinion. The risk of not detecting a material misstatement resulting from fraud is higher than for one resulting from error, as fraud may involve collusion, forgery, intentional omissions, misrepresentations, or the override of internal control.
- Obtain an understanding of internal control relevant to the audit in order to design audit procedures that are appropriate in the circumstances, but not for the purpose of expressing an opinion on the effectiveness of the Company's internal control.
- Evaluate the appropriateness of accounting policies used and the reasonableness of accounting estimates and related disclosures made by management.
- Conclude on the appropriateness of management's use of the going concern basis of accounting and, based on the audit evidence obtained, whether a material uncertainty exists related to events or conditions that may cast significant doubt on the Company's ability to continue as a going concern. If we conclude that a material uncertainty exists, we are required to draw attention in our auditor's report to the related disclosures in the financial statements or, if such disclosures are inadequate, to modify our opinion. Our conclusions are based on the audit evidence obtained up to the date of our auditor's report. However, future events or conditions may cause the Company to cease trading as a going concern.

- Evaluate the overall presentation, structure and content of the financial statements, including the disclosures, and whether the financial statements represent the underlying transactions and events in a manner that achieves fair presentation.

We communicate with those charged with governance regarding, among other matters, the planned scope and timing of the audit and significant findings, including any significant deficiencies in internal control that we identify during our audit.

We also provide those charged with governance with a statement that we have complied with relevant ethical requirements regarding independence, and to communicate with them all relationships and other matters that may reasonably be thought to bear on our independence, and where applicable, related safeguards.

From the matters communicated with those charged with governance, we determine those matters that were of most significance in the audit of the financial statements of the current period and are therefore the key audit matters. We describe these matters in our auditor's report unless law or regulation precludes public disclosure about the matter or when, in extremely rare circumstances, we determine that a matter should not be communicated in our report because the adverse consequences of doing so would reasonably be expected to outweigh the public interest benefits of such communication.

Report on Other Legal and Regulatory Requirements

[*As required by local law, regulation or national auditing standards*]

The engagement partner on the audit resulting in this independent auditor's report is Don Henman.

Wimble & Co

Wimble & Co, London

18 February 20X4

ISA 701 ***Communicating Key Audit Matters in the Independent Auditor's Report***

ISA 701 requires auditors of **listed companies** to determine key audit matters and to communicate those matters in the auditor's report.

Auditors of non-listed entities may voluntarily, or at the request of management or those charged with governance, include key audit matters in the audit report.

Key audit matters are those that in the auditor's professional judgment were of most significance in the audit and are selected from matters communicated to those charged with governance.

The purpose of including these matters is to assist users in understanding the entity, and to provide a basis for the users to engage with management and those charged with governance about matters relating to the entity and the financial statements. Each key audit matter should describe why the matter was considered to be significant and how it was addressed in the audit.

Key audit matters include:

- Areas of higher assessed risk of material misstatement, or significant risks identified in accordance with ISA 315.
- Significant auditor judgments relating to areas in the financial statements that involved significant management judgment, including accounting estimates that have been identified as having high estimation uncertainty.
- The effect on the audit of significant events or transactions that occurred during the period.

Specific examples include:

- Significant fraud risk
- Goodwill
- Valuation of financial instruments
- Fair values

- Effects of new accounting standards
- Revenue recognition
- Material provisions such as a restructuring provision
- Implementation of a new IT system, or significant changes to an existing system

Note that a matter giving rise to a qualified or adverse opinion, or a material uncertainty regarding going concern are by their nature key audit matters. However, they would not be described in this section of the report. Instead, a reference to the Basis for qualified or adverse opinion or the going concern section would be included.

If there are no key audit matters to communicate, the auditor shall:

- Discuss this with the engagement quality control reviewer, if one has been appointed.
- Communicate this conclusion to those charged with governance.
- Explain in the key audit matters section of the audit report that there are no matters to report.

Illustration 2: Key Audit Matter

Goodwill

Under IFRSs, the Group is required to annually test the amount of goodwill for impairment. This annual impairment test was significant to our audit because the balance of XX as of December 31, 20X1 is material to the financial statements. In addition, management's assessment process is complex and highly judgmental and is based on assumptions, specifically [describe certain assumptions], which are affected by expected future market or economic conditions, particularly those in [name of country or geographic area].

3 Forming an opinion

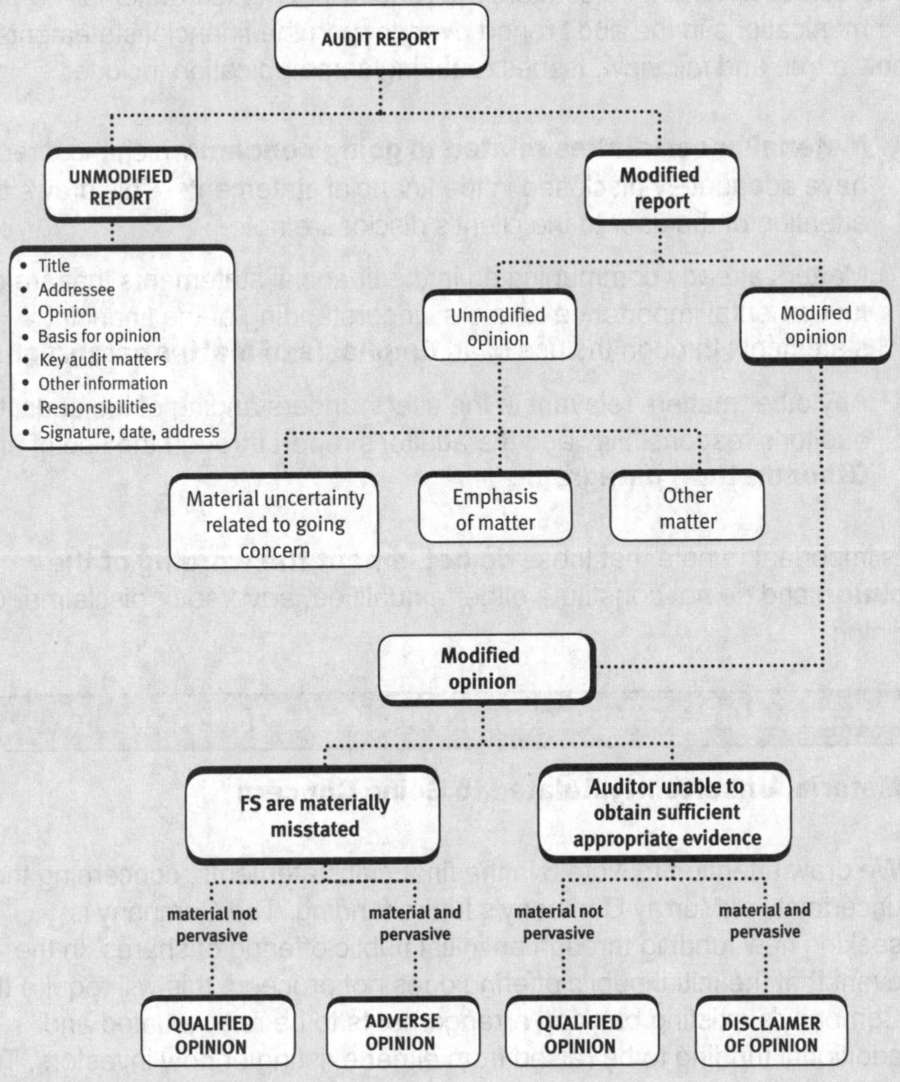

As can be seen from the diagram above, the report can be:

- Unmodified – the FS show a true and fair view. (ISA 700 Revised).
- Modified without modifying the opinion – the FS show a true and fair view but there is something that needs to be brought to the attention of the user by way of an additional paragraph. (ISA 570 (Revised) *Going Concern* and ISA 706 (Revised) *Emphasis of Matter Paragraphs and Other Matter Paragraphs in an Auditor's Report*).
- Modified with a modified opinion – the FS don't fully show a true and fair view or the auditor has not obtained sufficient appropriate evidence to make that conclusion. (ISA 705 (Revised) *Modifications to the Opinion in the Independent Auditor's Report*).

This chapter will take you through the different possibilities for the audit report.

4 Modified report with unmodified opinion

In certain circumstances auditors are required to make additional communications in the audit report even though the financial statements show a true and fair view. Issues requiring communication include:

- **Material uncertainties related to going concern** which the directors have adequately disclosed in the financial statements. This draws the attention of the user to the client's disclosure note.
- Matters already communicated in the financial statements that are of fundamental importance to users' understanding of the financial statements through the use of an **Emphasis of Matter paragraph**.
- Any other matters relevant to the users' understanding of the audit, the auditor's responsibility and the auditor's report through the use of an **Other matters paragraph**.

It is important to note that these **do not impact the wording of the opinion** and do not constitute either a qualified, adverse or disclaimer of opinion.

Illustration 3: Material Uncertainty Related to Going Concern

Material Uncertainty Related to Going Concern

We draw attention to Note 6 in the financial statements, concerning the uncertainty of Murray Company's future funding. The Company is seeking new funding through an initial public offering of shares. In the event that the initial public offering does not proceed, this will require the Company's existing banking arrangements to be renegotiated and additional funding to be raised from either existing or new investors. This condition indicates the existence of a material uncertainty which may cast significant doubt on the Company's ability to continue as a going concern. The financial statements do not include any adjustments that would result if the Company was unable to continue as a going concern. Our opinion is not modified in respect of this matter.

The Emphasis of Matter Paragraph

An Emphasis of matter paragraph is used to refer to **a matter that has been adequately presented or disclosed in the financial statements** by directors. The auditor's judgment is that these matters are **of such fundamental importance to the users' understanding** of the financial statements that the auditor should emphasise the disclosure.

Examples of such fundamental matters include:

- Where the financial statements have been prepared on a basis other than the going concern basis.
- An uncertainty relating to the future outcome of exceptional litigation or regulatory action.
- A significant subsequent event occurs between the date of the financial statements and the date of the auditor's report.
- Early application of a new accounting standard.
- Major catastrophes that have had a significant effect on the entity's financial position.
- Where the corresponding figures have been restated.
- Where the financial statements have been recalled and reissued or when the auditor provides an amended auditor's report.

It is important to note that the emphasis of matter paragraph can only be used when adequate disclosure has been made of the matters mentioned above. The auditor can only emphasise something that is already included.

Where adequate disclosure has not been made the opinion will need to be modified and an emphasis of matter paragraph **should NOT be used**.

An emphasis of matter paragraph should not be used to highlight an issue already included in the Key Audit Matters section of the report.

The heading can be amended to provide further context, for example, Emphasis of Matter – Subsequent event.

When a Key Audit Matters section is presented in the auditor's report, an Emphasis of Matter paragraph may be presented either directly before or after the Key Audit Matters section, based on the auditor's judgment as to the relative significance of the information included in the Emphasis of Matter paragraph.

An emphasis of matter paragraph is not used to draw attention to immaterial misstatements. The fact that they are immaterial means they do not warrant the attention of the shareholders.

Illustration 4: Emphasis of Matter Paragraph

Emphasis of Matter

We draw attention to Note 12 of the financial statements, which describes the effects of a fire at the premises of a third party warehouse provider. Our opinion is not modified in respect of this matter.

Other Matter Paragraph

An 'Other Matter' paragraph is included in the audit report if the auditor considers it necessary to communicate to the users regarding **matters that are not presented or disclosed in the financial statements** that, in the auditor's judgment, are **relevant to understanding the audit, the auditor's responsibilities, or the audit report**.

Examples of its use include:

- To communicate audit planning and scoping matters where laws or regulations require.
- To explain why the auditor has not resigned, when a pervasive inability to obtain sufficient appropriate evidence is imposed by management (e.g. denying the auditor access to books and records) but the auditor is unable to withdraw from the engagement due to legal restrictions.
- When law, regulation or generally accepted practice requires or permits the auditor to provide further explanation of their responsibilities.
- Where an entity prepares one set of accounts in accordance with a general purpose framework and another set in accordance with a different one (e.g. one according to UK and one according to International standards) and engage the auditor to report on both sets.
- To communicate that the auditor's report is intended solely for the intended users, and should not be distributed to or used by other parties.

An Other Matter paragraph does not include confidential information or information required to be provided by management.

The heading may be amended to provide further context, for example, Other Matter – Scope of the audit.

When an Other Matter paragraph is included to draw user's attention to a matter relating to other reporting responsibilities addressed in the auditor's report, the paragraph may be included in the Report on Other Legal and Regulatory Requirements section.

When relevant to all auditor's responsibilities or users' understanding of the auditor's report, the Other Matter paragraph may be included as a separate section following the Report on the Other Legal and Regulatory Requirements.

Illustration 5: Other Matter Paragraph

Other Matter

The financial statements of Murray Co for the year ended December 31, 20X3, were audited by another auditor who expressed an unmodified opinion on those statements on May 31, 20X4.

5 Modified report with modified opinion

Modifications to the audit opinion

The auditor may decide they need to modify the opinion when they conclude that:

- Based upon the evidence obtained **the financial statements** as a whole **are not free from material misstatement**. This is where the client has not complied with the applicable financial reporting framework.
- They have been **unable to gather sufficient appropriate evidence** to be able to conclude that the financial statements as a whole are free from material misstatement. This is evidence the auditor would expect to exist to support the figures in the financial statements.

The nature of the modification depends upon whether the auditor considers the matter to be material and, if so, whether it is pervasive to the financial statements.

Material and pervasive

A matter is considered '**pervasive**' if, in the auditor's judgment:

- The effects are not confined to specific elements, accounts or items of the financial statements
- If so confined, represent or could represent a substantial proportion of the financial statements; or
- In relation to disclosures, are fundamental to users' understanding of the financial statements.

In brief, a pervasive matter must be fundamental to the financial statements, therefore rendering them unreliable as a whole.

Qualified opinions

- If the misstatement or lack of sufficient appropriate evidence is **material but not pervasive**, a **qualified opinion** will be issued.
- This means the matter is material to the area of the financial statements affected but does not affect the remainder of the financial statements.
- **'Except for'** this matter, the financial statements give a true and fair view.
- Whilst significant to users' decision making, a material matter can be isolated whilst the remainder of the financial statements may be relied upon.

Adverse opinion

An **adverse opinion** is issued when a misstatement is considered material and pervasive. This will mean the financial statements **do not give a true and fair view**. Examples include:

- Preparation of the financial statements on the wrong basis.
- Non-consolidation of a subsidiary.
- Material misstatement of a balance which represents a substantial proportion of the assets or profits e.g. would change a profit to a loss.

Disclaimer of opinion

A **disclaimer of opinion** is issued when the auditor has not obtained sufficient appropriate evidence and the effects of any possible misstatements could be pervasive. The auditor **does not express an opinion** on the financial statements in this situation. Examples include:

- Failure by the client to keep adequate accounting records.

- Refusal by the directors to provide written representation.
- Failure by the client to provide evidence over a single balance which represents a substantial proportion of the assets or profits or over multiple balances in the financial statements.

Impact of a disclaimer of opinion

Where a disclaimer of opinion is being issued:

- the statement that sufficient appropriate evidence to provide a basis for the auditor's opinion has been obtained is not included.
- the statements regarding the audit being conducted in accordance with ISAs, and independence and other ethical responsibilities, are positioned within the Auditor Responsibilities section rather than the Basis for Disclaimer of Opinion section.
- the Key Audit Matters section is not included in the audit report as to do so would suggest the financial statements are more credible in relation to those matters which would be inconsistent with the disclaimer of opinion on the financial statements as a whole.

Basis for modified opinion

When the auditor decides to modify the opinion, they must amend the heading 'Basis for Opinion' to 'Basis for Qualified Opinion', 'Basis for Adverse Opinion' or 'Basis for Disclaimer of Opinion', as appropriate.

- The section will explain the reason why the opinion is modified e.g. which balances are misstated, which disclosures are missing or inadequate, which balances the auditor was unable to obtain sufficient appropriate evidence over and why.
- If possible, a quantification of the financial effect of the modification will be included.
- If the material misstatement relates to narrative disclosures, an explanation of how the disclosures are misstated should be included, or in the case of omitted disclosures, the disclosure should be included if the information is readily available.
- Where a qualified or adverse opinion is being issued, the auditor must amend the statement '...the audit evidence is sufficient and appropriate to provide a basis for the auditor's qualified/adverse opinion'.

The following table illustrates the impact on the audit opinion and audit report:

	Material but Not Pervasive	**Material & Pervasive**
Financial statements are materially misstated	Qualified Opinion Except for ... Basis for qualified opinion	Adverse Opinion FS do not give a true and fair view Basis for adverse opinion
Inability to obtain sufficient appropriate audit evidence	Qualified Opinion Except for ... Basis for qualified opinion	Disclaimer of Opinion Do not express an opinion Basis for disclaimer of opinion

Illustration 6: Murray Co Qualified opinion 1

Example where the auditor concludes that the financial statements are materially (but not pervasively) misstated:

Qualified Opinion

We have audited the financial statements of Murray Company (the Company), which comprise the statement of financial position as at 31 December, 20X4, and the statement of comprehensive income, statement of changes in equity and statement of cash flows for the year then ended, and notes to the financial statements, including a summary of significant accounting policies.

In our opinion, **except for the effects of the matter described in the Basis for Qualified Opinion section of our report, the accompanying financial statements give a true and fair view**.................. (remainder of wording as per an unmodified report).

Basis for Qualified Opinion

No allowance has been provided in the financial statements for a receivable for which recoverability is in doubt, which, in our opinion, is not in accordance with International Financial Reporting Standards. The allowance for the year ended 31 December 20X4 should be $211,000 based on the value of the receivable in current assets and the likely recoverability of the amount. Accordingly, current assets should be reduced by an allowance of $211,000 and the profit for the year and accumulated profit should be decreased by the same amount.

We conducted our audit in accordance with International Standards on Auditing (ISAs). Our responsibilities under those standards are further described in the Auditor's Responsibilities for the Audit of the Financial Statements section of our report. We are independent of the Company in accordance with the ethical requirements that are relevant to our audit of the financial statements in [jurisdiction], and we have fulfilled our other ethical responsibilities in accordance with these requirements. **We believe that the audit evidence we have obtained is sufficient and appropriate to provide a basis for our qualified opinion.**

Key Audit Matters

Except for the matter described in the Basis for Qualified Opinion section, we have determined that there are no other key audit matters to communicate in our report.

Illustration 7: Murray Co Qualified opinion 2

Example where the auditor concludes that they have been unable to gather sufficient appropriate evidence and the possible effects are deemed to be material but not pervasive:

Qualified Opinion

We have audited the financial statements of the Murray Company (the Company), which comprise the statement of financial position as at 31 December, 20X4, and the statement of comprehensive income, statement of changes in equity and statement of cash flows for the year then ended, and notes to the financial statements, including a summary of significant accounting policies.

In our opinion, **except for the possible effects of the matter described in the Basis for Qualified Opinion section of our report, the accompanying financial statements give a true and fair view**.................. (remainder of wording as per an unmodified report).

Basis for Qualified Opinion

As described in note 8 to the financial statements, Murray Company is the defendant in a lawsuit alleging constructive dismissal. The Company has filed a counter action, and preliminary hearings and discovery proceedings on both actions are in progress. The liability has been disclosed as contingent in accordance IAS 37 *Provisions and Contingent Liabilities.* We have been unable to obtain a response to our request for information from the solicitors representing Murray Company in the case. We were unable to confirm or verify by alternative means the likely success of the lawsuit and therefore unable to determine whether disclosure of a contingent liability is appropriate, or whether a provision for the value of the claim of $280,000 should be included in the statement of financial position as at 31 December 20X4 and an associated expense included in the statement of profit or loss for the year ended 31 December 20X4. Consequently, we were unable to determine whether any adjustments to these amounts were necessary.

We conducted our audit in accordance with International Standards on Auditing (ISAs). Our responsibilities under those standards are further described in the Auditor's Responsibilities for the Audit of the Financial Statements section of our report. We are independent of the Company in accordance with the ethical requirements that are relevant to our audit of the financial statements in [jurisdiction], and we have fulfilled our other ethical responsibilities in accordance with these requirements. **We believe that the audit evidence we have obtained is sufficient and appropriate to provide a basis for our qualified opinion.**

Key Audit Matters

Except for the matter described in the Basis for Qualified Opinion section, we have determined that there are no other key audit matters to communicate in our report.

Illustration 8: Murray Co Adverse opinion

Example where the auditor concludes that the financial statements are materially and pervasively misstated:

Adverse Opinion

We have audited the financial statements of the Murray Company (the Company), which comprise the statement of financial position as at 31 December, 20X4, and the statement of comprehensive income, statement of changes in equity and statement of cash flows for the year then ended, and notes to the financial statements, including a summary of significant accounting policies.

In our opinion, **because of the significance of the matter discussed in the Basis for Adverse Opinion section of our report, the accompanying financial statements do not give a true and fair view**...... (remainder of wording as per an unmodified report).

Basis for Adverse Opinion

As explained in note 12 to the financial statements, the financial statements have been prepared on the going concern basis. However, in our opinion, due to the number and significance of the material uncertainties, Murray Co is not a going concern in accordance with IAS 1 *Presentation of Financial Statements* and therefore the financial statements should not be prepared on the going concern basis.... [explanation of the various effects on the amounts presented in the financial statements].

We conducted our audit in accordance with International Standards on Auditing (ISAs). Our responsibilities under those standards are further described in the Auditor's Responsibilities for the Audit of the Financial Statements section of our report. We are independent of the Company in accordance with the ethical requirements that are relevant to our audit of the financial statements in [jurisdiction], and we have fulfilled our other ethical responsibilities in accordance with these requirements. **We believe that the audit evidence we have obtained is sufficient and appropriate to provide a basis for our adverse opinion.**

Key Audit Matters

Except for the matter described in the Basis for Adverse Opinion section, we have determined that there are no other key audit matters to communicate in our report.

Illustration 9: Murray Co Disclaimer of opinion

Example where the auditor concludes that they have been unable to gather sufficient appropriate evidence and the possible effects are deemed to be both material and pervasive.

Disclaimer of Opinion

We were engaged to audit the financial statements of Murray Company (the Company), which comprise the statement of financial position as at 31 December, 20X4, and the statement of comprehensive income, statement of changes in equity and statement of cash flows for the year then ended, and notes to the financial statements, including a summary of significant accounting policies.

We do not express an opinion on the accompanying financial statements. Because of the significance of the matter described in the Basis for Disclaimer of Opinion section of our report, **we have not been able to obtain sufficient appropriate evidence to provide a basis for an audit opinion on these financial statements.**

Basis for Disclaimer of Opinion

Due to a fire at a third party warehouse provider's premises, the records relating to inventory held there were destroyed. We were unable to confirm or verify by alternative means closing inventory of $1,054,000 deducted from cost of sales included in the statement of profit or loss for the year ended 31 December 20X4, and the inventory balance of $1,054,000 included in the statement of financial position as at 31 December 20X4.

As a result, we were unable to determine whether any adjustments to the financial statements might have been necessary in respect of recorded or unrecorded inventory or cost of sales, and the associated elements of the statement of changes in equity and statement of cash flows.

Responsibilities of Management and Those Charged With Governance for the Financial Statements

[Wording as per ISA 700]

Auditor's Responsibilities for the Audit of the Financial Statements

Our responsibility is to conduct an audit of the financial statements in accordance with International Standards on Auditing and to issue an auditor's report. However, because of the matter described in the Basis for Disclaimer of Opinion section of our report, we were not able to obtain sufficient appropriate evidence to provide a basis for an audit opinion on these financial statements.

We are independent of the Company in accordance with ethical requirements that are relevant to our audit of the financial statements in [jurisdiction], and we have fulfilled our other ethical responsibilities in accordance with these requirements.

Going concern reporting implications

Situation	Impact on audit opinion	Impact on audit report
No material uncertainty exists regarding going concern	Unmodified – FS give a TFV	Unmodified
Material uncertainty exists and is adequately disclosed by management	Unmodified – FS give a TFV	Modified with a section headed 'Material Uncertainty Related to Going Concern'.
Material uncertainty exists which is not adequately disclosed or is omitted altogether	Modified – qualified or adverse	Modified. Basis for modified opinion explaining the going concern issues management have failed to disclose adequately
Company is not a going concern and has prepared the FS on the break up basis appropriately and made adequate disclosure of this fact	Unmodified – FS give a TFV	Modified with emphasis of matter paragraph
Company is not a going concern and has prepared the FS on the going concern basis	Modified – adverse opinion	Modified. Basis for modified opinion explaining the going concern issues management have failed to account for appropriately
If the period assessed by management is less than twelve months from the statement of financial position date and management is unwilling to extend the assessment.	Modified – qualified or disclaimer due to an inability to obtain sufficient appropriate audit evidence regarding the use of the going concern assumption.	Modified. Basis for modified opinion explaining that sufficient appropriate evidence was not obtained to form a conclusion on the going concern assumption.

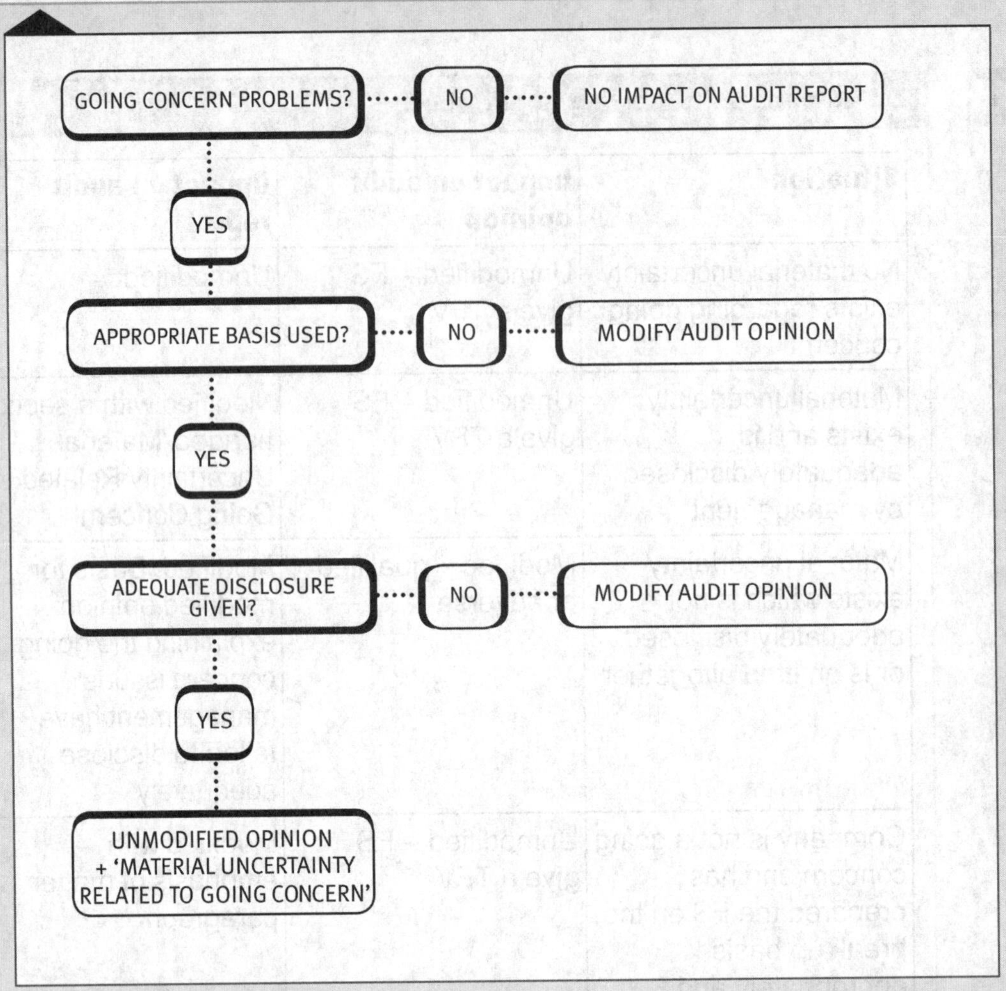

Management imposed limitation of scope

- If after accepting the engagement management impose a limitation of scope that will result in a modified opinion, the auditor will request management remove the limitation.
- If management refuse, the matter must be discussed with those charged with governance.
- The auditor should perform alternative audit procedures to obtain sufficient appropriate evidence, if possible.
- If the auditor is unable to obtain sufficient appropriate evidence and the matter is material but not pervasive, the auditor must issue a qualified audit opinion.
- If the matter is considered pervasive, the auditor must withdraw from the audit.
- If withdrawal is not possible before issuing the auditor's report, a disclaimer of opinion should be issued.
- If the auditor decides to withdraw from the audit, the auditor must communicate any material misstatements identified during the audit to those charged with governance before withdrawing.

6 ISA 720 Other information

ISA 720 (revised) ***The Auditor's Responsibilities Relating to Other Information*** states the objectives of the auditor are:

- To consider whether there is a material inconsistency between the other information and the FS.
- To consider whether there is a material inconsistency between the other information and the auditor's knowledge obtained during the course of the audit.
- To respond appropriately when the auditor identifies such inconsistencies.

The auditor must read and consider the other information to identify any materially inconsistencies with the financial statements or the auditor's knowledge obtained during the audit. Material misstatements or inconsistencies in the other information may undermine the credibility of the financial statements and the auditor's report. The auditor must not be knowingly associated with information which is misleading.

Other information refers to financial or non-financial information, other than the financial statements and auditor's report thereon, included in the entity's annual report, that are not necessarily subject to audit. Examples of other information include:

- Chairman's report
- Operating and financial review
- Social and environmental reports
- Corporate governance statements

Misstatement of other information exists when the other information is incorrectly stated or otherwise misleading (including because it omits or obscures information necessary for a proper understanding of a matter).

If the auditor identifies a material inconsistency:

- Perform limited procedures to evaluate the inconsistency.
- Discuss the matter with management and ask them to make the correction.

- If management refuse to make the correct, communicate the matter to those charged with governance.
- If the matter remains uncorrected the auditor should withdraw from the engagement if possible under applicable law or regulation as the issue casts doubt over management integrity.
- If withdrawal is not possible, the auditor must describe the material misstatement in the audit report.

Reporting implications

If the auditor obtains the final version of the other information before the date of the auditor's report, the auditor includes a separate section under the heading 'Other Information' in the audit report which:

- Identifies the other information obtained by the auditor prior to the date of the audit report.
- States that the auditor has not audited the other information and accordingly does not express an opinion or conclusion on that information.
- Includes a description of the auditor's responsibilities with respect to the other information.
- States either that the auditor has nothing to report, or, a description of the material misstatement if applicable.

The auditor must retain a copy of the final version of the other information on the audit file.

7 Reporting to those charged with governance

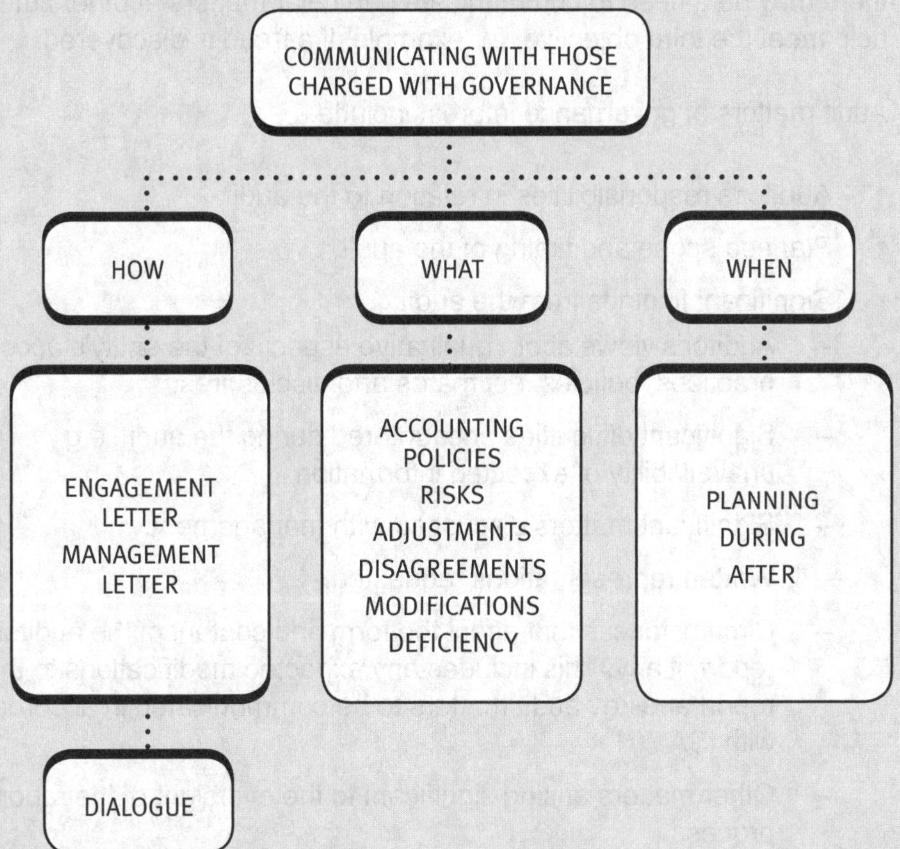

ISAs, in particular ISA 260 (Revised) *Communication with Those Charged with Governance* and ISA 265 *Communicating Deficiencies in Internal Control to Those Charged with Governance and Management*, require the external auditors to engage in communications with management.

The main forms of formal communication between the auditors and management are: the engagement letter (see 'Ethics and Acceptance' chapter); and another written communication, usually sent at the end of the audit, which is often referred to as 'the management letter.'

The objectives of these communications are:

- To communicate the responsibilities of the auditor and an overview of the scope and timing of the audit.
- To obtain, from those charged with governance, information relevant to the audit.
- To provide timely observations arising from the audit that are significant to the responsibilities of those charged with governance.
- To promote effective two-way communication between the auditor and those charged with governance.

Whilst a formal communication is usually sent at the conclusion of the audit there may be a need to communicate particular matters at other times to help meet the third objective, for example, if a fraud is discovered.

Audit matters of governance interest include:

- Auditor's responsibilities in relation to the audit.
- Planned scope and timing of the audit.
- Significant findings from the audit:
  - Auditor's views about qualitative aspects of the entity's accounting practices, policies, estimates and disclosures.
  - Significant difficulties encountered during the audit, e.g. unavailability of expected information.
  - Significant matters discussed with management.
  - Written representations requested.
  - Circumstances that affect the form and content of the auditor's report, if any. This includes any expected modifications to the audit report and key audit matters to be communicated in accordance with ISA 701.
  - Other matters arising significant to the oversight of the reporting process.
- Auditor independence.

Communication with those charged with governance

Timing of communications

Stage of audit	Communication required
Planning	Significant risks identified by the auditor. How the auditor plans to address the risks. Auditor's approach to internal control relevant to the audit. Application of materiality in the context of an audit.
During the audit	If any situation occurs and it would not be appropriate to delay communication until the audit is concluded.
Conclusion of audit	Major findings from audit work. Delays caused by management. Unreasonably brief time to complete the audit.

The auditor must take care not to compromise the effectiveness of the audit by communicating too much information about the planned scope and timing of the audit to such an extent that procedures become too predictable.

Test your understanding 1

In terms of audit reports, explain the term 'modified'.

(2 marks)

Test your understanding 2

ISA 260 *Communication with Those Charged with Governance* deals with the auditor's responsibility to communicate with those charged with governance in relation to an audit of financial statements.

Required:

(i) **Describe TWO specific responsibilities of those charged with governance; and**

(2 marks)

(ii) **Explain FOUR examples of matters that might be communicated to them by the auditor.**

(4 marks)

Test your understanding 3

Henry

(a) Aragon Co made a very poor attempt to conduct their inventory count. You attended, however there was insufficient evidence that the inventory valuation at $4 million is accurate. Sales revenue was $50 million and profit for the year was $15 million.

(b) Boleyn Co did not provide for a bad debt of $50,000 despite the fact that the customer went bankrupt just after the year end. Profit for the year was $500,000 and trade receivables $200,000.

(c) Seymour Co is being sued by a competitor company for the theft of intellectual property. The amount that Seymour is being sued for is material, but not a substantial amount, and the case could go either way. However, this is not mentioned anywhere in the financial statements.

(d) Howard Co is a cash retailer. There is no system to confirm the accuracy of cash sales.

(e) Cleves Co has neglected to include a statement of profit or loss in its financial statements.

(f) Parr Co is undergoing a major court case that would bankrupt the company if lost. The directors assess and disclose the case as a contingent liability in the accounts. The auditors agree with the treatment and disclosure.

Required:

For each of the above situations state what type of audit report should be issued and explain your choice.

(18 marks)

Test your understanding 4

You are the audit manager of Brakes Co, a listed client, and you are undertaking an overall review of the evidence obtained as part of the audit finalisation. Brakes Co is a global manufacturer of braking systems for use in domestic and commercial motor vehicles. $250,000 was raised through a new share issue in the year. Draft profit before tax is $9m and total assets are $37m.

(a) Explain the importance of the overall review of evidence obtained.

(3 marks)

(b) During your review you notice that one section of the file remains incomplete; that relating to share capital and reserves.

Required:

Describe audit procedures that should be performed in respect of Brake's share capital and reserves:

(4 marks)

(c) The following matters arising during the audit of Brakes Co have been noted on file for your attention:

(i) A customer of Brakes Co had to withdraw one of their family car models this year due to concerns over the safety of the braking system. The customer has lodged a legal claim against Brakes Co for $10m for the negligent supply of 'faulty' braking systems. The company's lawyers believe that there is an 80% chance that Brakes Co will lose the case but the directors believe that their quality control procedures have always been robust and that the braking systems will be proven to have been safe. They have however decided to disclose the matter in the accounts to provide additional information to shareholders.

(5 marks)

(ii) Brakes Co also produces and sells brake fluid. Another customer has recently returned a small batch of brake fluid because the fluid appeared to be contaminated with oil. Brakes Co issued the customer with a credit note for the full value ($137,500) and correctly accounted for this in the draft financial statements. As the brake fluid was returned before the year end, Brakes Co has included it in the year end inventory listing at cost ($125,000). Brakes Co may be able to re-filter and re-sell the brake fluid at the original price, but filtering will cost a further $62,500.

(4 marks)

(iii) Four months ago, Brakes Co began renting some additional warehouse space from a third party storage provider, Wheels Co. At the year end, a number of items of raw material belonging to Brakes were stored by Wheels Co. The directors of Brakes Co did not make you aware of the new third party storage facility. Consequently, no audit procedures were included in the audit plan to verify the quantity of raw material owned by Brakes Co but held by Wheels at the year end. $3.2m is included in inventory in Brakes Co draft financial statements, in respect of this raw material.

(4 marks)

Required:

Discuss each of these issues and describe the impact on the audit report if the above issues remain unresolved.

Note: The mark allocation is shown against each of the three issues above. Audit report extracts are NOT required.

(13 marks)

(Total: 20 marks)

Test your understanding 5 – OT Case 1

You are about to issue the audit report for Exmouth Co, a listed client. Half way through the year the company suffered a major computer systems failure which destroyed the accounting records for the year to date. Backups had not been kept and so the company has had to reconstruct the figures for the first six months.

(1) Which opinions are most appropriate in this situation?

A Qualified or adverse

B Unmodified or adverse

C Unmodified or disclaimer

D Qualified or disclaimer

(2) What it the purpose of the Basis for Opinion paragraph in an unmodified report?

A To state the opinion on the financial statements.

B To confirm the audit has been conducted in accordance with ISAs and ethical requirements.

C To highlight a material uncertainty relating to going concern which has been adequately disclosed.

D To highlight management's responsibilities to the users of the financial statements.

(3) Which of the following shows the correct order for the elements of the audit report given?

A Opinion, date, auditor's address, signature

B Title, opinion, signature, key audit matters

C Addressee, opinion, auditor's responsibilities, date

D Responsibilities of management, basis for opinion, date, addressee

(4) Which of the following describes a disclaimer of opinion?

A The financial statements give a true and fair view

B The financial statements do not give a true and fair view

C The auditor does not express an opinion on the financial statements

D Except for the matter described, the financial statements give a true and fair view

(5) Which of the following statements is correct in relation to the issue described?

A The Key Audit Matters section should be used to describe the matter giving rise to the modified opinion, in this case that the auditor has been unable to obtain sufficient appropriate evidence

B If a disclaimer of opinion is to be issued, the Key Audit Matters section should not be included in the audit report as to do so may suggest other aspects of the financial statements are reliable

C An Emphasis of Matter paragraph should be included to draw attention to the inability to obtain sufficient appropriate evidence

D The auditor will conclude that the financial statements do not give a true and fair view

Test your understanding 6 – OT Case 2

You are about to issue the audit report for two listed clients, Kalgoorlie Co and Cundeelee Co. The financial statements show the following:

	Kalgoorlie	Cundeelee
	$000	$000
Profit before tax	10	245
Total assets	2,300	6,500
Uncorrected misstatements:		
Overstatement of receivables due do an irrecoverable debt not being written off	15	
Overstatement of inventory due to failure to value at lower of cost and NRV		85

(1) Which of the following is the most appropriate opinion for Kalgoorlie Co?

A Adverse

B Disclaimer

C Qualified

D Unmodified

(2) Which of the following is the most appropriate opinion for Cundeelee Co?

A Adverse

B Disclaimer

C Qualified

D Unmodified

(3) How would your answer change for Cundeelee Co if the misstatement of inventory had been $10,000 instead of $85,000?

A Adverse opinion

B Unmodified opinion with emphasis of matter

C Qualified opinion

D Unmodified opinion and report

(4) You have also identified material uncertainties relating to going concern during your audit of Kalgoorlie Co. These have been adequately disclosed by management. How will this impact the audit report?

A The report should include a section titled 'Emphasis of Matter' which will refer to the management's disclosure note

B The report should include a section titled 'Material Uncertainty Related to Going Concern' which will refer to the management's disclosure note

C The report should include a section titled 'Going concern issues' which will refer to the management's disclosure note

D As management have adequately disclosed the uncertainties relating to going concern, the auditor does not need to modify the report as the financial statements include the appropriate information

(5) Included within the financial statements of Cundeelee Co is a provision for a legal case of which the outcome is uncertain at this date. Adequate disclosure of the matter has been included by management. The case represents a significant uncertainty and you have included an emphasis of matter in your audit report to refer to the client's disclosure of the uncertainty. What other modifications, if any, will be required to the report in respect of this matter?

A The opinion should be modified as a result of the significant uncertainty

B No further modifications to the report are required

C The Key Audit Matters section should describe the uncertainty

D The Basis for Opinion section should describe the uncertainty

8 Chapter summary

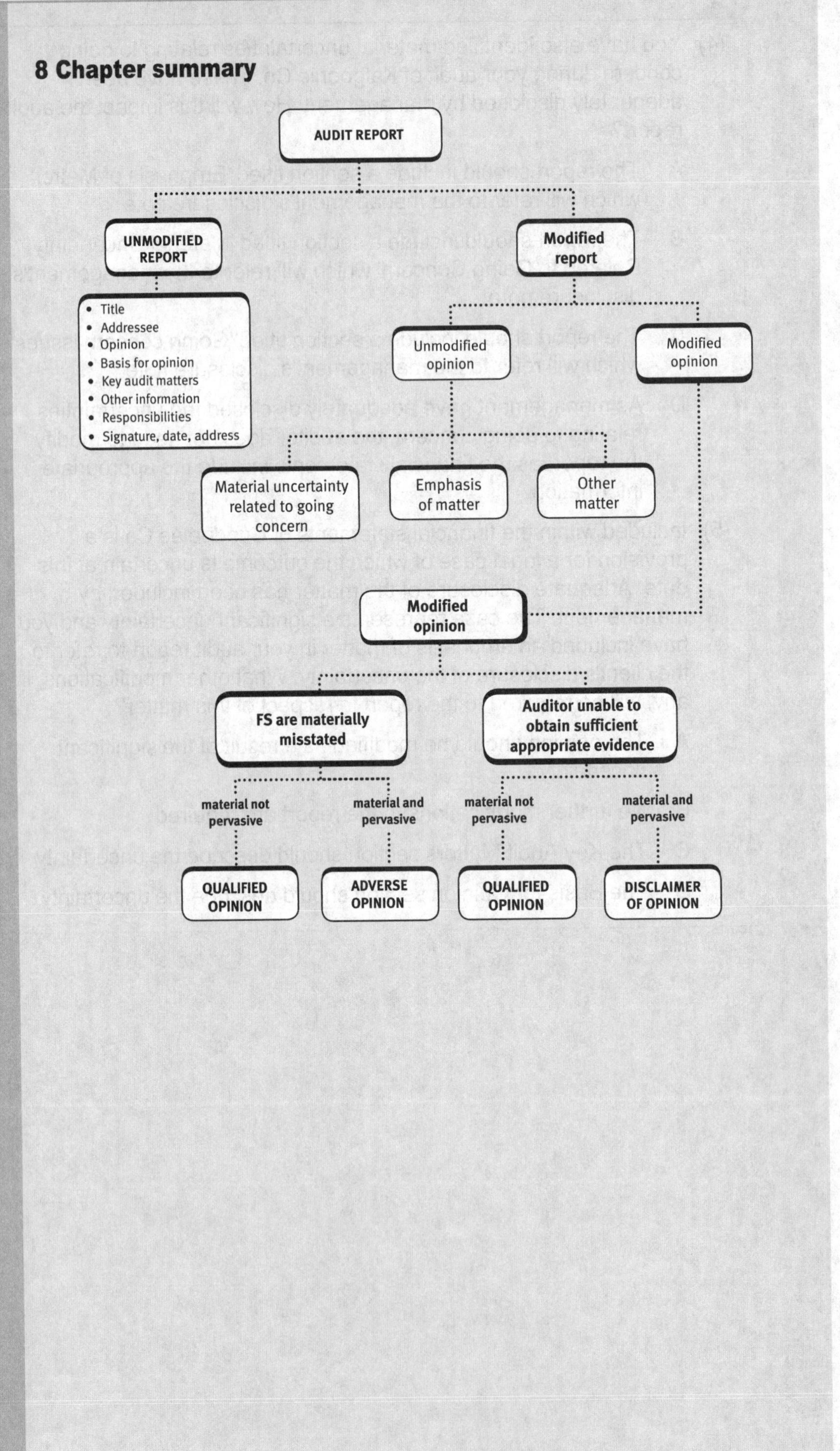

Test your understanding answers

Test your understanding 1

Audit report term

Modified. An auditor modifies an audit report in any situation where it is inappropriate to provide an unmodified report.

For example, the auditor may provide additional information in an emphasis of matter (which does not affect the auditor's opinion) or modify the audit opinion because the financial statements as a whole are not free from material misstatement or the auditor is unable to obtain sufficient appropriate evidence to conclude that the financial statements are free from material misstatement.

Test your understanding 2

(i) Those charged with governance are responsible for overseeing:

- the strategic direction of the entity
- obligations related to the accountability of the entity. This includes overseeing the financial reporting process
- promotion of good corporate governance
- risk assessment processes
- the establishment and monitoring of internal controls
- compliance with applicable law and regulations
- implementation of controls to prevent and detect fraud and errors.

(ii) General audit matters that might be communicated to those charged with governance are:

(1) The auditor's responsibilities in relation to financial statement audit. This would include:

- A statement that the auditor is responsible for forming and expressing an opinion on the financial statements.
- That the auditor's work is carried out in accordance with ISAs and in accordance with local laws and regulations.

(2) Planned scope and timing of the audit. This would include:

- The audit approach to assessing the risk of serious misstatement, whether arising from fraud or error.
- The audit approach to the internal control system and whether reliance will be placed on it.
- The timing of interim and final audits, including reporting deadlines.

(3) Significant findings from the audit. This could include:

- Significant difficulties encountered during the audit, including delays in obtaining information from management.
- Material deficiencies in internal control and recommendations for improvement.
- Audit adjustments, whether or not recorded by the entity, that have, or could have, a material effect on the entity's financial statements. For example, the bankruptcy of a material receivable shortly after the year-end that should result in an adjusting entry.

(4) A statement on independence issues affecting the audit. This would include:

- That the audit firm has ensured that all members of the audit team have complied with the ethical standards of ACCA.
- That appropriate safeguards are in place where a potential threat to independence has been identified.

Test your understanding 3

(a) There is a lack of sufficient appropriate audit evidence, specifically relating to the valuation of inventory. Inventory is a material amount since it is 8% of sales revenue and 27% of profit. A modified report with a qualified opinion will be issued (using the 'except for' wording) due an inability to obtain sufficient appropriate audit evidence.

(b) The financial statements are materially misstated as the event after the reporting date is an adjusting event in accordance with IAS 10 and therefore the debt should be written off. The debt of $50,000 is material since it is 10% of profit and 25% of the total receivables. A report with a qualified opinion will be issued (using the 'except for' wording) due to a material misstatement.

(c) The financial statements are materially misstated since this is a contingent liability in accordance with IAS 37 and so should be disclosed by note. The matter is material. A modified report with a qualified opinion will be issued (using the 'except for' wording) due to a material omission.

(d) There is a lack of sufficient appropriate audit evidence if there is no method available to confirm cash sales. The matter would be material and pervasive since if cash sales cannot be confirmed, it may also not be possible to verify other figures in the financial statements. A modified report with a disclaimer of opinion will be issued.

(e) The financial statements are materially misstated since legislation requires companies to publish a statement of profit or loss. The matter would material and pervasive. A modified report with an adverse opinion will be issued.

(f) An unmodified opinion would be issued since the auditors agree with the treatment and disclosure of the contingent liability. However, there is a fundamental uncertainty (the outcome of the court case will be determined in the future). The report would be modified with an emphasis of matter paragraph.

Note: Where a modified opinion is required, the 'Basis for Opinion' section will be amended to 'Basis for Qualified Opinion', 'Basis for Adverse Opinion' or 'Basis for Disclaimer of Opinion' to explain the reason for the modification. The Key Audit Matters section, if applicable, will reference the 'Basis for ... Opinion' section.

Test your understanding 4

(a) Reasons why the overall review of evidence obtained is important:

– It enables the auditor to satisfy themselves that sufficient appropriate evidence has been obtained.

– It enables the auditor to satisfy themselves that the evidence supports any conclusions reached, and is appropriately documented.

– It enables the auditor to ensure work has been performed in accordance with professional standards and applicable legal and regulatory requirements (quality control monitoring).

– For the appraisal and development of staff.

(b) Audit procedures regarding share capital and reserves

Share capital

- Agree authorised share capital and nominal value disclosures to underlying shareholding agreements/statutory constitution documents.
- Inspect cash book for evidence of cash receipts from share issues and ensure amounts not yet received are correctly disclosed as share capital called-up not paid in the financial statements.
- Inspect board minutes to verify issue of share capital during the year.

Reserves

– Agree opening reserves to prior-year closing reserves and reconcile movements.

– Agree movements in reserves to supporting documentation (e.g. revaluation reserve movements independently valuers report).

(c) Impact on audit report:

(i) Faulty brake systems

According to IAS 37 *Provisions, Contingent Liabilities and Contingent Assets*, if there is a present obligation, a probable outflow of resources to settle the obligation and a reliable estimate can be made of the obligation then a provision should be recognised. If the obligation is only possible, then a contingent liability should be disclosed.

It is probable that Brakes Co will lose the legal case and therefore the claim of $10m should be provided for in the financial statements. The amount of $10m is 111% ($10m/$9m) of profit before tax and is therefore material. The $10m provision would turn a profit of $9m into a loss of $1m and is also therefore pervasive.

Refusal to provide would change the whole view given by the financial statements and as a result an adverse opinion would be necessary.

The 'Basis for Adverse Opinion' section would describe the matter giving rise to the modification.

The Key Audit Matters section would reference the 'Basis for Qualified Opinion'.

(ii) Contaminated brake fluid

Inventory should be stated at the lower of cost and net realisable value, in accordance with IAS 2 *Inventories*.

The contaminated brake fluid cost $125,000. If sold at the original price charged of $137,500, the net realisable value will be $75,000 ($137,500 less $62,500 re-filtering costs). Inventory is therefore overstated by $50,000.

$50,000 is not material at 0.6% of profit ($50,000/$9m) and 0.1% of total assets ($50,000/$37m).

The misstatement should be brought to the attention of management and they should be asked to correct it.

However, as the misstatement is not material, the audit opinion would not be modified in respect of this matter and no reference to the misstatement would be made in the audit report.

(iii) Inventory held at third party premises

The auditor has not obtained sufficient appropriate evidence over the inventory held at third party premises.

The inventory is material to the statement of profit or loss at 36% of profit ($3.2m/$9m) and the statement of financial position at 8.6% of total assets ($3.2m/$37m)).

If alternative sources of evidence cannot be obtained, it will be necessary to modify the audit opinion due to an inability to obtain sufficient appropriate evidence.

A qualified opinion using the 'except for' wording would be necessary.

The 'Basis for Qualified Opinion' section would describe the matter giving rise to the qualification.

The Key Audit Matters section would reference the 'Basis for Qualified Opinion'.

Test your understanding 5 – OT Case 1

(1)	D	Qualified or disclaimer. Six months of accounting records have been lost meaning sufficient appropriate evidence will not be available. Whether the matter is deemed material or material and pervasive will depend on the auditor's assessment of the reconstruction of figures for the first six months.
(2)	B	A 'basis for....opinion' paragraph confirms the audit has been conducted in accordance with ISAs and ethical requirements.
(3)	C	Addressee, opinion, auditor's responsibilities, date.
(4)	C	A disclaimer of opinion is where the auditor does not express an opinion.
(5)	B	ISA 705 (revised) states that where a disclaimer of opinion is issued, the key audit matters section should not be included in the audit report.

Test your understanding 6 – OT Case 2

(1)	A	Whilst the misstatements represent less than 1% of total assets, they represent 150% of PBT and would turn the profit of $10,000 to a loss of $15,000 which is pervasive. Therefore an adverse opinion would be appropriate.
(2)	C	The misstatement represents 35% of PBT and 1.3% of total assets. This is material but not pervasive. A qualified opinion is appropriate.
(3)	D	The misstatement would represent 4.1% of PBT and 0.15% of total assets. This is not material. An unmodified report and opinion would be appropriate.
(4)	B	A section titled 'Material Uncertainty Related to Going Concern' will be included in the audit report.
(5)	B	No further modifications are required. The Key Audit Matters section should not describe matters already described in an Emphasis of Matter paragraph. The Basis for Opinion section would only describe matters giving rise to a modified opinion. As management have included the provision and disclosure of the legal case in the financial statements there is no reason to modify the audit opinion.

chapter

11

Corporate governance

Chapter learning objectives

This chapter covers syllabus areas:

- A3 – Corporate governance

1 Introduction

What is corporate governance?

Corporate governance is the means by which a company is **operated** and **controlled.**

The aim of corporate governance initiatives is to ensure that companies are run well in the interests of their shareholders and the wider community.

In response to major accounting scandals (e.g. Enron), regulators sought to change the rules surrounding the governance of companies, particularly publically owned ones.

In the US the Sarbanes Oxley Act (2002) introduced a set of rigorous corporate governance laws and at the same time the UK Corporate Governance Code introduced a set of best practice corporate governance initiatives into the UK.

External auditors in the UK are required to report on whether listed entities are compliant with the Code.

The principles of the Corporate Governance Code are considered best practise and are examinable for this paper.

2 The Corporate Governance Code

The Corporate Governance Code sets out the following main principles:

Leadership

- Each company should have an effective board who take collective responsibility for the long term success of the company.
- There should be clear division of responsibilities between running the board and the running of the company.
- No-one should have unfettered powers of decision.
- The chairman should lead the board and ensure it is effective.
- Non-executive directors should constructively challenge and help develop strategy.

Effectiveness

- The board should have the appropriate balance of skills, experience, independence and knowledge of the company.
- Appointment of directors should be made through a formal, transparent and rigorous process.
- Directors should allocate sufficient time to discharge their responsibilities.
- All directors should receive induction on joining the board and should regularly update and refresh their skills and knowledge.
- The board should be supplied with timely information in an appropriate form and quality.
- The board should undertake formal and rigorous evaluation of its performance and that of its committees and individual directors.
- All directors should be submitted for re-election at regular intervals subject to satisfactory performance.

Accountability

- The board should present a balanced and understandable assessment of the company's position and prospects.
- The board is responsible for determining the nature and extent of the significant risks it is willing to take in achieving its strategic objectives.
- The board should maintain sound risk management and internal control systems.
- The board should establish formal and transparent arrangements for applying principles for maintaining an appropriate relationship with the company's auditor.

Remuneration

- Levels of remuneration should be sufficient to attract, retain and motivate directors of the quality required but should not pay more than necessary.
- Remuneration should be designed to promote the long-term success of the company.
- The board should establish formal and transparent procedures for developing the policy for executive directors remuneration.
- No director should be involved in setting his own pay.

Relations with shareholders

- There should be dialogue with shareholders based on a mutual understanding of objectives.
- The board as a whole has responsibility for ensuring satisfactory dialogue with shareholders takes place.
- The board should use general meetings to communicate with investors and encourage their participation.

It is particularly important for publicly traded companies because large amounts of money are invested in them, either by 'small' shareholders, or from pension schemes and other financial institutions. The wealth of these companies significantly affects the health of the economies where their shares are traded.

3 Auditor reporting responsibilities

ISA 700 (UK and Ireland) requires the auditor to report by exception on the following matters in the audit reports of companies disclosing compliance with the UK Corporate Governance Code where the annual report includes:

- A statement given by the directors that they consider the annual report and accounts taken as a whole is fair, balanced and understandable and provides the information necessary for shareholders to assess the entity's performance, business model and strategy, that is inconsistent with the knowledge acquired by the auditor in the course of performing the audit.
- A section describing the work of the audit committee that does not appropriately address matters communicated by the auditor to the audit committee.
- An explanation, as to why the annual report does not include such a statement or section, that is materially inconsistent with the knowledge acquired by the auditor in the course of performing the audit.
- Other information that, in the auditor's judgment, contains a material inconsistency or a material misstatement of fact.

Other countries may have different reporting requirements in accordance with local legislation and regulations.

Enron

In the year 2000 Enron, a US based energy company, employed 22,000 people and reported revenues of $101 billion. In late 2001 they filed for bankruptcy protection. After a lengthy investigation it was revealed that Enron's financial statements were sustained substantially by systematic, and creatively planned, accounting fraud.

In the wake of the fraud case the shares of Enron fell from over $90 each to just a few cents each, a number of directors were prosecuted and jailed and their auditors, Arthur Andersen, were accused of obstruction of justice and forced to stop auditing public companies. This ruling against Arthur Andersen was overturned at a later date but the damage was done and the firm ceased trading soon after.

This was just one of a number of high profile frauds to occur at the turn of the millennium.

The Enron scandal is an example of the abuse of the trust placed in the management of publicly traded companies by investors. This abuse of trust usually takes one of two forms:

- the direct extraction from the company of excessive benefits by management, e.g. large salaries, pension entitlements, share options, use of company assets (jets, apartments etc.)
- manipulation of the share price by misrepresenting the company's profitability, usually so that shares in the company can be sold or options 'cashed in'.

In response regulators sought to change the rules surrounding the governance of companies, particularly publically owned ones. In the US the Sarbanes Oxley Act (2002) introduced a set of rigorous corporate governance laws and at the same time the Combined Code (now called the UK Corporate Governance Code) introduced a set of best practice corporate governance initiatives into the UK.

4 Corporate governance in action

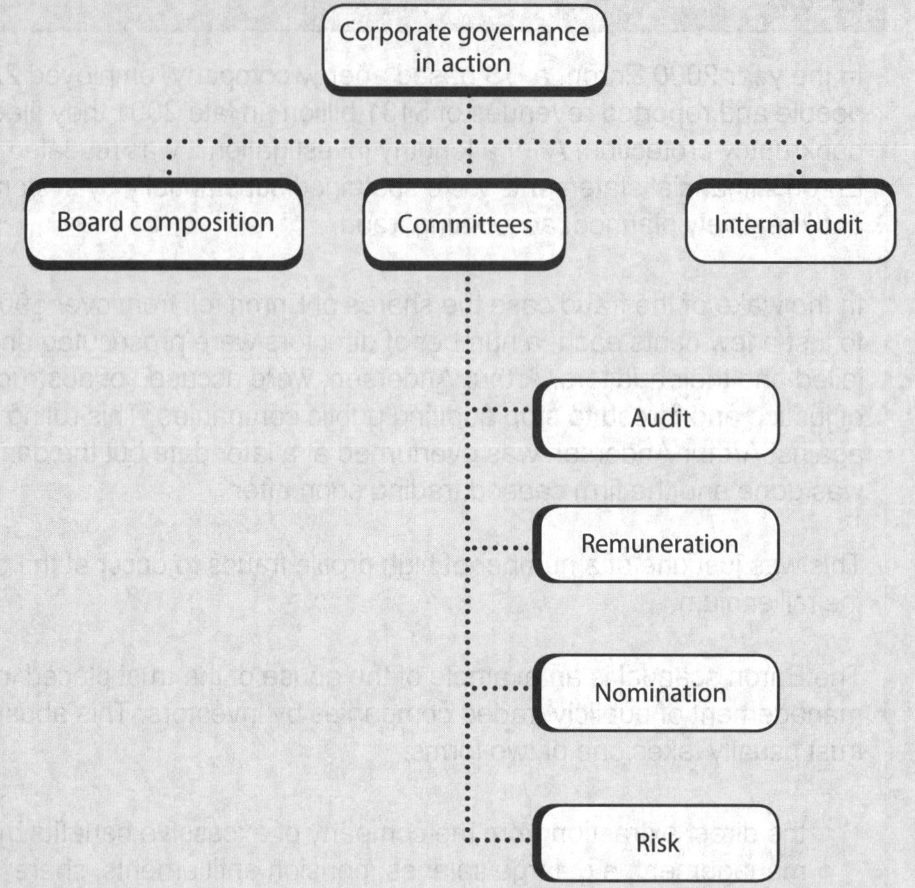

Segregation of roles

The roles of the Chairman and chief executive officer (CEO) should be held by two separate people to avoid concentration of power.

The chairman should preferably be independent to enhance effectiveness.

Board composition

The board should comprise of a balance of executive directors and non-executive directors. The executives run the company on a day to day basis. The non-executive directors monitor the executive directors and contribute to the overall strategy and direction of the organisation.

Audit committee

The audit committee will take responsibility for financial reporting and internal control matters. See below.

Remuneration committee

The role of the remuneration committee is to set the remuneration packages for the executive directors. This is to ensure that they are not paid excessive amounts but are paid fairly for their role. The committee will be comprised of non-executive directors.

Advantages:

- Decisions are based on agreement of several people, reducing the risk of bribes from directors in return for a higher package.
- No director is involved in setting his own pay.
- Performance related elements will be included to avoid the risk that directors are rewarded for poor performance.

Nomination committee

The role of the nomination committee is to decide on appointments of executive directors. This is to ensure the best person for the job is recruited. The committee will be comprised of non-executive directors.

Advantages:

- Reduces the risk of 'jobs for the boys'. Executive directors might appoint other directors who they are friends with or used to work with but wouldn't necessarily be the person with the skills required.
- Reduces the risk of improperly affecting board decisions. Executives might appoint people to the board they know will vote in favour of the same decisions as them and can therefore influence board decisions which may not be in the best interests of the company.

Risk committee

The risk committee will be responsible for assessing the risks of the company and deciding on the appropriate risk management approach. See below.

The roles of the board members

Segregation of roles

Best practice recommends that the roles of Chairman and Chief Executive Officer should be held be different people to reduce the power of prominent board members.

The chairman's role

- Head of the non-executive directors.
- Enables flow of information and discussion at board meetings.
- Ensures satisfactory channels of communication with the external auditors.
- Ensures the effective operation of sub-committees of the board.

The Chief executive's role

- Ensures the effective operation of the company.
- Head of the executive directors.

Non-executive directors

Non-executive directors are usually employed on a part-time basis and do not take part in the routine executive management of the company. Their role is as follows:

- Participation at board meetings.
- Provision of experience, insight and contacts to assist the board.
- Membership of sub-committees as independent, knowledgeable parties.

Advantages of participation by non-executive directors

- Oversight of the whole board.
- Often act as a 'corporate conscience'.
- They bring external expertise to the company.

Disadvantages

- They, and the sub-committees, may not be sufficiently well-informed or have time to fulfil the role competently.
- They are subject to the accusation that they are staffed by an 'old boy' network and may fail to report significant problems and approve unjustified pay rises.

Enron provides a cautionary note as its audit committee proved incapable of preventing the wrongdoing of the executive directors.

5 Audit committees

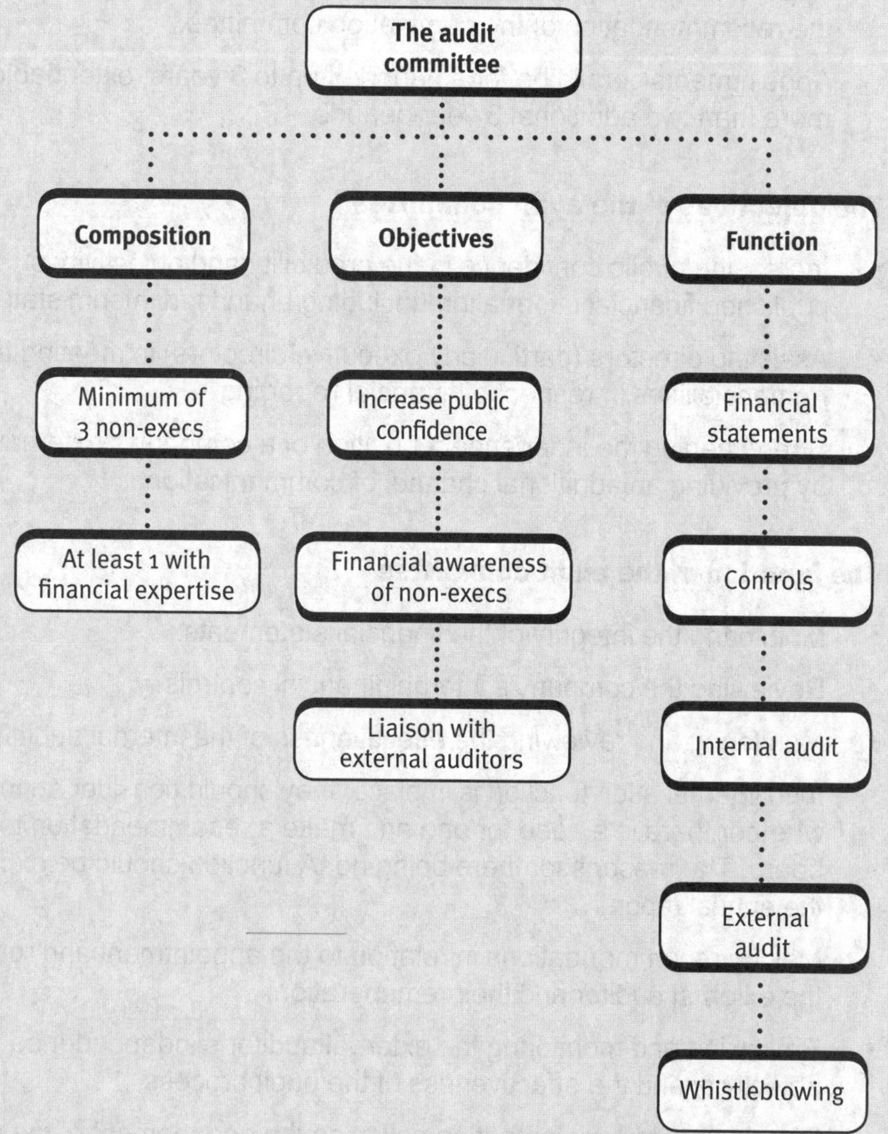

An audit committee is a committee consisting of non-executive directors which is able to view a company's affairs in a detached and independent way and liaise effectively between the main board of directors and the external auditors.

Membership of audit committees

- A group of independent, non-executive directors.
- The committee should have at least 3 members (2 for smaller companies).
- At least one member should have recent and relevant financial experience with an appropriate professional accountancy qualification.
- Committee members should be independent of operational management.
- Appointments to the audit committee should be made by the board on the recommendation of the nomination committee.
- Appointments should be for a period of up to 3 years, extendable by no more than two additional 3 year periods.

The objectives of the audit committee

- Increasing public confidence in the credibility and objectivity of published financial information (including unaudited interim statements).
- Assisting directors (particularly executive directors) in meeting their responsibilities in respect of financial reporting.
- Strengthening the independent position of a company's external auditor by providing an additional channel of communication.

The function of the audit committee

- Monitoring the integrity of the financial statements.
- Reviewing the company's internal financial controls.
- Monitoring and reviewing the effectiveness of the internal audit function.
- If no internal audit function is in place, they should consider annually whether there is a need for one and make a recommendation to the board. The reasons for there being no IA function should be explained in the annual report.
- Making recommendations in relation to the appointment and removal of the external auditor and their remuneration.
- Reviewing and monitoring the external auditor's independence and objectivity and the effectiveness of the audit process.
- Developing and implementing policy on the engagement of the external auditor to supply non-audit services.
- Reviewing arrangements for confidential reporting by employees and investigation of possible improprieties ('whistleblowing').

Benefits:

- Improved credibility of the financial statements, through an impartial review of the financial statements, and discussion of significant issues with the external auditors.
- Increased public confidence in the audit opinion, as the audit committee will monitor the independence of the external auditors.
- Stronger control environment, as the audit committee help to create a culture of compliance and control.
- The internal audit function will report to the audit committee increasing their independence and adding weight to their recommendations.
- The skills, knowledge and experience (and independence) of the audit committee members can be an invaluable resource for a business.
- It may be easier and cheaper to arrange finance, as the presence of an audit committee can give a perception of good corporate governance.
- It would be less burdensome to meet listing requirements if an audit committee (which is usually a listing requirement) is already established.

Problems:

- Difficulties recruiting the right non-executive directors who have relevant skills, experience and sufficient time to become effective members of the committee.
- The cost. Non-executive directors are normally remunerated, and their fees can be quite expensive.

FRC Guidance on audit committees

- This guidance is designed to assist company boards when implementing the Corporate Governance Code.
- Companies with a premium listing are required to comply with the Code or explain why they have not done so.
- Audit committee arrangements should be proportionate to the task and will vary according to size and complexity of the company.
- There should be a frank, open working relationship and a high level of mutual respect between audit committee chairman and board chairman, the chief executive and the finance director.
- Management is under an obligation to ensure the audit committee is kept properly informed. All directors must cooperate with the audit committee.

- The core functions of audit committees are oversight, assessment and review. It is not the duty of the audit committee to carry out functions that belong to others. For example, they should make sure there is a proper system in place for monitoring of internal controls but should not do the monitoring themselves.
- The board should review the audit committee's effectiveness annually.

The audit committee should:

- receive induction and training for new members and continuing training as required.
- hold as many meetings as the roles and responsibilities require and it is recommended that no fewer than three meetings are held.
- meet the external and internal auditors without management at least annually to discuss any issues arising from the audit.
- report to the board on how it has discharged its responsibilities.
- ensure the interests of the shareholders are properly protected in relation to financial reporting and internal control.
- review and report to the board on the significant financial reporting issues and judgments in connection with the preparation of the financial statements.
- consider the appropriateness of significant accounting policies, significant estimates and judgments.
- receive reports from management on the effectiveness of systems and the conclusions of any testing carried out by internal and external auditors.
- review the systems established by management to identify, assess, manage and monitor financial risks.
- monitor and review the effectiveness of the company's internal audit function. Where there is no internal audit function the audit committee should consider annually the need for one and make a recommendation to the board.
- review whistleblowing arrangements by which staff of the company may raise concerns about possible improprieties in financial reporting and other matters, in confidence.

Annual report

A separate section of the annual report should describe the work of the committee. Specifically:

- A summary of the role of the audit committee.
- The names and qualifications of all members of the audit committee during the period.
- The number of audit committee meetings.
- The significant issues that the committee considered in relation to the financial statements and how these issued were addressed.
- An explanation of how it has assessed the effectiveness of the external audit process and the approach taken to the appointment or reappointment of the external auditor.
- If the external auditor provides non-audit services, how auditor objectivity and independence is safeguarded.
- Where there is a disagreement between the audit committee and the board which cannot be resolved, the audit committee should have the right to report the issue to shareholders as part of its report within the annual report.
- The chairman of the audit committee should be present at the AGM to answer questions.

External audit matters

The audit committee is responsible for making a recommendation on the appointment, reappointment and removal of the external auditors. FTSE 350 companies should put the audit out to tender at least once every ten years to enable the audit committee to compare the quality and effectiveness of the services provided by the incumbent auditor with those of other firms.

The audit committee should:

- annually assess and report to the board on the qualification, expertise and resources, and independence of the external auditors and the effectiveness of the audit process.

- investigate reasons for the resignation of the external auditor and consider whether any action is required.
- assess the independence and objectivity of the external auditor annually.
- set and apply a formal policy specifying the types of non-audit service which are pre-approved, require approval or are not allowed.
- agree a policy for employment of former employees of the external auditor taking into account the Ethical Standards, paying particular attention to people who were part of the audit team. The audit committee should consider whether there has been any impairment of the auditors independence and objectivity in respect of the audit.
- monitor the external audit firm's compliance with ethical standards relating to partner rotation and fee levels.

The audit committee and internal audit

The audit committee should:

- Ensure that the internal auditor has direct access to the board chairman and to the audit committee and is accountable to the audit committee.
- Review and assess the annual internal audit work plan.
- Receive periodic reports on the results of internal audit work.
- Review and monitor management's responsiveness to the internal auditor's findings and recommendations.
- Meet with the head of internal audit at least once a year without the presence of management.
- Monitor and assess the effectiveness of internal audit in the overall context of the company's risk management system.

Risk management

Risk management in practice

Companies face many risks, for example:

- The risk that products may become technologically obsolete.
- The risk of losing key staff.
- The risk of a catastrophic failure of IT systems.
- The risk of changes in government policy.
- The risk of fire or natural disaster.

Companies need mechanisms in place to identify and then assess those risks. In so doing companies can rank risks in terms of their relative importance by scoring them with regard to their likelihood and potential impact. This could take the form of a 'risk map'.

A risk map enables the company to assess the likelihood or probability of a risk occurring and the likely impact to the company if it does happen.

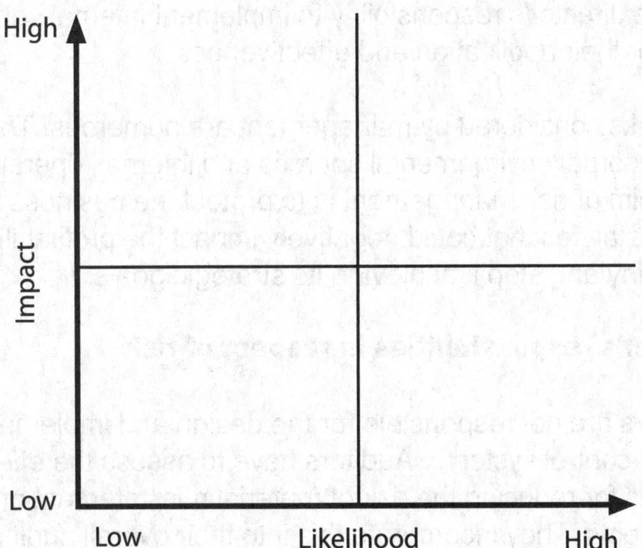

Once identified and assessed, the company must decide on appropriate ways to manage those risks.

Risk management can involve:

- Transferring the risk to another party e.g. by taking out insurance or outsourcing part of the business.
- Avoiding the risk by ceasing the risky activity.
- Reducing the risk by implementing effective controls.
- Accepting the risk and bearing the cost and consequence if the risk happens. This may be likely for risks which are deemed low in terms of probability or impact on the company.

A risk that ranked as highly likely to occur and high potential impact on the business would be prioritised as requiring immediate action. A risk that was considered both low likelihood and low impact might be ignored or insured against.

Internal controls and risk management

One way of minimising risk is to incorporate internal controls into a company's systems and procedures.

Director's responsibilities in respect of risk

It is the director's responsibility to implement internal controls and monitor their application and effectiveness.

The risks considered by management are numerous. They come from both external environmental sources and internal, operational ones. The main aim of risk management is to protect the business from unforeseen circumstances that could negatively impact the profitability of the company and stop it achieving its strategic goals.

Auditor's responsibilities in respect of risk

Auditors are not responsible for the design and implementation of their clients' control systems. Auditors have to assess the effectiveness of controls for reducing the risk of material misstatement of the financial statements. They incorporate this into their overall audit risk assessment, which allows them to design their further audit procedures.

In addition to this auditors are required, in accordance with ISA 265, to report significant deficiencies in client controls and any significant risks identified during the audit to those charged with governance.

Test your understanding 1 – OT Case

Cocklebiddy Co, a listed company, is currently reviewing its corporate governance practices to ensure they are compliant with regulations. The following is a description of the corporate governance policies they have in place:

- A remuneration committee comprising of 3 non-executive directors.
- An audit committee comprising of 2 non-executive directors, the finance director and the chief executive.
- Separate people taking on the roles of Chairman and chief executive.

(1) Which of the following best defines Corporate Governance?

A Corporate governance refers to the importance a company attaches to systems and controls.

B Corporate governance is the means by which a company is operated and controlled.

C Corporate governance is the extent to which a company is audited, both internally and externally.

D Corporate governance is an appraisal activity as a service to the entity.

(2) In terms of the structure of the audit committee of Cocklebiddy Co, which of the following actions should be taken to become compliant with corporate governance regulations?

A A minimum of one non-executive director should be recruited

B A minimum of one non-executive director should be recruited and the finance director should be removed

C A minimum of one non-executive director should be recruited and the finance director and chief executive should be removed

D No action necessary

(3) Which TWO of the following are functions of audit committees?

(i) Planning the annual external audit

(ii) Reviewing the effectiveness of internal financial controls

(iii) Reviewing and monitoring the external auditor's independence

(iv) Processing year end journal adjustments to the financial statements

A (i) and (iv)

B (i) and (iii)

C (ii) and (iv)

D (ii) and (iii)

(4) Cocklebiddy Co does not currently have an internal audit function. Which of the following summarises the requirements of corporate governance regulations in respect of internal audit?

A The audit committee must review the need for an internal audit function on an annual basis

B The audit committee must establish an internal audit committee as soon as possible

C There must either be an audit committee or internal audit function in place but there is no requirement to have both

D The finance director must review the need for an internal audit function and should make a request to the audit committee if it is decided that an internal audit function would be beneficial

(5) Which of the following is the main purpose of the remuneration committee?

A To ensure that the costs of the company are kept under control

B To ensure no director is involved in setting his own pay and the pay that is set is at an appropriate level

C To ensure decision making power for the company is not concentrated in the hands of one individual

D To ensure executives are paid a large basic salary irrespective of performance

Test your understanding 2

You are the audit manager of Tela & Co, a medium sized firm of accountants. Your firm has just been asked for assistance from Jumper & Co, a firm of accountants in an adjacent country. This country has just implemented the internationally recognised codes on corporate governance and Jumper & Co has a number of clients where the codes are not being followed. One example of this, from SGCC, a listed company, is shown below. As your country already has appropriate corporate governance codes in place, Jumper & Co have asked for your advice regarding the changes necessary in SGCC to achieve appropriate compliance with corporate governance codes.

Extract from financial statements regarding corporate governance:

Mr Sheppard is the Chief Executive Officer and board chairman of SGCC. He appoints and maintains a board of five executive and two non-executive directors. While the board sets performance targets for the senior managers in the company, no formal targets or review of board policies is carried out. Board salaries are therefore set and paid by Mr Sheppard based on his assessment of all the board members, including himself, and not their actual performance.

Internal controls in the company are monitored by the senior accountant, although detailed review is assumed to be carried out by the external auditors; SGCC does not have an internal audit department.

Annual financial statements are produced, providing detailed information on past performance.

Required:

(a) Explain why SGCC does not meet international codes of corporate governance.

(b) Explain why not meeting the international codes may cause a problem for SGCC.

(c) Recommend any changes necessary to implement those codes in the company.

(18 marks)

Test your understanding 3

(1) **What is meant by corporate governance?**

(3 marks)

(2) **Why are external auditors interested in corporate governance?**

(3 marks)

(3) **Who should make up a typical audit committee?**

(1 mark)

(4) **What is the committee's role?**

(2 marks)

(5) **Why would a company need an audit committee if it has a good relationship with its external auditors?**

(4 marks)

(6) **A company has identified one of its major risks as loss of key staff.**

Explain:

(a) **what they should do as a result of this?**

(b) **how they might reduce or even eliminate the risk?**

(c) **why the auditor is interested in this, given that it is not a direct financial risk?**

(5 marks)

6 Chapter summary

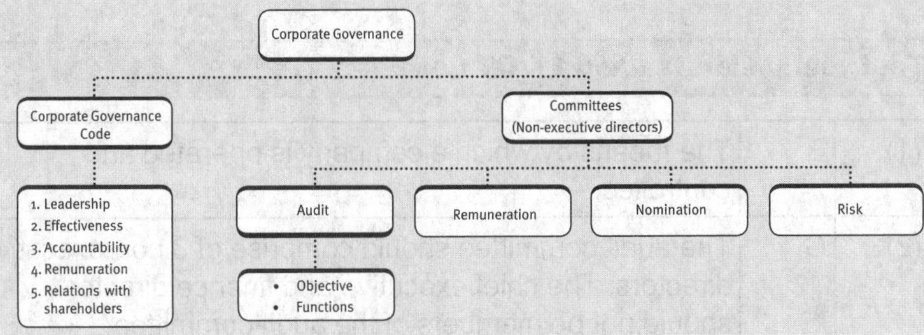

Test your understanding answers

Test your understanding 1 – OT Case

(1)	B	The means by which a company is operated and controlled.
(2)	C	The audit committee should comprise of 3 non-executive directors. The chief executive and finance director should not be members of the audit committee.
(3)	D	Reviewing the effectiveness of internal financial controls and reviewing and monitoring the external auditor's independence.
(4)	A	There is no requirement for a company to have an internal audit function. The audit committee should review the need for one on an annual basis if the company does not have one.
(5)	B	Directors should not be involved in setting their own pay. Remuneration should be performance related. Remuneration should be sufficient to attract, retain and motivate but should not be excessive.

Test your understanding 2

Why the corporate governance code is not met	Why this may cause problems	Recommendation
Mr Sheppard is chief executive and chairman of the company.	Mr Sheppard has too much power over the key decisions of the company.	Another person should be appointed as chairman as this role should be independent.
The board ratio is 5:2 in favour of the executive directors.	Executive directors can dominate board decisions which may not be in the best interests of the shareholders.	Three more non-executive directors should be appointed to balance the board.

Mr Sheppard appoints all directors to the board.	Mr Sheppard may appoint directors who will support his voting at board decisions. There may be no clear and transparent process for determining appointments.	A nomination committee comprising non-executive directors should be established to appoint directors and ensure there is no bias.
Mr Sheppard sets the pay of the directors as well as setting his own pay.	Mr Sheppard may pay directors more if they agree to back his decisions. He may pay himself more than he deserves.	A remuneration committee comprising non-executive directors should be established to set the pay of the executive directors. The committee should make sure the pay is based on performance of the company and the directors.
The board's performance is not reviewed.	If performance is not reviewed there is no accountability for poor performance.	Performance targets should be set and performance against these targets monitored on a regular basis. Directors should be required to explain any under-performance.
It is believed that the external auditor monitors the internal controls.	The external auditor will only look at controls relevant to the audit but this cannot be relied on to determine the effectiveness of the internal control systems across the company.	An internal audit function should be established to assess the effectiveness of the internal controls.
There is no audit committee.	Corporate governance codes require an audit committee to be established to take responsibility for the oversight of financial reporting and audit matters.	An audit committee should be established comprising of non-executive directors and they will be the main point of contact for internal auditors and external auditors.

Test your understanding 3

(1) What is meant by corporate governance?	The term corporate governance refers to the means by which a company is managed in the interests of all stakeholders. It will include consideration of: (1) directors' responsibilities (2) composition of the board of directors (3) audit requirements (internal and external).
(2) Why are the external auditors interested in corporate governance?	Corporate governance is the responsibility of the company's management and not its external auditors. However, it is the responsibility of the external auditors to form an opinion on the truth and fairness of the company's financial statements. If a company has good standards of corporate governance and is therefore managed well in the interests of all stakeholders, the auditors are likely to conclude that the risk of material misstatement in the financial statements is reduced. As a result of this they may well be able to reduce the extent of the audit procedures they carry out. The external auditor may have to report on whether the company is compliant with Corporate Governance requirements.
(3) Who should make up a typical audit committee?	The audit committee should be made up of non-executive directors and include someone with relevant financial experience.

(4) What is the audit committee's role?	The audit committee provides a channel of communication between the internal workings of the company and the external auditor. It also provides a channel of communication for employees who have concerns about the way the company is run.
(5) Why would a company need an audit committee if it has a good relationship with its external auditors?	A good relationship with external auditors is of immense help and support to an entity in complying with regulations, optimising controls and generally ensuring good corporate governance. However, the existence of an audit committee will enhance the company's corporate governance profile by: • improving public confidence • providing further support to directors • strengthening the independence of the external auditor • improving internal procedures e.g. management accounting, & communication generally.
(6) A company has identified one of its major risks as loss of key staff. Explain: • what they should do as a result of this? • how they might reduce or even eliminate the risk? • why the auditor is interested in this, given that it is not a direct financial risk?	The risk committee should discuss the issue and assess its seriousness in relation to its likelihood and potential impact. They should then decide what action is appropriate in order to manage the risk. This risk might be reduced by: • ensuring favourable employment packages for such individuals • ensuring training for other staff assists in case of succession issues • ensure key tasks are not carried out by just one person. The auditor must consider the possible impact of all significant risks as any of these could ultimately have financial consequences or going concern issues, hence impacting on the audit opinion.

chapter

12

Internal audit

Chapter learning objectives

This chapter covers syllabus areas:

- A5 – Internal audit and governance, and the differences between external audit and internal audit
- A6 – The scope of the internal audit function, outsourcing and internal audit assignments

Detailed syllabus objectives are provided in the introduction section of the text book.

1 The need for internal audit

Internal audit is an independent, objective assurance and consulting activity designed to add value and improve an organisation's operations.

Companies must create a strong system of internal control in order to fulfil their responsibilities.

However, it is not sufficient to simply have mechanisms in place to manage a business; their effectiveness must be regularly evaluated. All systems need some form of monitoring and feedback. This is the role of internal audit.

Having an internal audit department is generally considered to be best practice, but is not required by law. This allows flexibility in the way internal audit is established to suit the needs of a business.

In small, or owner managed businesses there is unlikely to be a need for internal audit because the owners are able to exercise more direct control over operations, and are accountable to fewer stakeholders.

The need for internal audit, therefore will depend on:

- Scale and diversity of activities. In a larger, diversified organisation there is a risk that controls don't work as effectively because of the delegation of responsibility down the organisation. Internal audit can report back to the audit committee if controls are not as effective as they should be.
- Complexity of operations. The more complex the organisation is, the greater the benefit obtained from having an IA function as there is greater risk of things going wrong. With larger organisations the consequences of poor controls/risk management/corporate governance practices are likely to be greater.
- Number of employees. The greater the number of employees the greater the risk of fraud.
- Cost/benefit considerations. It will only be worth establishing an IA function if the benefits outweigh the costs. For example a company might be losing money as a result of fraud, not using the most cost effective or reliable suppliers, incurring fines for non-compliance with laws and regulations. If these costs outweigh the cost of employing an IA function it will be beneficial to the company to establish a department.
- The desire of senior management to have assurance and advice on risk and control. The directors may wish to have the comfort that there is on-going monitoring of the organisation to help them discharge their responsibilities.

2 The difference between internal and external auditors

	External audit	Internal audit
Objective	Express an opinion on the truth and fairness of the financial statements in a written report.	Improve the company's operations by reviewing the efficiency and effectiveness of internal controls.
Reporting	Reports to shareholders.	Reports to management or those charged with governance.
Availability of report	Publicly available.	Not publicly available. Usually only seen by management or those charged with governance.
Scope of work	Verifying the truth and fairness of the financial statements.	Wide in scope and dependent on management's requirements.
Appointment and removal	By the shareholders of the company.	By the audit committee or board of directors.
Relationship with company	Must be independent of the company.	May be employees (which limits independence) or an outsourced function (which enhances independence).

3 The role of the internal audit function

The role of internal audit can vary depending on the requirements of the business.

Key activities of the internal audit function

- Assessing whether the company is demonstrating best practice in corporate governance.
- Evaluating the company's risk identification and management processes.
- Testing the effectiveness of internal controls.
- Assessing the reliability of financial and operating information.
- Assessing the economy, efficiency and effectiveness of operating activities (value for money).
- Assessing compliance with laws and regulations.
- Providing recommendations on the prevention and detection of fraud.

Most of these activities can be seen as supporting management comply with corporate governance requirements.

Additional roles

In addition to the above, internal audit will carry out ad hoc assignments, as required by management. For example:

- Fraud investigations – this may involve detecting fraud, identifying the perpetrator of a fraud and quantifying the loss to the company as a result of a fraud.
- IT systems reviews – performing a review of the computer environment and controls.
- Mystery shopper visits – for retail and service companies the IA staff can pose as customers to ensure that customer service is at the required level.
- Contract audits – making sure that where material or long term contracts are entered into by the organisation, the contract is written to protect the organisation appropriately and contractual terms are being adhered to by the supplier in line with the service level agreement.
- Asset verification – such as performing cash counts and physical inspection of non current assets to verify existence.
- Providing direct assistance to the external auditor – As seen in the 'Evidence' chapter, IA staff can help the external auditor with their procedures under their supervision, in accordance with ISA 610.

Qualities of an effective internal audit function

If the internal audit department is to be effective in providing assurance it needs to be:

- Sufficiently resourced, both financially and in terms of qualified, experienced staff.
- Well organised, so that it has well developed work practices.
- Independent and objective.
- Chief internal auditor appointed by the audit committee to reduce management bias.
- No operational responsibilities.
- Work plan agreed by the audit committee.
- No limitation on the scope of their work i.e. full access to every part of the organisation.

Limitations of internal audit

- Internal auditors may be employees of the company they are reporting on and therefore may not wish to raise issues in case they lose their job.
- In smaller organisations in particular, internal audit may be managed as part of the finance function. They will therefore have to report upon the effectiveness of financial systems that they form a part of and may be reluctant to say their department (and manager) has deficiencies.
- If the internal audit staff have worked in the organisation for a long time, possibly in different departments, there may be a familiarity threat as they will be audited the work of long standing colleagues and friends.

It is therefore difficult for internal audit to remain truly objective. However, acceptable levels of independence can be achieved through one, or more, of the following strategies:

- Reporting channels separate from the management of the main financial reporting function.
- Reviews of internal audit work by managers independent of the function under scrutiny.
- Outsourcing the internal audit function to a professional third party.

4 Outsourcing the internal audit function

In common with other areas of a company's operations, the directors may consider that outsourcing the internal audit function represents better value than an in-house provision.

Outsourcing is where the company uses an external company to perform its internal audit service instead of employing its own staff.

Advantages

- Greater focus on cost and efficiency of the internal audit function.
- Staff may be drawn from a broader range of expertise.
- Risk of staff turnover is passed to the outsourcing firm.
- Specialist skills may be more readily available.
- Costs of employing permanent staff are avoided.
- May improve independence.
- Access to new market place technologies, e.g. audit methodology software without associated costs.
- Reduced management time in administering an in-house department.

Disadvantages

- Possible conflict of interest if provided by the external auditors (In some jurisdictions – e.g. the UK, ethics rules specifically prohibit the external auditors from providing internal audit services where significant reliance will be placed on the work of the internal auditor).
- Pressure on the independence of the outsourced function due to, e.g. threat by management not to renew contract.
- Risk of lack of knowledge and understanding of the organisation's objectives, culture or business.
- The decision may be based on cost with the effectiveness of the function being reduced.
- Flexibility and availability may not be as high as with an in-house function.
- Lack of control over the standard of service.

5 Internal audit assignments

Internal auditors perform many different types of assignment. Common examples include:

- Value for money assignments
- The audit of IT systems
- Financial audit

Value for money

Value for money (VFM) is concerned with obtaining the best possible combination of services for the least resources. It is often referred to as a review of the three Es:

- **Economy** – obtaining the best quality of resources for the minimum cost.
- **Efficiency** – obtaining the maximum departmental/organisational outputs with the minimum use of resources.
- **Effectiveness** – achievement of goals and targets (departmental/organisational etc).

Comparisons of value for money achieved by different organisations (or branches of the same organisation) are often made using performance indicators that provide a measure of economy, efficiency or effectiveness. This is particularly common in the not-for-profit sector (i.e. public services and charities), but it can apply to any company.

For example, a company chooses the cheapest supplier for the materials it needs. The supplier has a lead time for delivery of 6 weeks. If the company needs a supplier that can deliver at short notice on a regular basis this will not be effective.

If a company sources lower quality materials at a price 10% cheaper than their current supplier but uses 50% more as a result of the lower quality, this is not efficient.

Value for money: hospital

Examples of value for money indicators for a hospital might include:

- Economy – cost of medical supplies per annum.
- Efficiency – number of patients treated per year, utilisation rate of beds/operating theatre.
- Effectiveness – recovery rates, number of deaths.

The audit of IT systems

The audit of IT systems

The external auditor considers IT systems from the perspective of whether they provide a reliable basis for the preparation of financial statements, and whether there are internal controls which are effective in reducing the risk of misstatement.

Internal audit will also consider this. However, their role is much wider in scope and will also consider whether:

- the company is getting value for money from their IT system
- the procurement process for the IT system was effective
- the ongoing management/maintenance of the system is appropriate.

Whilst this is an ongoing role, project auditing can be used to look at whether the objectives of a specific project, such as implementing new IT systems, were achieved.

Financial audits

Financial audit

The main aim of a financial reporting system, from a business' perspective; is to create accurate, complete and timely information to be used as a basis for internal decision making and business planning. This information is also needed to satisfy the requirements of actual and potential investors and trading partners.

Typical examples of financial information include:

- Annual financial statements
- Interim financial statements
- Monthly management accounts
- Forecasts and projections.

The main aim of internal financial audits is to ensure that the information produced is reliable and produced in an efficient timely manner. If not then executive decisions may be based upon unreliable information or, may not be possible at all.

The other aim of financial audit is to assess the financial health of a business. More importantly it is about ensuring there are mechanisms in place for the early identification of financial risk, such as:

- Adverse currency fluctuations
- Adverse interest rate fluctuations
- Cost price inflation.

In both cases the focus of internal audit will be on the processes and controls that underpin the creation of the various financial reports to ensure that they are as effective as possible for assisting decision making and the risk management processes of the company.

6 Reporting

Unlike an external audit report, the internal audit report does not have a formal reporting structure. It is likely that the format is agreed with the audit committee or board of directors prior to commencing the assignment.

These reports will generally be for internal use only. The external auditors may inspect them if they are intending on placing reliance on the work of internal audit.

A typical report will include:

- Terms of reference – the requirements of the assignment.
- Executive summary – the key risks and recommendations that are described more fully in the body of the report.
- Body of the report – a detailed description of the work performed and the results of that work.
- Appendix – containing any additional information that doesn't belong in the body of the report but which is relevant to the assignment.

In the exam you may be asked to take the role of an internal auditor performing an audit assignment to test controls or identify improvements in efficiency that can be made.

The internal audit report could be set out in the same way as the report to management that has been seen in the 'Systems and controls' chapter, describing the deficiencies identified, consequences of those deficiencies and recommendations for improvement.

Test your understanding 1

Murray Co's internal audit function

The internal audit function at Murray Co consists of a head of internal audit, two senior internal audit managers, four internal audit managers, seven internal auditors and an internal audit assistant. The head of internal audit has been in post for twelve years, and the other members of the team have varying lengths of service from two to fifteen years.

The head of internal audit is responsible for recruiting staff into the internal audit team. The head of internal audit was appointed by the audit committee.

The head of internal audit reports to the audit committee and agrees the scope of work for the internal audit function with the audit committee.

The internal audit staff have no operational responsibility. Where the staff have previously transferred from another department within Murray Co, the head of internal audit ensures that another member of the team carries out the audit of that system.

Murray Co's internal audit function follow the International Standards for the Professional Practice of Internal Auditing issued by the Global Institute of Internal Auditors.

Barker Co's internal audit function

The internal audit function at Barker Co consists of a chief internal auditor, one senior internal audit managers, one audit manager, one auditor and an audit assistant. The chief internal auditor has been in post for ten years, and the other members of the team have varying lengths of service from five to nine years.

The finance director is responsible for recruiting all staff into the internal audit function. The chief internal auditor reports to the finance director and agrees the scope of work for the internal audit function with the him.

The internal audit team spend 50% of their time carrying out internal audit assignments and 50% of their time working in the finance department. Due to the limited number of staff in the team, this has resulted in the internal auditors reviewing their own work.

Barker Co's internal audit team follow a variety of standards, in accordance with their own professional training.

Exercise:

Compare and contrast the effectiveness of Murray Co and Barker Co's internal audit functions.

Test your understanding 2

You are the senior manager in the internal audit department of Octball, a limited liability company. You report to the chief internal auditor and have a staff of six junior auditors to supervise, although the budget allows for up to ten junior staff.

In a recent meeting with the chief internal auditor, the difficulty of staff recruitment and retention was discussed. Over the past year, five junior internal audit staff have left the company, but only two have been recruited. Recruitment problems identified include location of Octball's head office in a small town over 150 kilometres from the nearest major city and extensive foreign travel, often to cold climates.

Together with the chief internal auditor you believe that outsourcing the internal audit department may be a way of alleviating the staffing problems. You would monitor the new outsourced department in a part-time role taking on additional responsibilities in other departments, and the chief internal auditor would accept the post of Finance Director (FD) on the board, replacing the retiring FD.

Two firms have been identified as being able to provide the internal audit service:

- The NFA Partnership, a local firm specialising in provision of accountancy and internal audit services. NFA does not audit financial statements or report to members, and
- T&M, Octball's external auditors, who have offices in 75 countries and employ in excess of 65,000 staff.

Required:

(a) **Discuss the advantages and disadvantages of appointing NFA as internal auditors for Octball.**

(8 marks)

(b) **Discuss the matters T&M need to consider before they could accept appointment as internal auditors for Octball.**

(7 marks)

(c) **Assume that an outsourcing company has been chosen to provide internal audit services. Describe the control activities that Octball should apply to ensure that the internal audit service is being maintained to a high standard.**

(5 marks)

(Total: 20 marks)

Test your understanding 3

Flylo is an airline. The company owns some of its fleet of aircraft. Other aircraft are leased from third parties. Flylo has an internal audit function that has recently been expanded. Your firm is the external auditor to Flylo. Your firm has been asked to investigate the extent to which it may be able to rely on the work of internal audit in the following areas:

- sales and ticketing
- fleet acquisition and maintenance
- trade payables and long-term debt financing (borrowings).

The company outsources its in-flight catering and payroll functions to different service organisations.

Required:

(a) **Explain why the work of the internal auditors, in the three areas noted above, is likely to be useful to you as the external auditor.**

(9 marks)

(b) **Explain how the quality of the internal audit function is likely to influence the extent of your reliance on internal audit work.**

(5 marks)

(c) **Describe the audit evidence you will seek relating to internal controls over the out-sourced functions (in-flight catering and payroll).**

(6 marks)

(Total: 20 marks)

Test your understanding 4 – OT Case

You and an audit senior working at Monkey, Mia & Co. You have been seconded to your firm's internal audit department to broaden your experience. You have been assigned to an internal audit assignment to test the effectiveness of the computer systems at a large company. Your firm won the contract to provide internal audit services to the company after it took the decision to outsource its internal audit function and make the existing internal audit staff redundant.

(1) Internal audit reports have to be produced in a standardised format as set out by the financial reporting framework. Is this statement false or true?

A False

B True

(2) Which TWO of the following statements are correct?

(i) Internal auditors always report directly to shareholders.

(ii) The format of external audit reports is determined by management.

(iii) Internal auditors work may be determined by management.

(iv) All external audits must be planned in accordance with International Auditing Standards and other regulatory requirements.

A (i) and (iv)

B (i) and (iii)

C (ii) and (iii)

D (iii) and (iv)

(3) Which of the following is NOT part of the role of internal audit?

A Risk identification and monitoring

B Expression of opinion to the shareholders on whether the annual financial statements give a true and fair view

C Fraud investigations

D Assessing compliance with laws and regulations

(4) What of the following is not a valid reason to outsource the internal audit function?

A Expected efficiencies from having the external auditor providing internal audit services as the staff will already have a good understanding of the company

B Outsourcing may be more cost effective as compared with employing staff and providing training and other employment benefits

C A professional firm is likely to be more experienced and able to provide better recommendations for improvements

D Greater independence of an external service provider

(5) With which of the following should the internal auditor not be involved?

A Identifying deficiencies in internal controls

B Providing recommendations to management on how to overcome the deficiencies identified

C Implementing the new controls recommended

D Monitoring the effectiveness of the new controls implemented

7 Chapter summary

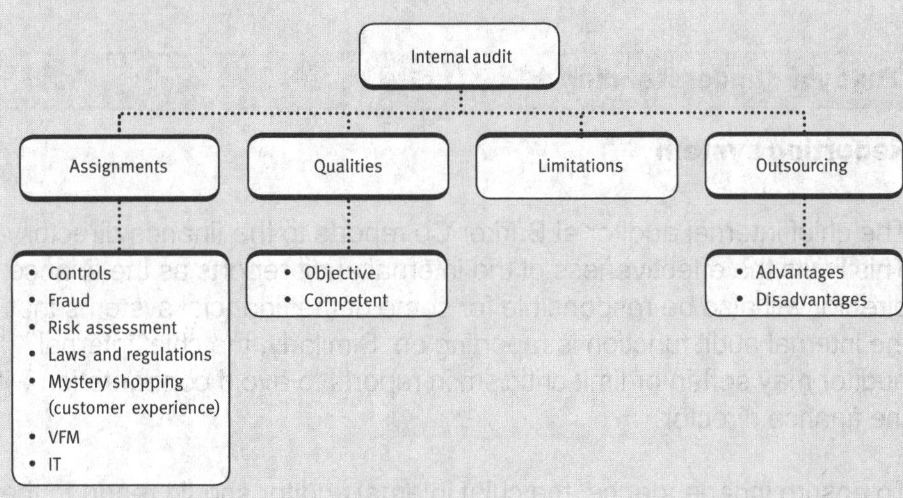

Test your understanding answers

Test your understanding 1

Reporting system

The chief internal auditor at Barker Co reports to the finance director. This limits the effectiveness of the internal audit reports as the finance director will also be responsible for some of the financial systems that the internal audit function is reporting on. Similarly, the chief internal auditor may soften or limit criticism in reports to avoid confrontation with the finance director.

To ensure independence, the chief internal auditor should report to the Audit Committee, as the head of internal audit at Murray Co does.

Recruitment of staff

All of the internal audit team at Barker Co are recruited by the finance director. The finance director may appoint personnel who are less likely to criticise his work. To ensure independence, the head of internal audit should be appointed by the audit committee, and they should then recruit and appoint the rest of the team, as at Murray Co.

Scope of work

The scope of work of internal audit at Barker Co is decided by the finance director in discussion with the chief internal auditor. This means that the finance director may try and influence the chief internal auditor regarding the areas that the internal audit department is auditing, possibly directing attention away from any contentious areas that the director does not want auditing.

To ensure independence, the scope of work of the internal audit department should be decided by the chief internal auditor, perhaps with the assistance of an audit committee, as at Murray Co.

Audit work

The internal audit team at Barker Co review their own work. This limits independence as the auditor may overlook or fail to identify errors or deficiencies in those areas. This is a self-review threat.

If possible, the internal audit team should not have operational responsibility. However, if this is not possible, the internal audit work should be arranged so that no member of the team reviews areas where they have operational responsibility, as Murray Co does.

Lengths of service of internal audit staff

The internal audit team staff of both companies have been employed for a long time. This may limit their effectiveness as they will be very familiar with the systems being reviewed and therefore may not be sufficiently objective to identify errors in those systems.

However, there are sufficient staff at Murray Co to ensure that the team can be rotated into different areas of internal audit work, and their work can be independently reviewed. Due to the small number of staff in the internal audit team, Barker Co may not be able to achieve this.

Given the extent of limitations, it may be appropriate for Barker Co to outsource its internal audit function.

Variation of standards

Individual staff at Barker Co follow the auditing standards they are familiar with. Standards of internal audit are not uniform across the profession. This could lead to inconsistency in the way internal audit is performed across different assignments, and it can lead to manipulation of internal audit aims and measurement. Barker Co should follow an agreed, recognised set of professional internal audit standards, such as those followed by Murray Co.

Test your understanding 2

(a) **Benefits of outsourcing to NFA**

Expertise available

The NFA partnership will be able to provide the necessary expertise for internal audit work. They may be able to provide a broader range of expertise as they serve many different clients therefore staff may be available for specialist work that Octball could not afford to employ.

Buy-in skills as necessary

If internal audit is only required for specific functions or particular jobs each year then the expertise can be purchased as required. Taking this approach will minimise in-house costs.

Independence

As an independent firm which does not perform the audit of the financial statements it is likely that they can provide a high level of service with appropriate objectivity. In particular, there will be no self review threats.

Audit techniques – training

Outsourcing will remove the need for training internal staff. Effectively training will be provided for 'free' as the outsourcing firm will be responsible for keeping staff up-to-date with new auditing techniques and processes.

Continuity of service – staffing

As provision of audit services is the NFA partnership's main activity, they should also be able to budget for client requirements. As a larger internal auditing firm, they may be able to offer staff better career progression which should assist staff retention.

Problems with outsourcing to NFA

Fee pressure

NFA may experience some fee pressure, but only in respect of maintaining cost effectiveness of the internal audit department. The relationship needs to be managed carefully to ensure that NFA do not decrease the quality of their work due to insufficient fees.

Knowledge

The NFA partnership will not have any prior knowledge of Octball. This will be a disadvantage as this will mean the partnership will need time to ascertain the accounting systems and controls etc in Octball before commencing work. However, provision of an independent view may identify control deficiencies etc that the current internal audit department have missed.

Location

The NFA partnership may not be able to provide this service to Octball as they are a local firm and therefore the issue of travel and working away from home would remain.

(b) **Matters to be considered by T&M**

Independence

T&M need to ensure that independence can be maintained in a number of areas:

– Independence regarding recommending systems or preparing working papers and subsequent checking of those systems or working papers. While the internal audit department may need to carry out these functions, T&M must ensure that separate staff are used to provide the internal and external audit functions.

– Staff from T&M will be expected to follow the ethical guidance of ACCA which means that steps will be taken to avoid conflicts of interest or other independence issues such as close personal relationships building up with staff in Octball. Any real or perceived threats to independence will lower the overall trust that can be placed on internal audit reports produced by T&M.

Skills

T&M must ensure that they have staff with the necessary skills and sufficient time to undertake the internal audit work in Octball. As a firm of auditors, T&M will automatically provide training for its staff as part of the in-house compliance with association regulations (e.g. compulsory CPD). T&M will need to ensure that staff providing the internal audit function to Octball are aware of relevant guidance for internal auditors.

Fee pressure

There may be fee pressure on T&M, either to maintain the cost effectiveness of the internal audit department, or to maintain the competitiveness of the audit fee itself in order to keep the internal audit work.

Knowledge

As external auditors, T&M will already have knowledge of Octball. This will assist in establishing the internal audit department as systems documentation will already be available and the audit firm will already be aware of potential deficiencies in the control systems.

(c) Controls to maintain the standard of the internal audit department

- If T&M are appointed, ensure that the internal and external audit is managed by different departments in the firm.
- Setting and review of performance measures such as cost, areas reviewed, etc with explanations obtained for any significant variances.
- Use of appropriate audit methodology, including clear documentation of audit work carried out, adequate review, and appropriate conclusions drawn.
- Review of working papers, ensuring adherence to International Standards on Auditing where appropriate and any in-house standards on auditing.
- The work plan for internal audit is agreed prior to work commencing and this is followed by the outsourcing company.

Test your understanding 3

(a) **Use of the work of the internal auditors by external auditors**

Sales and ticketing

(i) The sales function is likely to be integrated with the accounting and internal control system used to produce the figure in the financial statements for revenue, on which the external auditor reports and is therefore useful.

(ii) The internal auditors' work on the ticketing system is less likely to be useful because it relates to an operational area which does not have a direct impact on the financial statements. There are, however, regulatory matters that may need to be considered by the external auditor. Ticketing may also have an indirect effect because it is likely to be integrated with the sales system and there is likely to be some crossover between the controls over ticketing and controls over sales generally. The work of the internal auditors is therefore likely to be of some use to the external auditor.

Fleet acquisition and maintenance

(iii) The internal auditors' work on the fleet acquisition system is likely to be very relevant to the external auditors because owned aircraft and leased aircraft will constitute a substantial element of statement of financial position assets and liabilities, and depreciation and finance charges in the statement of profit or loss.

(iv) Much of the internal auditors' work is likely to relate to ensuring that company policy has been complied with. Policy will relate to the authorisation for and acquisition of aircraft, and accounting for aircraft in terms of the correct classification of leases (operating or financing) and depreciation policy, for example. Company policy is likely to be extensive and detailed for such material items and external auditors will be concerned to ensure that it is both appropriate and has been complied with.

(v) It is also possible that the internal auditors' work may involve some verification of the statement of profit and loss and statement of financial position figures. Given the likely materiality of the amounts involved, this work will also be of interest to the external auditors.

(vi) It is possible that the internal auditors' work may also relate to the quality of aircraft, and other operational aspects of fleet management. These issues may also be relevant to the external auditors, at least insofar as they relate to compliance with laws and regulations.

(vii) In relation to maintenance, the internal auditors' work is likely to relate to the authorisation and correct accounting for maintenance expenditure (capitalisation or expensing), and on the operational side, to the quality thereof, as for fleet acquisition (above). Maintenance expenditure in the statement of profit or loss may well be material and the work of the internal auditors is therefore of interest to external auditors.

Trade payables and long term debt financing

(viii) The extent of the external auditor's interest in the internal auditors' work on trade payables and long term financing will depend on the materiality of the amounts involved. Trade payables (for certain types of routine maintenance, and payables due to the service organisations, for example) may be material. Long term debt financing is very likely to be material as many airlines have substantial debt financing.

(ix) Internal audit work on trade payables is likely to involve ensuring that routine internal controls are properly designed and are operating. The external auditors may well be interested in the internal auditors' work in this area.

(x) There are substantial financial statement disclosures required for debt financing. The internal auditors' assistance with ensuring that disclosures are properly made, as well as with ensuring that any covenants have been complied with and that the accounting for the financing is appropriate, may also be helpful to the external auditors.

(b) **Quality of internal audit function: extent of reliance**

(i) The quality of the internal audit function will have a significant effect on the extent of the external auditor's reliance. If the quality of work is not adequate, reliance will not be possible, regardless of the extent and relevance of the work performed.

(ii) The firm will seek to ensure that there is an appropriate structure within the department itself, with appropriate reporting lines outside the department, preferably reporting to the audit committee.

(iii) The internal audit function has recently been expanded and there are likely to be changes in the way that it is organised. The function should have operational independence within the organisation and formal terms of reference that encompass the recent changes made.

(iv) The function should have a clearly defined set of operating procedures, as well as a work program. Proper documentation of all work performed is essential.

(v) Staff should be appropriately trained, experienced and qualified. The head of such an important department should preferably be a professionally qualified.

(c) **Audit evidence: outsourced functions**

(i) Internal controls exercised by the company over in-flight catering and payroll must be properly designed and operated. The firm will seek to review documentation of controls and internal audit reports. It will seek to obtain evidence that controls have been applied.

(ii) A breach of regulations or a deterioration in the quality of catering could both have a significant effect on the financial statements, particularly if fines were payable or adverse publicity was likely. Enquiries into both areas and a review of relevant documentation provided by, for example, food licensing authorities to the company or the service organisation, and company lawyers (in relation to passenger complaints, perhaps), will be necessary.

(iii) Evidence of controls sought by the firm will include:

- controls over the selection of the service organisations selected (e.g. by competitive tendering).
- evidence relating to the completeness, accuracy and timeliness of information provided to, and received from, the payroll organisation (e.g. batch summaries and exception reports).
- evidence relating to the security measures taken by the payroll organisation to ensure that confidential information is kept confidential.
- evidence relating to the security measures taken by the catering organisation to ensure that health and safety standards are maintained and that no sabotage of the food can take place.

Test your understanding 4 – OT Case

(1)	A	False. Internal audit reports will be in the format required by the audit committee or management.
(2)	D	Internal audit work may be determined by management or the audit committee if there is one. External audits must be conducted in accordance with ISAs.
(3)	B	An audit opinion presented to the shareholders must be expressed by an independent external auditor.
(4)	A	Ethical guidance issued to external auditors requires separate teams to provide internal and external services. Therefore the internal audit staff assigned will not have existing knowledge gained from the external audit.
(5)	C	Internal auditors should not implement new controls as this would create a self-review threat when the controls are tested at a later date.

chapter

13

Summary of key ISAs

Chapter learning objectives

This section is designed to help you with the key requirements of the International Auditing Standards.

200 series: General principles and responsibilities

ISA 200 ***Overall Objectives of the Independent Auditor and the Conduct of an Audit in Accordance with International Standards on Auditing***

Objectives of the auditor:

- To obtain reasonable assurance whether financial statements as a whole are free from material misstatement, whether due to fraud or error.
- To express an opinion on whether the financial statements are prepared, in all material respects, in accordance with a relevant financial reporting framework.
- To report on the financial statements, and communicate as required, in accordance with the auditor's findings.

Responsibilities of management:

- Preparation of the financial statements in accordance with the applicable financial reporting framework, including their fair presentation.
- Internal control necessary to enable preparation of financial statements that are free from material misstatement, whether due to fraud or error.
- To provide the auditor with:
  - access to all information relevant to the preparation of the financial statements
  - unrestricted access to persons from within the entity whom the auditor determines it necessary to obtain evidence.

Risk:

- Audit: risk of issuing an inappropriate opinion.
- Inherent: susceptibility of an assertion about a class of transaction (e.g. revenue) or account balance (e.g. receivables) to material misstatement before the consideration of any related internal controls.
- Control: risk that material misstatement not detected by entity's internal control.
- Detection: risk that audit procedures do not detect material misstatements.

Inherent limitations of audit:

Audit evidence is persuasive rather than conclusive because of:

- the nature of financial reporting
- the nature of audit procedures
- the need to conduct audit a within reasonable time and at reasonable cost.

ISA 210 ***Agreeing the terms of audit engagements***

The auditor should accept or renew an engagement only if the preconditions for an audit are present:

- An appropriate financial reporting framework is to be applied in the preparation of the financial statements; and
- Management's acknowledgement and understanding of its responsibilities.

Contents of engagement letter:

- The objective and scope of the audit.
- The responsibilities of the auditor.
- The responsibilities of management.
- The identification of an applicable financial reporting framework.
- Reference to the expected form and content of any reports to be issued.

ISA 220 ***Quality Control for an Audit of Financial Statements***

The firm should have a system of quality control to ensure:

- compliance with professional standards, and
- reports issued are appropriate in the circumstances.

The engagement partner takes overall responsibility for the overall quality of the engagement including the direction, supervision and performance of the engagement.

An engagement quality control reviewer must be assigned for listed entities and high risk engagements focusing on significant matters and areas involving significant judgment.

The firm's quality control processes must be monitored to ensure they are relevant, adequate and operating effectively.

ISA 230 *Audit documentation*

Objective of documentation:

- Sufficient appropriate record of basis for audit report
- Evidence that audit planned and performed in accordance with ISAs and legal/regulatory requirements.

Content should enable an experienced independent auditor to understand:

- Nature, timing & extent of audit procedures:
  - Specific items tested.
  - Who performed work and when.
  - Who reviewed work and when.
- Results of audit procedures.
- Significant conclusions and professional judgments.

ISA 240 The auditor's responsibilities relating to fraud in an audit of financial statements

- Identify risks of material misstatement in FS due to fraud.
- Obtain sufficient appropriate evidence regarding assessed risks.
- Respond appropriately to fraud or suspected fraud identified.

Fraud: intentional act involving use of deception to obtain unjust/illegal advantage.

Two types of fraud:

- Fraudulent financial reporting.
- Misappropriation of assets.

Professional scepticism: an attitude of a questioning mind; a critical assessment of audit evidence.

Audit procedures to identify:

- Appropriateness of journal entries.
- Review of accounting estimates.
- Identify significant transactions outside normal course of business.

Examples of fraud risk factors:

- High degree of competition.
- Need to obtain additional financing.
- Low morale amongst senior staff.
- Large amounts of cash on hand.

ISA 250 *Consideration of laws and regulations in an audit of financial statements*

Auditor's responsibilities:

- Obtain general understanding of legal/regulatory framework applicable to entity.
- Obtain sufficient appropriate evidence regarding compliance with provisions of laws/regulations that may materially affect FS.

ISA 260 *Communication with those charged with governance*

Those charged with governance:

- Those with responsibility for overseeing the strategic direction of the entity.

Matters to be communicated:

- Auditor's responsibility in relation to the FS audit.
- Planned scope and timing of audit.
- Significant findings from audit.
- Auditor's independence (listed companies).
- Circumstances that affect the form and content of the auditor's report, if any.

ISA 265 ***Communicating deficiencies in internal control to those charged with governance and management***

Reporting responsibilities:

- Significant deficiencies, to those charged with governance.
- Other deficiencies, to an appropriate level of management.

What makes deficiencies significant:

- Likelihood of material misstatement in FS.
- Susceptibility to loss/fraud of related asset.
- Volume of activity in related account balance.
- Interaction of deficiency with other deficiencies.

300 & 400 series: Assessment and response to assessed risks

ISA 300 ***Planning an audit of financial statements***

Objectives of planning:

- Help auditor to devote appropriate attention to important areas of audit.
- Help identify and resolve issues on a timely basis.
- Assist in selection of suitable audit team.
- Help direction and supervision of audit team.

Content of audit strategy:

- Scope of engagement (e.g. input of other auditors).
- Reporting objectives of assignment (e.g. reporting timetable).
- Nature/timing/extent of resources.

Content of audit plan:

- Risk assessment procedures.
- Detailed planned audit procedures.

ISA 315 ***Identifying and Assessing the Risks of Material Misstatement Through Understanding the Entity and its Environment***

Required understanding of entity and environment:

- Industry/regulatory factors affecting FS
- Nature of entity:
  - operations
  - ownership and governance
  - financing.
- Accounting policies.
- Objectives and strategy.

IT controls, risks:

- Unauthorised changes to data in master files.
- Unauthorised access to programs.
- Inappropriate manual intervention.

Financial statement assertions:

- Account balances and related disclosures: Completeness; rights and obligations; accuracy, valuation & allocation; existence; classification; presentation.
- Transactions and events and related disclosures: Occurrence; completeness; accuracy; cut-off; classification; presentation.

ISA 320 ***Materiality in planning and performing an audit***

Materiality: Misstatements, including omissions, are considered to be material if they, individually or in the aggregate, could reasonably be expected to influence the economic decisions of users taken on the basis of the financial statements.

Performance materiality: an amount set at less than materiality for the FS as a whole, to reduce to an appropriately low level the probability that the FS as a whole are materially misstated.

ISA 330 The auditor's responses to assessed risks

The auditor shall design and perform audit procedures whose nature, timing and extent are based on and are responsive to the assessed risks of material misstatement.

Test of controls: to evaluate operating effectiveness of controls in preventing, or detecting and correcting material misstatements at the assertion level.

Substantive procedures: to detect material misstatements at assertion level, comprising tests of details and analytical procedures.

ISA 450 ***Evaluation of misstatements identified during audit***

A misstatement is: A difference between the amount, classification, presentation, or disclosure of a reported financial statement item and the amount, classification, presentation, or disclosure that is required for the item to be in accordance with the applicable financial reporting framework. Misstatements can arise from error or fraud.

Requirements:

- Accumulate identified misstatements.
- Determine whether audit strategy needs to be revised.
- Communicate misstatements to appropriate level of management on a timely basis.
- Evaluate effect of uncorrected misstatements on FS.
- Request written representation that uncorrected misstatements are not material.

500 series: Evidence

ISA 500 ***Audit evidence***

Characteristics:

- Appropriateness: quality, linked to relevance and reliability.
- Sufficiency: quantity, linked to quality and to risk of material misstatement.

Relevance: linked to FS assertions.

Reliability:

- Independent better than internal.
- Auditor generated better than indirectly obtained.
- Documentary better than oral.
- Originals better than photocopies.

ISA 501 ***Audit Evidence – Specific Considerations for Selected Items***

The auditor should obtain sufficient appropriate evidence regarding:

- existence and condition of inventory
- completeness of litigation and claims involving the entity
- presentation and disclosure of segment information.

ISA 520 ***Analytical Procedures***

Definition:

- Evaluation of financial information.
- By analysing plausible relationships.
- Among financial and non-financial data.

May be used as a substantive procedure to assess the reasonableness of the balance in the FS.

Must be used at the completion stage to ensure the financial statements are consistent with the auditor's understanding.

ISA 530 ***Audit Sampling***

Definitions:

- Audit sampling: application of audit procedures to less than 100% of population to provide auditor with reasonable basis to draw conclusions on entire population.
- Sampling risk: risk of an unrepresentative sample.

- Non-sampling risk: of erroneous conclusion from representative sample.
- Statistical sampling: random sampling plus use of probability theory to evaluate results.
- Tolerable misstatement: A monetary amount set by the auditor in respect of which the auditor seeks to obtain an appropriate level of assurance that the monetary amount set by the auditor is not exceeded by the actual misstatement in the population.

Factors increasing sample size:

- Increase in risk of material misstatement.
- Increase in tolerable misstatement.
- Increase in expected misstatement.

ISA 540 *Auditing accounting estimates, including fair value accounting estimates and related disclosures*

Audit approach:

- Review events after the reporting period.
- Test management's estimate:
  – Appropriateness of method.
  – Reasonableness of assumptions.
- Develop an independent estimate.
- Obtain evidence from an expert.

ISA 560 *Subsequent events*

Obtain sufficient appropriate evidence about whether events occurring between the date of the financial statements and the date of the auditor's report that require adjustment of or disclosure in the financial statements are appropriately reflected in those financial statements.

ISA 570 *Going Concern*

Definition – entity is viewed as continuing in business for the foreseeable future.

Auditor must assess:

- whether the basis of preparation is appropriate.
- whether disclosure of going concern uncertainties are adequately disclosed
- consider implications for the audit report if not.

ISA 580 *Written representations*

Content:

- Management responsibility for preparation of FS.
- Auditor provided with all relevant information.
- All transactions recorded in FS.
- Plans that may affect the carrying value of the assets.
- As required by other ISAs e.g. ISA 240, 250, 450, 560, 570, 580.

600 series: Using the work of others

ISA 610 (Revised) *Using the work of internal auditors*

The external auditor must evaluate:

- the extent to which the internal audit function's **organisational status** and relevant policies and procedures support the **objectivity** of the internal auditors)
- the **competence** of the internal audit function
- whether the internal audit function applies a systematic and disciplined **approach**, including quality control.

They also have to plan adequate time to review the work of the internal audit function to evaluate whether:

- the work was properly planned, performed, supervised, reviewed and documented
- sufficient appropriate evidence has been obtained
- the conclusions reached are appropriate in the circumstances
- the reports prepared are consistent with the work performed.

Using internal audit to provide direct assistance

The external auditor may use the internal audit function to provide direct assistance with the external audit under the supervision and review of the external auditor.

- Internal auditor must be objective and competent.
- Internal auditor must observe confidentiality.
- Management must agree not to intervene with the work.
- External auditor must not use the internal auditor excessively.
- External auditor must not assign work which is judgmental, a high risk of material misstatement or which the internal auditor has been involved with.
- Direct assistance cannot be provided in countries where national law prohibits such assistance.

ISA 620 *Using the work of an auditor's expert*

The external auditor must assess an expert's:

- independence and objectivity
- competence.

The auditor must assess the expert's work including:

- the consistency of the findings with other evidence
- the significant assumptions made
- the use and accuracy of source data.

700 series: Audit conclusions and reporting

ISA 700 (Revised) *Forming an opinion and reporting on the financial statements*

Content of audit report:

- Title:
  - reference to independent auditor
- Addressee:
  - shareholders/members
- Audit Opinion:
  - FS prepared in accordance with IFRS
  - FS give true and fair view
- Basis for Opinion:
  - Audit conducted in accordance with ISAs and ethical requirements
- Going concern
  - Reference to any going concern disclosures made by management
- Key Audit Matters
  - Significant matters to be drawn to the user's attention
- Responsibilities of Management:
  - Preparation of FS
  - Internal controls
- Auditor responsibilities:
  - To express an opinion on the FS
- Name of engagement partner
- Signature
- Location of auditor's office
- Date

ISA 701 ***Communicating Key Audit Matters in the Independent Auditor's Report***

Key audit matters are those that in the auditor's professional judgment were of most significance in the audit and are selected from matters communicated to those charged with governance.

The purpose of including these matters is to assist users in understanding the entity, and to provide a basis for the users to engage with management and those charged with governance about matters relating to the entity and the financial statements.

ISA 705 ***Modifications to the audit opinion in the Independent Auditor's report***

Definitions:

- Modified: qualified, adverse or disclaimer.
- Pervasive: not confined to specific elements or representing a substantial proportion of a single element.

Modifications:

- FS as a whole not free from material misstatement
  - Material: qualified
  - Pervasive: adverse
- Unable to obtain sufficient appropriate evidence
  - Material: qualified
  - Pervasive: disclaimer

ISA 706 ***Emphasis of matter paragraphs and other matter paragraphs in the Independent Auditor's report***

Emphasis of matter: refers to matter fundamental to user's understanding of FS. Can only be used to highlight a matter already disclosed in the FS.

Other matter: refers to matters relevant to the audit, the audit report or the auditor's responsibilities.

ISA 720 ***The auditor's responsibilities relating to other information in documents containing audited financial statements***

Responsibilities:

- Read other information to identify material inconsistencies with the FS.
- If inconsistencies identified:
  - If FS are wrong, propose adjustment. If refused consider modifying audit opinion.
  - If other information is wrong, propose adjustment. If refused consider:
    - referring to the matter in audit report.
    - withholding audit report.
    - resignation.

chapter

14

Summary of IFRSs

Chapter learning objectives

This section is designed to help you with the key requirements of the IFRSs examinable for paper F8.

IAS 1 Presentation of financial statements

IAS 1 provides standard formats for the statement of profit or loss and other comprehensive income, statement of financial position, statement of cash flows and statement of changes in equity as well as setting out six overall accounting principles that should be applied:

- going concern
- accruals
- consistency of presentation
- materiality and aggregation
- offsetting
- comparative information.

Accounting policies should be selected so that the financial statements comply with all international standards and interpretations.

An entity must make an explicit statement in the notes to the accounts that the financial statements comply with IFRS.

IAS 1 also requires classification of items of other comprehensive income between those which:

- will not be reclassified to profit or loss; and
- which may be reclassified to profit or loss in future reporting periods.

IAS 2 Inventories

IAS 2 Inventories requires that inventories should be valued at the lower of cost and net realisable value.

Cost includes all of the costs associated with bringing items of inventory to their present condition and location.

Cost includes:

- purchase price including import duties, transport and handling costs
- any other directly attributable costs, less
- trade discounts, rebates and subsidies
- costs which are specifically attributable to units of production, e.g. direct labour

- direct expenses and subcontracted work
- production overheads (which must be based on the normal level of activity)
- other overheads, if any, attributable in the particular circumstances of the business to bringing the product or service to its present location and condition.

Cost excludes:

- abnormal waste
- storage costs
- administrative overheads which do not contribute to bringing inventories to their present location and condition
- selling costs.

Some entities can identify individual units of inventory (e.g. vehicles can be identified by a chassis number). Those that cannot should keep track of costs using either the first in, first out (FIFO) or the weighted average cost (AVCO) assumption.

Some entities may use standard costing for valuing inventory. IAS 2 permits the use of standard cost for convenience, where it is a close approximation to actual cost, and is regularly reviewed and revised in the light of current conditions.

IAS 7 Statement of cash flows

The statement of cash flows provides an important insight into the ways in which the entity has created and applied cash during the period. The fact that a business generated profit during a period means that it has created wealth, but wealth is not necessarily reflected by cash. The fact that a business is liquid according to the statement of financial position at the year-end does not explain the cash movements that occurred during the year. IAS 7 requires a cash flow statement to show cash flows generated from operating, investing and financing activities.

IAS 10 Events after the reporting period

- Events after the reporting period are those events, favourable and unfavourable, that occur between the statement of financial position date and the date when the financial statements are authorised for issue.
- Adjusting events after the reporting period are those that provide evidence of conditions that existed at the statement of financial position date.
- Non-adjusting events after the reporting period are those that are indicative of conditions that arose after the reporting period.

Accounting treatment

- Adjusting events affect the amounts stated in the financial statements so they must be adjusted.
- Non-adjusting events do not concern the position at the statement of financial position date so the accounts are not adjusted. If the event is material then the nature and its financial effect must be disclosed.

Examples of adjusting events

- The sale of inventory after the date which gives evidence about the inventory's net realisable value at the reporting date.
- The bankruptcy of a customer after the date that confirms that a provision is required against a receivable balance at the reporting date.
- The discovery of fraud or errors that show that the financial statements are incorrect.
- The settlement after the reporting period of a court case that confirms that the entity had a present obligation at the statement of financial position date. This would require a provision to be recognised in the financial statements (or an existing provision to be adjusted).

Examples of non-adjusting events that would require disclosure

- A major business combination after the date or disposing of a major subsidiary.
- Announcing a plan to discontinue an operation.
- Major purchases and disposals of assets.
- Destruction of a major production plant by a fire after the reporting date.
- Announcing or commencing a major restructuring.
- Abnormally large changes after the reporting date in asset prices or foreign exchange rates.

Dividends

- Ordinary dividends declared after the date are not recognised as liabilities at the reporting date.
- If the liability did not exist at the reporting date, then it cannot be recognised.
- This is consistent with IAS 37 and the definition of a liability in the Framework.

IAS 16 Property plant and equipment

Cost and depreciation of an asset

Property, plant and equipment is initially recognised at cost. An asset's cost is its purchase price, less any trade discounts or rebates, plus any further costs directly attributable to bringing it into working condition for its intended use.

- Subsequent expenditure on non current assets may be capitalised if it:
  - enhances the economic benefits of the asset e.g. adding an new wing to a building
  - replaces part of an asset that has been separately depreciated and has been fully depreciated; e.g. furnace that requires new linings periodically
  - replaces economic benefits previously consumed, e.g. a major inspection of aircraft.

- The aim of depreciation is to spread the cost of the asset over its life in the business.
  - The depreciation method and useful life of an asset should be reviewed at the end of each year and revised where necessary in accordance with IAS 8. This is not a change in accounting policy, but a change of accounting estimate.
  - If an asset has parts with different lives, (e.g. a building with a flat roof), the component parts of the asset should be capitalised and depreciated separately.

Revaluation of property, plant and equipment

- Revaluation of non-current assets is optional. However, if one asset is revalued, all assets in that class must be revalued, i.e. no cherry-picking.
- Valuations should be kept up to date to ensure that the carrying amount does not differ materially from the fair value at each statement of financial position date.
- Revaluation gains are credited to other comprehensive income unless the gain reverses a previous revaluation loss of the same asset previously recognised in the statement of profit or loss.
- Revaluation losses are debited to the statement of profit or loss unless the loss relates to a previous revaluation surplus, in which case the decrease should be debited to other comprehensive income to the extent of any credit balance existing in the revaluation reserve relating to that asset.

Accounting for revaluations

Steps:

(1) Restate asset from cost to valuation amount: Dr Non-current asset (valuation – cost)

(2) Remove any existing depreciation: Dr Accumulated depreciation

(3) Include increase in other comprehensive income: Cr Revaluation gain within other comprehensive income (valuation – old carrying value).

Depreciation is charged on the revalued amount less residual value (if any) over the **remaining useful life** of the asset.

An entity may choose to make an annual transfer of excess depreciation from revaluation reserve to retained earnings. If this is done, it should be applied consistently each year.

Note that assets **held for sale** are recognised at the lower of carrying amount and fair value less costs to sell in accordance with IFRS 5.

IAS 18 Revenue

Revenue is the gross inflow of economic benefits during the period arising from the ordinary activities of the entity.

The standard relates to revenue arising from:

(i) the sale of goods

(ii) the rendering of services

(iii) the use by others of entity assets yielding interest, royalties and dividends.

The primary issue is determining when to recognise revenue. Revenue is recognised when:

- it is probable that future economic benefits will flow to the entity, and
- these benefits can be measured reliably.

It may be necessary to apply the recognition criteria to the separately identifiable components of a single transaction, to two or more transactions together, or (more normally) to a single transaction in its entirety.

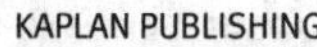

Recognition

In addition to the recognition criteria described above:

- Revenue from the sale of goods can be recognised when the seller transfers the risks and rewards of ownership to the buyer.
- Revenue from the rendering of services is recognised by reference to the stage of completion at the statement of financial position date. When the outcome of the transaction cannot be estimated reliably, revenue shall be recognised only to the extent of the expenses recognised that are recoverable.
- In both cases above, the amount of revenue and costs incurred must able to be measured reliably.
- Revenue from interest, royalties and dividends should be recognised, as follows:
  - interest is recognised using the effective interest method.
  - royalties are accrued in accordance with the relevant contract.
  - dividends are recognised when the shareholders right to receive payment is established.

Measurement

- Revenue should be measured at the fair value of consideration received or receivable. Fair value is the amount for which an asset could be exchanged, or liability settled between knowledgeable parties on an arm's length basis.
- In most cases this will be the amount agreed between the two parties as the price, adjusted for discounts if necessary.

If the time value of money is material, then the revenue should be discounted to present value and the unwinding of the discount treated as interest income in the statement of profit or loss. In this case, there are effectively two transactions – the sale of the goods and the provision of finance.

IAS 27 Separate financial statements

IAS 27 (revised) applies when an entity has interests in subsidiaries, joint ventures or associates and either elects to, or is required to, prepare separate **non-consolidated financial statements**.

If the financial statements are not consolidated, they must therefore present interests in other entities at cost, using the equity method.

IAS 28 Investments in associates and joint ventures

A **joint venture** is a joint arrangement whereby the parties have joint control of the arrangement and have rights to the net assets of the arrangement. This will normally be established in the form of a separate entity to conduct the joint venture activities (IFRS 11).

An **associate** is an entity over which the investor has significant influence and that is neither a subsidiary nor an interest in a joint venture.

Significant influence is the power to participate in the financial and operating policy decisions of the investee but is not control or joint control over those policies.

The definition of significant influence is very broad. You may have to read the question very carefully in order to decide whether an investment creates should be recognised as either an associate or as a joint venture.

It is normally assumed that significant influence exists if the holding company has a shareholding of 20% to 50%. That does not, however, guarantee that the investing entity has any real influence. For example, a 40% shareholding might actually offer very little real influence if the remaining 60% is in the hands of a controlling investor.

Equity accounting

In the consolidated financial statements of a group:

- Acquisition accounting is used to account for subsidiaries.
- Equity accounting is used to account for associates and joint ventures.

Unlike acquisition accounting, which combined the holding company's figures with those of the subsidiary or subsidiaries, equity accounting involves single figure adjustments to the consolidated statement of profit or loss and the consolidated statement of financial position.

An interest in an associate or joint venture should be accounted for in the separate financial statements of an entity in accordance with accordance with IAS 27 (Revised).

Statement of profit or loss

The consolidated statement of profit or loss and other comprehensive income includes the **investor's share** of the associate or joint venture's results.

Statement of financial position

In the consolidated statement of financial position, the associate or joint venture is initially shown at cost and then increased by the investor's share of the post-acquisition reserve movement.

Balances with the associate

The associate or joint venture is considered to be outside the group. Therefore balances between group companies and the associate or joint venture will remain in the consolidated statement of financial position. If a group company trades with the associate or joint venture, the resulting payables and receivables will remain in the consolidated statement of financial position.

Sales to and from associates

Sales between group members and associates or joint ventures are left in the consolidated statement of profit or loss.

Unrealised profit in inventory

The group share of unrealised profit in closing inventory arising from sales between group members and associates or joint ventures should still be cancelled.

Dividends from associates

Dividends from associates and joint ventures are not included in the consolidated statement of profit or loss. This is because the dividend is effectively being paid out of the group's share of the associate or joint venture's profit, which has already been recognised in the group accounts.

IAS 37 Provisions, contingent liabilities and contingent assets

- A provision is a liability of uncertain timing or amount.
- A contingent liability is a possible obligation arising from past events whose existence will only be confirmed on the occurrence of uncertain future event outside of the entity's control.
- A contingent asset is a possible asset that arises from past events and whose existence will only be confirmed on the occurrence of uncertain future events outside of the entity's control.

Provisions

Recognition

Recognise when:

- an entity has a present obligation (legal or constructive) as a result of a past event,
- It is probable that an outflow of resources embodying economic benefits will be required to settle the obligation, and
- a reliable estimate can be made of the amount of the obligation.

Measurement

- The amount recognised as a provision should be the best estimate of the expenditure required to settle the present obligation at the SFP date
- Where the time value of money is material, the provision should be discounted to present value.

Contingent liabilities should not be recognised. They should be disclosed unless the possibility of a transfer of economic benefits is remote.

Contingent assets should not be recognised. If the possibility of an inflow of economic benefits is probable they should be disclosed.

Specific guidance

Future operating losses

- Provisions should not be recognised for future operating losses.

Onerous contracts

- Provisions should be recognised for the present obligation under the contract.
- E.g. non-cancellable lease, provide for the unavoidable lease payments.

Restructuring

- Provisions can only be recognised where an entity has a constructive obligation to carry out the restructuring.
- A constructive obligation arises: when there is a detailed formal plan, identifying at least:
  - the business concerned,
  - the principal location, function, and approximate number of employees being made redundant,
  - the expenditures that will be incurred,
  - when the plan will be implemented; and
  - There is a valid expectation that the plan will be carried out by either implementing the plan or announcing it to those affected.

IAS 38 Intangible assets

An **intangible asset** is an identifiable non-monetary asset without physical substance.

Accounting treatment

An intangible asset is initially recognised at cost if all of the following criteria are met.

(1) It is identifiable – it could be disposed of without disposing of the business at the same time.

(2) It is controlled by the entity

– the entity has the power to obtain economic benefits from it, for example patents and copyrights give legal rights to future economic benefits.

(3) It will generate probable future economic benefits for the entity

– this could be by a reduction in costs or increasing revenues.

(4) The cost can be measured reliably

– this is straightforward if the asset was purchased outright. If the asset was acquired in a business combination then the initial cost will be the fair value.

- If an intangible does not meet the recognition criteria, then it should be charged to the statement of profit or loss as it is incurred. Items that do not meet the criteria are internally generated goodwill, brands, mastheads, publishing titles, customer lists, research, advertising, start-up costs and training.
- Intangible assets should be amortised, normally using the straight line method, over the term of their useful lives.
- If it can be demonstrated that the useful life is indefinite no amortisation should be charged, but an annual impairment review must be carried out.
- Intangible assets can be revalued but fair values must be determined with reference to an active market. This will have homogenous products, willing buyers and seller at all times and published prices. In practical terms, most intangible assets are likely to be valued using the cost model.
- The recognition of internally generated intangible assets is split into a research phase and a development phase. Costs incurred in the research phase must be charged to the statement of profit or loss as they are incurred. Costs incurred in the development phase should be recognised if they meet the following criteria:

  (a) the project is technically feasible

  (b) the asset will be completed then used or sold

(c) the entity is able to use or sell the asset
(d) the asset will generate future economic benefits (either by internal use or there is a market for it)
(e) the entity has adequate technical, financial and other resources to complete the project
(f) the expenditure on the project can be reliably measured.

- Amortisation of development costs will occur over the period that commercial benefits are expected to be received.

IFRS 3 Business combinations

IFRS 3 requires that on acquisition both the cost of investment and the net assets acquired are recorded at their fair value. Assets and liabilities must be recognised if they are separately identifiable and can be reliably measured. The future intentions of the acquirer must not be taken into account when calculating fair values.

Fair value is the amount for which an asset could be exchanged, or a liability settled, between knowledgeable, willing parties in an arm's length transaction.

Fair value of the cost of acquisition

The cost of acquisition is:

(a) the amount of cash paid, plus
(b) the fair value of other purchase consideration given by the acquirer.

Note:

- If payment of cash is deferred it should be discounted to present value using a rate at which the acquirer could obtain similar borrowing.
- If the acquirer issues shares, fair value is normally the market price at the date of acquisition.
- IFRS 3 requires the acquirer to recognise the acquisition date fair value of contingent consideration as part of the consideration.

Goodwill and the non-controlling interest

The standard allows the acquirer (parent) to measure any non-controlling interest (NCI) in one of two ways:

- at fair value – this measures goodwill for the entity as a whole, or
- at the NCI's proportionate share of the acquiree's (subsidiary's) identifiable net assets.

Negative goodwill

If the net assets acquired exceed the fair value of consideration, then negative goodwill arises.

After checking that the calculations have been done correctly, negative goodwill is credited to the statement of profit or loss and other comprehensive income immediately.

Other adjustments

Other consolidation adjustments need to be made, including:

- dividends declared by the subsidiary or associate and not accounted for by the parent.
- interest on intercompany loans that has not been accounted for by the receiving party.
- intercompany management charges that have not been accounted for by the receiving party.
- intercompany sales, purchases and unrealised profit in inventory.
- intercompany transfer of non-current assets and unrealised profit on transfer.
- intercompany receivables, payables and loans that need eliminating.

IFRS 10 Consolidated financial statements

IFRS 10 requires consideration of whether or not an entity is controlled by another entity, to determine if it is a subsidiary that should be consolidated.

Control consists of three components:

(1) **Power** over the investee: this is normally exercised through the **majority of voting rights**, but could also arise through other contractual arrangements. Power relates only to substantive, rather than protective rights. The former arises where there is practical ability to exercise rights of control at the time when relevant decisions are made. The latter may arise where control can be exercised only upon pre-determined circumstances arising at some later date.

(2) **Exposure** or rights to variable returns (positive and/or negative) from involvement, and

(3) The **ability to use power** over the investee to affect the amount of investor returns. The ability to use power over an investee to affect returns is regarded as a crucial determinant in deciding whether or not control is exercised.

This definition should be subject to **continuous assessment**, and should be considered at least at each reporting date to determine that control continues to apply.

[illegible]

IFRS 10 [illegible] definition of whether or not an entity is controlled, [illegible] should be [illegible] determine if it is a subsidiary that should be consolidated.

Control consists of three components:

(1) **Power**: Power in most cases is normally exercised through the **majority of voting rights**, but could also arise through other contractual arrangements. Power relates to rights that are substantive rather than protective rights. The [illegible] has the practical ability to exercise rights [illegible] decisions [illegible] may arise where control can be exercised only when [illegible] circumstances [illegible].

(2) **Exposure** or rights to variable returns (both positive and negative) from involvement [illegible].

(3) The **ability to use power** over the investee to affect the amount of investor returns. The ability to use power over an investee to affect such returns [illegible] whether or not actually exercised.

The definition should be subject to **continuous assessment** and should be considered at least at each reporting date to determine that control continues to apply.

chapter

15

Additional practice questions

Test your understanding 1 – Conflicts of interest

Your firm is the external auditor to two companies. One is a hotel, Tourex, the other is a food wholesaler, Pudco, that supplies the hotel. Both companies have the same year-end. Just before that year-end, a large number of guests became ill at a wedding reception at the hotel, possibly as a result of food poisoning.

The guests have taken legal action against the hotel and the hotel has taken action against the food wholesaler. Neither the hotel nor the food wholesaler have admitted liability. The hotel is negotiating out-of-court settlements with the ill guests, the food wholesaler is negotiating an out-of-court settlement with the hotel. At the statement of financial position date, the public health authorities have not completed their investigations.

Lawyers for both the hotel and the food wholesaler say informally that negotiations are 'going well' but refuse to confirm this in writing. The amounts involved are material to the financial statements of both companies.

Required:

(a) **Describe how ACCA's Rulebook apply to this situation and explain how the external auditors should manage this conflict of interest.**

(5 marks)

(b) **Outline the main requirements of IAS 37 *Provisions, Contingent Liabilities and Contingent Assets* and apply them to this case.**

(5 marks)

Test your understanding 2 – Ethics

Professional ethics are relevant to both external auditors and internal auditors.

You work for a medium-sized firm of Chartered Certified Accountants with seven offices and 150 employees. Your firm has been asked to tender for the provision of statutory audit and other services to Billington Travel, a private company providing discounted package holiday services in the Mediterranean. The company is growing fast and would represent a substantial amount of fee income for your firm. The finance director has explained to you that the company would like the successful firm to provide a number of different services. These include the statutory audit and assistance with the preparation of the financial statements. The company is also struggling with a new computer system and the finance director considers that a systems review by your firm may be helpful. Your firm does not have much experience in the travel sector.

Required:

(a) **Explain why it is necessary for external auditors to be and be seen to be independent of their audit clients.**

(3 marks)

(b) **With reference to the ACCA Rulebook, describe the ethical matters that should be considered in deciding on whether your firm should tender for:**

(i) **the statutory audit of Billington Travel**

(4 marks)

(ii) **the provision of other services to Billington Travel.**

(4 marks)

You are a student Chartered Certified Accountant and you are one of four assistant internal auditors in a large manufacturing company. You report to the chief internal auditor. You have been working on the review of the payables system and you have discovered what you consider to be several serious deficiencies in the structure and operation of the system. You have reported these matters in writing to the chief internal auditor but you are aware that none of these matters have been covered in his final report on the system which is due to be presented to management.

Required:

(c) **List the actions you might take in these circumstances.**

(6 marks)

(d) **Explain the dangers of doing nothing in these circumstances.**

(3 marks)

(Total: 20 marks)

Test your understanding 3 – Audit risk

You are an audit senior in Staple and Co and you are commencing the planning of the audit of Smoothbrush Paints Co for the year ending 31 August 20X0.

Smoothbrush Paints Co is a paint manufacturer and has been trading for over 50 years, it operates from one central site, which includes the production facility, warehouse and administration offices.

Smoothbrush sells all of its goods to large home improvement stores, with 60% being to one large chain store Homewares. The company has a one year contract to be the sole supplier of paint to Homewares. It secured the contract through significantly reducing prices and offering a four-month credit period, the company's normal credit period is one month.

Goods in/purchases

In recent years, Smoothbrush has reduced the level of goods directly manufactured and instead started to import paint from South Asia. Approximately 60% is imported and 40% manufactured. Within the production facility is a large amount of old plant and equipment that is now redundant and has minimal scrap value. Purchase orders for overseas paint are made six months in advance and goods can be in transit for up to two months. Smoothbrush accounts for the inventory when it receives the goods.

To avoid the disruption of a year end inventory count, Smoothbrush has this year introduced a continuous/perpetual inventory counting system. The warehouse has been divided into 12 areas and these are each to be counted once over the year. At the year end it is proposed that the inventory will be based on the underlying records. Traditionally Smoothbrush has maintained an inventory allowance based on 1% of the inventory value, but management feels that as inventory is being reviewed more regularly it no longer needs this allowance.

Finance Director

In May 20X0 Smoothbrush had a dispute with its finance director (FD) and he immediately left the company. The company has temporarily asked the financial controller to take over the role while they recruit a permanent replacement. The old FD has notified Smoothbrush that he intends to sue for unfair dismissal. The company is not proposing to make any provision or disclosures for this, as they are confident the claim has no merit.

Required:

(a) **Explain the audit risks identified at the planning stage of the audit of Smoothbrush Paints Co.**

(8 marks)

(b) **Discuss the importance of assessing risks at the planning stage of an audit.**

(6 marks)

(c) **Describe THREE substantive procedures the auditor of Smoothbrush Paints Co should perform at the year end in confirming each of the following:**

(i) **The valuation of inventory**

(ii) **The completeness of provisions or contingent liabilities.**

(6 marks)

(Total: 20 marks)

Test your understanding 4 – Inventory count

DinZee Co assembles fridges, microwaves, washing machines and other similar domestic appliances from parts procured from a large number of suppliers. As part of the interim audit work two weeks prior to the company year-end, you are testing the procurement and purchases systems and attending the inventory count.

On the day of the inventory count, you attended depot nine at DinZee. You observed the following activities:

Prenumbered count sheets were being issued to client's staff carrying out the count. The count sheets showed the inventory ledger balances for checking against physical inventory.

All count staff were drawn from the inventory warehouse and were counting in teams of two.

Three counting teams were allocated to each area of the stores to count, although the teams were allowed to decide which pair of staff counted which inventory within each area. Staff were warned that they had to remember which inventory had been counted.

Information was recorded on the count sheets in pencil so amendments could be made easily as required.

Any inventory not located on the pre-numbered inventory sheets was recorded on separate inventory sheets – which were numbered by staff as they were used.

At the end of the count, all count sheets were collected and the numeric sequence of the sheets checked; the sheets were not signed.

Required:

(a) **Describe FOUR audit procedures that an auditor will normally perform prior to attending the client's premises on the day of the inventory count.**

(4 marks)

(b) **Identify the deficiencies in the control system for counting inventory, explain why it is a deficiency and state how each deficiency can be overcome.**

(12 marks)

(c) **State the aim of a test of control and the aim of a substantive procedure and in respect of your attendance at DinZee Co's inventory count, state one test of control and one substantive procedure that you should perform.**

(4 marks)

(Total: 20 marks)

Test your understanding 5 – Controls 1

There are a number of key procedures which auditors should perform if they wish to rely on internal controls and reduce the level of substantive testing they perform. These include:

(i) Documentation of accounting and internal control systems

(ii) Walk-through testing

(iii) Audit sampling

(iv) Testing internal controls

(v) Dealing with deviations from the application of control procedures.

Required:

Briefly explain each of the procedures listed above.

(10 marks)

NB: (i) to (v) above carry equal marks

Test your understanding 6 – Controls 2

Your firm is the external auditor of Bestwood Engineering, a privately owned incorporated business, which manufactures components for motor vehicles and sells them to motor vehicle manufacturers and wholesalers. It has sales of $10 million and a profit before tax of $400,000.

The company has a new chief financial officer who has asked your advice on controls in the company's purchases and accounts payable system.

Bestwood Engineering has separate accounts, purchasing and goods received departments. Most purchases are required by the production department, but other departments are able to raise requisitions for goods and services. The purchasing department is responsible for obtaining goods and services for the company at the lowest price which is consistent with the required delivery date and quality, and for ensuring their prompt delivery.

The accounts department is responsible for obtaining authorisation of purchase invoices before they are input into the computer which posts them to the accounts payable ledger and the general ledger. The accounting records are kept on a computer and the standard accounting software was obtained from an independent supplier. The accounting software maintains the accounts payable ledger, accounts receivable ledger, general ledger and payroll. The company does not maintain inventory records, as it believes the costs of maintaining these records outweigh the benefits.

The chief financial officer has explained that services include gas, electricity, telephone, repairs and short-term rental (hire) of equipment and vehicles.

Required:

(a) **Describe the controls which should be in operation in the purchasing department in respect of the purchase and receipt of goods.**

(8 marks)

(b) **Describe the controls the accounts department should exercise over obtaining authorisation of purchase invoices before posting them to the accounts payable ledger.**

(6 marks)

(c) **Explain how controls over the purchase of services, from raising the purchase requisition to posting the invoice to the accounts payable ledger, might differ from the procedures for the purchase of goods, as described in your answers to parts (a) and (b) above.**

(6 marks)

(Total: 20 marks)

Test your understanding 7 – Controls 3

Flowers Anytime sells flowers wholesale. Customers telephone the company and their orders are taken by clerks who take details of the flowers to be delivered, the address to which they are to be delivered, and account details of the customer. The clerks input these details into the company's computer system (whilst the order is being taken) which is integrated with the company's inventory control system. The company's standard credit terms are payment one month from the order (all orders are despatched within 48 hours) and most customers pay by bank transfer. An accounts receivable ledger is maintained and statements are sent to customers once a month. Credit limits are set by the credit controller according to a standard formula and are automatically applied by the computer system, as are the prices of flowers.

Required:

(a) **Describe and explain the purpose of the internal controls you might expect to see in the sales system at Flowers Anytime over the:**

(i) **Receipt, processing and recording of orders.**

(6 marks)

(ii) **Collection of cash.**

(4 marks)

(b) **Describe how you would test each of the controls identified in part (a).**

(10 marks)

Test your understanding 8 – CAATs

(a) Computer Assisted Audit Techniques (CAATs) are used to assist an auditor in the collection of audit evidence from computerised systems.

Required:

List and briefly explain four advantages of CAATs.

(4 marks)

(b) Porthos, a limited liability company, is a reseller of sports equipment, specialising in racquet sports such as tennis, squash and badminton. The company purchases equipment from a variety of different suppliers and then resells this using the Internet as the only selling media. The company has over 150 different types of racquets available in inventory, each identified via a unique product code.

Customers place their orders directly on the Internet site. Most orders are for one or two racquets only. The ordering/sales software automatically verifies the order details, customer address and credit card information prior to orders being verified and goods being despatched. The integrity of the ordering system is checked regularly by ArcherWeb, an independent Internet service company.

You are the audit manager working for the external auditors of Porthos, and you have just started planning the audit of the sales system of the company. You have decided to use test data to check the input of details into the sales system. This will involve entering dummy orders into the Porthos system from an online terminal.

Required:

List the test data you will use in your audit of the financial statements of Porthos to confirm the completeness and accuracy of input into the sales system, clearly explaining the reason for each item of data.

(6 marks)

(c) **You are also considering using audit software as part of your substantive testing of the data files in the sales and inventory systems of Porthos.**

(i) **List and briefly explain some of the difficulties of using audit software.**

(4 marks)

(ii) **List the audit tests that you can program into your audit software for the sales and inventory system in Porthos, explaining the reason for each test.**

(6 marks)

(Total: 20 marks)

Test your understanding 9 – Audit risk NFP

(a) **Explain the term 'audit risk' and the three elements of risk that contribute to total audit risk.**

(4 marks)

The EuKaRe charity was established in 1960. The charity's aim is to provide support to children from disadvantaged backgrounds who wish to take part in sports such as tennis, badminton and football.

EuKaRe has a detailed constitution which explains how the charity's income can be spent. The constitution also notes that administration expenditure cannot exceed 10% of income in any year.

The charity's income is derived wholly from voluntary donations. Sources of donations include:

- Cash collected by volunteers asking the public for donations in shopping areas,
- Cheques sent to the charity's head office,
- Donations from generous individuals. Some of these donations have specific clauses attached to them indicating that the initial amount donated (capital) cannot be spent and that the income (interest) from the donation must be spent on specific activities, for example, provision of sports equipment.

The rules regarding the taxation of charities in the country EuKaRe is based are complicated, with only certain expenditure being allowable for taxation purposes and donations of capital being treated as income in some situations.

Required:

(b) **Identify areas of inherent risk in the EuKaRe charity and explain the effect of each of these risks on the audit approach.**

(12 marks)

(c) **Explain why the control environment may be weak at the charity EuKaRe.**

(4 marks)

(Total: 20 marks)

Test your understanding 10 – NFP audit

Ajio is a charity whose constitution requires that it raises funds for educational projects. These projects seek to educate children and support teachers in certain countries. Charities in the country from which Ajio operates have recently become subject to new audit and accounting regulations. Charity income consists of cash collections at fund raising events, telephone appeals, and bequests (money left to the charity by deceased persons). The charity is small and the trustees do not consider that the charity can afford to employ a qualified accountant. The charity employs a part-time bookkeeper and relies on volunteers for fund raising. Your firm has been appointed as accountants and auditors to this charity because of the new regulations. Accounts have been prepared (but not audited) in the past by a volunteer who is a recently retired Chartered Certified Accountant.

Required:

(a) **Describe the risks associated with the audit of Ajio under the headings risk of material misstatement (inherent and control risks) and detection risk and explain the implications of these risks for overall audit risk.**

(10 marks)

(b) **List and explain the audit tests to be performed on income and expenditure from fund raising events.**

(10 marks)

Note: You are not required to deal with the detail of accounting for charities in either part of the question.

(Total: 20 marks)

Test your understanding 11 – Audit reports

You are currently engaged in reviewing the working papers of several audit assignments recently carried out by your audit practice. Each of the audit assignments is nearing completion, but certain matters have recently come to light which may affect your audit opinion on each of the assignments. In each case the year end of the company is 30 September 20X2.

(a) **Jones** (Profit before tax $150,000)

On 3 October 20X2 a letter was received informing the company that a customer, who owed the company $30,000 as at the year end had been declared bankrupt on 30 September. At the time of the audit it was expected that unsecured creditors, such as Jones, would receive nothing in respect of this debt. The directors refuse to change the financial statements to provide for the loss, on the grounds that the notification was not received by the statement of financial position date.

Total debts shown in the statement of financial position amounted to $700,000.

(5 marks)

(b) **Roberts** (Profit before tax $500,000)

On 31 July 20X2 a customer sued the company for personal damages arising from an unexpected defect in one of its products. Shortly before the year end the company made an out-of-court settlement with the customer of $10,000, although this agreement is not reflected in the financial statements as at 30 September 20X2. Further, the matter subsequently became known to the press and was extensively reported. The company's legal advisers have now informed you that further claims have been received following the publicity, although they are unable to place a figure on the potential liability arising from such claims which have not yet been received. The company had referred to the claims in a note to the financial statements stating, however, that no provision had been made to cover them because the claims were not expected to be material.

(5 marks)

(c) **Griffiths** (Net profit before tax $250,000)

The audit work revealed that a trade investment stated in the statement of financial position at $500,000 had suffered a permanent fall in value of $300,000. The company admitted that the loss had occurred, but refused to make an allowance for it on the grounds that other trade investments (not held for resale) had risen in value and were stated at amounts considerably below their realisable values.

(5 marks)

(d) **Evans** (Net profit before tax $100,000)

This client is a construction company, currently building a warehouse on its own premises, and using some of its own workforce. The cost of labour and materials has been included in the cost of the non-current asset in the statement of financial position, the total figure being based on the company's costing records. The warehouse is almost complete and the cost shown in the statement of financial position includes direct labour costs of $10,000. However, during audit testing it was discovered that the costing records, showing the direct labour costs for the warehouse in the early part of the year, had been destroyed accidentally.

(5 marks)

Required:

Discuss each of the cases outlined above, referring to materiality considerations and, where appropriate, relevant accounting principles and appropriate accounting standards. You should also indicate, with reasons, the kind of audit report (including the type of modification, if necessary) which you consider would be appropriate in each case.

You are not required to produce the full audit reports, and you may assume that all matters other than those specifically mentioned are considered satisfactory.

(Total: 20 marks)

Test your understanding 12 – Fraud

Fraud and error present risks to an entity. Both internal and external auditors are required to deal with risks to the entity. However, the responsibilities of internal and external auditors in relation to the risk of fraud and error differ.

Required:

(a) **Explain how the internal audit function helps an entity deal with the risk of fraud and error.**

(5 marks)

(b) **Explain the responsibilities of external auditors in respect of the risk of fraud and error in an audit of financial statements.**

(8 marks)

(c) Stone Holidays is an independent travel agency. It does not operate holidays itself. It takes commission on holidays sold to customers through its chain of high street shops. Staff are partly paid on a commission basis. Well-established tour operators run the holidays that Stone Holidays sells. The networked reservations system through which holidays are booked and the computerised accounting system are both well-established systems used by many independent travel agencies.

Payments by customers, including deposits, are accepted in cash and by debit and credit card. Stone Holidays is legally required to pay an amount of money (based on its total sales for the year) into a central fund maintained to compensate customers if the agency should cease operations.

Describe the nature of the risks to which Stone Holidays is subject arising from fraud and error.

(7 marks)

(Total: 20 marks)

Test your understanding 13 – Quality control

You are the partner responsible for quality control within your firm. You are reviewing the findings from a recent post-issuance (cold) review performed by your firm's compliance department. The following issues were identified on a number of audits:

Client A

A review of working papers found that on some working papers had not been signed off by the team member that had completed the working paper. Some working papers were not dated and some did not have a signature confirming they had been reviewed.

Client B

A mandatory procedure included in the audit plan which required a written representation letter to be obtained, had not been completed. A comment had been added by the audit manager stating that there were no issues requiring a written representation from management.

Client C

An audit test over purchases required a sample of 30 invoices to be tested. 27 had been tested and found to be recorded accurately and completely. 3 invoices could not be found. No further invoices were identified for testing and a conclusion was drawn based on the 27 items tested.

Client D

The audit of a material provision was performed by the audit junior as the audit manager was too busy finishing off work for the previous client on which they had been working.

Client E

The planning section of the file has not been completed. The audit procedures performed were copied over from the previous year's file and the same approach and sample sizes have been used to conduct this year's audit.

Required:

Describe the quality control issues arising from each of the findings.

(10 marks)

Test your understanding answers

Test your understanding 1 – Conflicts of interest

(a) Managing conflicts of interest

The ACCA Rulebook states that auditors should avoid conflicts of interest (both conflicts between the firm and clients, and conflicts between clients) wherever possible. In some cases, such as these, they are unavoidable.

Full disclosure is important and both companies should be fully aware that the firm is acting for the other party.

One or both companies may object to the firm acting for the other company and the auditor may be forced to make a decision as to which company to resign from. However, this is not an attractive course of action because the audits may already have commenced and it may be difficult for one of the companies to find a new auditor, quickly.

The auditor should probably not, therefore, resign unless forced to do so – this might be prejudicial to the interests of one of the clients.

It is important in such cases that different teams of staff, and different engagement partners work on the respective audits.

Internal procedures within the firm should be set up to prevent confidential information from one client being transferred to the other and the interests of one firm damaging the interests of the other. Such procedures are known as information barriers. This can be achieved by having the different audit teams from two completely separate offices.

(b) IAS 37 states that a provision is a liability of uncertain timing or amount. It should only be recognised when there is a present obligation (legal or constructive) arising from past events and it is probable that a transfer of economic benefits will be required to settle the obligation and a reliable estimate of the amount can be made. If the firm can obtain sufficient appropriate audit evidence to show that Tourex and/or Pudco are likely to have to make a payment, and that the amount can be reliably estimated, a constructive obligation seems to exist and provision should be made.

IAS 37 states that a contingent liability is either a possible obligation arising from past events whose existence will be confirmed by uncertain future events outside the control of the entity or, a present obligation arising from past events that is not recognised because a transfer of economic benefits is not probable, or because the amount of the obligation cannot be measured with sufficient certainty. If Tourex and/or Pudco are uncertain as to whether a payment will have to be made, or if they are certain but the amount cannot be estimated, a contingent liability should be disclosed in the accounts.

IAS 37 states that a contingent asset is a possible asset arising from past events whose existence will be confirmed by uncertain future events outside the control of the entity. Contingent assets can be disclosed when an inflow of economic benefit is probable. When they are virtually certain, a contingency does not exist; the income may be accrued. This might apply to Tourex in its claim against the food company. It seems unlikely that there is sufficient certainty relating to the claim and therefore no disclosure should be made.

It also states that expected reimbursements (such as those arising from insurance contracts) should be recognised only where they are virtually certain, and treated as separate assets. The net expense may be recognised in the statement of profit or loss. If either Tourex or Pudco hold insurance against such events, and it is probable that the insurance claim will be met, a contingent asset may need to be disclosed. If there is any uncertainty, there should be no disclosure. If it is virtually certain that the claim will be met, a separate asset should be recognised.

A brief description of the nature of each class of contingent liability should be made unless the possibility of the transfer of benefits is remote. Where practical, an estimate of the financial effect, an indication of the relevant uncertainties, and the possibility of any reimbursement should be disclosed. Similar rules apply to contingent assets.

Test your understanding 2 – Ethics

(a) **Independence**

(i) It is important for external auditors to be independent of their audit clients because external auditors act on behalf of the owners of the business (normally the shareholders) and report on the financial statements prepared by the management for the benefit of shareholders.

(ii) If external auditors are not independent of their clients, for example if they hold shares in the companies that they audit, their ability to form an objective opinion on the financial statements is impaired.

(iii) External auditors must also be seen to be independent because if they are not, the owners of the business will not have confidence in the audit reports that the auditors issue.

(iv) The ACCA Rulebook requires that auditors are independent, and that they are seen to be independent. The Rules cover a number of areas in which the auditors' independence may be, or be seen to be, impaired.

(v) National legislation also normally requires external auditors to be independent.

(b) **Billington Travel**

(i) The statutory audit

- The Rulebook states that it is important that the firm is competent to undertake the audit; it must have adequate resources in terms of staff with sufficient experience in this sector. The fact that the services to be provided would constitute a substantial amount of fee income indicates that the firm might not, at present, have those resources.
- It may be appropriate to consider whether experience in this sector can be brought in, by the recruitment of additional staff.
- The firm should consider whether staff are available at the right time of year and whether the work fits in with the firm's existing obligations.
- The Rules also state that the firm must be independent of its clients; in particular, this means that it must not take too much of its fee income from one client (or group of clients).

- Generally, for non-public interest clients, the fee income (including income from additional services) should not exceed 15% of the gross practice income. If that figure is exceeded, it may be possible to consider providing some, but not all, of the services requested.

(ii) The provision of other services

- Preparation of financial statements: it is generally acceptable under the Rulebook for auditors to provide assistance with the preparation of financial statements for private company clients, provided that the client takes full responsibility for the accounting records and financial statements.
- It is important to know why the company needs assistance in this area and it would be preferable in the long run for the company to be able to prepare its own financial statements.
- It is important that those preparing the financial statements are independent of those performing the audit as far as possible, in order that the firm is seen to remain independent.
- Systems review: the external auditor is often well placed to provide assistance with such reviews as the firm obtains a working knowledge of systems during the course of the audit.
- However, there is always the danger that the firm finds itself in the position of having to report on a system that it has helped to improve, and it may be difficult in such circumstances to be critical of the system. This detracts from the firm's ability to remain independent, and in this case, given that it is the first year of audit and that assistance is also needed with the preparation of financial statements, it seems preferable not to tender for the systems review, this year.

(c) **Actions to be taken**

(i) It may be appropriate to discuss the matter, discreetly, with other staff members to establish whether or not it is of concern to them, as well as to you. It would be preferable to discuss the matter with persons who are known to be reliable.

(ii) If the concerns are shared, or if the other staff have no knowledge of the matter, or if you are still concerned about the matter, it may be appropriate to discuss the matter with the chief internal auditor to try and establish why the matter has not been reported, as there may be a good reason. If other staff support you in your view, it may be appropriate to take another member of staff along to the discussion.

(iii) If the chief internal auditor is able to reassure you (either that it is not necessary to report the matter, or that the matter will be reported), no further action will be necessary, although it may be useful to make a brief note of the discussion.

(iv) If you are not satisfied, or if the chief internal auditor undertakes to report the matter but does not do so within a reasonable time, the situation may be more serious and it is more important in such circumstances to make notes of any discussions. It may be appropriate to have further discussions with the chief internal auditor.

(v) If you are still not satisfied, and you consider that the matter is sufficiently serious, it may be appropriate to approach a more senior member of management to voice your concerns. You may wish to avoid this situation but it may be necessary in order to protect yourself.

(vi) On the assumption that the matter is one of internal concern to the company and there is no question of illegality, the question of reporting the matters to third parties outside the organisation does not arise.

(d) **Doing nothing**

(i) The principal danger in doing nothing lies in the possibility that you may be accused of not bringing attention to the matter or even of being actively involved in a 'cover-up'.

(ii) Professional ethics do not permit chartered certified accountants to take no action at all where serious matters are concerned and to do nothing might, in extreme circumstances, involve you in disciplinary proceedings by the ACCA, even as a student.

(iii) To do nothing might also mean that the business of the company you work for is damaged, and therefore your own employment prospects.

Test your understanding 3 – Audit risk

(a) **Audit risks**

Inventory valuation

Smoothbrush supplies 60% of its goods to Homewares at a significantly reduced selling price, hence inventory may be overvalued.

Receivables

Smoothbrush has extended its credit terms to Homewares from one month to four months. There is an increased risk as balances outstanding become older that they may be irrecoverable resulting in overstatement of receivables.

Plant and equipment

The production facility has a large amount of unused plant and equipment. As per IAS 16 *Property, Plant and Equipment* and IAS 36 *Impairment of Assets*, this plant and equipment should be stated at the lower of its carrying value and recoverable amount, which may be at scrap value depending on its age and condition. Plant and equipment may be overvalued.

Cut-off

Smoothbrush imports goods from South Asia and the paint can be in transit for up to two months. The company accounts for goods when they receive them. Therefore at the year end only goods that have been received into the warehouse should be included in the inventory balance and a respective payables balance recognised. Cut-off of purchases and inventory may not be accurate.

Inventory system

New inventory system introduced in the year. This could result in inventory balances being misstated if the records and new system have not initially been set up correctly.

Inventory allowance

Previously Smoothbrush maintained an inventory allowance of 1%, however, this year it has decided to remove this. Unless all slow moving/obsolete items are identified at the year end and their value adjusted, there is a risk that the overall value of inventory may be overstated.

Legal action

The company's finance director (FD) has left and is intending to sue Smoothbrush for unfair dismissal. However, the company does not intend to make any provision/disclosures for sums due to the FD. Provisions/contingent liability disclosures may not be complete.

Lack of FD

Inherent risk is higher due to the changes in the finance department. The financial controller has been appointed as temporary FD and this lack of experience could result in increased risk of errors arising in the financial statement. In addition, the previous FD is not available to help with the audit.

Inventory may be misstated if the perpetual inventory counts are not complete and accurate. The inventory counts should cover all of the inventory lines but if any of the warehouses are not counted then this will need to be done at the year end. In addition, inventory adjustments arising from the counts must be verified and updated by an appropriate member of the finance team to ensure the records are accurate.

(b) **Importance of assessing risks**

- ISA 315 *Identifying and Assessing the Risks of Material Misstatement Through Understanding the Entity and Its Environment,* requires auditors 'to identify and assess the risks of material misstatement, whether due to fraud or error, at the financial statement and assertion levels'.
- It is vitally important for auditors to assess engagement risks at the planning stage, this will ensure that attention is focused early on the areas most likely to cause material misstatements.
- A thorough risk assessment will also help the auditor to fully understand the entity, which is vital for an effective audit. Any unusual transactions or balances would also be identified early, so that these could be addressed in a timely manner.
- In addition, as most auditors adopt a risk based audit approach then these risks need to be assessed early in order for the audit strategy and detailed work programmes to be developed.
- Assessing risks early should also result in an efficient audit. The team will only focus their time and effort on key areas as opposed to balances or transactions that might be immaterial or unlikely to contain errors.

- In addition assessing risk early should ensure that the most appropriate team is selected with more experienced staff allocated to higher risk audits and high risk balances.
- A thorough risk analysis should ultimately reduce the risk of an inappropriate audit opinion being given. The audit would have focused on the main risk areas and hence all material misstatements should have been identified, resulting in the correct opinion being given.
- It should enable the auditor to have a good understanding of the risks of fraud, money laundering, etc. Assessing risk should enable the auditor to assess whether the client is a going concern.

(c) **Audit procedures**

Substantive procedures to confirm valuation of inventory

- Select a representative sample of goods in inventory at the year end, agree the cost per the records to a recent purchase invoice and ensure that the cost is correctly stated.
- Select a sample of year end goods and review post year end sales invoices to ascertain if NRV is above cost or if an adjustment is required.
- For a sample of manufactured items obtain cost sheets and confirm:
  - raw material costs to recent purchase invoices
  - labour costs to time sheets or wage records
  - overheads allocated are of a production nature.
- Review aged inventory reports and identify any slow moving goods, discuss with management why these items have not been written down.
- Compare the level/value of aged product lines to the total inventory value to assess whether the provision for slow moving goods of 1% should be reinstated.
- Review the inventory records to identify the level of adjustments made throughout the year for damaged/obsolete items. If significant consider whether the year end records require further adjustments and discuss with management whether any further write downs/allowance may be required.

– Follow up any damaged/obsolete items noted by the auditor at the inventory counts attended, to ensure that the inventory records have been updated correctly.

– Perform a review of the average inventory days for the current year and compare to prior year inventory days. Discuss any significant variations with management.

– Compare the gross margin for current year with prior year. Fluctuations in gross margin could be due to inventory valuation issues. Discuss significant variations in the margin with management.

Substantive procedures to confirm completeness of provisions or contingent liability

– Discuss with management the nature of the dispute between Smoothbrush and the former finance director (FD), to ensure that a full understanding of the issue is obtained and to assess whether an obligation exists. Review any correspondence with the former FD to assess if a reliable estimate of any potential payments can be made. Write to the company's lawyers to obtain their views as to the probability of the FD's claim being successful.

– Review board minutes and any company correspondence to assess whether there is any evidence to support the former FD's claims of unfair dismissal.

– Obtain a written representation from the directors of Smoothbrush confirming their view that the former FD's chances of a successful claim are remote, and hence no provision or contingent liability is required.

Credit will be awarded for any substantive procedures which test for additional provisions or contingent liabilities of Smoothbrush.

Test your understanding 4 – Inventory count

(a) **Audit procedures prior to inventory count attendance**

Procedure

- Review prior year working papers to identify any issues encountered which the auditor should be prepared for this year.
- Obtain inventory count instructions from the client to ascertain whether appropriate controls and procedures will be in place during the count.
- Enquire of the client whether any inventory is held at third parties and assess whether attendance is required at those sites.
- Book audit staff to attend the inventory count ensuring that staff with the right experience are booked and the right number of staff for the size of the client.

(b) **Deficiencies in counting inventory**

Deficiency	**Reason for deficiency**	**How to overcome deficiency:**
Inventory sheets stated the quantity of items expected to be found in the store	Count teams will focus on finding that number of items making undercounting of inventory more likely – teams stop counting when 'correct' number of items found.	Count sheets should not state the quantity of items so as not to pre-judge how many units will be found.
Count staff were all drawn from the stores	Count staff are also responsible for the inventory. There could be a temptation to hide errors or missing inventory that they have removed from the store illegally.	Count teams should include staff who are not responsible for inventory to provide independence in the count.
Count teams allowed to decide which areas to count	There is a danger that teams will either omit inventory from the count or even count inventory twice due to lack of precise instructions on where to count.	Each team should be given a precise area of the store to count.
Count sheets were not signed by the staff carrying out the count	Lack of signature makes it difficult to raise queries regarding items counted because the actual staff carrying out the count are not known.	All count sheets should be signed to confirm who actually carried out the count of individual items.

Inventory not marked to indicate it has been counted	As above, there is a danger that inventory will be either omitted or included twice in the count.	Inventory should be marked in some way to show that it has been counted to avoid this error.
Recording information on the count sheets in pencil	Recording in pencil means that the count sheets could be amended after the count has taken place, not just during the count. The inventory balances will then be incorrectly recorded.	Count sheets should be completed in ink.
Count sheets for inventory not on the pre-numbered count sheets were only numbered when used	It is possible that the additional inventory sheets could be lost as there is no overall control of the sheets actually being used. Sheets may not be numbered by the teams, again giving rise to the possibility of loss.	All inventory sheets, including those for 'extra' inventory, should be pre-numbered.

(c) (i) The aim of a test of control is to check that an audit client's internal control systems are operating effectively.

The aim of a substantive procedure is to ensure that there are no material errors at the assertion level in the client's financial statements.

(ii) Regarding the inventory count:

Test of control

Observe the count teams ensuring that they are counting in accordance with the client's inventory count instructions.

Substantive procedure

Record the condition of items of inventory to ensure that the valuation of those items is correct on the final inventory summaries.

Test your understanding 5 – Controls 1

Key procedures

(i) *Documentation of accounting and internal control systems*

Auditors document accounting and internal control systems in order to evaluate them for their adequacy as a basis for the preparation of the financial statements and to make a preliminary risk assessment of internal controls.

In very simple systems with few internal controls where auditors do not intend to perform tests of internal controls, it is not necessary to document the internal control system in detail. It is always necessary, however, to have sufficient knowledge of the business to perform an effective audit.

For large entities, where the client has already documented the system, it is not necessary for the auditors to repeat the process if they can satisfy themselves that the client's documentation is adequate.

(ii) *Walk through tests*

The purpose of walk-through tests is for the auditors to establish that their recording of the accounting and internal control system is adequate.

Auditors trace a number of transactions from source to destination in the system, and vice versa. For example, customer orders can be traced from the initial documentation recording the order, through to the related entries in the daybooks and ledgers.

It is common for walk-through tests to be performed at the same time as tests of controls, where auditors are reasonably confident that systems are recorded adequately.

(iii) *Audit sampling*

Auditors perform tests of controls and substantive testing on a sample basis in order to form conclusions on the populations from which the samples are drawn.

It is not possible in anything but the very smallest of entities to take any other approach, as testing 100% of a population may be impractical, not cost effective and not accurate because populations are too large and because of human error.

Samples can be selected in a number of ways – either statistically or on the basis of auditor judgment. In all cases, the sample selected must be representative of the population as a whole.

(iv) *Testing internal controls*

Auditors test internal controls in order to establish whether they are operating effectively throughout the period under review. If controls are operating effectively, auditors can reduce the level of substantive testing on transactions and balances that would otherwise be required.

In testing internal controls, auditors are checking to ensure that the stated control has been applied. For example, auditors may check that there is a grid stamp on a sales invoice with various signatures inside it that show that the invoice has been approved by the credit controller, that it has been checked for arithmetical accuracy, that the price has been checked, and that it has been posted to the sales ledger. The signatures provide audit evidence that the control has been applied.

Auditors are not checking to ensure that the invoice is, in fact, correct. This would be a substantive test. Nevertheless, it is possible to perform tests of control and substantive tests on the same document at the same time.

(v) *Dealing with deviations from the application of control procedures*

Where it appears that an internal control procedure has not been applied, it is necessary to form an opinion as to whether the deviation from the application of the procedure is an isolated incident, or whether the deviation represents a systematic breakdown in the application of the control procedure. This is usually achieved by selecting a further sample for testing.

If it cannot be shown that the non-application of the procedure is isolated (i.e. there are no further instances in which the control has failed), it is necessary either to find a compensating control that can be tested, or to abandon testing of controls and to take a wholly substantive approach. Where there is a breakdown in internal controls it is also necessary to reassess the auditor's preliminary risk assessment. Abandoning tests of control may place strains on the budget for the audit and auditors should always consider the possibility of compensating controls before abandoning tests of controls.

Test your understanding 6 – Controls 2

(a) **Purchasing department – procedures to control the purchase and receipt of goods**

The controls the purchasing department should exercise over ordering and control over receipt of goods and services should include:

– For all goods ordered, there should be a purchase requisition from a user department. The purchasing department should not be permitted to raise purchase requisitions, as this would create a deficiency in the division of duties. For goods required by the purchasing department, they should request another department (e.g. the accounts department) to raise a purchase requisition. Before raising the purchase requisition, the accounts department should ensure it is for goods the purchasing department require and are authorised to order.

– The purchasing department should check the purchase requisition is for goods the user department is authorised to buy or consume. If the value of the order is substantial, the purchasing department should ensure there is a need for such a large order, by checking current inventory levels and future orders to determine whether so large a quantity or value is required.

– The purchase requisition should use a standard form and be signed by an authorised signatory.

– The purchasing department should order the goods from an authorised supplier. Where there is a choice of supplier or a new supplier is required, the purchasing department should obtain the product from the supplier who provides the product or service at the best price, quality and delivery. For audit purposes, it is desirable for staff in the purchasing department to record details of the suppliers contacted, the price, delivery date and perceived quality, and the decision on which supplier was finally chosen.

– The purchasing department should raise the purchase order which should be signed by the purchasing manager. For large value purchases, a director may be required to sign the purchase order. The purchase order should be sent to the supplier, the goods received department, the user department and the accounts department. The purchasing department should ensure the goods are received on time. This may require them to contact the supplier a week before the expected delivery date to ensure they are received on time, and allow action to be taken if the delivery date is later than specified on the purchase order.

- When the goods are received, the purchasing department should receive a copy of the goods received note (GRN) from the goods received department. They should record the goods received against the order. From this information, they will be able to take action when there are short deliveries or the goods are received late. Frequently purchasing departments file purchase orders in three types of file:
  - where none of the goods have been received
  - where some of the goods ordered have been received
  - where all the goods ordered have been received (i.e. 'dead' purchase orders).
- The purchasing department may be part of the system which authorises purchase invoices. They should check the goods on the invoice are consistent with the purchase order and the price per unit is correct.
- The purchasing department should be informed about short deliveries (i.e. the quantity of goods received is less than on the purchase order or advice note) and when there are quality problems. From this information, they can contact the supplier so that corrective action is taken. Also, such details may be helpful in determining whether the supplier should be used for future orders.
- The purchasing department should be informed of situations when goods or services are received but no purchase order has been raised. With this information, the purchasing department should contact the 'offending' department and ensure that in future a purchase order is raised for all the goods they order. The supplier should be contacted and informed that an authorised purchase order must be received by them (the supplier) before any goods or services are provided by the supplier.

(b) **Controls over obtaining authorisation of purchase invoices**

- The accounts department will receive the purchase invoice, which they should record in a register.
- The invoice expense will be included on the invoice (for posting to the general ledger). The expense analysis will be checked by an independent department (e.g. the purchasing or user department).

- The accounts department will either match the purchase invoice to the goods received note and delivery note or ask the goods received department to check and authorise the purchase invoice.
- The purchasing department will be asked to confirm the goods are as described on the purchase order and the price per unit is correct.
- The user department may be asked to authorise the purchase invoice.
- An appropriate responsible official will be asked to authorise the purchase invoice.
- Provided these checks are satisfactory, the accounts department should input the invoice details into the computer which will post it to the accounts payable ledger and the general ledger.

Where there is a problem with the invoice (e.g. concerning the quantity, quality or price of the goods received) the accounts department should put the invoice in a 'hold' file. They should contact the supplier (sometimes with the help of the purchasing or user department) and try to resolve the problem. When either a credit note is received or the correct quantity and quality of goods have been received, the accounts department will get authorisation (e.g. from the purchasing department) that the situation is resolved and they should input the purchase invoice into the computer (and credit note if this is required).

Periodically, an independent person should check suppliers' statements against the balances on the accounts payable ledger. Differences between these two balances should be recorded. If the transaction which created the difference is close to the date of the check, it is probable that no action will be taken. However, older items should be investigated to ensure that action is being taken to resolve the problem.

(c) **Controls over the purchase of services**

Frequently, procedures over receiving services are less strong and less effective than those over receiving goods.

For some types of service, such as receipt of electricity, gas, water and telephone charges there may be no system for raising purchase orders. However there should be a system for reviewing these costs, by comparing them with the previous year (or period), with budget and with amounts charged by alternative suppliers. In this way, the company can ensure these services are received at the most economical cost.

For some of these services it may be possible to suggest ways in which these costs can be reduced (e.g. by turning off lights and reducing the temperature settings in winter).

Costs of gas, electricity and water can be monitored by checking the meter readings monthly and determining whether the consumption is reasonable. For telephone expenses, the system should provide information on the cost for each department, and each department manager should review his/her department's costs. A risk with telephone systems is that they can be abused by staff, who make personal telephone calls using the company's telephone system. The department managers should be made responsible for checking this abuse is kept to a minimum.

For receipt of all other services, before the service is obtained, a purchase requisition should be raised by the user department, and the purchasing department should raise a purchase order. In emergency situations, it may be acceptable to raise a purchase requisition and order after the service has been received (e.g. the repair of a vehicle which has broken down). There should be a system whereby action is taken when no purchase order has been raised for a service which has been received. In many situations when a service has been received, it is probably appropriate that the department receiving the service should issue a goods received note and send it to the purchases accounts and the purchasing departments. In this way, the same system can be used for processing receipt of services as for receipt of goods.

Test your understanding 7 – Controls 3

(a) **Controls**	(b) **Test of Control**
Receipt, processing and recording	
All orders taken should be recorded on a pre-numbered multi-part document generated by the computer. One part might be a copy for the customer, one might form the invoice, one might be for the despatch department and one might be retained for accounts receivable ledger purposes. Manual or computer systems should perform checks on the completeness of the sequence of pre-numbered documents at various stages. Any documents unaccounted for should be traced and investigated.	Review a sample of the sequence checks performed.
The computer system should apply the credit limits set by the credit controller and the system should reject any orders that exceed customer credit limits at the point at which the order is taken, so that the customer can be advised. Any override of credit limits should be authorised by the credit controller.	Try to enter an order that would put a customer over the credit limit and check that the system rejects it.
From time to time, there should be an independent check to ensure that the credit limits within the system are being properly calculated and properly applied to individual transactions. Similar considerations apply to prices maintained within the system.	Take a sample of prices in the system and compare to the authorised price list.
The computer system should also reject any order for which there are no flowers available so that orders cannot be taken for flowers that cannot be delivered.	Try to input an order for flowers which are not available to check that it is rejected.
All invoices should be posted to the sales daybook, the accounts receivable ledger and the accounts receivable control account automatically by the system. The accounts receivable ledger and the accounts receivable control account should be reconciled each month in order for sales and receivables records to be kept up to date.	Review the reconciliations to ensure they are performed regularly and they are reviewed by a supervisor.

There should be controls in place to deal with credit notes and other discrepancies involving the price, type or quality of flowers delivered in order to maintain the accuracy of records and customer goodwill.	Review a sample of credit notes or other adjustments made for evidence of an authorisation signature.
Collection of cash	
At the end of each period, the system should produce a list of overdue receivables. There should be procedures for chasing these customers and for putting a 'stop' on accounts where amounts are significant in order to control bad debts.	Review the list of overdue receivables. Review correspondence chasing these customers.
When bank transfers are received from customers, they should be input into the system and matched with individual transactions and controls should ensure that the correct amounts are allocated to the correct customers and transactions.	Review the bank statement and check that all transfers have been matched with customers.
An exception report should be produced for any unallocated bank transfers. Exceptions should be promptly investigated. This will ensure that receivables information is accurate and up to date and that customers are not chased for amounts that have been paid.	Review the exception report. Check that all matters were resolved promptly.
A bank reconciliation should be performed on a monthly basis in order to ensure that the company's cash records are complete, accurate and up to date.	Review bank reconciliations to ensure they are performed regularly and reviewed by a supervisor.

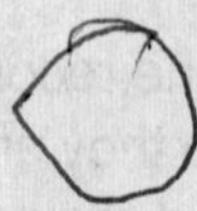

Test your understanding 8 – CAATs

(a) The advantages of Computer-Assisted Audit Techniques (CAATs) are that they:

- Enable the auditor to test program controls – if CAATs were not used then those controls would not be testable.
- Enable the auditor to test a greater number of items quickly and accurately. This will also increase the overall confidence for the audit opinion.
- Allow the auditor to test the actual accounting system and records rather than printouts which are only a copy of those records and could be incorrect.
- Are cost effective after they have been set up as long as the company does not change its systems.
- Allow the results from using CAATs to be compared with 'traditional' testing – if the two sources of evidence agree then this will increase overall audit confidence.

(b)

Test Data	**Reason for Test**
Input of an order for a negative number of tennis racquets	Ensures that only positive quantities are accepted – tennis racquets although the company cannot despatch negative quantities anyway.
Input of an order for ten tennis racquets	There are reasonableness checks in the system to identify possible input errors. A warning message should appear on screen asking the customer to confirm any order for more than say two racquets.
Input of an order without payment details	Ensures that orders are paid for prior to despatch – being completed this also limits the number of bad debts.
Input of invalid inventory code	Ensures that the computer detects the invalid code and presents an error message rather than taking the nearest code and accepting that.
Input of invalid customer credit card details	Online checking of credit card details to the credit card company ensures that goods cannot be despatched without payment. This will also limit the number of bad debts.

Input of invalid address	Ensures that the address and post code are valid, possibly by accessing a database of valid codes. If the code is not valid an error message should be displayed. This ensures that goods are only despatched to valid addresses.

(c) **Audit software**

(i) Difficulties of using audit software

- Substantial setup costs because the client's procedures and files must be understood in detail before the audit software can be used to access and interrogate those files.
- Audit software may not be available for the specific systems set up by the client, especially if those systems are bespoke. The cost of writing audit software to test those systems may be difficult to justify against the possible benefits on the audit.
- The software may produce too much output either due to poor design of the software or using inappropriate parameters on a test. The auditor may waste considerable time checking what appear to be transactions with errors in them when the fault is actually in the audit software.
- Checking the client's files in a live situation. There is the danger that the client's systems are disrupted by the audit program. The data files can be used offline, but this will mean ensuring that the files are true copies of the live files.

(ii) **Audit Software**	**Reason for Test**
Calculation check of the sales day book	Ensures that the computerised sales day book has been cast correctly and helps to verify the sales balance in the financial statements.
Analysis of the aging of items in the inventory ledger	Help to detect inventory items which are relatively old which may need valuing at net realisable value rather than cost.
Selecting a sample of inventory at the end of the year as part of the physical verification	Removes bias from sample selection as well as being quicker than selecting the items manually.

Selecting a sample of sales invoices for checking to despatch documentation	Removes bias from sample selection as well as being quicker than selecting the items manually.
Checking completeness of sales invoice numbers	Ensures that all sales invoices are recorded in the sales day book.
Check that all sales invoices have been paid for	All sales are paid for on ordering, unpaid sales would be a violation of systems rules and would need to be investigated by the auditor.
List large credit notes (perhaps more than five racquets) for investigation by the auditor	The auditor will find reasons for the return – this is also a check on the accuracy of the ordering system – ordering errors may result in customers returning goods later.

Test your understanding 9 – Audit risk NFP

(a) **Audit risk**

Audit risk is the risk that an auditor gives an incorrect opinion on the financial statements being audited.

Inherent risk is the susceptibility of an assertion to a misstatement that could be material individually or when aggregated with misstatements, before considering any related controls. The risk of such misstatement is greater for some assertions and related classes of transactions, account balances, and disclosures than for others.

Control risk is the risk that a material error could occur in an assertion that could be material, individually or when aggregated with other misstatements, will not be prevented or detected on a timely basis by the company's internal control systems.

Detection risk is the risk that the auditors' procedures will not detect a misstatement that exists in an assertion that could be material, individually or when aggregated with other misstatements.

(b) **Inherent risks and effect on audit approach**

Area of inherent risk	**Effect on audit approach**
Income is from voluntary donations only. It will be difficult to estimate future income. There is a risk that disclosure of going concern issues is not adequate in the FS.	Going concern procedures such as enquiry with the trustees and management of the charity to ascertain how their fundraising plans for the future. Written representation will be required from the trustees that they believe the charity can continue in existence for the foreseeable future.
Risk to completeness of income as cash donations may be stolen in the absence of any controls. No invoices will be raised and therefore no evidence of the income received.	Assess what controls exist over cash donations (if any). Test the controls in place. There may need to be a modified opinion due to lack of sufficient appropriate evidence.
There is a risk that the funds are not spent in accordance with the aims of the charity (regularity audit)	Inspect the constitution of the charity to understand its aims. Review of breakdown of expenditure to ensure it is in line with the constitution.
The taxation rules are quite complex for the charity resulting in a risk to the reasonableness of the tax accrual at the year end.	Use of a tax expert or audit staff with relevant knowledge to assess the tax rules and recalculation of the tax charge and liability to ensure arithmetical accuracy.
According to the constitution of the charity, only 10% of expenditure can be on administration. There is a risk that admin costs are manipulated to ensure this restriction is met.	Inspect the constitution of the charity to understand its aims. Review of breakdown of other types of expenditure to identify any admin costs incorrectly classified if the 10% limit has been exceeded.
Some donations are made for an intended purpose. There is a risk that these restricted funds are not shown as such in the financial statements.	Documentation for any donation will need to be obtained and then expenditure agreed to the terms of the documentation. Any discrepancies will have to be reported to management.

(c) **Weak control environment**

Lack of segregation of duties

There is normally a limited number of staff working in the charity meaning that a full system of internal control including segregation of duties cannot be implemented.

Volunteer staff

Many staff are volunteers and so will only work at the charity on an occasional basis. Controls will be performed by different staff on different days making the system unreliable.

Lack of qualified staff

Selection of staff is limited as people tend to volunteer for work when they have time and so they are unlikely to have professional qualifications or experience to implement or maintain good control systems.

No internal audit department

Any control system will not be monitored effectively, mainly due to the lack of any internal audit department. The charity will not have the funds or experience to establish internal audit.

Attitude of the trustees

It is not clear how the charity's trustees view risk. However, where trustees are not professionally trained or have little time to devote to the charity, then there may be an impression that controls are not important. The overall control environment may therefore be weak as other charity workers do not see the importance of maintaining good controls.

Test your understanding 10 – NFP audit

(a) **Risks and implications for audit risk**

Inherent and control risks

(i) Charities can be viewed as inherently risky because they are often managed by non-professionals and are susceptible to fraud, although many charities and the volunteers that run them are people of the highest integrity who take a great deal of care over their work. The assessment of this aspect of inherent risk depends on each individual charity, and the areas in which it operates.

(ii) Charities are also at risk of being in violation of their constitutions which is important where funds are raised from public or private donors who may well object strongly if funds are not applied in the manner expected. Other charities and regulatory bodies supervising charities may also object. Again, the auditors will assess the level of risk. The involvement of a recently retired Chartered Certified Accountant in the preparation of accounts in the past may lower the auditor's assessed inherent risk to an extent.

(iii) Most small charities have a high level of control risk because formal internal controls are expensive and are not often in place. This means that donations are susceptible to misappropriation. Charities rely on the trustworthiness of volunteers. The auditors will assess the level of risk.

Detection risk

(iv) Detection risk comprises sampling risk and non-sampling risk. It is possible in this case that all transactions will be tested and therefore sampling risk (the risk that samples are unrepresentative of the populations from which they are drawn) is not present.

(v) Non-sampling risk is the risk that auditors will draw incorrect conclusions because, for example, mistakes are made, or errors of judgment are made in interpreting results, or because the auditors are unfamiliar with the client, as is the case here.

Audit risk

(vi) Audit risk is the product of inherent risk, control risk and detection risk and is the risk that the auditors will issue an inappropriate audit opinion. This risk can be managed by decreasing detection risk by altering the nature, timing and extent of audit procedures applied. Where inherent risk is high and controls are weak (as may be the case here) more audit work will be performed in appropriate areas in order to reduce audit risk to an acceptable level.

(b) **Audit tests – fund raising events**

(i) Attend fund raising events and observe the procedures employed in collecting, counting, banking and recording the cash. This will help provide audit evidence that funds have not been misappropriated and that all income from such events has been recorded. Sealed boxes or tins that are opened in the presence of two volunteers are often used for these purposes.

(ii) Perform cash counts at the events to provide evidence that cash has been counted correctly and that there is no collusion between volunteers to misappropriate funds.

(iii) Examine bank paying in slips, bank statements and bank reconciliations and ensure that these agree with records made at events. This also provides evidence as to the completeness of income.

(iv) Examine the records of expenditure for fund raising events (hire of equipment, entertainers, purchase of refreshments, etc.) and ensure that these have been properly authorised (where appropriate) and that receipts have been obtained for all expenditure. This provides evidence as to the completeness and accuracy of expenditure.

(v) Review the income and expenditure of fund raising events against any budgets that have been prepared and investigate any significant discrepancies.

(vi) Ensure that all necessary licences (such as public entertainment licences) have been obtained by the trustees for such events in order to ensure that no action is likely to be taken against the charity or volunteers.

(vii) Obtain representations from the trustees to the effect that there are no outstanding unrecorded liabilities for such events – again for completeness of expenditure and liabilities.

Test your understanding 11 – Audit reports

(a) **Jones**

Materiality

The amount of the loss at $30,000 represents 20% of pre-tax profit and more than 4% of accounts receivable; it would therefore seem to be material in both statement of profit or loss and statement of financial position terms, although it is clearly more material in relation to profit.

Relevant accounting principles

The bankruptcy of the customer indicates that the company has overstated profit and assets as at the year-end by $30,000. This letter provides evidence of a condition existing at the statement of financial position date (IAS 10). It should therefore be treated as an adjusting event. The loss should be provided for in full in the financial statements at 30 September 20X2.

Form of audit report

Management's refusal to adjust for the loss means that the financial statements are materially misstated. In such a case, the auditor has to make a decision as to whether the misstatement is 'material and pervasive' or 'material but not pervasive'. Without more facts being available, it is difficult to draw conclusions satisfactorily in this area, but on the face of it a qualified opinion would appear appropriate as the true and fair view would not be entirely destroyed if the loss were to remain unadjusted.

The 'Basis for Opinion' section will be amended to a 'Basis for Qualified Opinion' to explain the reason for the qualified opinion.

The Key Audit Matters section will reference the Basis for Qualified Opinion.

(b) **Roberts**

Materiality

The amount of $10,000 represents only 2% of the stated profit before tax of $500,000 and does not, in itself, appear to be material in terms of its impact on the financial statements. Unfortunately, however, the potential losses may be very much more significant than the figure of $10,000, since other claims are now pending, and the auditor may have to conclude that the whole legal matter is potentially material.

Relevant accounting principles

There is clearly a contingent liability in respect of potential claims arising from the product defect. The potential loss which is material should be accrued in the financial statements where it is probable that future events will confirm the loss and that the loss can be estimated with reasonable accuracy (except where the possibility is remote).

Form of audit report

There is clearly uncertainty with regard to the outcome of the pending claims and the potential liability which they represent. The auditor will have to decide whether or not the possibility of loss is likely or remote. Management has apparently chosen to ignore both the actual loss (which is not individually material) and the potential loss (which may well be material). If the auditor can be convinced that management's view is acceptable and the disclosure in the notes is adequate, then a modification may be completely avoidable. The auditor should be aware, however, that items which are not material when considered individually may well have a cumulative effect which is material in total.

If the auditor does not believe that the management's view is acceptable, or does not think that the disclosure is adequate, then a qualified (except for) opinion due to a material misstatement is probably sufficient. However, if the auditor believes that the claims are likely to be successful and are likely to be substantial then it may be necessary to issue an adverse opinion (FS do not show a true and fair view).

The 'Basis for Opinion' section will be amended to a 'Basis for Qualified Opinion' or 'Basis for Adverse Opinion' to explain the reason for the modified opinion.

The Key Audit Matters section will reference the 'Basis for ... Opinion'.

(c) **Griffiths**

Materiality

The fall in value is clearly material. In fact, the auditor would probably have to view the matter as pervasive, because providing for the loss would have the effect of converting a profit before tax of $250,000 into a loss of $50,000.

Relevant accounting principles

Long-term investments should be written down where there has been an impairment in value. Falls in the value of one asset must not be offset against increases in the value of another asset. Each asset has to be considered separately.

The directors should ensure adequate allowance is made for all known liabilities (expenses and losses). The accounting treatment adopted, offsetting known losses against unrealised profits, is unacceptable. As the company admits that a permanent fall in value has taken place, it should make full allowance against the loss. Further, as the other trade investments (with reputedly high realisable values) are permanent investments not held for resale, the accounting treatment adopted for them could be amended.

Form of audit report

As mentioned above, it is likely that the auditor would have to view the misstatement as both material and pervasive. The auditor will probably be forced to give an adverse opinion, stating that the financial statements do not show a true and fair view.

The 'Basis for Opinion' section will be amended to a 'Basis for Adverse Opinion' to explain the reason for the adverse opinion.

The Key Audit Matters section will reference the 'Basis for Adverse Opinion'.

(d) **Evans**

Materiality

The $10,000 represents 10% of the reported profit before tax, and so would appear to be material. However, the actual materiality of this item in relation to profit is, in fact, a somewhat judgmental matter. The auditor would probably conclude that the possible error in calculating the $10,000 was not material in relation to the profit of $100,000, since the amount of any error will probably be substantially less than the full amount included in the accounts. Further since the accounting records were only destroyed for the early part of the year, the auditor would still be able to confirm the calculations for the later part of the year. In these particular circumstances, therefore, the auditor may consider that the amount of any error (which is likely to be considerably less than $10,000) is not material.

Relevant accounting principles

It is perfectly acceptable for the company to add the cost of its own labour and materials in the construction of the warehouse, since these have been used to create a capital asset. This is following the 'matching' or 'accruals' concept as set out in IAS 1 and applied in IAS 16.

Form of audit report

The accounting treatment is generally acceptable and the amount of any error is not likely to be considered material, the auditor will probably be able to give a standard unmodified audit report i.e. The FS show a true and fair view.

Test your understanding 12 – Fraud

(a) **Internal audit function: risk of fraud and error**

(i) Internal audit can help management manage risks in relation to fraud and error, and exercise proper stewardship by:

- commenting on the process used by management to identify and classify the specific fraud and error risks to which the entity is subject (and in some cases helping management develop and implement that process)
- commenting on the appropriateness and effectiveness of actions taken by management to manage the risks identified (and in some cases helping management develop appropriate actions by making recommendations)
- periodically auditing or reviewing systems or operations to determine whether the risks of fraud and error are being effectively managed
- monitoring the incidence of fraud and error, investigating serious cases and making recommendations for appropriate management responses.

(ii) In practice, the work of internal audit often focuses on the adequacy and effectiveness of internal control procedures for the prevention, detection and reporting of fraud and error. Routine internal controls (such as the controls over computer systems and the production of routine financial information) and non-routine controls (such as controls over year-end adjustments to the financial statements) are relevant.

(iii) It should be recognised however that many significant frauds bypass normal internal control systems and that in the case of management fraud in particular, much higher level controls (those relating to the high level governance of the entity) need to be reviewed by internal audit in order to establish the nature of the risks, and to manage them effectively.

(b) **External auditors: fraud and error in an audit of financial statements**

(i) External auditors are required by ISA 240 *The Auditor's Responsibilities Relating to Fraud...* to consider the risks of material misstatements in the financial statements due to fraud. Their audit procedures will then be based on that risk assessment. Regardless of the risk assessment, auditors are required to be alert to the possibility of fraud throughout the audit and maintain an attitude of professional scepticism, notwithstanding the auditors' past experience of the honesty and integrity of management and those charged with governance. Members of the engagement team should discuss the susceptibility of the entity's financial statements to material misstatements due to fraud.

(ii) Auditors should make enquiries of management regarding management's assessment of fraud risk, its process for dealing with risk, and its communications with those charged with governance and employees. They should enquire of those charged with governance about the oversight process.

(iii) Auditors should also enquire of management and those charged with governance about any suspected or actual instance of fraud.

(iv) Auditors should consider fraud risk factors, unusual or unexpected relationships, and assess the risk of misstatements due to fraud, identifying any significant risks. Auditors should evaluate the design of relevant internal controls, and determine whether they have been implemented.

(v) Auditors should determine an overall response to the assessed risk of material misstatements due to fraud and develop appropriate audit procedures, including testing certain journal entries, reviewing estimates for bias, and obtaining an understanding of the business rationale of significant transactions outside the normal course of business. Appropriate written representations should be obtained.

(vi) External auditors are only concerned with risks that might cause material error in the financial statements. External auditors might therefore pay less attention than internal auditors to small frauds (and errors), although they must always consider whether evidence of single instances of fraud (or error) are indicative of more systematic problems.

(vii) It is accepted that because of the hidden nature of fraud, an audit properly conducted in accordance with ISAs might not detect a material misstatement in the financial statements arising from fraud. In practice, routine errors are much easier to detect than frauds.

(viii) Where auditors encounter suspicions or actual instances of fraud (or error), they must consider the effect on the financial statements, which will usually involve further investigations. They should also consider the need to report to management and those charged with governance.

(ix) Where serious frauds (or errors) are encountered, auditors need also to consider the effect on the going concern status of the entity, and the possible need to report externally to third parties, either in the public interest, for national security reasons, or for regulatory reasons. Many entities in the financial services sector are subject to this type of regulatory reporting and many countries have legislation relating to the reporting of money laundering activities, for example.

(c) **Nature of risks arising from fraud and error: Stone Holidays**

(i) Stone Holidays is subject to all of the risks of error arising from the use of computer systems. If programmed controls do not operate properly, for example, the information produced may be incomplete or incorrect. Inadequate controls also give rise to the risk of fraud by those who understand the system and are able to manipulate it in order to hide the misappropriation of assets such as receipts from customers.

(ii) All networked systems are also subject to the risk of error because of the possibility of the loss or corruption of data in transit. They are also subject to the risk of fraud where the transmission of data is not securely encrypted.

(iii) All entities that employ staff who handle company assets (such as receipts from customers) are subject to the risk that staff may make mistakes (error) or that they may misappropriate those assets (fraud) and then seek to hide the error or fraud by falsifying the records.

(iv) Stone Holidays is subject to problems arising from the risk of fraud perpetrated by customers using stolen credit or debit cards or even cash. Whilst credit card companies may be liable for such frauds, attempts to use stolen cards can cause considerable inconvenience.

(v) There is a risk of fraud perpetrated by senior management who might seek to lower the amount of money payable to the central fund (and the company's tax liability) by falsifying the company's sales figures, particularly if a large proportion of holidays are paid for in cash.

(vi) There is a risk that staff may seek to maximise the commission they are paid by entering false transactions into the computer system that are then reversed after the commission has been paid.

Test your understanding 13 – Quality control

Client A

Failure to sign off a working paper makes it difficult to identify the person responsible for the work in case of any query. If the working papers had been reviewed the reviewer should have identified this issue and investigated who had performed the work and asked them to sign off the working papers.

Completion dates of audit work are essential in order to identify the information that would have been available to the auditor at the time the procedures were completed. With the passage of time more information can come to light which would change the conclusion. If the working papers had been reviewed the reviewer should have identified this issue and asked the preparer to date the working papers.

Review of the working papers is an important quality control procedure. Every team member's work should be reviewed by someone more senior to ensure it has been performed properly and to the appropriate standard. If a review has not been performed there could be material misstatements that have not been detected during the audit which could result in an inappropriate audit report being issued.

Client B

Written representations are required by ISA 580. By not obtaining a written representation the audit firm does not have sufficient appropriate evidence to support the audit opinion.

Written representations should include matters such as the management confirming they have prepared financial statements that give a true and fair view and that they have provided the auditor with all of the information required for the audit.

The audit partner should not have signed the audit report without the written representation being on file.

The comment on the file stating that there are no matters requiring written representation would indicate that the audit manager does not understand the professional standards that should be followed during an audit, specifically, the requirements of ISA 580.

1	A	Briefing of the audit teams forms part of the direction of the audit.
2	C	Engagement quality control review is part of the engagement performance.
3	D	Quality is important for upholding the reputation of the profession and the firm in order to maintain investor confidence. Avoiding punishment is not the primary reason for ensuring a quality audit is performed.
4	B	An EQCR should be performed by someone independent of the engagement and someone of suitable authority such as a senior manager, director or partner.
5	B	The firm should perform its own quality control reviews and take action as necessary to ensure quality control procedures are followed.

Client C

A sample of 30 was chosen for a purchases test yet only 27 were tested and a conclusion drawn from those items.

Sample sizes are chosen to ensure sufficient appropriate evidence has been obtained. As only 27 items were tested instead of 30, sufficient appropriate evidence has not been obtained in this instance.

The three missing invoices could be evidence of a wider control deficiency or a material fraud. Further investigation should have been performed to discover the reason for the missing invoices.

The issue may indicate a lack of supervision if the audit team member was unsure how to proceed after discovering the issue.

The issue would also indicate a lack of review as the matter was not identified during the review process.

Client D

Provisions are inherently risky as they are often determined by the judgment of management. As such they should be audited by someone with suitable experience and judgment.

An audit junior should not have been assigned this task. This raises questions about the selection and direction of the audit team. Tasks should be allocated to team members of appropriate experience and competence. Junior members of staff are usually allocated lower risk areas which require little experience and judgment. More senior members of the team should be assigned the riskier areas of the audit.

It is stated that the audit manager was too busy to perform the audit of the provision due to other client work. This may indicate that the workload of staff is not manageable. Audit quality could have been affected on both clients as work may be rushed to get it completed which may result in material misstatements going undetected.

Client E

Planning is an important and compulsory part of the audit process. ISA 300 requires the audit to be planned in order to ensure that the audit is performed in an efficient and effective manner and an appropriate audit approach is taken which addresses the risks of the audit.

The auditor should not simply copy last year's procedures and approach as this may not be appropriate for this year's circumstances.

By failing to plan the audit properly, ISA 300 has not been complied with and therefore the audit has not been performed in accordance with professional standards.

General points

The quality control issues identified raise doubts over the performance of several audits conducted by the firm.

If it is discovered that an inappropriate audit report was issued in any of these cases the firm could face action by the ACCA and by the client.

Any action taken against the firm could damage their reputation as well as result in a loss of clients and financial penalties.

The firm's policies and procedures should be communicated again to staff to remind them of the requirements and the importance of them.

Further training is recommended to ensure staff are aware of how to comply with the requirements.

Disciplinary action may be necessary in respect of staff have been found to be deliberately disregarding company policy.

Index

Index

Index